TRIVIUM

TRIVIUM

THE CLASSICAL LIBERAL ARTS OF
GRAMMAR, LOGIC, & RHETORIC

BLOOMSBURY
NEW YORK · LONDON · OXFORD · NEW DELHI · SYDNEY

WOODEN
BOOKS

CONTENTS

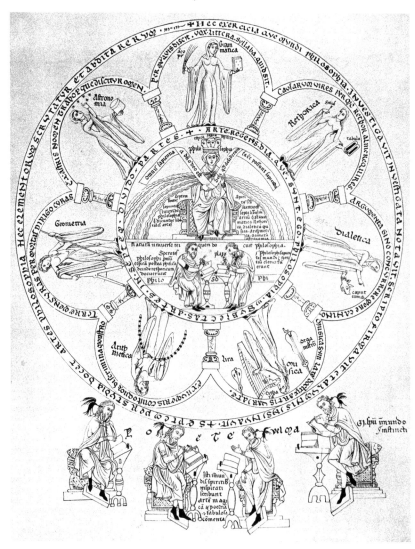

The seven liberal arts. Clockwise from top, Grammar, Rhetoric, Dialectic, Music, Arithmetic, Geometry, and Astronomy. From the Hortus Deliciarum, *1185, by Herrad of Landsberg, Hohenburg, Alsace.*

EDITOR'S PREFACE

THE TRIVIUM is a body of learning that was perfected in the medieval period, but whose roots go back much further, into the classical Roman and Greek world and perhaps earlier. At its core, it deals with language and the various ways we humans use it to communicate, reason, and persuade. Superficially divided into grammar, logic, and rhetoric, the trivium has also encompassed euphonics, poetics, and ethics in its long history, and sections on these subjects have been included in these pages.

Seven books from the Wooden Books series have been combined to produce *Trivium*. First up is John Michell's *Euphonics*, which playfully demonstrates the innate qualities of the various letters of the alphabet. Next, Dr. Rachel Holley artfully presents *Grammar*, placing English grammar in the context of general grammar, gently building from words to clauses, and ultimately to the unit of the sentence. Joining sentences together, Octavia Wynne then introduces *Poetic Meter and Form*, where language arguably finds its most beautiful expression. Next up, in *Logic,* Dr. Earl Fontainelle investigates the rules by which truth and falsity are commonly deduced and inferred, exposing some nasty fallacies along the way. Less straightforward tools used by professional persuaders to bamboozle, charm, and dazzle are to be found in our delightful guide to *Rhetoric*, by Adina Arvatu and Prof. Andrew Aberdein. Finally, as a reminder of the highest purpose of such a potent toolkit, we present *Ethics,* by Prof. Gregory Beabout and Dr. Mike Hannis. Further appendices cover Theophrastus' *Characters, The Art of Memory, Narrative Structure*, and finally *Proverbs*, by Alice O'Neill.

Thank you to Anne Hechle for the calligraphic cover, Merrily Harpur for the cartoons, and to Paul Taylor and Rembrandt Duits at the Warburg Institute for help with picture research. I am also particularly indebted to Stephen Parsons, Jan Suchanek, and Trent Halliday for their assistance. Additional thanks to George Gibson, Polly Napper, and Laura Phillips at Bloomsbury, and to Jane Smith, Daud Sutton, Hector McDonell, Adam Tetlow, Woody Rivers, Kenneth Wilson, and David Wade for their help.

Apologies to sensitive readers on both sides of the pond, but we have adopted a mostly Canadian mixture of transatlantic spelling and punctuation conventions for this jointly printed edition. For example, we like the way Americans maximize 'z's and spell 'judgment', but we also like the 'u' in British 'colour' and 'honour' (*see page 395*). Finally, we've chosen to use the serial comma throughout: it's cleaner, clearer, and smarter.

Trivium, which covers the liberal arts of language and thinking, is the sister volume to *Quadrivium*, which deals with the arts concerned with number. Between them, they cover as much of the syllabus of the seven liberal arts as we could fit into the space. These volumes do not describe the history or the story of the liberal curriculum; instead they simply aim to present elements of the arts themselves to a modern readership.

At the heart of the liberal arts curriculum lies the classical Greek idea that while many subjects have a utilitarian function—thus law, chemistry, medicine, engineering, accountancy, economics, and carpentry are 'servile' arts, studied in order to work in the world—there are a few subjects which can not be legitimized this way, and which instead train and refine core faculties of the learner. Mastery of these special subjects 'liberate' a person into rational, intellectual, and civic life (hence 'liberal' arts), and provide a foundation from which all other subjects may be learned.

Some semblance of the trivium first appears in the oratorical schools of the Sophists in ancient Greece from c.600 BC, and notably that of Isocrates

[436–338 BC]. Distrustful of rhetoric, Plato [c.424–348 BC] attempted to separate 'true' dialectic from 'false' sophistry, but it was Aristotle [384–322 BC] who finally laid out grammar, logic, and rhetoric in the systematic manner familiar to us today. Notable grammarians who followed include Aristarchos [c.217–145 BC], Dionysius Thrax [170–90 BC], and later in Latin Varro [116–27 BC], Donatus [fl.350 AD], and Priscian [fl.500 AD]. Rhetoric was later further developed in Rome, notably by Cicero [106–43 BC] and Quintilian [c.35–100 AD].

From Roman times and through the middle ages the quadrivium arts (mathematics, geometry, music, and astronomy) were poorly understood. Compilations by St. Augustine [354–430], Martianus Capella [fl.410–420], Boethius [c.480–524], Cassiodorus [c.485–585], and Isidore of Seville [c.560–636] show these subjects, and even logic, struggling without Greek mathematics. Add to this the suspicion by churchmen of pagan rhetoric, and it is easy to see how, by the eleventh century, grammar ruled supreme.

It was not until the twelfth century, as missing texts by Euclid, Plato, Aristotle, Archimedes, and others began to find their way into Latin via Arabic and Greek that the ancient curriculum began to be restored and developed into the synthesis that we have today. This was achieved by a variety of figures, such as John of Salisbury [1176–1180], Thomas Aquinas [1225–1274], Petrarch [1304–1374], Marsilio Ficino [1433–1499], and Pico della Mirandola [1463–1494] as the Renaissance gathered pace.

The trivium is, remarkably, a 2500-year-old course in clear thinking which is still fresh today. In the well-chosen words of Sister Miriam Joseph [1898-1982]: "Logic is the art of thinking; grammar, the art of inventing symbols and combining them to express thought; and rhetoric, the art of communicating thought from one mind to another, the adaptation of language to circumstance."

BOOK I

EUPHONICS

A POET'S DICTIONARY OF
ENCHANTMENTS

John Michell

illustrations by Merrily Harpur

Hand-drawn alphabets, by Don Moyer, 2010

INTRODUCTION

NAMES ARE IMPORTANT, particularly in public life and when one is young and self-conscious. Actors, politicians, and businessmen are prone to worry about such things, and adolescents who suffer under a name they deem ridiculous or inappropriate commonly exchange it for one which better expresses their personality, as they see it.

Personal names acquire historical associations (Winston, Marilyn) and sometimes express moral qualities (Faith, Prudence), which make them more or less popular at different periods. But apart from the flow of fashion, names may be seen as having their own peculiar characters, formed by nothing more substantial than the logic of alliteration. So parents agonize about the right names for their children, whether Polly sounds too pert or Deirdre rather depressing, Bill too blunt, Willie too weak, or whether nicknames might produce a cheeky Charlie, big Bertha, or slippery Sid.

This may seem childish and neurotic, but behind such trivia lies a feature of language which poets have always, more or less consciously, acknowledged. Names and words are made up of sounds, and each sound has some kind of natural meaning, expressing and evoking a certain human emotion. In some cases even the shapes of letters—the serpentine, sibilant S for example—seem to accord with the sounds they denote. Academic linguists and etymologists, amid their serious studies of secular derivations and verbal migrations, have no time for such whimsical notions; but to a poet this aural approach to language is all-important. Every sensitive writer is concerned not only with the proclaimed meaning of words, but also with their esoteric, subliminal qualities, their pitch and ring and the irrational feelings produced by the sound, and sometimes by the sight of them.

Onomatopoeia as defined in the *Oxford English Dictionary* is, 'Formation of names or words from sounds that resemble those associated with the object or action to be named, or that seem naturally suggestive of its qualities.' The example given is 'cuckoo', and there are many other words, such as plop, click, buzz, purr, hiss, hem, and haw, which are obvious attempts at imitating a sound. Similar attempts are made in all languages. The question which then arises is to what extent these imitative sounds influence the meanings of the longer, composite words in which they occur. This Dictionary is designed to assist its readers' individual judgements on the matter. Its usefulness will be apparent to poets, dramatists, ritualists, occultists, advertisers, orators, and all who require to choose words and sounds for their powers of invocation.

A previous essay on *The Poetical Alphabet* forms a chapter in a book called *Pluriverse* by the idiosyncratic American philosopher Benjamin Paul Blood [1832–1919]. He begins by telling of a discussion he once had as to why an icicle could not fitly be called a tub, nor vice versa. It is in the nature of its name, he concluded, for a tub to be short and stubby whereas an icicle sounds spindly and slim. At the sound of 'icicle' the irrational mind throws up the word 'bicycle', which is also spindly, and often cold, explaining perhaps the popular acceptance of that word to name a pedal-cranked two-wheeler.

Such verbal associations are notorious afflictions on mental patients, and they also haunt the poetic mind. As part of his dangerous game the poet is forced to receive these germs of madness, to make them welcome and find profit in their visitations. He will also cultivate the art (or nervous compulsion) of rhyming, together with alliteration (commonly used in Teutonic and Old English verse), where consonance is in the first rather than the last syllables of words. Alliteration and the spontaneous associations of sounds and meanings are then brought together to constitute poetic euphonics. By that word is implied the most subtle and magical of the ancient sacred sciences, to do with the psychological effects of sound, and the use of music and sonorous speech for the spreading of enchantments.

The primary text in euphonics is Plato's *Cratylus*, a Socratic dialogue about the origins of language and the influence of archetypal sounds on the formation of words. It is subtitled 'On the Correctness of Names'. The debate is between Socrates and two other characters, Cratylus, who claims to know the science of nomenclature and what there is in a name which makes it correct or otherwise, and Hermogenes, who denies that there is any science or inherent correctness in naming things. His contention is that "whatever name you choose to give anything is its right name". The third party, Socrates, examines both arguments and comes down on the side of Cratylus.

The dialogue is long, intricate, and in parts quite mystifying. In speculating about the original forms and derivations of names, Socrates teases his listeners with outrageous puns and obscure allusions which modern scholars are at a loss to interpret. He claims no special knowledge of the subject but offers the view that "a name appears to be a vocal imitation, and a person who imitates something with his voice names that which he imitates". There are good names and bad ones, and a good name is one that contains the "proper letters". Letters are appropriate or not in a name according as they serve to represent, through their sounds, the qualities of whatever is being named. Thus the proper name for a thing is a composition of those sounds which imitate the ideas associated with it.

Near the end of the dialogue (426C) Socrates speaks about the inherent meanings in individual sounds. The R sound, he says, is made by the tongue at its most agitated and it is therefore expressive of rapid movement.

It also, he adds later, stands for hardness. The Greek words containing R with which Socrates illustrates his statement justify modern interest in this subject, for the English translations also feature the letter R. They include *rhein* (to run or stream), *rhoe* (current), *tromos* (trembling), *trechein* (run, rush, hurry, race) and the words for rend, crush, and whirl. Among other examples given are the L sound, which has a sleek, gliding motion, and the G sound which is gummy and glutinous. The passage is regrettably short, and Socrates does not go on to complete the sonic alphabet.

An objection raised by Hermogenes is that quite different words for the same thing are used in both Greek and foreign languages. Socrates replies that many words have become corrupt over the period since they were designed, and no longer contain the appropriate sounds. This leads to the question of who it was that composed words in the first place. Socrates reasons that it must have been someone skilled in the art, having a talent for making verbal imitations of things. He observes that if a number of painters are all asked to paint the same scene or object, each of their pictures will look different from the others. Similarly with the word-artists: each of them will think up a different word or compilation of sounds to represent the same idea. The fact that in the languages of the world the same things are called by many different names, some of which seem more appropriate than others, is due partly to corruption of the original forms and partly to the differing tastes and whims of the artists who composed the words of each language.

The poet who gives names to things, according to Socrates (389 D), "must know how to embody in sounds and syllables the name of each object which is naturally appropriate to it. Surely, if he is to be an authoritative name-giver, he must make up and bestow all his names with his eye fixed on the absolute or ideal name of what he is naming". Thus the Socratic doctrine of ideal patterns or archetypes which generate the apparent forms of creation is here extended to names. The nature of archetypes is not such as allows them to be copied in perfect detail; human craftsmen can aspire merely to reflect some of their aspects. In the same way, Socrates' ideal names are in the transcendental language of the gods, which is beyond human ken or utterance. The most that name-givers can do, therefore, is to contemplate the essential nature of whatever it is they require to name, and express it as far as possible in the sounds of the word by which they decide to call it. Here again is the lesson, repeated throughout the Platonic works, that the best results in all the arts of life, from carpentry to statesmanship, are obtained through study and imitation of abstract ideals.

That style of philosophy, and the mystical sciences that flourish with it, have a natural and traditional appeal to poets—much to the bafflement of their academic commentators. Rationalism spawns few verses; poets are inclined to cut the professors and turn their backs on the eminent likes of Newton, Locke, Marx and Darwin in favour of more congenial company. William Blake inveighed against the 'single vision' of academic theorists and adopted the comprehensive world-view of Plato and Plotinus. The darling studies of the poets are commonly those which their learned contemporaries have considered morbid or discredited. Dante acknowledged the influence of Dionysius and Areopagite, Milton that of Hermes Trismegistos, while Spenser, Shelley, Yeats, Coleridge, and Wordsworth were among those who found a prime source of inspiration in the mystical theology of the Neoplatonists. The tradition on which they all drew was that which is most firmly rooted in human nature and has, by its long endurance, earned itself the epithet 'perennial'. Springing to light in the songs of Orpheus and the ancient law-giving bards, and channelled through a golden succession of sages, mystics and devout scholars, it forms that invisible stream which has fertilized the noblest works of literature and wells up spontaneously in the mind of a natural poet.

In the spirit of ancient scholarship, this Dictionary is not definitive, authoritative, exclusive or didactic. As one name-giver, says Socrates, will differ from others in the sounds he chooses to make up his verbal imitations, so readers may find other associations than those here attached to the various sounds. A few relevant words in foreign languages have been included, but for the most part the following verbal illustrations are in English, a composite tongue where the adaptation to rich onomatopoetic effect of words from many different sources has clearly been the work of that shrewd, ever-active name giver, the native genius.

In light and humorous verse the use of alliteration, onomatopoeia and suchlike devices may well be exaggerated, as for example in Hood's *Ben Battle was a soldier bold*, where the blustering B is repeated to comic effect. Coarse rhymes and alliterations are also appropriate in the lowest of poetic forms, the warcry or slogan. Thus: *Power to the people!*, *Ban the bomb!*, and *No taxation without representation!* In higher forms the medium poets are inclined not to flaunt such techniques , but rather to evade pedantic analysis by concealing their art. Yet on every level the art of poetry is bound up with euphonics and the subtle relationships between sound and meaning. The subject of this Dictionary is thus of assured interest to all who in any way practise that art, and the Compiler anticipates the approval of all poets towards his purpose, however inadequate the results. His hopes are for readers' pleasure in the wisdom and humour which lie in the Socratic philosophy of names, or at least that they may derive some amusement and stimulation from these pages.

A

a daring aviator aloft in the atmosphere

Vowels express emotions and feelings, while consonants hold thoughts and the intellect. A Japanese sage gives the explanation of why people falling off buildings shout 'Aaaaaa!' on their way downwards. It is because they naturally wish to ascend, and the Aaaaa! sound is characteristic of uplift, whether in body or spirit.

A gives a sense of alacrity, of *active, happy, alert, agile, attentive, aware, awake lads* and *lasses*. The appropriate bird is the lark, which might thus be addressed:

Audacious avian arise!
Ascend aloft to azure skies!
Alert to your angelic strain
Our aspirations soar again.

B

big-breasted and broad in the beam

The shape of the letter B can be described as double or *binary*. It is an oval squashed into two *bumps*, like *bi-focal* spectacles, and the B sound is predominant in the names, both proper and vulgar, given to the *bipartite bulges* of the body: *bust, bosom, breasts, boobs, bubs, bum, buttocks, butt, base, beam, bottom,* and *backside*. A bull has *balls* or *bollocks*, and a *beer-bibber* grows a *big belly* (*Bierbauch*) like a *tub, barrel,* or *bloated bladder*.

An image evoked by the B sound is of *balloons blown* up near to *bursting*. They are *broad, bluff, burly, obese, bulging, bulbous, burgeoning, billowing, blooming, blubbery blimps*. These *bouncing* orbs attract adjectives of *bounty: blessed, benevolent, benign, abundant, bland, buttery* and *beautiful*.

But *bulbous bubbles* also have the sound of *bumptious bullies, bold, brash, brazen, bothersome, beefy, brawny, bellicose, brutal bigots* or *bossy bounders*, given to *brawling, blustering, blundering, squabbling, slobbering, blubbering, biffing, bashing, brow-beating, butting, bumping,* and *boring*. *Bucolic* and *flabby buffoons*, they *boom, bawl, bray, bleat,* and *bellyache*. They are *boastful, bombastic blundering braggarts, babbling bullshit, blah-blah,* and *balderdash*.

Big Bill was as broad
   as a barrel of beer;
At bruising and boozing
   he hadn't a peer.
A burly club bouncer
   he drubbed one and all,
Until clobbered and bashed
   in a brutal pub brawl.

C

cringing in the corner

The hard C pertains to the *core, coeur* or *centrum*, the symbolic locus of the goddess or receptive principle in nature. Thus *cloister, sanctuary, cathedral, crypt, cradle, cozy cot,* and *castle keep* are epithets of the mystical center, gateway to the chthonic realm of the earth spirit, the *crucible* wherein life is generated. *Close, confined,* and *covered* in, the names of its symbols include *cove, chasm, cavern, oracular cave, cleft, crack, creek, cranny, corridor, crevice, recess, nook, chink, cavity, crater, corner, closet, cubby-hole, cubicle, cupboard, catacomb,* and *carapace.* Carrying water it is a *culvert, cundy, cunette,* or *conduit.*

The common reference of these words is to concealed chambers and channels and thus to *cunnus,* which echoes through European languages as the Basque *kuna,* the Norse *kunta* and the old English *cunt.* The Roman goddess Cunina was in charge of the *cunabula, cradle,* or *crib,* and she offered *care, comfort, concern, contentment, consolation, cover,* and *protection, coddling, cuddling, cosseting, crooning, confiding, kissing, clinging,* and *clasping.* There is also the *canny, cunning* woman, one with an *oracular knack.*

The C sound implies a *cautious, careful, circumspect* approach, as in *crawl, creep, cringe* and *cower,* associated with low types, *crooks, creeps, craven cowards, cranks, criminals,* and *corrupt occultists.*

> Kind Cunina's chthonic cavity,
> Cavern sacred to depravity
> Succours in its covered nooks,
> Cowards, creeps, and cunning crooks;
> Craving sanctuary and care,
> Outcasts seek protection there.

CK

cutting corn with a sickle

An emblem of Ceres, goddess of corn, was the sickle. Many other names for cutting, cleaving, and culling instruments are built round the (usually) hard 'C', which was associated in the previous entry with certain aspects of the female principle. For instance: *cutters, clippers, chopper, scissors, sickle, secateurs, scythe, scimitar, scalpel,* and—one to relish—*snickersnee.*

Related to cleaving, culling or cutting are *scar, snick, cicatrice, score, scotch, scratch, scalp, schism, incision, dissection,* and *curtailment.*

A sickle was the instrument with which Kronos mutilated his father, Uranos, and awareness of castration seems to be one of the feelings evoked by the hard 'C'.

It is also present in cutting remarks, which are *scathing, scolding, sceptical, scornful, caustic, sarcastic, scurrilous, acute, acerbic, acid,* and *acrimonious.*

Ken is a critic,
   A scurrilous scold.
His comments are sceptical,
   Acid, and cold.
By caustic remarks
   And discouraging sneers
He's scarred and curtailed
   Many coming careers.

CH

cheap and cheerful but itching to scratch

Ch at the beginning of a word gives a chirpy sound, as of *cheeky chicks* and *chappies* who *cheep, chirp, chaff, chant, chortle, chuckle,* exchange *chit-chat,* and are cherished for their *cheery charm.* In the last syllable of a word the *ch* or *tch* sound is of an irritating fidget, as in *itch, stitch, scratch, twitch,* a *hitch,* a *catch,* a *tetchy, touchy bitch,* and *wretched kitsch.* Its petulant, crotchety air is heard in:

"Richard," said Bridget,
  "Don't fidget and twitch,
Stop scratching your chin,
  Give your britches a hitch.
You look such a wretch
  with that blotch on your boot
And I'm itching to chuck out
  that cheap checkered suit."

D

down in the dumps or dead as dodo

D has the ring of *death, doomsday*, and sad *endings*. As an initial it implies loss or lessening, *demotion, dismissal, diminution*, or *degradation*. As a final letter it tells of *deeds dead and done. Dread*, with a D at each end, sums it up. The *depressing* effect of D may be detected in the following incantation:

> Dim, dumb, dingy, droop, done down,
> dark, dank, drear, disgraceful, drown,
> damp, dump, dismal, damned, dire dread,
> drop, dope, doleful, doddering, dead.

Particularly dreary is the DGE sound, as in *dredge, drudge, trudge, dungeon, sludge, smudge, stodgy porridge, curmudgeon, grudge*, and *dudgeon*. See also G.

> Down in a dungeon,
>   Dank and dread,
> Dreary despondent,
>   Droops my dismal head.
> A dark, depressing death
>   Will be my dire doom,
> Abandoned underground,
>   This dug-out for my tomb.

E

elegant elves and eerie evils

The short and simple E has an *ephemeral* and *elegant* quality. It is *elevated*, *erudite*, *elated*, *epic* even *effervesent*, a quality present in *engaging eloquence*, *exquisite esteemed elite education* and the *enigmatic elemental elixirs*, *enticing essential essences*, *electric elegies* and *esoteric echoing entrances* of *enchanting elderly elves*, *eligibly elected* due to their *evidently excellent ethics*.

As the E-sound lengthens though, it darkens, as in *evening*, *ebony* and *elegy*, until the long E, drawn out in the cry of *eeeee*, becomes a sound of grief and supernatural terror, puting a shiver in *creepy*, *weird*, *eerie*, *fearsome*, *feverish dreams* of *evil demons eating keening banshees* and in verbs of distress, such as *keen*, *weep*, *shriek*, *scream*, *screech*, *squeak*, *squeal*, *plead*, and *beseech*.

A classic example of the use of the E and other long vowel sounds to brew up a dense, solemn, uncanny atmosphere is in the opening lines of Poe's *The Raven* ('Once upon a midnight dreary...', *see page 135*):

Once from dreams of mystic meaning,
*   I awoke to sounds of keening,*
Sounds which seemed to echo
*   from a being with a greenish gleam.*
Flickering o'er its evil features
*   Scenes of weird demonic creatures*
Teased my brain ... I could but scream.
The doctor said, "You'll be all right.
*   Just turn the TV off at night."*

F

footloose and fancy-free

F has a frightfully flippant sound, especially in conjunction with L. It seems to imitate a *flag unfurled, flapping* in the wind. It is applied to flappers of all kinds, from those that fly to those who are flighty, who *frolic* and *flirt* with *fops* and are called *flibbertigibbets* or *footloose* and *fancy-free*.

   A fabulous image of F is a *frivolous flock* of *fowls*, a *flight* of *feathered fools*. In *fantastic fashion* they *flash, flail, fan,* and *flutter* their *flimsy finery, fussed* and *flustered* as they *fidget, flit, flounce, drift,* and *float free, flourishing* their *flim-flam frippery* and *flaunting* their *fleecy, flossy, frilly taffeta frocks, fringed* with *ruffles, flaring, flaming, flagrant,* and *flamboyant*. Such *flippant, fashionable, frothy folk* are *famous* for *flair* and *effervescence*.

Frivolous, flighty fairies
   flutter by,
Frisk and flirt and flaunt
   their frilly stuff,
Flustering the flitting
   butterfly,
Floating free as feathers,
   foam, or fluff.

FA
Fanny's failure

A sound of fizzling out is sometimes heard in words with F, often when A is also present. In the word *failure* the F which precedes the wailing sound suggests that before the *fiasco* there was a certain amount of *fun*, *folly*, or *futile* effort. The word for a brief flight and a spattering *fall* is, aptly, *flop*!

Fanny fancied flying
  But her flaps were false and frail.
She flailed and fluttered feverishly
  For fear that she might fail.
Finally she faltered,
  Forced by fits and faints to stop,
And fell down feeling foolish,
  A fiasco and a flop.

G

bogged down in a greasy quagmire

Socrates, in *Cratylus*, said that when the first inventor of names observed that the slide of the tongue was blocked by the G sound, he made use of that sound to form words such as *glischron* (glutinous), *gluku* (glucose, sweet), and *gloiodes* (gluey). The type of movement indicated by G is a *sluggish oozing of disgusting, congealing grease.*

The gist or nitty-gritty of a *bog*, slough or *quagmire* is of *grey-green, greasy, grimy, gloomy, grisly, grim, glum, grievous, gummy, glutinous, gooey, soggy, clogging, plugging, gurgling globs of grunge.* The exclamation of one who falls into it is a *hoggish grunt, ugh!*

Sounds of GH and KH occur in expressions of disgust and in names of things which provoke them: *Yukh! Gross greedy pigs!* Filth in Welsh is *achawi*, in French *ca-ca*, and a true note of revulsion is heard in the Yiddish *schmuck*, wherein is heard another sound of disgust, the SCH.

George and Gert began to slog
  Through a grisly, gurgling bog.
"Gosh," gasped George,
  "What gummy muck."
"George," gulped Gert,
  "Good grief, I'm stuck."

H

heavenly hopes and hellish horrors

The aspirate H often tends to give spiritual uplift to words, even where it is barely heard, as in *ghost*. Its poetic effect is illustrated by such phrases as: *heavenly hosts, ghostly choir, harmony of the spheres, ethereal charm, breath of enchantment, rushing whirlwind, refreshing honesty, heaving a hopeful sigh, ha-has, hurrahs, harking halos, high hopes,* and *happy holidays.*

At other times, though, the H sound can invoke *Halloween horrors, hollow, haunted, hidden, heavy, hooting, howlings, of hideous, hellish, half-hewn, hacking, hair-raising hullaballos* from *Hades!*

Here, however, is an aspirated, pneumatic, philosophical rhyme:

Holy Pythagoras made his charts
 To humanize the heavenly arts.
His highest hope, to charm our ears
 With echoes of the chanting spheres
Which chime in every heart from birth
 In chorus with the breath of earth.
But no ear hears, no eye can see
 The whole ethereal harmony.

1

The sound of the short I expresses light affection or derision. Its diminishing trivializing effect is illustrated in the once popular song which described a yellow polka-dot bikini as 'itsy-bitsy'. The sound T adds extra pettiness.

An infant imp

Shrivelled and skinny is Sid,
    And Kitty is thin as a kipper,
And Willie their rickety kid
    Is a whimpering wisp of a nipper.
He's hideous, wizened, and vicious,
    Goes rigid or livid or limp,
And Kitty and Sid are suspicious
    He was switched for a pixie or imp.
They took him to Jimmy the wizard,
    And Biddy his wife, who said "Who
Is this miserable skin of a lizard?
    He's the image of Sidney and you!"

I

I'm a private individual

The letter I is the symbol of the first person, number 1. It is heard in *myself*, *my identity*, and what I *opine, my private ideology*. It is also in one's self-*image* and *independent existence* as a *single individual*. In psychoanalysts' parlance the instinctive self is the Id, and an egomaniac is one who makes I into an idol. There is an obvious link between the I and inwardness, prompting associations as: *inherent, I'm in here, my inheritance*.

Poets who speak in the first person have to be careful with the I sound. It creates a pompous, didactic effect. This effect is exaggerated in the following imitation of a self-important proprietor.

As a private individual
  I'm not inclined to mingle.
I prize my independence,
  I insist on biding single.
In my isolated island
  I'm the idol of my minions
Who identify themselves
  With my ideas and my opinions.

I

the egg and eye

The I, the eye, and the German *Ei* (egg) are homophones, and each of them has a similar traditional meaning as representing alike the divine I am, whose symbol is a radiant eye, egg, or orb, and the individual as microcosm.

The Greek and Latin I is *ego*, a word made up of the egg and its oval or *ovum* shape—egg-O. The I, the eye and the egg thus seem to be ancient companions. Some verbal connections between them are pictured below.

I and O are the sounds which link the solitary self with the totality of things, as in I alone, or I all one. Similarly in German, the *Alleinsein* (solitude) divides into *all ein sein* (to be all one). Unity is *Einheit* and one's own is *eigen,* wherein occurs the egg sound which is also in *Auge* (eye). See also O.

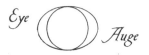

The single visionary eye
Its macrocosm may descry.
At one are those who can atone,
For the All One revolves alone.

J
a jolly jingle

The pure French J, as in *jeune, joli, jeu, jouet*, seems better adapted to express the *jaunty, jingle-jangle* associations of the letter than the clogged sound of its English pronunciation, which is as DJ or DGE. That sound at the end of a word has a deadening effect, like sludge (see D), but the initial J imparts a *jerky, jittery* form of *jubilation*, as in: a *jovial joke, jest* or *jape*, a *jag, jamboree, jubilee* or *junket, jazz, jive, jig, jog, judder* and *jitterbug*, a *jabbering jay, jolly Jack, jumping for joy*.

These words have an air of somewhat garish jollity, and the harshness of the J sound is heard in *jarring jabber* and *jeering jingles*. Its associated colour, *jaune*, or orange, becomes sickly in *jaundice* and *jealousy*.

Here is a Jubilee jaunt:

a *Jubilee jaunt*

Jill and Julian Gee enjoyed a joyful jamboree
 With a jaunt along the hedges to rejoice
In the jangling, jarring bray of the jerky popinjay
 And the jewel-hijacking jackdaw's jeering voice.
When their jubilation faded, feeling just a trifle jaded,
 They adjourned to Jilly's uncle, Major Plunket.
He's a jovial jackanapes and his jugglings, jinks, and japes
 Made a jolly, jokey ending to their junket.

K

a quick flick of the whisk

The K sound is a clarion call, like a startled blackbird's ke-ke-ke-ke-ke, commanding attention in: *quick! awake! hark! look! prick* your ears, and *perk* up!

The words *quick* and *click*, which sound K at both ends, epitomize its function in denoting movements and noises which are brusque, brisk, and ephemeral. Its staccato crack is heard after the swishing sound in *whisking skirts*, and gives a feeling of sparkling spirits in words such as: *lark, prank, caper, high jinks, jokey, skipping, skimming, skating, skittish, frisky, kittenish, scamper, scatter-cash, jocular, lucky, cocky, chic, spic and span,* and *cocktail-shaker.*

The trivializing effect of K is apparent in *knick-knacks, kick-shaws, bric-a-brac, trinkets, keepsakes, crackpots, fickle chicks* and *gimcrack sparklers, tinkling, twinkling,* and *flickering.* Names of small sharp or stinging things tend to be built on the K sound, hence *pick, pike, prickle, spike, beak, stick, crop, cane, icicle,* and *flick-knife.* Other cutting instruments are listed under C. With these are administered short, sharp chastisements, generally minor: *spank, shake, smack, crack, whack, hack, yank, attack, tweak, jerk, peck, wreck, break, kick, nick, flick, prick, lick, tick-off, tickle, poke, sock, rock,* and *knock.*

a false alarm

Quick, Jack! Wake up and act!
Pick up your walking-stick! Look, we're attacked!
Good luck and be plucky! They're wicked and slick,
But poking and tickling them may do the trick.
Alick, you brick, you take the stick,
Unbuckle your flick-knife and cut them off quick!
But hark! there's no tinkling of muskets or tanks.
Despicable trickster! It's one of your pranks.

L

lingering by a limpid lagoon

The L sound expresses light and clarity; its corresponding motion is of languidly gliding liquid, as in a placid, limpid lagoon. Its feeling is leisurely, lazy, flaccid, loose, lax, lounging, laid-back, and dilly-dallying.

Preceded by the S sound it becomes slurred, and its character then is slinky and slippery like a slimy slob. Heard in it is a slow, slurping, slithering, slipping, sliding sound as of sleek, slothful slugs. See SL.

Languid lovers lie
   in Lethe's valley.
Lethargic, lotus-like,
   they laze and dally.
Idly the listless loafers,
   slaked with pleasure
Slump on the lawns,
   recline and sleep at leisure.
Stealthy oblivion
   lulls each slothful soul.
The swelling floods glide up
   and o'er them roll.

M

warm meals, home comforts, and mother's moods

The double-arched shape of the letter M in its mother's eyebrows and breasts is the first pattern to be experienced by an infant, and its first sound is likely to be a *murmured, muttered* M, which seems a natural symbol of *mammals* and *maternity*. *Mother* is *mild, merciful, mollifying,* and *mollicoddling.* Her *home* is *humble* but *warm* and *comfortable* as the *womb.* Sometimes it is moderately *merry* and *mirthful,* yet home can become *monotonous, hum-drum* and *gloomy,* making one *morose, miserable, mean, mouldy, melancholy, mournful, moody, mopey, dim, grim,* and *glum.*

The association between the cycles of women and the *moon* that *measures* the *month* has caused these words in many different languages to be dominated by the M sound. Under the moon occur *mysteries, romances, marvels, miracles, magic,* and the *mantic* arts, *stimulating imagination* or *madness* and *monomania.* The M sound evokes images of the dark, *mysterious* aspect of the female spirit, such as the *mystic moon-maiden,* the *Madonna,* and the *gloomy chasm.*

Mother's plump and matronly
  and humbly domestic,
Her home is warm and comforting,
  but modest, not majestic.
She used to dream of mysteries,
  of glamour and romance,
But muddling her money matters
  made her miss her chance.

N

inwardly denying

The N sound is widely used for negation, as in *no, nay, non, nein, ne,* and *niet.* Socrates identified it as an inward sound, and it does seem appropriate to those who are *negative, niggling, introvert, mean,* and *stingy, nagging, narrow-minded, nit-picking, snide, sneering, sneaky,* and *nasty.* It has an air of denigration which, as Mr. Blood observed, "is intensified by drawing up of the muscles of contempt at the sides of the nose."

"No, you naughty knave," nagged Nurse,
"Nasty Sneak! I've known none worse.
Don't deny you nicked my ring,
Sinful, mean, indecent thing."

O

our noble mother

The shape of the letter O is the shape of the mouth producing the round O sound. It is a *noble, rolling, resounding, overawing* sound, used to effect in the translation of Homer's invocation to "Ocean, the source and origin of the gods".

O is old, a proto-sound, symbol of the original womb or of the oval world-egg (*ovum, oeuf*). It dominates words meaning either the whole or a hole, totality or void. The whole is the *cosmos, world, dome* of heaven, *globe*, or *orb*; a hole is an *orifice* (*trou*). The womb sound echoes in the names of other round containers: *bowl, bower, pot, retort, bottle, oven*, and finally the *gloomy tomb*. Protuberances are also expressed by O, as *mound, nob, knob, knoll, blob, bobble*, and one who is *overblown is pompous, bloated, obese, orotund, roly-poly, obsessed* by *glory*. In some of these words the O sound is combined with B to create a blustering effect.

The *orb of the moon*, the *womb of our mother*, and the *rolling downs* are poetic phrases typifying the effect of the O sound.

O, *goddess of the whole round globe,*
  Noble in glorious, glowing robe,
 Enthroned beneath a golden dome,
   Your womb our source, come, call me home.

P

the pride of the progenitor

The sound of the letter P is proud, imperious, and priapic. As B suggests the binary bulges of the body and hard C and soft M invoke aspects of the female, so P denotes the emblems of *paternity*, the *penis*, *prick*, *pecker*, *impregnator*, and the letter is shaped accordingly. It proclaims male *priority* and *pre-eminence* and is heard in *principalities* and *powers*, *emperors* and *potentates*. With reference to the P sound are named things which are *perpendicular* and *rampant*, such as *piles*, *poles*, *posts*, *props*, *supports* and *uprights*, *pikes*, *peaks*, *pales*, *pimples*, *pinnacles*, *pillars*, and *pedestals*.

a Paternal parade

Papa, the President, the *principle* *personage* in our *Republic*, *proudly* *parades* his *powerful* troops *past* the imperial *palace*, *prinking* and *preening* in *peacock* *plumes* and *prancing* importantly on his *prize* *palfrey*.

Papa is a prime politician
And proud of his powerful position.
When people implore
his support for the poor
He spurns and pooh-poohs their petition.

P

pompous little pipsqueak

When persons become puffed-up, pompous, and pretentious they attract
the derisory effect of the P sound and are called *poor, puny, piffling, piddling,
pitiful, petty, pushy, impertinent pups, peanuts, pipsqueaks,* and *poltroons.* Another
kind of pride makes people *prim* and *proper, prissy, pernickety,* and *precious.*
They are apt to be contemptuous and pooh-poohing, and their particular
exclamation is *pshaw!* In contrast to the B people who bash and batter, the
spiteful P folk *pinch, poke pins, prick, pry,* and *prod.* Given the same treatment,
they turn *peevish* and *pine, pule, puke,* and complain *pathetically.*

Pride precedes comeuppance

"Proper little popinjay!"
  the population cried
As he pirouetted past them
  in his panoply of pride.
He preened his purple plumage,
  posed in postures prim to pert,
Then tripped and sprawled and splattered
  in a putrid pool of dirt.

Q

quaint and quizzical

The Q with its curlicue or curlie *queue* is a funny looking letter, and the odd quirkiness of its appearance seems to extend to its meaning. It sounds in the last syllable of words with a slightly outmoded, whimsical air, such as *picturesque, baroque, exquisite, antique,* and the words to which it provides the initial are *quaint, queer, quirky, queasy, quaking,* and *quivering.* It is a bit of a fraud in *quack* doctors, *chequered* careers, and things which are *quasi,* or not quite what they seem, and it is *quizzical, questioning,* and *querulous* in *quids* and *quiddities, qualms* and *quandaries, quests, quips,* and *quibbles.* In Latin languages it queries: *quis? que? quoi? quad? quando?*

A-quiver with zest we embarqued on a quest,
But its quirks made us queer and uneasy,
Querulous, havering, questioning, quavering,
Quarrelsome, quibbling and queasy.

R

running round the rugged rocks

The R sound, said Socrates, denotes *rapidity* and *hardness*. The first is illustrated by numerous words such as *hurry, scurry, rush,* and *tear, run a race, whirr round, revolve, raging torrent,* and *roaring current.* Hardness and R go together in phrases like: *rigid, firm,* and *rugged* as a *rock* of *granite.* The two qualities are combined in words for *rough abrasive* actions such as *break, rend, crush, crumble* (given in *Cratylus*), *crack, fracture, rupture, grind, rub, rip, roll, wreck, crash, scrape,* and *crunch.*

Roughly runs the raging torrent
Over rocks and crags abhorrent,
Rolling rapid with a roar
Bursting on the rugged shore.

SL
swine slurping swill

The sibilant S can be amiable, as in *whispering* and *whistling*, but it is the hostile *hiss* of a snake or cat which is heard in spiteful words as, *Piss off you stupid ass, stinking skunk!* Further disgust is added when the sound is SCH or SL. Combining these with the other common sounds of disgust, G or GH, one arrives at the perfect word for expressing contempt and loathing—*schlugh!* This ideal was approached by Shakespeare when he named Shylock, and it is rivalled by several Yiddish words of contempt such as *schlock, schlepp,* and *schmuck.*

Associations of *sludge* and the *slimy* serpent (in German *Schlange*) are in words such as *slither, slip, slop, slide, slurp, sleaze, slug, sloth, slur, sly, slouch, slovenly,* and *sulky.* In these words the gliding, limpid liquid represented by the L sound is sullied by the S, making it a *sluggish* ooze or *slough.*

"Since you're such a slippery slug,"
Hissed Sally with a sullen shrug,
"Slink to Susie's sluttish slum.
  She's your sort you slimy scum."

SP

spirit of spring

The SP sound of spitting is heard at or near the beginning of many verbs which describe liquid *spluttering* or *splashing* out in *spate*, like *sparkling* water from a *spa* or *spume splurging* from a champagne bottle. They include: *spew, spurt, spray, spate, spring, spill, spout, explode, expectorate, expel,* and *spit out*.

Spring and spirit are words which sum up the qualities of SP. Spring is to do with jumping up. In *springtime sprouts* and *sprigs spurt* ahead and one feels *spruce, spry, sprightly, spicy, spic and span, sparky, spunky, speedy, spontaneous, splendid, inspired, spurred* on, ready to *sprint* at a *spanking* pace or go on a *sporting spree*.

A spirited person is either full of *aspirations, expectations,* and *espoir,* or has *spasms* of *spite, spleen* and *waspishness*.

In *spring* the *aspidistras sprout,*
Sprightly sprigs and sprays spurt out.
Spleen is spent; the sparkling air
Dispatches spite, expels despair.

STR

strict instructions

The STR sound is strongly connected with straightness and strictness of conduct. Among the names of things which are *straight* when *stretched* out are *street*, *strand*, *strip*, *stripe*, *streak*, and *string*. In *striding*, *strutting*, and *straining* ahead one naturally goes *straight*.

Stringency and the *striking* down of those who ignore *strictures* or *instructions* are displayed in the German words, *Strafe* (punishment) and *streng* (stern). Wrong-doers are given *strokes* of the *strap* or *strop* or put under *constraint*.

A poetic image of the STR sound is a streak of light (German *Strahl*) *streaming* or *striking straight* down a *stretch* of *strand*.

The Schoolmaster

My strategy is stern but straight:
  Obstructive, strident, obdurate
Striplings who strike or stroll in late
  I strap or treat to strictures.
But those who stringently abide
  by my instructions, strict applied,
Who strive ahead with strenuous stride,
  I take them to the pictures.

T

a tintinabulation of tiny, tinny trinkets

T has a light tinkling sound, *stimulating slightly pleasant* or *irritated* feelings, as in the phrases: *pretty ditties and tinkling tunes on the spinet; trilling, twittering titmice; titivating chatterers, talkative tell-tales, tittle-tattling* over the *tea-table; tasty tart, trifle* or *titbit to tickle, tempt,* and *titillate the appetite.* A *trip for two to tea in Tooting* gives the general impression.

    The type of motion implied by T is *dainty* and *fastidious, tripping, trotting, tip-tapping, tottery.* It is the opposite of purposeful and is apt to be called *trivial, stupid, futile, pretentious, affected, stuttering, tedious,* and *tiresome.* The T sound is applied scornfully to those who are thought to be *pretty, trite, tarty, tatty* little *upstarts, wretches, chits, sluts, twits, gits, twats, twerps,* and *nitwits.* When *teased, tortured, twitted,* or *tantalized,* such people become *irritable, testy, tetchy,* and *spiteful* and throw *fits* and *temper tantrums.*

Tim and Terry take a cottage
  near the tiny town of Wittering,
Replete with dainty ornaments
  and bits of tinsel glittering.
Through the pretty little patio
  you trip onto the terrace
Which it's Timmy's task to tidy
  when to set the tea is Terry's.

TR

trouble in store

The tremulous sound in T, combined with long vowels and various other consonants, particularly R, gives *terror* to words such as *storm, torrent, trouble, tumult, tornado, tirade, tempest, tantrum,* and the *twisting, twirling tourbillon* (whirlwind).

In high winds and rough seas sailors are *tossed, turned, tormented, terrified,* and made to *twitch* and *tremble.*

This town is tormented in terrible forms
By torrents, tornadoes, and trumpeting storms.
The traders are troubled and tremble afraid
When the thunders intone their tremendous tirade.

U

utterly uncouth

In his essay on *The Poetical Alphabet* Mr. Blood amusingly illustrates the blunt, mundane effect of the short U sound:

U, gutteral, or flat, is a humorous savage, best described in his own words: *a huge, lubberly, blundering dunderhead, a blubbering numskull and a dunce, ugly, sullen, dull, clumsy, rugged, gullible, glum, dumpish, lugubrious; a stumbler, mumbler, bungler, grumbler, jumbler; a drudge, a trudge, he lugs, tugs, sucks, juggles and is up to all manner of bulls; a musty, fussy, crusty, disgusting brute, whose head is his mug, his nose is a snub or a pug, his ears are lugs, his breasts dugs, his bowels guts, his vitals grub, his garments duds, his hat a plug, his child a cub, his dearest diminutive is chub or bub or runt; at his best he is bluff, gruff, blunt; his doublet is of sturdy buff and though not sword, is 'cudgel proof'; budge he will not, but will drub you with a club, or a slug, nub, stub, butt, or rub you with mud, for he is ever in a muss or a fuss, and should you call him grudging curmudgeon he gulps up 'ugh, fudge, stuff, rubbish, humbug' in his dudgeon; he is a rough, a blood-tub, a bummer, and a 'tough cuss' all around; he has some humour, more crudity, but no delicacy; of all nationalities you would take him for a Dutchman.* - Benjamin Paul Blood [1832-1919]

Doug, the Dutchman in our pub,
Sups a mug and stuffs his grub.
"Ugh!" he gulps and rubs his gut,
Stumbling glumly to his hut.

V

vital and vigorous but vain and vicious

Vitality is in words which relate to the Latin *vita* (life), *vis* (force) and *vigor*. In English are *vim* and *vigour*, *vitality*, and *velocity*. The effect of V can be described as *very vivacious*.

Like several other sounds V has a second, opposite meaning. In accordance with its relationship to the sounds W and F, it is sometimes weak and flustered (German *verwirrt*), as in the words *vain*, *vacuous*, *vapid*, *vague*, *vacillate*, *vagrant*, *vaporous*, *vertigo*, *veer*, and *vary*.

Weakness leads to *vice*, and so to a *vile*, *vicious*, *depraved*, *evil*, *vindictive*, *violent*, *virulent*, *vexacious*, *vengeful*, *voracious villain*, *virago*, *vermin*, *viper*, *vampire*, and *devil*.

Venomous is best descriptive of the *malevolent* aspect of V.

Ravished, violently defiled,
　　Savaged, chivvied, vexed, reviled,
Vows of love I rive and sever.
　　Vicious vamp! Forgive I'll never.

W

washed away by waves of water

The shape of the letter W can be described as *wavy* and *watery*, and so can the type of motion it implies. In liquids it is an *aqueous flow*, as in *swelling billows*. In air it is of *whisps* of *wool* or *down*, *wafted away*, *blown* on the *winds*.

Wavering is the state of mind reflected in the W sound; it is *weak, wet, weary, weedy, wobbly, wandering, woeful, wistful, willowy, wishy-washy*, and *querulous*.

The sense and image of W are depicted in a switchback railway.

a Watery walk

When the weather is wet and windy the wells overflow and waves of water wash over the weir. Wearing wellingtons we waddle through the squelchy swamp, wondering which way to wander, whether to wade or swim.

X

the box of tricks

The form of the letter X, a cross as of two sticks laid one across the other, depicts a paradox, a meeting of opposites as in sex. Its sound suggests an eccentricity, a box of tricks, by which one is *perplexed, vexed, hexed, jinxed, foxed, mixed* up, and put in a *fix*.

There is a teasing quality to the X sound, as in:

Pixy is a foxy minx,
  Full of vexing tricks, a jinx,
Yet she cooks and fixes clocks,
  A perplexing paradox!

Y

yowling yobbos

Y at the end of a word is a sound of familiarity, affectionate or derisive, like the short I. A *merry ditty* for a *pretty baby* typifies its associations.

Y as an initial has a coarse, rustic, jeering ring. Curs and rude youths torment with *yaps, yelps, yowls, yells, baying,* and *yammering.* Makers of such noises are called *yobs* or *yoiks,* or *yokels* (rustic clods). Swift's name for human animals in *Gulliver's Travels* was *yahoos.* People of similar kind in America have been called *yippies,* and those of another class *yuppies.* In English novels they yodel *yoo-hoo,* or *yoicks* if huntsmen, or *yo-ho-ho* if pirates.

Yeah! yah! ya-boo! yaroo! are among many expressions of leering mockery based on the Y sound. It is heard in *yid,* a nasty name for a Jew, also in a nasty epithet for timid folk, *yellow.* 'You young ...' followed by some disobliging term, is a style of address traditionally used by irate fathers-in-law.

In German the Y sound is denoted by the letter J and occurs in words of yowling and yelping such as *jammern, janken,* and *jaueln.*

Yowling yobs

Yelping, yapping puppies,
Gangs of jeering kids,
Yelling names at yuppies,
Yokels, Yanks, and yids.

Z

dazzled by the puzzle of the fizzle

There is a line in a half-remembered song which recalls "those lazy, hazy, crazy days of summer". It illustrates the effect of the Z sound in conjuring up the muzzy, fuzzy atmosphere of a hot summer's day, when bees are buzzing, one's eyes are glazed, and the mind feels *dizzy, dazy, fazed, bemused, woozy,* and *dowsy.* From the heads of *dozing, snoozing* (perhaps *boozed*) cartoon characters issue the letters zzzzzzzz.

The Z sound has a quizzical, zealously inquisitive air, apparent in words such as *puzzle* (which looks a bit like a puzzle), *quiz, tease,* and *maze,* or *miz-maze,* which can make one *crazy, zany,* or *frenzied.* The Z shape recalls the crooked pathway of a maze, also the crooked *business wizard,* by whom one is *swizzled, chizzled,* and *bamboozled.* It is the shape of the zig-zag flash of *blazing, fizzing, sizzling, dazzling* lightning in a *blizzard.* With this image come the words *whizz, zing, zip, zoom,* and *zap.*

Impressions given by the Z sound are of a person with zest, trying busily to escape from a maze, or of someone in a *tizzy, dazed* by a *bizarre puzzle* and *gazing* at it in *amazement.*

Sizzle or doze?

Lizzie's always busy, dizzy, buzzing round like crazy.
Ebenezer's zonked and sozzled, dozy, dazed, and lazy.
Here's the quiz and puzzle: if bamboozled and confused
Do you zoom and sizzle or get hazy and bemused?

BOOK II

Above: Grammar holding the key to the door of the seven liberal arts.
From Margarita Philosophica by Gregor Reisch, 1508.

GRAMMAR

THE STRUCTURE OF LANGUAGE

Rachel Holley

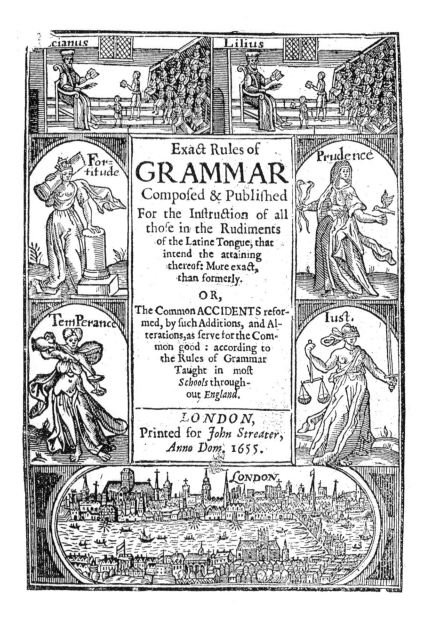

cianus   Lilius

For=
titude

Prudence

Exact Rules of

GRAMMAR

Compoſed & Publiſhed

For the Inſtruction of all
thoſe in the Rudiments
of the Latine Tongue, that
intend the attaining
thereof: More exact,
than formerly.

OR,

The Common ACCIDENTS refor-
med, by ſuch Additions, and Al-
terations, as ſerve for the Common good : according to
the Rules of Grammar
Taught in moſt
Schools through-
out England.

LONDON,
Printed for *John Streater*,
Anno Dom. 1655.

TemPerance

Iuſt.

LONDON

INTRODUCTION

IF YOU ARE READING this book, you already have some notion of grammar. As your eyes scan this page, your brain derives meaning from the symbols printed here, knowing that words come in a certain order, and that different types of word fulfil different functions.

Language is humanity's primary vehicle for thought and communication, both internal and external. Indeed, the ability to learn the complex system of symbols and rules which underlie syntax and grammar is arguably the most distinctive feature of the human race. Grammar enables us to inform, edify, and entertain; it allows us to reason, debate, and argue; it helps us study, build, and use complex things, from recipes to spaceships.

Aristotle and the Stoics thought that grammar, although patterned, was also essentially messy, whereas later grammarians, such as Dionysius Thrax, Varro, and Priscian, praised and encouraged regularities in language. In 14th century Northern Europe, a group know as the Modistae were the first to propose a universal grammar, prefiguring the work of Noam Chomsky.

In the medieval period, grammar was seen as the foundation subject on which all other knowledge depended, and it dominated the studies of pupils between the ages of seven and fourteen. As had been the practice since Classical times, students would painstakingly work through famous texts, analyzing them syllable by syllable.

Logic asks: *when is a sentence true?* Rhetoric asks: *which is the right sentence?* Grammar purely asks: *when is a sentence correct?* I hope that these pages will at least whet your appetite for grammar, if not turn you into a most ardent and impassioned grammarian.

LETTERS AND SCRIPTS
alphabet systems and languages

The word 'grammar' comes from the Greek term *gramma* (a letter), itself related to *grapho* (to draw or write). The invention of *script*, around 3000 BC in Sumeria and India, suddenly made it possible to write and read texts of law, commerce, ritual, poetry, history, philosophy, and science. And, perhaps most important of all, it gave birth to the detailed discussion of the *correct form* of such texts.

Broadly speaking, scripts come in two types. LOGOGRAPHIC systems try to depict the *meaning* of a text without relating to the sound of language (the Chinese script being a prime example). PHONOGRAPHIC systems, on the other hand, record text as it would *sound* when spoken. The Roman alphabet, which we use to write English and other Western European tongues, is phonographic, as are the scripts used for Hebrew, Russian, Greek, Arabic, and Sanskrit. Today's *International Phonetic Alphabet* is used for correctly writing the pronunciation of languages.

Every natural language uses a distinct set of sounds as building blocks, these generally being classified as either *consonants* or *vowels*. Distinguishing how and with which parts of our speech organs these sounds are formed can be of great help in the acquisition of a language. The science of sounds in speech and language is called *phonetics*.

漢 汉 **ABC** देवनागरी 𓀀 אלפבית ひ カ
字 字 αλφάβητο Кириллица أبجدية ら タ
⋮⋮⋮⋮⋮ ตัวอักษรไทย 𐤀𐤋𐤐𐤀𐤓𐤊 한 글 が カ
な ナ

𒀭 𒄑 𒆠 𒂊 𒀸 𒈗 𒉺 𒅗 𒐀 𒐊 𒐓 𒐤 𒑊 𒐴 𒁹 𒁹

PETROGLYPH | HIEROGLYPH | SYLLABIC | ALPHABETS

PALEOLITHIC 15,000–12,000 B.C. MESOLITHIC 12,000–7,000 B.C. NEOLITHIC 7,000–5,000 B.C. ARMENIA	CHALCOLITHIC ROCK CARVING COPPER–BRONZE AGE 5000–2000 B.C. ARMENIA	METZAMOR INSCRIPTION 2000–1800 B.C.	HYKSOSIAN INSCRIPTION 1750–1580 B.C.	HAIKAZIAN INSCRIPTION 1500 B.C.? ARMENIA	URARTIAN SYMBOLS 1270–550 B.C. ARMENIA	ARMAVIR INSCRIPTION ARMENIA	CHOLAGERD INSCRIPTION 850–750 B.C. ARMENIA	URARTIAN CUNEIFORM 855–450 B.C. ARMENIA	HYKSOSIAN after 1720 B.C. SINAI	HAIKAZIAN OLD ARMENIAN 7–14th Cent. A.D. SINAI	ODESSIAN 5–6th Cent. B.C. SINAI	MESROBIAN 406 A.D.–PRESENT ARMENIA	NAME	PHONETIC VALUE

Left: Examples of various script forms, ancient and modern, from around the world.
Above: A suggestive interpretation of the evolution of the Armenian Indo-European alphabet.

EARLY GRAMMAR
Sanskrit, Greek, and Latin

One of the earliest written languages for which governing rules were established is Indian Sanskrit (Sanskrit hymns are among the oldest written texts on earth), and the first compilation of its rules was made by Panini around 450 BC. One of the most prominent features of Sanskrit is *inflection,* where words undergo changes to express relationships. In English *he* might become *his* or *him,* while in Sanskrit *deva* (meaning *god*) might become *devasya* (*of the god*). Sanskrit is the oldest recorded language of a branch of tongues called the *Indo-European Language Family.* Our own ancestors probably spoke a language very similar to Sanskrit.

The first concise grammar in the West is attributed to Dionysius Thrax [170–90 BC], who taught in Alexandria, Egypt. He found that words in classical Greek change according to rules, and when Latin later came to dominate the Western world, scholars noticed that it too was similar. We now know that Sanskrit, Greek, and Latin share a common ancestor and that other members of this family include Indo-Iranian, Balto-Slavic, Celtic, and Germanic. Although classical Latin disappeared, its dialects became today's Romance languages. This means that our language now has a quite extensive family tree.

Broadly speaking, older languages have more complex systems of inflection, while the grammar of younger languages is more simplified. Immigration, trade, invasions, and occupations may have forced villagers to learn more languages over time, and, rather than mastering the intricacies of any particular tongue, they muddled along with a simplified speech which later became the rule. Perhaps the finest example of such a process and its result is English.

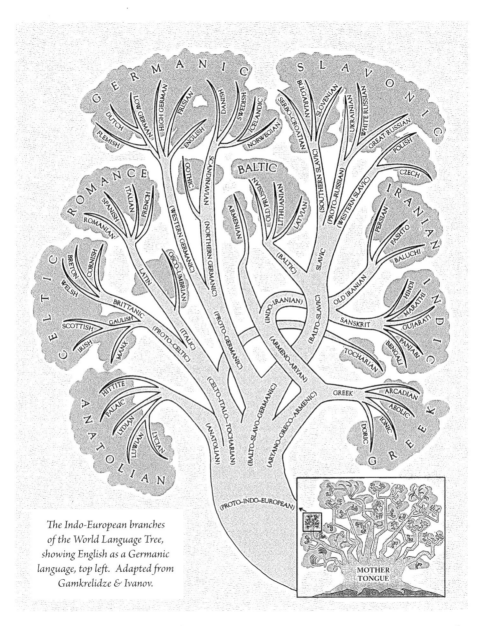

The Indo-European branches
of the World Language Tree,
showing English as a Germanic
language, top left. Adapted from
Gamkrelidze & Ivanov.

THE STORY OF ENGLISH
into the melting pot

The British Isles, at the northwestern tip of the European peninsula of the Eurasian continent, have experienced many waves of immigration in their long history, both as invasions and peaceful settlements. The first settlers arrived in the early Stone Age, and of their language we have no trace. However, at the time of the Roman conquest, we know that Celtic languages were spoken. Then, after the Romans departed in 410 AD, a huge wave of Anglo-Saxon immigration from what is now northern Germany and Denmark brought with it a language known as Old Saxon, with many of the words we use today. Further plundering, settlement, and trading by Norsemen brought in yet more foreign words, resulting in the fascinating blend of Old English.

Just as the language was beginning to settle down, the Norman conquest of 1066 brought in a plethora of new French terms which soon changed the language forever. French words in English include *judge, government, brunette, nation, parliament, voyage, president, route, inhabitant,* and *arrive*. Luckily, Norman French and Old English broadly shared the rules of inflection common to all Indo-European tongues, but their two systems were still somewhat incompatible, so most people soon began to ignore both systems, resulting in the fact that there is little inflectional grammar left at all in English today. Modern English thus emerged as a hybrid language, about 28% Latin, 28% French, 25% Germanic (Saxon, Dutch, and Norse), 6% Greek, 4% proper names and 6% from elsewhere. It continues today to absorb and transmit words, and its grammar and pronunciation remain in flux. It now functions primarily through the combination of predominantly inflexible words, much like Chinese.

INDO-EUROPEAN   URALO-ALTAIC

CHAMITO-
SEMITIC

SINO-THAI

NIGER-
CONGO

DRAVIDIAN

AMERINDIAN

AUSTRONESIAN

BANTU

PAPUAN AND AUSTRALIAN

Above: The primary distribution of native language across the planet. Notice the language island Finland and Estonia create within the Indo-European grouping. Note too Madagascar.

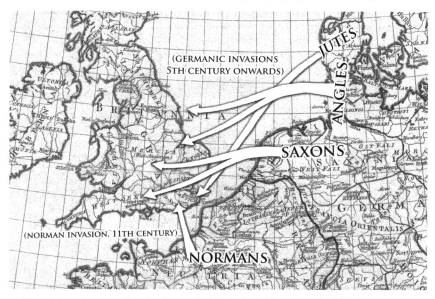

(GERMANIC INVASIONS
5TH CENTURY ONWARDS)

JUTES

ANGLES

SAXONS

(NORMAN INVASION, 11TH CENTURY)

NORMANS

Above: The main waves of peoples that resulted in the English language. The Celtic languages, once spoken throughout this same area, are today confined to the extremities.

MAKING SENSE
putting words together

Languages combine sounds to express meanings, and grammar describes the rules of this process. There are at least five different ways to do this:

COMBINATION. So, *un* and *lock* can combine to form the word *unlock*.

CONNECTING WORDS. For example, the words *key* and *lock* can be combined using a preposition: *key in lock*.

WORD ORDER. Languages that use a lot of inflection, like Sanskrit or Russian, have a less strict word order, while English makes heavy use of word order—compare *Tom loves Anya* to *Anya loves Tom*.

ACCENT, STRESS, INTONATION, and **PITCH.** Modern Indo-European languages use changes in stress, intonation, or pitch to convey emotional content, or to denote a question. In languages such as Chinese, however, the same syllable can have completely different meanings depending on the shape of tone contour (e.g. rising, peaking, dipping, or falling).

INFLECTION. Here, words change to express a different relation; so the word *see* can be inflected to *saw*, conveying tense (*p. 82*) and aspect (*p. 89*). Indo-European languages all share similar rules on how to inflect nouns (*declension*) and verbs (*conjugation*), though English has lost much of this over time. For example, the old intimate second person singular *thou* (*thou art*) has largely been dropped, where in Middle English it once became *thee* (*I give thee*) for the accusative and dative, and *thy* (*thy hand*) or *thine* (*thine eyes*) for the possessive.

The example below shows how the conjugations of the verb *to make* have changed in English over the centuries:

OLD ENGLISH	MIDLE ENGLISH	MODERN ENGLISH
ich make	I make	I make
þu makest	thou makst	you make
he makeþ	he maketh	he makes
we maken	we make	we make
ge maken	ye make	you make
hio maken	they make	they make

And here is another example, showing how the declensions of the noun *angel* have likewise changed over time.

	LATIN	OLD ENGLISH	MODERN
NOMINATIVE (I, angel)	angelus	engel	angel
ACCUSATIVE (I saw the angel)	angelum	engel	angel
GENITIVE (my or his angel)	angeli	engles	angel
DATIVE (to the angel)	angelo	engle	angel

English, in fact, is becoming more and more like Chinese, which uses no inflection and is comprised of one-syllable particles—similar to the following English sentence: *She just has to go for this! It's a piece of cake for her! She can do it!* So, in English, many of the early grammatical rules today explain the exceptions, rather than serving as rules, and declension remains, for the most part, merely in the personal pronouns. An exception is the genitive, which remains as *'s*, the apostrophe indicating where the *e* dropped out, as in *engles* (above), so today we speak of *the angel's wings*.

CATEGORIES & TERMS
the five building blocks

Language can communicate both *thoughts* and *emotions*, but while emotions can also be conveyed by music or facial expressions, thoughts are more intrinsically linked to language and the use of symbols. When a word is not just a combination of sounds, but has a certain meaning, it is called a TERM. Speakers and listeners who agree on the meaning of a word have *come to terms*—they understand what they are talking about. Each term can be expanded or refined, and set in relation to other terms.

There are different types of terms: those which describe *objects* (or *substances*), those which describe *actions*, and those which *quantify relations*. It was Aristotle who first began to categorize words, listing nouns (describing substances) and verbs (describing actions) as the parts of speech. Philosophers later began to wonder if these categories were somehow more fundamental than grammar itself? A substance, for example, appears timeless, while a verb, in contrast, always happens in time. Today we still distinguish between words that describe objects and words that describe actions, as well as between words that describe qualities and those that indicate relation in number, time, space, and causation.

A NOUN stands for a object, whether an *observed object*, like a *butterfly*, or an *abstract thing* which may be explained by other words learned earlier, such as *the mind*. A noun term generally invokes an image of a *substance*, e.g. *tree* conjures not a specific tree, but a general idea. Some qualities are then intrinsic to the idea *tree* and can be listed in a definition.

A VERB describes the action concerning or linking one or more substance, e.g. *the tree grows*. Some actions can be demonstrated, like *to fly*, and others cannot, e.g. *to postpone*. Actions are always associated with substances—in most cases they are what speech is really about. In the sentence *the man drives a car* there are two such substances: *the man*, and *the car*. One is *subject* to the action, in this case, the man: what he is and does is here completely determined by the act of driving. The other is *object* to the action, in this case, the car: it is controlled by the action, but is also challenging the action, as it needs to be controlled.

A QUALIFIER is a word or phrase which attributes a quality to another word. When a qualifier is applied to a noun, it is called an *adjective*, as in *tall tree*; and when applied to a verb it is called an adverb, as in *running quickly*. Pronouns and determiners, like *a, the, he, she* are also qualifiers.

A RELATION WORD, such as *with, before*, or *behind*, creates a relation between other words. We tend to learn relation words by example.

There are thus five main building blocks of language (*italicized below*). English grammar also works at five levels: SENTENCES are made up of CLAUSES, which are made up of PHRASES, which consist of WORDS, which are composed of MORPHEMES.

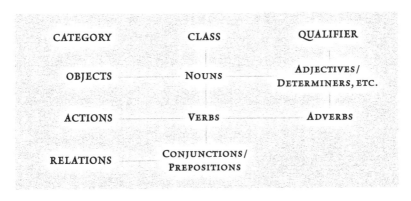

CATEGORY	CLASS	QUALIFIER
OBJECTS	NOUNS	ADJECTIVES/ DETERMINERS, ETC.
ACTIONS	VERBS	ADVERBS
RELATIONS	CONJUNCTIONS/ PREPOSITIONS	

THE PARTS OF SPEECH
classifying words

By the end of the 2nd century BC, grammarians were identifying eight categories of words. In 500 AD, Priscian added a new category of 'interjection'. Today, auxiliary verbs (*is, a, are, see page 87*) are separated from main verbs, and words are often grouped into ten classes (parts of speech) in two categories:

CONTENT:	**NOUNS** – naming words	
(*open*)	**ADJECTIVES** – modify nouns	
	MAIN VERBS – express actions and states	
	ADVERBS – modify verbs, adjectives, or other adverbs	
	INTERJECTIONS – expressions of emotion; *wow!*	
STRUCTURE:	**PRONOUNS** – words that stand in for nouns	
(*closed*)	**DETERMINERS** – articles, modify nouns	
	AUXILIARY VERBS – express actions and states	
	CONJUNCTIONS – connecting words	
	PREPOSITIONS – show the relationship between words	

Content words carry the meaning of a sentence. The classes for these words are *open*, meaning new words are readily added. An example is the new noun *locavore*, meaning 'one who eats locally grown food'.

Structure words structure a sentence, e.g. *it, the, was, and, to,* and these classes are generally *closed* and very limited in number, rarely admitting new words.

Content words and structure words each make up about 50% of most pieces of writing. The most commonly used English content words are: *say, make, like, time, know, take, people, year, good, see, look, come, think, work, want, give, day.*

The investigation of the meaning of words is the beginning of education. — Antisthenes

DETERMINERS
identify yourself

I pass by THESE walls, THE walls of Layla
And I kiss THIS wall and THAT wall
It's not Love of THE houses that has taken MY heart
But of THE One who dwells in THOSE houses

— poem attributed to Qays ibn al-Mulawwah

Determiners, including *articles*, come before nouns and tell us something about their number, definiteness, proximity, and ownership. Classes are:

DEFINITE ARTICLE — *the*
INDEFINITE ARTICLE — *a / an, any, some, that, those, this, whichever, whatever*
DEMONSTRATIVE DETERMINERS — *this, that, these, those*
POSSESSIVE DETERMINERS — *my, your, his, her, its, our, their*
RELATIVE DETERMINERS — *whose, whichever, whatever*
INTERROGATIVE DETERMINERS — *whose, which, what*
S-GENITIVE — *Harold's*
NUMERALS — Cardinal or ordinal numerals before a noun; *two donkeys, first night*

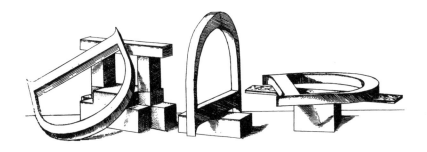

THE NOUN PHRASE
the thing itself

The noun phrase within a sentence is a word or a group of words describing something of substance (rather than an action), e.g. *the horse*. At its core is usually a noun, e.g. *horse* or *Peter*, or a pronoun that has taken its place, e.g. *it* or *he*. Adjectives may also be present, e.g. *the tall horse*. Rules now apply:

Logical rules deal with content, and so with terms rather than words. For example, *the solid air* is illogical, since air is by definition not solid. Some qualities are also intrinsic to nouns and need not be specified once we understand the term. For example, a statement such as *the sphere is round* is essentially redundant if we understand its terms.

Grammatical rules deal with certain qualities that words carry. For example, the word *house* conveys the fact that a singular object is being discussed; while in the word *houses* the annexed *s* denotes a plurality. Inflections (changed spellings) like these in nouns (as well as pronouns and adjectives) are known as DECLENSION, and in the inflecting Indo-European languages, nouns carry three such intrinsic qualities, *number*, *gender*, and *case*.

NUMBER, e.g. *house/houses:* While English uses SINGULAR and PLURAL, some Indo-European languages also have a DUALITY declension for things appearing in pairs, a bit like *the twain*, or *a pair of scissors* or *trousers*.

GENDER: English does not use gender, preserving the idea in only a few words (e.g. ships are often FEMININE). However, other Indo-European languages have two or even three genders: in German, *der Mond* (the moon) is MASCULINE, while *das Mädchen* (the maiden) is NEUTER. Note, grammatical gender is not the same as the sex of an object (e.g. *priest/priestess*).

CASE, e.g. *Peter/Peter's* (genitive): Here, a word gets slightly altered to express a certain function or relation it is performing in its clause. English uses only nominative and genitive, but older Indo-European languages may possess three or more of the following cases:

NOMINATIVE - the term is the agent of an action; *the horse* ran.

GENITIVE - the term is possessor of another term; *the horse's* stable.

DATIVE - the term is receiver of something or indirect object of an action; he gave something *to the horse*.

ACCUSATIVE - the term is the direct object of an action; she rode *the horse*.

ABLATIVE - the term is the origin of the action; he fell *from the horse*.

INSTRUMENTAL - the term is a tool of an action; she rode the horse *with a saddle*.

LOCATIVE - the term is the location of something; he rode the horse *on the track*.

VOCATIVE - the term is directly addressed; *Oh horse!*

The English word *horse* does not change in these examples, but consider them in Latin: *equus* (nom); *equi* (gen); *equo* (dat); *equum* (acc); *eque* (voc), or German: *das Pferd* (nom), *des Pferdes* (gen), *dem Pferde* (dat), *das Pferd* (acc).

To summarize, in the noun phrase the noun and all extensions of the noun (i.e. the determiner and adjectives) must agree in case, gender, and number, e.g. in French compare *la maison verte* (the green house) with *le tapis vert* (the green cover).

In English, declension is limited to **SINGULAR** *vs.* **PLURAL** number (*cat/cats*) and **NOMINATIVE** *vs.* **GENITIVE** case (*the cat* or *the cat's*). There are, however, some exceptions, as a few nouns do take **GENDER** forms (*prince/princess*) while others are sometimes considered female (*ship/moon*).

ENGLISH NOUNS
the name of the game

Over half the words in the *Oxford English Dictionary* are nouns, and nouns form the largest part of the average English speaker's vocabulary. Nouns take many different forms, as illustrated by the examples opposite, and the emphasized words below:

When ICICLES hang by the WALL
    And DICK the SHEPHERD blows his NAIL,
And TOM bears LOGS into the HALL,
    And MILK comes frozen HOME in PAIL;

When BLOOD is nipt and WAYS be foul,
    Then nightly sings the staring OWL
Tuwhoo! Tuwhit! Tuwhoo! A merry NOTE!
    While greasy JOAN doth keel the POT.

When all aloud the WIND doth blow
    And COUGHING drowns the PARSON's SAW,
And BIRDS sit brooding in the SNOW,
    And MARIAN's NOSE looks red and raw;

When roasted CRABS hiss in the BOWL
    Then nightly sings the staring OWL
Tuwhoo! Tuwhit! Tuwhoo! A merry NOTE!
    While greasy JOAN doth keel the POT.

— William Shakespeare

GRAMATICA

Nouns name people, things, places, or ideas that are:

ANIMATE
Joan, parson, owl

INANIMATE
pail, snow, logs, fork, newspaper

CONCRETE
milk, bread, piano, music

ABSTRACT
freedom, anger, happiness, glory

PROPER NOUNS refer to persons, places, geographical features, or various periods of time; *William Shakespeare, Marian, Asia, the Amazon River, Sunday*.

COMMON NOUNS refer to general entities. Most have a singular and a plural form; *crab / crabs, rose / roses, liberty / liberties, man / men, child / children*.

COUNT NOUNS denote things that can be counted; one *person*, two *glasses*, many *problems*, several *books*.

NONCOUNT (OR MASS) NOUNS refer to inanimate entities or constructs and are usually only expressed in singular form; *thunder, cotton, milk, luggage, hair*.

COLLECTIVE NOUNS define groups composed of individual members referred to collectively; *team, class, electorate, parliament, flock, herd, army*.

PRONOUNS

I, me, myself, and you, we, and them

PRONOUNS are words that stand in for nouns or other pronouns. They allow us to refer to a word that has already been mentioned without having to repeat it. Pronouns can also be used to refer to people or things which have no antecedent in the text. **PERSONAL PRONOUNS** refer to the people or things involved in a text, and change to reflect person, number, gender, and case.

SUBJECTIVE	OBJECTIVE	REFLEXIVE	POSSESSIVE
I	Me	Myself	My
You	You	Yourself	Your
He/She/It	Him/Her/It	Him/Her/Itself	His/Hers/Its
We	Us	Ourselves	Our
You	You	Yourselves	Your
They	Them	Themselves	Their

SUBJECTIVE PRONOUNS act as the *subject* of a sentence or clause,

> I'm nobody! Who are YOU?
> Are YOU nobody, too?

OBJECTIVE PRONOUNS are used as the *object* of a sentence or clause.

> Then there's a pair of US — don't tell!
> They'd banish US, you know.
>
> — Emily Dickinson

REFLEXIVE PRONOUNS are used when the object of the sentence is the same as the subject, and can also be used for emphasis.

> I am, indeed, a king, because I know how to rule MYSELF. — Pietro Aretino

> If you make YOURSELF understood, you're always speaking well. — Molière

POSSESSIVE PRONOUNS show personal possession. They substitute for a possessive adjective and a noun.

His money is twice tainted: 'taint YOURS *and 'taint* MINE. — Mark Twain

Other types of pronouns include:

RECIPROCAL PRONOUNS, which express mutual action or relationship. In
English: *each other*, or *one another*.

> *Words are but symbols for the relations of things to* ONE ANOTHER *and to us;*
> *nowhere do they touch upon absolute truth.* — Friedrich Nietzsche

DEMONSTRATIVE PRONOUNS identify nouns; *this, that, these, those, such.*

> *There are three classes of people:* THOSE *who see,* THOSE *who see when*
> *they are shown,* THOSE *who do not see.* — Leonardo da Vinci

> *Always do right.* THIS *will gratify some people and astonish the rest.* — Mark Twain

> SUCH *as we are made of,* SUCH *we be.* — William Shakespeare

INTERROGATIVE PRONOUNS are used to ask questions; *who, what, why, where,
when, whatever.*

> WHAT'*s in a name? That which we call a rose*
> *By any other name would smell as sweet.* — William Shakespeare

INDEFINITE PRONOUNS refer to people or things in a vague or general way;
*any, anything, anybody, anyone, some, something, somebody, someone, none, no one,
nothing, nobody, none, either, neither, both, each, all, everything, everybody, everyone.*

> *Trying to please* EVERYBODY, *I pleased* NOBODY. — Richard Wright

RELATIVE PRONOUNS introduce relative clauses (*see page 107*). They refer to a
noun that has already been mentioned, and give more information about
it; *who, whose, whom* are used for people, *which, what, that* refer to things.

> *The person, be it gentleman or lady,* WHO *has not pleasure in a good*
> *novel, must be intolerably stupid.* — Jane Austin

> *Knowledge* WHICH *is acquired under compulsion obtains no hold on the mind.* — Plato

ADJECTIVES
and other ways to expand a noun

Every noun evokes an idea, the essence of its term. For example, the essence or definition of wine is *alcoholic beverage made by the fermentation of grape juice*. Plato thought of nouns as representing *ideas* rather than *things*, and nouns demonstrate that the easiest way to evoke a thought about something is to name it, so if I say *Shakespeare*, you may immediately visualize someone. This doesn't work with general words like *cat*, or abstract concepts like *reality*. For example, if I say *woman*, of whom am I speaking? We need some quality or relation to distinguish her. Is she perhaps *the tall woman in the red dress on the left?* The noun phrase has expanded around the noun *woman* using attributives, *tall, in the red dress, on the left*.

The most common ways of expanding NOUN PHRASES are:

ARTICLES: Particles that precede a noun, e.g. *the* tree, or *a* tree (compare with *those trees* or *any tree*). The main function of articles is to define whether we are talking about one specific element of the idea, *the car* or *their car*, or any member, *a car*.

DECLENSION: Many languages (but not English) include qualities in a noun's declension which must agree in *number, gender,* and *case,* e.g. *goose/geese, count/countess (see pp. 70–71)*. Other signifiers can also be included; for example relative size in German, where *das Haus* means *the house,* while the diminutive *das Häuschen* means *the tiny house.*

ADJECTIVES: Any other qualifiers closely related to the noun. Adjectives in English do not take a specific form, although there are various adjectival suffixes, e.g. *-ful* or *-ly* as in *beautiful* or *friendly.* In many languages, e.g.

Spanish, adjectives need to agree with the noun in declension and gender. Word order also plays an important role: *the responsible person* or *the person responsible*. The standard order of adjectives is *colour, origin, material,* and *purpose: the red, French, leather riding boots.*

Qualities already included in a term's definition tend not to be added again, as doing so would produce a redundancy: *alcoholic wine, female woman;* neither are qualities contradicting its essence: *the straight curve;* nor logically false contradictory adjectives: *the black white swan.*

Adjectives in many languages are gradable and can be modified: *a very tall person, a taller person, quite a tall person, a slightly tall person, an absurdly tall person, the tallest person.* Adjectives make a language more pictorial, and convey judgements about the substances in a sentence. In Japanese the negative forms of verbs *are* adjectives, while the *beautiful* language of English uses many *clearly descriptive* adjectives, for example:

The poulterers' shops were still HALF OPEN, and the fruiterers' were RADIANT in their glory. There were GREAT, ROUND, POT-BELLIED baskets of chestnuts, SHAPED like the waistcoats of JOLLY OLD gentlemen, lolling at the doors, and tumbling out into the street in THEIR APOPLECTIC opulence. There were RUDDY, BROWN-FACED, BROAD-GIRTHED SPANISH Onions, shining in the fatness of their growth like SPANISH Friars, and winking from their shelves in WANTON slyness at the girls as they went by, and glanced demurely at the HUNG-UP mistletoe. There were pears and apples, CLUSTERED high in BLOOMING pyramids; there were bunches of grapes, made, in the shopkeepers' benevolence to dangle from CONSPICUOUS hooks, that people's mouths might water gratis as they passed; there were piles of filberts, MOSSY and BROWN, recalling, in THEIR fragrance, ANCIENT walks among the woods, and pleasant shufflings ANKLE DEEP through WITHERED leaves; there were NORFOLK Biffins, SQUAB and SWARTHY, setting off the yellow of the oranges and lemons, and, in the GREAT compactness of THEIR JUICY persons, urgently entreating and beseeching to be carried home in PAPER bags and eaten after dinner. — Charles Dickens, *A Christmas Carol*

ENGLISH ADJECTIVES
attributive and predicative

Adjectives describe, modify, and give information about nouns and pronouns. In English, adjectives may be *attributive* or *predicative*.

ATTRIBUTIVE ADJECTIVES are qualitative adjectives which are placed in front of the noun that they modify.

> A LARGE nose is the mark of a WITTY, COURTEOUS, AFFABLE, GENEROUS and LIBERAL man. — Cyrano de Bergerac

> She sent for one of those SQUAT, PLUMP LITTLE cakes called "PETITES madeleines..." — Marcel Proust

PREDICATIVE ADJECTIVES follow such linking verbs as *be, seem, become,* or *appear* and give information about the subject.

> The roots of education are BITTER, but the fruit is SWEET. — Aristotle

> I am INVISIBLE, understand, simply because people refuse to see me.
> — Ralph Waldo Ellison

Some adjectives can only be used attributively:

> It is not enough to have a good mind; the MAIN thing is to use it well. — René Descartes

while others are restricted to the predicative: We can say I am afraid / asleep / unwell / alive, but not I am an afraid / asleep / unwell / alive person.

CENTRAL ADJECTIVES can be used both attributively and predicatively.

> Every day I hear STUPID people say things that are not STUPID. — Michel de Montaigne

> The fool doth think himself WISE, but the WISE man knows himself to be a fool.
> — William Shakespeare

> There is nothing more SILLY than a SILLY laugh. — Gaius Valerius Catullus

QUALITATIVE ADJECTIVES can be graded to express degrees of qualities. By adding modifiers before or after a noun, we can speak of:

A FAIRLY *large nose,*
A RATHER *large nose,*
A VERY LARGE *nose,*
An EXTREMELY *large nose,*
Or *a nose that is large* ENOUGH

Adjectives can also be used to make comparisons between two or more people, things, or ideas. The three degrees of comparison are:

POSITIVE	*fair*	*happy*	*good*	*graceful*
COMPARATIVE	*fairer*	*happier*	*better*	*more graceful*
SUPERLATIVE	*fairest*	*happiest*	*best*	*most graceful*

... my love is as FAIR. *As any mother's child ...* — William Shakespeare

You shall be yet far FAIRER *than you are.* — William Shakespeare

The FAIREST *I have yet beheld.* — William Shakespeare

Adjectives can be:

QUALITATIVE – *round, jolly, outrageous, thin, crafty, powerful, dramatic*
DEMONSTRATIVE – *this, that, these, those*
DISTRIBUTIVE – *each, every, either, neither*
QUANTITATIVE – *a, some, any, no, none, little, few, many, much, 1, 2, 3 ...*
INTERROGATIVE – *which, what, whose*
POSSESSIVE – *my, your, his, her, its, our, their*
CLASSIFYING – *annual, French, chief, principal, unique, pregnant*

We are armed with language ADEQUATE *to describe each leaf of the field,*
but not to describe HUMAN *character.* — Henry David Thoreau

The Verb Phrase
action!

Words which describe the action in a sentence are called "verbs," from the Latin *verbum* "word". The **Verbal Phrase** of a sentence is a syntactic unit which involves at least one verb and its dependents, e.g. *planted the tree* or *read him his last rites*. While nouns name substances, verbs do more than just name actions, they can convey a wealth of information in five key ways:

PERSON: In the act of speaking I may refer to actions involving myself, whomever I am speaking to, or others. In English, the categories of *first*, *second*, and *third* person *singular* (I, thee, he/she/it), and *plural* (We, ye, they) denote *person*. However, in heavily-inflected languages, such as Polish, verbs have different endings for I, You, He, She, It, We both, We all, You both, You all, They both, They all, etc.

TENSE: While substance is eternal, action is change, and happens in time. Any action can therefore either have already happened, be happening, or happen in the future: *past*, *present*, and *future*. The *tense* of a verb describes the position of the action in time relative to the speaker (*see pages 82-3*). Different languages employ different tenses—in the Navajo language there are seven: the **Imperfective**, I *was walking*, the **Perfective**, I *walked*, the **Progressive**, I *am walking*, the **Future**, I *shall walk*, the **Usitative**, I *usually walk*, the **Iterative**, I *always walk*, and the **Optative**, I *hope I walk*.

VOICE: For every action there is a reason, sometimes conscious, sometimes not: If I *hold a sword*, I have probably made a conscious decision to do so, but if *The wind blows*, there may or may not be a being originating the action. If the agent is uncertain, we can say It *is raining*. However, the agent of an action is not necessarily its prime cause: If I *smell a flower*, I might just have walked past it. Sentences express our experience of cause and effect, and verbs assist this through *active* and *passive* voices (*see page 88*). Compare The *lion caught the mouse* (active) vs. *The mouse was caught by the lion* (passive).

ASPECT: The ancient Greeks used two words for time, *chronos* for a stretch of time and *kairos* for a moment. A verb's aspect colours the action, describing whether it is perfected, *the farmer has ploughed the field*, or ongoing, *the farmer was ploughing the field*. In some languages, like Chinese, neither tense nor aspect is differentiated, while the Navajo use twelve possible aspects with ten subaspects. In other languages, aspects can describe actions as repetitive, successful, defective, resumptive or accidental (*see appendix, page 396*). In Slavic languages, aspect is conveyed via prefixes and suffixes to the verb and counts more heavily than either tense or mood. In English, verb aspect simply describes whether an action is simple, ongoing, completed, or will be completed (*see pages 83 and 89*).

MOOD: Actions can really be taking place, or be only proposed, stated, or hypothetical in other ways. These are the moods of a verb (*see page 90*); compare I *insist I am involved* vs. I *insist I be involved*.

In many languages verbs change their form quite radically with the sentence's subject and time reference, and in verbs such inflections are called CONJUGATION. *Am, are, is,* and *was* are all conjugated forms of *to be*. Older verbs tend to retain their strong (or irregular) conjugation, but most English verbs show very little inflection, e.g. I *laugh, he laughs*.

ENGLISH VERB TENSES
about time too

The **TENSE** of a verb refers to the location of an action or event in time.

The **PRESENT TENSE** is used to indicate something that is happening or existing now, is a recurring event, or is true at all times.

> But soft! What light through yonder window BREAKS?
> It IS the East, and Juliet IS the sun! — William Shakespeare

> Every time a child SAYS "I don't believe in fairies" there is
> a little fairy somewhere that falls down dead. — James M. Barrie

> He who OPENS a school door, CLOSES a prison. — Victor Hugo

> Don't grieve. Anything you lose COMES round in another form. — Jalaluddin Rumi

The **PAST TENSE** indicates that something happened or existed in the past.

> The world's bright candle, early Spring, CAME new
>   And BROUGHT the bounteous gift of life restored,
> And SPREAD afar its veil of pearly blue,
>   And URGED the nightingale to trill its song;
> SPREAD far the limped wine of morning dew,
>   And FILLED the open'd tulip's crimson cup;
> INFLAMED the rose that in the garden BLEW
>   Agleam with turquoise and the ruby's glow. — Mohammed Fuzuli (tr. Sofi Nuri)

The **FUTURE TENSE** does not have inflected forms in English, unlike in most other languages. *Future time can be expressed in a variety of ways:*

> This suspense is terrible. I hope it WILL LAST. — Oscar Wilde

By *putting forward the hands of the clock*
you **SHALL NOT ADVANCE** *the hour.* — Victor Hugo

You have to have an idea of what you **ARE GOING TO DO,**
but it should be a vague idea. — Pablo Picasso

Tomorrow, every Fault **IS TO BE AMENDED;**
but that Tomorrow never comes. — Benjamin Franklin

The possible tenses of an English verb, combined with its possible aspects, create a grid of distinct possibilities:

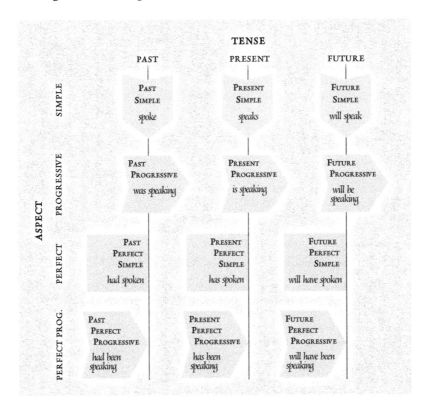

ENGLISH VERB FORMS
the five forms

All verbs inflect, or change their form, to express changes in tense, person, number, and voice. The majority of verbs in the English language are **REGULAR VERBS** and follow a set pattern of five forms:

BASE INFINITIVE	PRESENT TENSE	SIMPLE PAST	PRESENT PARTICIPLE	PAST PARTICIPLE
TO	-s	-ED	-ING	HAVE -ED
to walk	walk/walks	walked	walking	have/has/had walked
to dream	dream/dreams	dreamed	dreaming	have/has/had dreamed
to dance	dance/dances	danced	dancing	have/has/had danced

IRREGULAR VERBS also have five forms, but follow different patterns:

to be	am/is/are	was/were	being	been
to have	have/has	had	having	had
to do	do/does	did	doing	did
to go	go/goes	went	going	gone
to eat	eat/eats	ate	eating	eaten
to speak	speak/speaks	spoke	speaking	spoken

Finite TO FAIL, but infinite TO VENTURE. — Emily Dickinson

There are two key classes of verb: *main verbs* (also known as *lexical verbs*) and *auxiliary verbs*.

MAIN VERBS express the meaning of a clause. They show action, possession, or states of being.

> I THINK *therefore* I AM. — René Descartes

AUXILIARY VERBS add information to the main verb in order to refer to actual events or situations in the past or the present. The primary auxiliaries are *be, have,* and *do* (and their corresponding conjugated forms).

> *Happy he who, like Ulysses,* HAS COMPLETED *a great journey.* — Du Bellay les Regrets

> *I was angry with my friend: I told my wrath, my wrath* DID END.
> *I was angry with my foe: I told it not, my wrath* DID GROW. — William Blake

> *In the world through which I travel,*
> I AM *endlessly* CREATING *myself.* — Frantz Fanon

The primary auxiliaries also can stand alone as the main verb of a clause.

> "I HAVE *no name* / I AM *but two days old."* / *What shall I call thee?*
> "I *happy* AM, *Joy* IS *my name."* / *Sweet joy befall thee!* — William Blake

> *Nature* DOES *nothing uselessly.* — Aristotle

MODAL AUXILIARY VERBS help the main verb to express a range of meanings, including possibility, probability, desirability, permission, requests, suggestions, instructions, wants, wishes, obligations, and necessity; *will, would, shall, should, may, might, can, could, must, ought* (to).

> *Men* WOULD *live exceedingly quiet if these*
> *two words, 'mine' and 'thine', were taken away.* — Anaxagoras

> *We* SHOULD *come home from adventures, and perils,*
> *and discoveries every day with new experience and character.* — Henry David Thoreau

> *Like weather, men's fortune* MAY *change by the evening.* — Luu Mengsheng

TO BE

or not

		PRESENT	PAST
SINGULAR	I	*am*	*was*
	you	*are*	*were*
	he/she/it	*is*	*was*
PLURAL	*we*	*are*	*were*
	you	*are*	*were*
	they	*are*	*were*

INFINITIVE: *to be*   **PARTICIPLE:** *being*

The verb *to be* describes a state, rather than an action, and takes very irregular forms in accordance with the subject of the sentence.

To be can be used as a main verb: *There is something in the cupboard*; but it also functions as a copula, in that it connects terms expressing identity, location, class membership, and predication (among other things): *One and one is two; stars are celestial objects; the house is big enough; this is true.* When used with another verb in the infinitive, *to be* can also express obligation or fate: *He is to be executed.*

However, the most frequent use of *to be*, in English as well as in many other Western European languages, is as an auxiliary verb in various cases including continuous forms and the passive voice, such as: *I am going; we were running; the city was destroyed.*

People have been contemplating the essence of *to be* for thousands of years, and the connection it suggests between action and existence. As we all know, existence is a complicated affair!

TO HAVE
and do go on

		PRESENT	PAST
SINGULAR	I	have	had
	you	have	had
	he/she/it	has	had
PLURAL	we	have	had
	you	have	had
	they	have	had

INFINITIVE: *to have*   **PARTICIPLE:** *having*

The irregular verb *to have* also regularly serves as an auxiliary: *If she had noticed the mistake, she would have corrected it.* As a main verb, it has various meanings: In *I have a cold,* it describes a state of being; in *I have to go,* it denotes obligation; in *I have a car,* it expresses possession or belonging, much like the possessive genitive form (*see pages 65 and 71*) of a noun or pronoun: *my father's car; his car.* It can also express obligation via the infinitive: *You have to bow;* or the participle: *I am having this fixed.* Most notably, English uses *to have* to form the perfect aspect a verb: *I have pondered.*

Other irregular verbs also have special roles: *To do* can stand in for an action previously referred to (much like a pronoun stands for a noun we already know about): *I love swimming; So do I.* Sometimes it can appear as a main *and* auxiliary verb: *How do you do?*

To go also has a special role. Since English lacks a specific form for the future tense, it instead uses *to go* and modal verbs such as *will* and *shall* to suggest the future: *I am going to swim; they are going to miss the boat.*

VERB VOICE
active and passive

The *active voice* and *passive voice* express whether the action is being done or received by the subject. The two voices may occur in any tense.

ACTIVE VOICE is used in a clause whose subject is performing the action:

How could youths better LEARN to live than by at once
trying the experiment of living? — Henry David Thoreau

The things which I HAVE SEEN I now can SEE no more. — William Wordsworth

It was high counsel that I once HEARD given to a young person,
"always do what you are afraid to do." — Ralph Waldo Emerson

PASSIVE VOICE is used in a clause whose subject is the recipient of the action:

A man's character MAY BE LEARNED from the adjectives
which he habitually uses in conversation. — Mark Twain

I am the one, whose art WAS SEEN by the blind,
and whose words WERE HEARD by the deaf. — Al Mutannabi

VERB MOOD
a manner of speaking

The *mood* of a verb expresses the conditions under which an action or condition is taking place. It refers to the attitude or manner of the person who is speaking or writing. In English there are three moods.

The **INDICATIVE MOOD** is used to express fact or opinion.

> Love IS a serious mental disease. — Plato

> Behind every successful man STANDS a surprised mother-in-law. — Voltaire

The **IMPERATIVE MOOD** is used to give orders, commands, and directives, or to make requests.

> LIVE your life, DO your work, then TAKE your hat. — Henry David Thoreau

> Friends, Romans, countrymen, LEND me your ears. — William Shakespeare

> DON'T COUNT your chickens before they are hatched. — Aesop

The **SUBJUNCTIVE MOOD** expresses wishes, commands, desires, possibility, necessity, and hypothetical supposition.

> I would my horse HAD the speed of your tongue. — William Shakespeare

> Suppose you WERE an idiot and suppose you WERE a member of Congress. But I repeat myself. — Mark Twain

> We would often be sorry if our wishes WERE granted. — Aesop

The **FORMULAIC SUBJUNCTIVE** uses set formulas.

> BE that as it may; far BE it from me; PERISH the thought; SUFFICE it to say; if it PLEASE the court; truth BE told; Long LIVE the Queen; God BLESS you.

Verb Aspect
simple, progressive, and perfect

***

The *aspect* of a verb expresses the status of an action or state, essentially whether it is indefinite (unknown), has been completed, or is still in progress.

The indefinite **SIMPLE ASPECT** merely indicates an action.

> What you SEEK is seeking you. — Jalaluddin Rumi

The **PROGRESSIVE ASPECT** indicates continuing action, past, present, or future.

> While I thought THAT I WAS LEARNING how to live,
> I have been learning how to die. — Leonardo da Vinci

> We have watered the trees that blossom in the summer-time. Now let's sprinkle those whose flowering time is past. That will be the better deed, because WE SHALL NOT BE WORKING for the reward. — Kalidasa

The **PERFECT ASPECT** indicates that an action has been completed, or will be completed at some point in the future.

> I know many books which HAVE BORED their readers,
> but I know of none which has done real evil. — Voltaire

> All the fruit will be off the Christmas tree then; the crackers WILL HAVE CRACKED OFF; the almonds WILL HAVE BEEN CRUNCHED; and the sweet-bitter riddles WILL HAVE BEEN READ; the lights will have perished off the dark green boughs; the toys growing on them WILL HAVE BEEN DISTRIBUTED, FOUGHT FOR, CHERISHED, NEGLECTED, BROKEN. — William Makepeace Thackeray

The perfect and progressive aspects can be combined.

> Hetty HAD BEEN DECEIVING herself in thinking that she could love and marry him: SHE HAD BEEN LOVING Arthur all the while: and now, in her desperation at the nearness of their marriage, she had run away. — George Eliot

COMPLEX ASPECTS
in auxiliary verb phrases

The tenses and aspects of the English language combine using auxiliaries to create a matrix of verb forms. Up to five positions may be identified in a verb phrase. The modal verb comes first (*might, could, should, would*), the main verb last, and between them up to three auxiliary verbs may specify aspect and tense. The table below shows some examples of complex English verb phrases including modal verbs.

	1	2	3	4	5
It	*might*				*explode*
She		*has*			*vanished*
They			*were*		*singing*
He		*had*	*been*		*skating*
It	*will*	*have*		*been*	*dropped*
We	*may*	*have*	*been*	*being*	*followed*
TYPE	*modal v.*	*perfect aux.*	*progr. aux.*	*passive aux.*	*main verb*
MAIN VERB	*base form*	*-ed participle*	*-ing part.*	*-ed part.*	
MEANING	*modalized*	*perfect aspect*	*progr. asp.*	*is passive*	

In a similar fashion, for its future tenses, English uses either the present tense with a future time phrase, or modals, e.g. *we are leaving tomorrow*, or I *will/shall leave tomorrow*. The same technique also provides constructions for further tenses such as the future perfect, I *will have left by tomorrow*, and the future progressive, *he will be waiting* (*see page 83*).

NEGATIVES
don't, won't, can't!

In English, auxiliary and modal verbs are required to form *negative sentences*, so we say I *do not believe that* rather than I *not believe that* or I *believe not that*. Main verbs are never negated in main prose English; instead the word *not* appears after auxiliaries or modals. So I *go* negates as I *am not going*, and I *like* negates to I *do not like*, and I *will help* negates to I *will not help*.

There are, however, two cases in which negation does not adhere to this rule. One is with the main verb *hope*, and its corollaries, *pray*, and *think*: thus I *hope he wins* negates as I *hope not*. The other is the modal *must*: You *must go* is negated as You *don't have to go* instead of You *must not go*.

The negations of auxiliary and modal words often have *contracted forms*, and although these are common in spoken English, they are frowned upon in writing: *can* + *not* = *cannot* or *can't*; *do* + *not* = *don't*; *will* + *not* = *won't*; *have* + *not* = *haven't*.

Verb Transitivity
to take or not to take

Transitive verbs require an object to complete their meaning.

> You *can* CUT *all the flowers but you cannot* KEEP *spring from coming.*
> — Pablo Neruda

> *By putting forward the hands of the clock*
> *you shall not* ADVANCE *the hour.* — Victor Hugo

Intransitive verbs do not require an object, but may be accompanied by an adverbial word or phrase.

> *Some* RISE *by sin, and some by virtue* FALL. — William Shakespeare

> *A man* KNOWS *when he is growing old because*
> *he* BEGINS *to look like his father.* — Gabriel Garcia Marquez

Some verbs can be used transitively or intransitively.

> *The sun, with all those planets revolving around it and dependent on it, can still* RIPEN
> *a bunch of grapes as if it had nothing else in the universe to do.* — Galileo Galilei

> *The wise man does not grow old, but* RIPENS. — Victor Hugo

Ditransitive verbs take a *direct object* and an *indirect object* at the same time.

> GIVE *every man thy ear, but few thy voice.* — William Shakespeare

> *By plucking her petals, you do not* GATHER
> *the beauty of the flower.* — Rabindranath Tagore

FINITE & COPULAR VERBS
alone or linking

A **FINITE VERB** has a subject and shows tense and number. It can stand by itself as the main verb of a sentence.

> Hope IS the thing with feathers / That PERCHES in the soul
> And SINGS the tune without the words / And never STOPS at all. — Emily Dickinson

> If a thing LOVES, it IS infinite. — William Blake

A **NON-FINITE VERB** (VERBAL) cannot stand alone as a main verb of a sentence. The non-finite verb forms are: the *infinitive*, and the *present* and *past participles*.

> Clouds come FLOATING into my life, no longer TO CARRY rain or USHER
> storm, but TO ADD colour to my sunset sky. — Rabindranath Tagore

> DANCING begets warmth, which is the parent of wantonness. — Henry Fielding

> Of all the noises KNOWN to man, opera is the most expensive. — Molière

> Everything CONSIDERED, work is less boring than amusing oneself. — Baudelaire

COPULAR VERBS are linking verbs such as *be, seem, appear, feel, remain, become, smell,* and *look* which join a subject to its complement.

> When a thought takes one's breath away,
> a grammar lesson SEEMS an impertinence. — Thomas W. Higginson

> My pen IS my harp and my lyre;
> my library IS my garden and my orchard. — Judah Ha-Levi

Is it a Verb?
confusion in class

Words can belong to more than one class, depending on the role they play in a sentence. For example, some words can be either **a Noun or a Verb**:

How can we know the dancer from the DANCE? — William Butler Yeats

Let us read and let us DANCE—two amusements
that will never do any harm to the world. — Voltaire

A Noun or an Adjective:

Happiness resides not in possessions and not in GOLD,
happiness dwells in the soul. — Democritus

Rich and rare were the gems she wore,
And a bright GOLD ring on her hand she bore. — Thomas Moore

An Adverb, Preposition, or Conjunction:

A great part of courage is the courage of having
done the thing BEFORE. — Ralph Waldo Emerson

A dreamer is one who can only find his way by moonlight, and his punishment
is that he sees the dawn BEFORE the rest of the world. — Oscar Wilde

The woods are lovely, dark and deep. But I have promises to keep,
and miles to go BEFORE I sleep. — Robert Frost

Or even an Adverb, Adjective, Noun, and Verb.

Try Again. Fail again. Fail BETTER. — Samuel Beckett

He does it with BETTER grace, but I do it more natural. — William Shakespeare

When we our BETTERS see bearing our woes —William Shakespeare

If we are to BETTER the future we must disturb the present. — Catherine Booth

ADVERBIALS & ADVERBS
adding to the action

Adverbials are used to modify verbs, adjectives, or other adverbs. They can take the form of a single word (an *adverb*) or a group of words (an *adverbial phrase* or *adverbial clause*). In English, many adjectives can be converted into adverbs by adding *-ly*, e.g. *he slowly stood* (although some adjectives already end in *-ly*, e.g. *friendly*). Adverbs, like adjectives, can be modified by other adverbs such as *quite, very, mildly, extremely* in order to add further clarification. Adverbs provide information about:

TIME — ADVERBS: *always, now, eventually, immediately, yesterday, soon, forever*
  ADVERBIALS: *in the morning, all of a sudden, just then, after a while*

PLACE — ADVERBS: *there, here, anywhere, nowhere, hither, yon, thence, upstairs*
  ADVERBIALS: *Over there, in the distance, far away, in the box, around the room*

MANNER — ADVERBS: *happily, carefully, badly, silently, carefully, disdainfully*
  ADVERBIALS: *without a sound, as fast as he could, like a butterfly*

FREQUENCY — ADVERBS: *always, seldom, never, often, rarely, regularly*
  ADVERBIALS: *Once or twice, never in my life, every second*

DEGREE — ADVERBS: *very, extremely, slightly, more, less, perhaps, maybe*
  ADVERBIALS: *nearly asleep, utterly joyous, totally overwhelmed*

PURPOSE — ADVERBS: *consequently, therefore, hence, because, since*
  ADVERBIALS: *as a result, due to rain, for her country, because he was ugly*

A true friend unbosoms FREELY, advises JUSTLY, assists READILY, adventures BOLDLY, takes all PATIENTLY, defends COURAGEOUSLY, and continues a friend UNCHANGEABLY. — William Penn

It's NEVER the wrong time to call on Toad. EARLY or LATE he's ALWAYS the same fellow. — Kenneth Grahame

Poets have been MYSTERIOUSLY *silent on the subject of cheese.* — G. K. Chesterton

CONJUNCTIVE ADVERBS link two clauses: *moreover, however, accordingly, otherwise, undoubtedly:*

> *Lies are essential to humanity. They are perhaps as important as the pursuit of pleasure and* MOREOVER *are dictated by that pursuit.* — Marcel Proust

INTERROGATIVE ADVERBS ask *why, where, how, when:*

> HOW *shall a man escape from that which is written;*
> HOW *shall he flee from his destiny?* — Ferdowsi

> WHY *should we be in such desperate haste to succeed, and in such desperate enterprises? If a man does not keep pace with his companions, perhaps it is because he hears a different drummer.* — Henry David Thoreau

Adverbs can be used to emphasize, amplify, or tone down adjectives or other adverbs.

> *History books that contain no lies are* EXTREMELY *dull.* — Anatole France

> *I like my body when it is with your body. It is* SO QUITE *new a thing.*
> *Muscles better and nerves more.* — e. e. cummings

Adverbs are usually optional, and can be removed without affecting grammatical structure or meaning.

> *And what he* (GREATLY) *thought, he* (NOBLY) *dared.* — Homer

Most adverbs can be placed at the beginning, middle, or end of a sentence.

> SOMETIMES *small things lead to great joys.* — Shmuel Agnon

> *It is in our idleness, in our dreams, that the submerged truth* SOMETIMES *comes to the top.* — Virginia Woolf

> *'Tis healthy to be sick* SOMETIMES.
> — Henry David Thoreau

LITTLE WORDS
a limited list

Since English, like Chinese, uses so little inflection to express relations between its terms, it instead relies heavily on *form words* or *copula* to express these relations. Spoken English uses a huge number of these little words, *conjunctions* (*and, or*), *prepositions* (*at, in*), and *interjections* (*yes!, wow!*), compared to one someone speaking a heavily inflected language like Sanskrit or Polish.

While nouns, verbs, adjectives, and adverbs are open classes, with new words entering the vocabulary on a daily basis, conjunctions and prepositions are closed classes, so can be listed in their entirety, which begs a question:

> *Are these all the possible relations between substances and actions, or are there further relations, which we only have difficulty imagining due to a lack of words?*

Conjunctions and prepositions have been compared to seeds. It is possible that the original primitive language of our ancestors comprised of a small collection of simple sounds, the smallest building blocks of meaning. Then, like atoms combining to make molecules, these sounds, or *morphemes*, combined into words. Finally, as time passed and pronunciations changed, we lost knowledge of exactly what these building blocks were.

CONJUNCTIONS
joining together

Conjunctions join words, phrases, or clauses together and show the relationship between them.

COORDINATING CONJUNCTIONS join two items (words, phrases, or clauses) of equal grammatical status: *for, and, nor, but, or, yet, so.*

> *The rose AND the thorn, AND sorrow AND gladness are linked together.* — Saadi

CORRELATIVE CONJUNCTIONS always appear in pairs and are used to link equivalent sentence elements: *both...and, either...or, neither...nor, not only ...but also, so...as, whether...or.*

> *It is NOT ONLY what we do, BUT ALSO what we do not do for which we are accountable.* — Molière

SUBORDINATING CONJUNCTIONS link two items of unequal grammatical status and indicate the nature of the relationship among the independent clause(s) and the dependent clause(s):

*after, as, as if, as long as,
as much as, as soon as, as though,
because, before, by the time,
even if, even though, if,
in order that, in case, lest*

*once, only if, provided that,
since, so that, than, that, though,
till, unless, until, when, whenever,
where, wherever, while*

> *Some cause happiness WHEREVER they go;
> others WHENEVER they go.* — Oscar Wilde

> *AS LONG AS a word remains unspoken,
> you are its master; ONCE you utter it,
> you are its slave.* — Solomon Ibn Gabirol

PREPOSITIONS
little relationships

Prepositions are used to link two parts of a clause or sentence, and show a relationship in space, time, cause, manner, or means.

PREPOSITIONS OF SPATIAL LOCATION: *at* (point), *on* (surface), *in* (volume).

PREPOSITIONS OF SPATIAL DIRECTION: *to, onto, into, through, out of, toward, away from, up, down, around.*

PREPOSITIONS OF SPATIAL RELATIONSHIP: *by, off, along, across, against, among, beside, near, next to, between, among, ahead of, in front of, in the middle of, inside, round, opposite, behind, from, beyond, off, within, over, on top of, above, below, beneath, under, underneath, to the left of, to the right of, following.*

PREPOSITIONS OF TIME: *on, at, in, after, before, since, for, by, from, until, during, within, throughout.*

PREPOSITIONS OF CAUSE, MANNER, AND MEANS: *as, of, about, but, despite, except, than, with, without, minus, plus, like, unlike, via, because of, apart from, along with, as for, instead of, up to, in case of, according to.*

He said the pleasantest manner OF *spending a hot July day was lying* FROM *morning* TILL *evening* ON *a bank* OF *heath* IN *the middle* OF *the moors,* WITH *the bees humming dreamily* ABOUT AMONG *the bloom, and the larks singing high* UP OVERHEAD, *and the blue sky and bright sun shining steadily and cloudlessly.* — Emily Brontë

SUBJECT & PREDICATE
a little logic

We are now in a position to begin putting together the various elements of our book. Every complete *sentence* consists of a *subject*, which performs the action of a verb, and a *predicate* which modifies the subject. In English the subject comes at, or near, the beginning of a clause, and precedes the verb.

A **SIMPLE SUBJECT** can be a noun or pronoun.

> MOONLIGHT *is sculpture.* — Nathaniel Hawthorne

> HE *was happily married — but his wife wasn't.* — Victor Borge

A **COMPLETE SUBJECT** can be a noun phrase or clause, and includes the noun or pronoun, plus any modifiers.

> *Have patience.* ALL THINGS *are difficult before they become easy.* — Saadi

> THE MAN WHO DOES NOT READ GOOD BOOKS *has no advantage over the man who cannot read them.* — Mark Twain

The **SIMPLE PREDICATE** consists of the main verb and any auxiliary verbs.

> *The flower that smells the sweetest* IS *shy and lowly.* — William Wordsworth

> *A mule* WILL LABOUR *ten years willingly and patiently for you, for the privilege of kicking you once.* — William Faulkner

The **COMPLETE PREDICATE** includes the verb, along with any direct or indirect objects, complements, and adverbials.

> *All the ills of mankind, all the tragic misfortunes that fill the history books, all the political blunders, all the failures of the great leaders,* HAVE ARISEN MERELY FROM A LACK OF SKILL AT DANCING. — Molière

THE FIVE PHRASES
putting it all together

A *phrase* is a word, or a small group of related words, that functions as a grammatical unit. In English grammar, we distinguish five types of phrase which take their names from their central element, or *head word*. In addition to the head word, phrases may have pre- and post-head strings composed of determiners, modifiers, objects, or complements.

A NOUN PHRASE, as we have already seen (*pp. 70-71*), consists of a noun or a pronoun head-word, and any determiners and modifiers.

> THE INSUFFERABLE ARROGANCE OF HUMAN BEINGS *to think that Nature was made solely for their benefit, as if it was conceivable that the sun had been set afire merely to ripen* MEN'S APPLES *and head* THEIR CABBAGES.
> — Cyrano de Bergerac

A VERB PHRASE is composed of a verb head word, which may be preceded by a *negative* word such as *not* or *never*, as well as any auxiliaries.

> *Whenever you* ARGUE *with another wiser than yourself in order that others* MAY ADMIRE *your wisdom, they* WILL DISCOVER *your ignorance.* — Saadi

> *You* MIGHT, *from your appearance,* BE *the wife of Lucifer. Nevertheless,* YOU SHALL NOT GET *the better of me. I* AM *an Englishwoman.* — Charles Dickens

An ADJECTIVE PHRASE has an adjective as the head word, and may include an adverb or adverb phrase as the pre-head string.

> *The person, be it gentleman or lady, who has not pleasure in a* GOOD *novel, must be* INTOLERABLY STUPID. — Jane Austen

> *It is a* VERY SAD *thing that nowadays there is* SO LITTLE USELESS *information.* — Oscar Wilde

I really do not know that anything has ever been MORE EXCITING *than diagramming sentences.* — Gertrude Stein

An **ADVERB PHRASE** has an adverb as the *head word*, with modifiers before, after or both.

Who you are speaks SO LOUDLY I *can't hear what you're saying.*

— Ralph Waldo Emerson

The universe is full of magical things, PATIENTLY *waiting for our wits to grow sharper.* — Eden Phillpotts

A **PREPOSITIONAL PHRASE** consists of a preposition, a noun or pronoun that serves as its complement, and any modifiers.

A Christmas frost had come AT MIDSUMMER; *a white December storm had whirled* OVER JUNE; *ice glazed the ripe apples, drifts crushed the blowing roses;* ON HAYFIELD AND CORNFIELD *lay a frozen shroud: lanes which last night blushed full of flowers, today were pathless* WITH UNTRODDEN SNOW *and the woods, which twelve hours since waved leafy and flagrant as groves* BETWEEN THE TROPICS, *now spread, waste, wild, and white as pine-forests* IN WINTRY NORWAY. — Charlotte Brontë

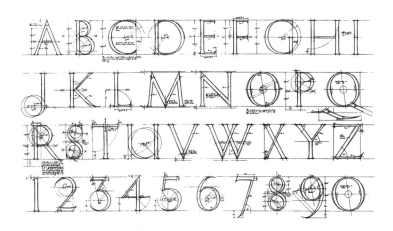

CLAUSES
elements

A *clause* is a sentence or sentence-like construction. In the English language, there are seven clause elements:

The **SUBJECT** gives the clause its theme or topic, and may be a noun, a noun phrase, a participial form, or another clause. The subject performs the action of a verb (*see too page 70*).

> **LIFE** *shrinks or expands in proportion to one's courage.* — Anais Nin
>
> **WHAT I LIKE TO DRINK MOST** *is wine that belongs to others.* — Diogenes

The **VERB** indicates the occurrence or performance of an action, or the existence of a state or condition. The verb must agree with the subject in person and number (*see too page 80*).

> *Whatever you* **CAN DO***, or* **DREAM** *you* **CAN***,* **BEGIN** *it. Boldness* **HAS** *genius, power, and magic in it.* **BEGIN** *it now.* — J. W. von Goethe

A **DIRECT OBJECT** directly receives the action of or is affected by the verb. Like the subject, the object of a clause can be a noun, pronoun, noun phrase, present participle, or another clause.

> *Every day we should hear at least* **ONE LITTLE SONG***, read* **ONE GOOD POEM***, see* **ONE EXQUISITE PICTURE***, and, if possible, speak* **A FEW SENSIBLE WORDS***.* — J. W. von Goethe

An **INDIRECT OBJECT** receives the action of or benefits from the direct object.

> *If you want to annoy your neighbours, tell the truth about* **THEM***.* — Pietro Aretino

A **COMPLEMENT** is a word, phrase or clause which is necessary to complete the meaning of a word. A **SUBJECT COMPLEMENT** follows a copular (linking) verb and completes the meaning of the subject.

Friendship is THE SHADOW OF THE EVENING, *which increases with the setting sun of life.* — Jean De La Fontaine

A book is A GARDEN, AN ORCHARD, A STOREHOUSE, A PARTY, A COMPANY BY THE WAY, A COUNSELLOR, A MULTITUDE OF COUNSELLORS. — Charles Baudelaire

The **OBJECT COMPLEMENT** is a noun, noun phrase, adjective, or adjective phrase that modifies or refers to the direct object.

I do not say a proverb is amiss when aptly and reasonably applied, but to be forever discharging them, right or wrong, hit or miss, renders conversation INSIPID AND VULGAR. — Miguel de Cervantes

A ruffled mind makes A RESTLESS PILLOW. — Charlotte Brontë

ADVERBIALS provide more information about a clause and can be an *adverb, adverb phrase, prepositional* and *noun phrase,* as well as a *subordinate clause.* A clause may contain more than one adverbial.

Do not train a child TO LEARN BY FORCE OR HARSHNESS; *but direct them* TO IT BY WHAT AMUSES THEIR MINDS, *so that you may be* BETTER ABLE TO DISCOVER WITH ACCURACY *the peculiar bent* OF THE GENIUS OF EACH. — Plato

Not every clause needs an adverbial, but some verbs are grammatically incomplete without one.

Aspects are WITHIN US, *and who seems* MOST KINGLY *is king.* — Thomas Hardy

Words mean MORE THAN WHAT IS SET DOWN ON PAPER. *It takes the human voice* TO INFUSE THEM WITH DEEPER MEANING.

— Maya Angelou

TYPES OF CLAUSE
in a nutshell

An **INDEPENDENT CLAUSE** is a simple sentence that can stand alone.

The creation of a thousand forests is in one acorn. — Ralph Waldo Emerson

The greater part of the world's troubles are due to questions and grammar.
— Michel de Montaigne

A **COORDINATE CLAUSE** is a clause linked to another clause by a *coordinating conjunction*: And, But, Nor, Or, Then, Yet.

A mother's arms are made of tenderness AND CHILDREN SLEEP SOUNDLY IN THEM. — Victor Hugo

If you do not expect the unexpected you will not find it, FOR IT IS NOT TO BE REACHED BY SEARCH OR TRAIL. — Heraclitus

A **SUBORDINATE** or **DEPENDENT CLAUSE** is linked to a main clause by a *subordinating conjunction*. When one clause complements another clause, it is subordinate to it. There are subordinating conjunctions of:

TIME — *After, Before, As soon as, Since, When, Whenever, While*

All men WHILST THEY ARE AWAKE *are in one common world: but each of them,* WHEN HE IS ASLEEP, *is in a world of his own.* — Plutarch

WHEN I GET A LITTLE MONEY, *I buy books.*
And if there is any left over, I buy food. — Desiderius Erasmus

CONCESSION — *Al/though, Even though, Despite, Except that, Much as, Not that, Whereas, While/whilst*

It is the part of a gallant man to say nothing, THOUGH HE MAY INDICATE *that he could say a great deal.* — Sir Arthur Conan Doyle

CONDITION — If, Provided that, As long as, Unless

"IF YOU LIVED ON CABBAGE, you would not be obliged to flatter the powerful." To which the courtier replied, "IF YOU FLATTERED THE POWERFUL, you would not be obliged to live upon cabbage."
— Diogenes, *Advice to a Young Courtier*

REASON — Because, Since, As

A bird doesn't sing BECAUSE IT HAS AN ANSWER, it sings BECAUSE IT HAS A SONG. — Maya Angelou

RESULT — So, Thus

I love you without knowing how, or when, or from where.
I love you straightforwardly, without complexities or pride;
SO I LOVE YOU BECAUSE I KNOW NO OTHER WAY. — Pablo Neruda

and COMPARISON — Than, As

Better by far you should forget and smile THAN THAT YOU SHOULD REMEMBER AND BE SAD. — Christina G. Rossetti

A clause can be FINITE or NON-FINITE, according to its type of verb.

A RELATIVE CLAUSE is a dependent clause generally introduced by a *relative pronoun* such as Who, Whom, That, Which, Whose, When, Where.

I would venture to guess that Anon, WHO WROTE SO MANY POEMS WITHOUT SIGNING THEM, was often a woman. — Virginia Woolf

The REDUCED RELATIVE CLAUSE, has no relative pronoun, and the verb is non-finite.

But words are things, and a small drop of ink,
FALLING LIKE DEW, upon a thought, produces
That which makes thousands, perhaps millions, think. — George Gordon Byron

SENTENCES
putting it all together

The *sentence* is the largest unit of grammar. It is often defined as the expression of a complete thought, although one person's complete thought may not be another's. Perhaps the simplest way to define sentence is to say that it is a meaningful string of words with a capital letter at the beginning, and a stop of some kind at the end.

> *Oh Romeo! Romeo! Wherefore art though Romeo?*
> > *Deny thy father and refuse thy name:*
> *Or if thou wilt not, be but sworn my love*
> > *And I'll no longer be a Capulet.* — William Shakespeare

There are four different types of sentences:

EXCLAMATORY SENTENCES express strong feelings or emotion:

> *Oh Romeo! Romeo!*

INTERROGATIVE SENTENCES request information or ask questions:

> *Wherefore art thou Romeo?*

IMPERATIVE SENTENCES request action, or give directives or commands:

> *Deny thy father and refuse thy name.*

DECLARATIVE SENTENCES make statements, or convey information:

> *I'll no longer be a Capulet.*

Sentences can also vary in complexity:

The **SIMPLE SENTENCE** has a single verb phrase and is made up of one independent clause:

> *Necessity has the face of a dog.* — Gabriel García Márquez

Brevity is the soul of wit. — William Shakespeare

A **COMPOUND SENTENCE** contains two or more independent clauses, which may be linked by coordination, a conjunct, or a comma or semi-colon.

She might have beguiled the loneliness of her days with old songs and poems, but she really did not have much feeling for such things. — Murasaki Shikibu (trans. G. Seidensticker)

Age considers; youth ventures. — Rabindranath Tagore

A **COMPLEX SENTENCE** consists of one main clause and at least one subordinate clause.

When we remember we are all mad, the mysteries disappear and life stands explained. — Mark Twain

How did it happen that their lips came together? How does it happen that birds sing, that snow melts, that the rose unfolds, that the dawn whitens behind the stark shapes of trees on the quivering summit of the hill? A kiss, and all was said. — Victor Hugo

A **COMPOUND-COMPLEX SENTENCE** is a compound sentence with more than one main clause and at least one subordinate clause.

We are not satisfied with real life; we want to live some imaginary life in the eyes of other people and to seem different from what we actually are. — Blaise Pascal

What is life? A madness. What is life? An illusion, a shadow, a story. And the greatest good is little enough; for all life is a dream, and dreams themselves are only dreams. — Pedro Calderon de la Barca

Beyond Grammar
a few small thoughts

Most written clauses express statements, for example when making a legal point, presenting an argument, or leading a philosophical discussion. However, in everyday language the situation is rather different. In slang, dialect, and common communication, long grammatically correct sentences are the exception rather than the rule. If you were to record everything you said during a day, how many whole sentences would there be? Most utterances consist merely of short phrases, questions and answers, idioms, slang, imperatives, or even single words: *You coming; Not yet; What a huge car; Could be worse; Get in; Oh wow; Yeah right; Let's go; Hmm.*

Grammarians have only relatively recently started looking more carefully into everyday language. Only recently too has the science of grammar finally broken free from natural tongues through the study of artificial languages such as Esperanto, computer languages (pioneered by Alan Turing), and the linguistic interpretation of other information such as DNA.

Modern grammar has two branches. The first uses mathematical and computational techniques to delve into how information is coded, interpreted, and translated from one medium to another. Can we reduce the content of a spoken sentence to an ideal language or code to help translate it into any other language (a subject pioneered by Noam Chomsky)? It appears that the human brain is primed at birth to learn language and grammar quickly, so a child who has not been exposed to language by the age of four will never learn to speak properly. There seems to be something common to all human

010011010110111101110011011011101000010000001110111011100100110100101110100011010001100101011011100010000001100011011011000110000101110101011100110110010010111001100100000011001010101110000111000001110010011001010110011011100110010000000111001101110100001100001011101011

minds in structuring thoughts, something categorical, involving elemental differentiations between substance, action, space, and time.

The second modern approach to grammar is more humanistic and interaction-based, focusing on the speaker and listener. Known as Speech Act Theory, it asks *what is somebody actually doing when they say something?* Here is a minimum list of speech acts:

REPRESENTATIVES: speech acts that commit a speaker to the truth of the expressed proposition, e.g. statements in court or in a paper.

DIRECTIVES: speech acts that aim to cause the hearer to take a particular action, e.g. requests, commands, and advice.

COMMISSIVES: speech acts that commit a speaker to some future action, e.g. promises and oaths.

EXPRESSIVES: speech acts that express a speaker's attitudes and emotions toward the proposition, e.g. congratulations, excuses, and thanks.

DECLARATIONS: speech acts that change the reality in accord with the proposition of the declaration, e.g. baptisms, pronouncing someone guilty, or pronouncing off-side in football.

The science of grammar can be viewed as loose (descriptive), or tight (normative/ prescriptive), or it may be enlarged to the rules and devices governing communication and persuasion on a larger scale, in which case we enter the realms of logic and rhetoric, covered elsewhere in this volume (*see pages 177–231 and 237–291*).

BOOK III

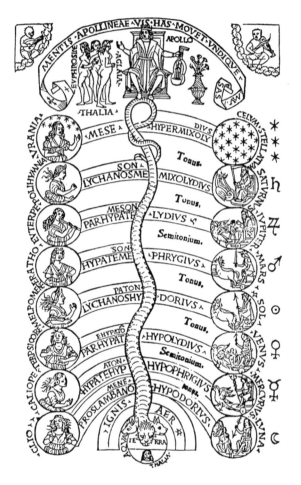

Musica Universalis *from Gafurius's* Practica Musice, *1496. Apollo is shown presiding over the Muses and tones (left), and modes and planetary spheres (right). On the left the Three Graces, Euphrosine (mirth), Aglaea (splendour), and Thalia (comedy, also a muse) stand over the other eight muses: Urania (astronomy); Polyhymnia (hymns); Euterpe (music, song & elegiac poetry); Erato (lyric poetry); Melpomene (tragedy); Terpsichore (dance); Calliope (epic poetry); Clio (history).*

POETIC
METER AND FORM

Octavia Wynne

Above: Après la Marne, Joffre visita le front en auto, *Tommaso Marinetti,* 1915. *A visual and sound poem presented like a military map to show the journey of General Joffre. Visual poems objectify their text and use line length, grouping, indentation, punctuation, capitalisation, typefaces, and size changes to effect shifts in tone, topic, and perspective to heighten awareness of the process of reading.*

INTRODUCTION

PEOPLE HAVE BEEN WRITING poems for a very long time. The Sanskrit epic *Ramayana* dates to around 300 BC and is still popular throughout India, Cambodia, Indonesia, and Thailand. The Chinese *Shih-ching*, or *Book of Songs*, contains 305 poems dating from the 11th to 7th centuries BC. Poems meaningfully pattern the musical features of language, using rhythm, pitch, and timbre (texture) and often grasp at truths that resist the logical pen of prose. This book looks at the patterns of poetry, its shapes and rhythms, through foot, meter, and form.

The word 'poetry' derives via Latin from the Greek term *poiein* ('to make'). In the Archaic Period [800–480 BC], poetry was largely improvised orally, often accompanied by *music* (derived from the Greek word *mousikê*, 'having to do with the Muses'). In the Classical Period [480–323 BC], poetry began to be performed with the other verbal arts, *rhetoric* (public speaking) and *drama*, and some poems were memorized and written down.

Ancient European poetry was often sung: land songs, Anglo Saxon oar songs, Celtic smith songs, Greek altar songs, medieval court songs, and children's songs. The vast majority of pre-12th century English poetry is lost, but the Anglo-Saxons and Vikings brought with them a canon of verse full of epic myth which rolled and rowed to a four-beat turn with a stress on the first syllables of words, forming an earthy rhythm. Other settlers who followed them sometimes emphasized the ends of words, encouraging rhymes and a lilting upward beat. These two opposing styles combined in the daily rhythms of speech, poetry, and song. Later, the Crusades and the Renaissance brought with them the Greek and Roman classics, encouraging poets of the time to imitate the ancient forms.

PATTERNS IN LANGUAGE
rhythm, meter, rhyme, and form

Listen to people speaking in any language and one can immediately detect patterns of various kinds, for language itself is innately suited for song and chant, and its spoken form is an echo of ancient music and poetry.

The most basic pattern of language is its *rhythm*, heard as a beat:

BEAT   1   &   2   &   3   &   4   &
Pít-*ter* **Pát**-*ter* **Pít**-*ter* **Pát**-*ter*

In poetry, rhythm is most clear when spoken aloud, mainly as the effect of *syllables* and *stresses*. The majority of European Romance languages, derived from Latin, are *syllable-timed*, their natural rhythm resting on the number of syllables in words, phrases and sentences.

e.g. French: **Cá-ná-dá** (all syllables stressed equally).

English, on the other hand, is derived from West Germanic languages, and relies heavily on the *stresses* placed on syllables—it is *stress-timed*. It is as though, when walking, the basic rhythmical *left/right* pattern develops a bias towards one or other foot, a little like the way the British often accent the first syllable of a word, while Americans emphasize the second/last:

UK: **Dé**bris   US: Deb**rís**

In *prosody*, these different kinds of rhythmically stressed units are known as *feet*. Add some sway into your walk and a longer foot emerges:

LÉFT, *two, three* | **RÍGHT**, *two, three*

Accented syllables (marked *áéíóúý*) and the feet they define (divided by |) became the foundation of post-13th century English poetry. We will meet the various feet in the pages which follow (*pages 122–129*), and learn how they may be formally combined into a line of two, three, four, five, six, seven, or eight feet, which is then said to have a *poetic meter* (*pages 130–135*).

Poetic lines combine into larger units, *stanzas* (*pages 146–155*), which can be two lines (*couplets*), three (*triplets*), four (*quatrains*), or more, sometimes with occasional lines repeated as *refrains*. A finished poem may contain anywhere between one and over 2,000 stanzas, with some poetic forms dictating exactly how many stanzas are required (*closed* or *fixed forms*), and others allowing the poet more flexibility (*open forms*). The final part of this book examines some of the more popular poetic forms (*pages 156–169*).

There is a second obvious pattern of language: *rhyme*. This might be thought of as a natural phenomenon, since language uses a limited number of sounds to create words, yet two-thirds of the world's languages do not use poetic rhyme. The earliest known use of rhyme dates back to the *Book of Songs* (*see page 117*), and it arrived in Europe from China via Middle Eastern trade routes, through ancient Rome and Persian mystery cults and from Celtic Ireland around the 3rd–4th centuries BC. During the Middle Ages, English poetic rhyme was based on *alliteration*, where words start with the same stressed consonant (*five/feet*); and *assonance*, where words share the same vowel sounds (*black/hat*), but by the 14th century *perfect rhyme* (*bright/night/light*) was found in all European poetry, becoming ubiquitous in English verse around the 16th–17th centuries (*see pages 142–143*).

There are other interesting patterns that words make, and which poets use, and these are explored later in the book (*pages 170–171*). Indeed, the building blocks and tools of poetry are reflections and refinements of natural patterns already present in language. Poetry may require effort and skill to write, but we all experience the simple delight of words which beat and rhyme, and which, at the right time, can find easy passage into hearts and minds.

ACCENTUAL OR SYLLABIC
all about the rhythm

Meter is counted in different ways. *Accentual* meter is a natural mode of English verse and appears in Irish/Celtic, Old Norse, Anglo-Saxon, and Middle English poetry such as *Beowulf* and *Sir Gawain and the Green Knight*, as well as nursery rhymes, football chants, traditional ballads, and literary imitations (by Coleridge, Hopkins, Yeats, and others). For example:

ACCENTUAL VERSE - EXAMPLE WITH 2 BEATS PER LINE

Báa, baa, bláck sheep,	(4)	Óne for the máster,	(5)
Háve you any wóol?	(5)	And óne for the dáme,	(5)
Yés sir, yés sir,	(4)	And óne for the líttle boy	(7)
Thrée bags fúll;	(3)	Who líves down the láne.	(5)

Note how the number of stresses remains constant despite the changing syllable-count—since accentual verse counts only the stresses in a poetic line there may be any number of weak syllables in any part (*see too page 140*).

Syllabic verse, by contrast, purely counts the number of syllables in a line and is common in syllable-timed languages such as Spanish, French, Italian, the Baltic and Slavic languages, Turkish, Cantonese, and Japanese. For example, Dylan Thomas' 1946 poem *In My Craft or Sullen Art* uses seven syllables in each line but has no regular stress pattern.

SYLLABIC VERSE - EXAMPLE WITH 7 SYLLABLES PER LINE

In my cráft or súllen árt	(7)	I lábour by sínging líght	(7)
Éxercised in the stíll níght	(7)	Nót for ámbition or bréad	(7)
When ónly the móon ráges	(7)	Or the strút and tráde of chárms	(7)
And the lóvers líe abéd	(7)	On the ívory stáges	(7)
With áll their griefs in their árms,	(7)	Bút for the cómmon wáges	(7)
		Of théir most sécret héart.	(6)

The strictest form of poetic meter is *accentual-syllabic*. Here, both the number of stresses and the number of syllables are fixed. If most lines in a poem have the same number of syllables *and* stresses, or a poem has repeating patterns of them, then it is accentual-syllabic verse, as in this 1963 example from *The Gashlycrumb Tinies*, by Edward Gorey.

ACCENTUAL-SYLLABIC VERSE - DACTYLIC TETRAMETER *dúm diddy* ●○○ × 4

Á is for| Ámy who| féll down the| stáirs   ●○○ ●○○ ●○○ ●
B́ is for| Básil as|sáulted by| béars   ●○○ ●○○ ●○○ ●
Ć is for| Clára who| wásted á|way   ●○○ ●○○ ●○○ ●
D́ is for| Désmond thrown| óut of a| sléigh   ●○○ ●○○ ●○○ ●

In *quantitative meter*, used in ancient Greek, Roman, and Sanskrit poetry, it is the length of syllables in time that counts. Feet are durational rather than accentual, and each syllable is either long (*longis*) ■ or short (*brevis*) □. Syllables in English are likewise of different lengths, but although these lengths do affect the rhythm of speech, they disappear alongside the strong rhythms created by the patterns of stressed and unstressed syllables. Some Renaissance poets attempted to write English verse in quantitative meter, though with limited success. In the example below, from Edmund Spenser's 1579 poem *Iambicum Trimetrum*, notice the rhythms of duration over stresses.

QUANTITATIVE VERSE - QUANTITATIVE IAMBIC TRIMETER *di dummm* □■ × 3

Unha<u>ppy</u> verse, the <u>witness</u> of my unh<u>appy state,</u>   □■ □■ □■
Make <u>thy self</u> flutt'ring <u>wings</u> of thy <u>fast flying</u>   □■ □■ □■
Thought, and <u>fly forth</u> unto <u>my love,</u> wheres<u>oever she be</u> ...   □■ □■ □■

There are a few other examples. However, in this short book, in order to achieve our purpose, we will learn our feet and meters via more easily scannable poems, primarily employing the familiar rhythms of English accentual-syllabic verse.

The Spondee
dum dum

The basic element of meter is a *foot*, which consists of stressed (classically long) and/or unstressed (classically short) beats or syllables. The punchiest of the feet, and the symbol of rhythm itself, is the *spondee*. With two stressed beats, ●●, it KICKS HARD. Rare in poems, you are more likely to hear it in political slogans or football chants, or read it on road signs:

THE SPONDAIC FOOT - dúm dúm (●●)

SLOW DOWN!	●●	GIVE WAY!	●●
TURN RIGHT!	●●	THINK BIKE!	●●

The repetitive stress of the spondee may be heard in stressful situations, e.g. JUMP! JUMP! or compounded as: MAYDAY! MAYDAY! Shakespeare uses it in *Troilus and Cressida*: Crý, crý! Tróy búrns, or élse let Hélen gó.

Spondees are often mixed with less forceful feet to make a point: COME COME *you answer with an idle tongue*, or to create a stop at the end of a line: True ease in writing comes from art NOT CHANCE.

Two spondees placed together make a *dispondee*. Examples are the giant's call Fée Fýe Fóe Fúm or the multiple-rhyming Hów Nów BrównCów?

A rare example of a dispondaic poem is E.J. Thribb's 1967 *Bonfire Song*:

DISPONDAIC VERSE - dúm dúm (●●) × 2

Sún shíne| Móon cúrl	●●	●●
Ráin wásh| Eárth whírl	●●	●●
Fíre fórk| Aír fúrl	●●	●●
Sóng bóy| Síng gírl	●●	●●

The spondee is the most insistent syncopation of meter.

THE PYRRHIC
di di

The opposite of the spondee is the *Pyrrhic* foot. Like the hollow victory to which the word now alludes, the pyrrhic consists of two unstressed syllables. Edgar Allan Poe [1809–49] dismissed it entirely as a chimerical foot, an irrational nonentity, for it is almost impossible to construct an entirely Pyrrhic line or poem out of things like:

THE PYRRHIC FOOT - diddy (○○)

is a	○○	*into*	○○
and the	○○	*any*	○○

Instead these little feet work best combined and contrasted with more stressed feet to punctuate the line. Welsh blues poet Dylan Evans combines a Pyhrric foot with a spondee to form a *minor ionic* in *Old Coals*, 1952.

PYRRHIC + SPONDEE = MINOR IONIC - diddy dúm dúm (○○●●)

See a| déad mán	○○ ●●
In a| bláck hóle	○○ ●●
In the| héartbréak	○○ ●●
Of a| lóne sóul	○○ ●●

A spondee *in front* of a Pyrrhic foot creates the rare and exciting *major ionic*:

SPONDEE + PYRRHIC = MAJOR IONIC - dúm dúm diddy (●●○○)

Squéeze tíght,| it's a	●● ○○
Hót níght,| and the	●● ○○

The Pyrrhic foot is suggestive of further hidden rhythms, as well as other syllables which may be so weak as to be silent or missing altogether.

THE TROCHEE
dum di

A poetic unit consisting of a stressed syllable followed by an unstressed one, ●○, is called a *trochee*. In musical terms it is a strong beat followed by a weaker one, a long note preceding a shorter one. Imagine a sergeant major shouting "LEFT *right*, LEFT *right*, LEFT *right*, ...". The emphasis may be slight, but many of us put our best foot first and walk in trochees.

Linguists speculate that there may be a trochaic bias in early childhood, with baby words like *múmmy, dáddy, háppy, cúddle, húngry, bédtime, íPad*, following this pattern. 'Dr.' Theodor Seuss Geisel [1904–91] used it widely:

SIMPLE TROCHAIC VERSE - dúm di (●○)

ONE Fish	●○	BLACK *fish*	●○
TWO Fish	●○	BLUE *fish*	●○
RED Fish	●○	OLD *fish*	●○
BLUE Fish	●○	NEW *fish*	●○

When trochees are compounded they form trochaic verse. Many nursery rhymes use four trochees per line, e.g. *Simple Simon* or:

TROCHAIC TETRAMETER - dúm di (●○) ×4

Péter,| Péter,| púmpkin| éater	●○ ●○ ●○ ●○
Hád a| wífe but| cóuldn't| kéep her	●○ ●○ ●○ ●○

Lines of trochaic meter often lose weak stresses at the ends of lines (*catalectic*), or add extra stresses to the beginnings of lines (*hypercatalectic*):

TROCHAIC TETRAMETER/TRIMETER

Máry| hád a| líttle| lámb	●○ ●○ ●○ ●
Its fléece was| whíte as| snów	○ ●○ ●○ ●

THE IAMB
di dum

The inverse of the trochee is the *iamb*, an unstressed syllable followed by a stressed one, ○●, the most common foot in English verse. Like the trochee, the iamb reflects the natural rise and fall of speech. Words like *behóld, amúse, aríse, eléct, retúrn*, and *insíst* are all iambs. In his poem *Upon His Departure Hence*, Robert Herrick [1591–1679] uses a single iambic foot for each line.

SIMPLE IAMBIC VERSE - di dúm (○●)

Thus Í	○●	As óne	○●	I'm máde	○●
Pass bý	○●	Unknówn	○●	A sháde,	○●
And díe	○●	And góne	○●	And láid	○●

When several iambs are placed one after the other they create an iambic rhythm, *di-dum di-dum di-dum di-dum*. In this satirical example, Samuel Johnson [1709–84] alternates four and three iambs (*a ballad stanza, page 148*):

IAMBIC TETRAMETER/TRIMETER - di dúm (○●) ×3/4

I pút| my hát| upón| my héad,	○● ○● ○● ○●
And wálked| intó| the Stránd,	○● ○● ○●
And thére I mét anóther mán	○● ○● ○● ○●
Whose hát was ín his hánd.	○● ○● ○●

Five iambs form Shakespeare's mighty *iambic pentameter*: If músic bé the fóod of lóve play ón. Lines of six and seven are popular too, but why stop there? Here are lines of eight iambs by W. S. Gilbert, from *The Pirates of Penzance*:

IAMBIC OCTAMETER - di dúm (○●) ×8

I ám\| the vé\|ry mó\|del óf\| a mó\|dern Má\|jor-Gé\|nerál,
I've ín\|formá\|tion vég\|etá\|ble, án\|imál,\| and mí\|nerál

THE DACTYL
dum diddy

The *dactyl* is the three-fold equivalent of the trochee, and has a strong beat followed by two weak ones, ●○○. This makes for a waltzing rhythm "ONE two three, ONE two three, ...". Words like *búffalo*, *stráwberry*, *pát-a-cake*, *éverywhere*, *sýnthesis*, and *mérrily* are dactylic. The word *dactyl* comes from the Greek for finger, *daktylos*, since a long bone is followed by two short ones.

Two dactyls form a *double dactyl*, and this forms the basis of a poetic form designed by Anthony Hecht and John Hollander in 1966:

DOUBLE DACTYL - dúm diddy (●○○) ×2

Híggeldy| Píggledy	●○○ ●○○	Féw realístically	●○○ ●○○
Sérgei Rach|máninov	●○○ ●○○	Cán pianístically	●○○ ●○○
Wróte his con|cértos for	●○○ ●○○	Dígitallístically	●○○ ●○○
Hándspans like| wíngs.	●○○ ●○○	Pláy the damned thíngs.	●○○ ●○○

Four dactyls make *dactylic tetrameter*. In *The Bride of Abydos* Lord Byron [1788–1824] omits many unstressed catalectic syllables at the ends of his lines, adding them as hypercatalectic syllables to the beginning of the next:

DACTYLIC TETRAMETER - dúm diddy (●○○) ×4

Knów ye the| lánd where the| cýpress and| mýrtle	●○○ ●○○ ●○○ ●○
Are émblems of| déeds that are| done in their| clíme -	○ ●○○ ●○○ ●○○ ●
Where the ráge of the| vúlture, the| lóve of the| túrtle	○○ ●○○ ●○○ ●○○ ●○
Now mélt into| sóftness, now| mádden to| críme?	○ ●○○ ●○○ ●○○ ●○○
Knów ye the| lánd of the| cédar and| víne,	●○○ ●○○ ●○○ ●
Where the flówers ever| blóssom, the| béams ever| shíne;	○○ ●○○ ●○○ ●○○ ●○○

Six dactyls form *dactylic hexameter*, one of the primary meters of the Classical world, widely used by Homer and Virgil (*see page 134*).

THE ANAPEST
diddy dum

A grouping of three syllables which saves its kick until the end is called an *anapest*. This waltz goes ○○●, "*one two* THREE, *one two* THREE, *one two* THREE, ...". Anapestic words like *violín*, *indiréct*, *misconcéive*, *realígn*, and *untowárd* are examples of this foot. Two anapests make *anapestic dimeter* and here is Dr. Seuss again, from his 1954 book *Horton Hears a Who*:

> ANAPESTIC DIMETER · diddy dúm (○○●) × 2
>
> On the fíf|teenth of Máy   ○○● ○○●   In the héat of the dáy   ○○● ○○●
> In the Jún|gle of Nóol   ○○● ○○●   In the cóol of the póol   ○○● ○○●

Four anapests form *anapestic tetrameter*, a fine example of which is Lord Byron's *Destruction of Sennacherib*, first published in 1815.

> ANAPESTIC TETRAMETER · diddy dúm (○○●) × 4
>
> The Assý|rian came dówn| like the wólf| on the fóld,   ○○● ○○● ○○● ○○●
> And his có|horts were gléam|ing in púr|ple and góld;
> And the shéen of their spéars was like stárs on the séa,
> When the blúe wave rolls níghtly on déep Galilée.

A variation appears in the well-known *The Night Before Christmas*, by Clement Clarke Moore [1779–1863]. Note the omission of the first syllables of lines 3 and 4, which produces *acephalous*, or *headless*, lines.

> ANAPESTIC TETRAMETER · diddy dúm (○○●) × 4
>
> 'Twas the níght| before Chríst|mas, when áll| through the hóuse   ○○● ○○● ○○● ○○●
> Not a créa|ture was stír|ring, not é|ven a móuse.   ○○● ○○● ○○● ○○●
> The stó|ckings were húng| by the chím|ney with cáre,   ○○● ○○● ○○● ○○●
> In hópes| that St Ních|olas sóon| would be thére.   ○○● ○○● ○○● ○○●

The Amphibrach
di dum di

The third place where emphasis can fall in a three-syllable unit is in the center, ○●○, to form an *amphibrach*, "one **Two** three, one **Two** three, one **Two** three, ...", as in im*á*gine, el*é*ctron, impr*ó*per, fore*bé*arance, pet*ú*nia, and corr*é*ctly. Amphibrachs (along with anapests) also form the basis of limericks:

CATALECTIC AMPHIBRACHIC DI/TRIMETER - di dúm di (○●○) × 2/3

There wás an| old mán from| Perú	○●○ ○●○ ○●
Who dréamed he| was éating| his shóe.	○●○ ○●○ ○●
He wóke in| the níght	○●○ ○●
With a térri|ble fríght	○ ○●○ ○●
And fóund that| his dréam had| come trúe!	○●○ ○●○ ○●

Four amphibrachs gallop along, as here in Dr. Seuss' *If I Ran the Circus*:

AMPHIBRACHIC TETRAMETER - di dúm di (○●○) × 4

And NÓW comes\| an áct of\| Enórmous\| Enórmance!   ○●○ ○●○ ○●○ ○●○
No fórmer perfórmer's perförmed this perförmance!

Amphibrachs are a common meter in Russian poetry, where the final syllable is often omitted, as here in Thomas Hardy's *The Ruined Maid*:

CATALECTIC AMPHIBRACHIC TETRAMETER - di dúm di (○●○) × 4

"O 'Mélia\|, my déar, this\| does évery\|thing crówn!   ○●○ ○●○ ○●○ ○●
Who cóuld have\| suppósed I\| should méet you\| in Tówn?

The inversion of the amphibrach is the rare *amphimacer*, ●○●, *dúm-di-dúm*:

AMPHIMACER - dúm di dúm (●○●), from *The Oak*, by Lord Tennyson [1809-92]

Líve thy lífe / Yóung and óld / Líke yon oák / Bríght in Spríng / Líving góld.

	FOOT	LENGTH	KEY	RHYTHM	EXAMPLE
MONO	brach	1	●	strong	*bíg, stár, béat, hóle*
	macer	1	○	weak	*a, the, in, to, by*
BINARY	iamb	2	○●	rising	*alíve, becóme, contról, a bírd, to séek*
	trochee	2	●○	falling	*mústard, pívot, wéaving, fínd it*
	spondee	2	●●	emphatic	*ráinbów, cúckóo, lóve sóng*
	pyrrhic	2	○○	quiet	*any, into, of a, in the*
TERNARY	anapest	3	○○●	rising	*disagrée, incorréct, violín*
	dactyl	3	●○○	falling	*émphasis, flíckering, móckingbird*
	amphibrach	3	○●○	galloping	*eléctron, enchántment, insístence*
	amphimacer	3	●○●	galloping	*místletóe, lá-di-dáh, mén-at-árms*
	bacchius	3	○●●	rising	*abúndánce, my héart áches*
	antibacchius	3	●●○	falling	*óutsíder, flátfóoted*
	molossus	3	●●●	emphatic	*bómbárdmént*
	tribrach	3	○○○	quiet	*anyway, in and out, into it*
QUATERNARY	tetrabrach	4	○○○○	quiet	*innit yeah sis, insy-winsy*
	primus paeon	4	●○○○	galloping	*dífficulties, génuinely, sécularist*
	secundus paeon	4	○●○○	galloping	*abnórmally, comédian, discóvery*
	tertius paeon	4	○○●○	emphatic	*acquisítion, deconstrúction, incohérent*
	quartus paeon	4	○○○●	emphatic	*misunderstánd, undersubscríbed*
	major ionic	4	●●○○	falling	*péjorative, pré-éminent, próféssional*
	minor ionic	4	○○●●	rising	*with the lóve sóng, anacrúsis*
	ditrochee	4	●○●○	falling	*circulátion, idiótic, váriátion*
	diiamb	4	○●○●	rising	*leviathán, buffóonerý, assíduous*
	choriamb	4	●○○●	galloping	*múrmuring sílk, óde to the wést,*
	antispast	4	○●●○	galloping	*besíde bóttom, abóve cótton*
	first epitrite	4	○●●●	emphatic	*tomáto sóup! behóld Kíng Bíll!*
	second epitrite	4	●○●●	rising	*chóco yúm yúm, háppy bírthdáy!*
	third epitrite	4	●●○●	galloping	*fóotbáll inspíres, píck úp that gún*
	fourth epitrite	4	●●●○	falling	*chíldhóod swéetheart, báthróbe fálling*
	dispondee	4	●●●●	emphatic	*wígwám súnshíne, básebáll tóothbrúsh*

METER

dimeter and trimeter

Poetic feet combine to produce poetic *meter,* and each meter has its own distinctive quality, melody, and musical meaning. Likewise, a subject, mood, or feeling may suggest an appropriate meter. In general, meters are formed from a single repeated foot, although some meters are combinations of different feet (*e.g. the Sapphic, see page 164*).

Meters are named after the Greek number and type of foot of which they are comprised; thus with one foot per line a poem is described as being in *monometer* (*see examples on pages 124–5*) and with two feet per line it is an example of *dimeter,* and so on. Such simple meters are rare outside children's verse. However, lines of three feet, *trimeter,* are more common.

Here is some iambic trimeter from William Blake's 1777 *I Love the Jocund Dance* (note the hypercatalectic syllable at the start of the fourth line).

IAMBIC TRIMETER - di dúm (○●) ×3

I lóve| the jóc|und dánce,   ○● ○● ○●
The sóft|ly bréa|thing sóng,   ○● ○● ○●
Where ínn|ocent éyes| do glánce,   ○● ○● ○●
And where lísps| the mái|den's tóngue.   ○○● ○● ○●

The waltzing quality of trimeter is doubly apparent in this poem by William Cowper, published in 1782:

ANAPESTIC TRIMETER - di di dúm (○○●) ×3

I am óut| of humán|ity's réach,   ○○● ○○● ○○●
I must fín|ish my jóur|ney alóne,   ○○● ○○● ○○●
Never héar| the sweet mú|sic of spéech;   ○○● ○○● ○○●
I stárt| at the sóund| of my ówn.   ○○● ○○● ○○●

Meter	No.	FOOT		SYLL.	EXAMPLE
Dimeter	2	Trochaic	●○ × 2	4	Úp the válleys / Dówn the cányons
	2	Iambic	○● × 2	4	And só to dréam / How still the dáy
	2	Anapaestic	○○● × 2	6	From the céntre all sóund / and all silence is fóund
	2	Dactylic	●○○ × 2	6	Cánnon to ríght of them / Cánnon to léft of them
Trimeter	3	Trochaic	●○ × 3	6	Glíding clóse to héaven / sóaring óver Dévon
	3	Iambic	○● × 3	6	The ónly néws I knów / is búlletins all dáy
	3	Anapaestic	○○● × 3	9	And I láugh to see thém whirl and flée
	3	Dactylic	●○○ × 3	9	Túrning and gálloping wéarily
Tetrameter	4	Trochaic	●○ × 4	8	Bý the shóres of Gítchee Gúmee
	4	Iambic	○● × 4	8	And báts went róund in frágrant skies
	4	Anapaestic	○○● × 4	12	The Assýrian came dówn Like the wólf on the fóld
	4	Dactylic	●○○ × 4	12	Grínd away, móisten and másh up thy páste I say
Pentameter	5	Trochaic	●○ × 5	10	Sítting sínging quíetly bý the ríver
	5	Iambic	○● × 5	10	And súmmer's léase hath áll too shórt a dáte
	5	Anapaestic	○○● × 5	15	Like the ówl in the níght who was thínking some míce might be níce
	5	Dactylic	●○○ × 5	15	Chórus oh síng with the sún as she ríses and shínes on us
Hexameter	6	Trochaic	●○ × 6	12	Hóly, hóly, hóly, áll the sáints adóre thee
	6	Iambic	○● × 6	12	Did nów but fréshly spring, and sílken blóssoms béare
	6	Anapaestic	○○● × 6	18	As a slóop with a swéep of immáculate wings on her délicate spine
	6	Dactylic	●○○ × 6	18	Fáint was the áir with the ódorous bréath of magnólia blóssoming
Heptameter	7	Trochaic	●○ × 7	14	Cúrsèd bé the síckly fórms that érr from hónest náture
	7	Iambic	○● × 7	14	Oh sóme are fónd of Spánish wine and sóme are fónd of Frénch
	7	Anapaestic	○○● × 7	21	For the móon never béams without brínging me dréams of the béautiful Ánnabel Lée
	7	Dactylic	●○○ × 7	21	Dówn in the válley of Ávon so péaceful, so périlous, wáited young Willoughby
Octameter	8	Trochaic	●○ × 8	16	Thén, methóught, the áir grew dénser, pérfumed fróm an únseen cénser
	8	Iambic	○● × 8	16	My sélfish héart its véil now rípped, yet rhýthm héals what bróken strips
	8	Anapaestic	○○● × 8	24	As a pínnacle cárven and gílded of mén; for the dáte of its dóom is no móre than an hóur's
	8	Dactylic	●○○ × 8	24	Hére is a wónderful cúmbersome spéctacle strúggling to próve it is crédibly póssible

TETRAMETER
four foot

Lines of four feet are known as *tetrameter* (Greek *tetra* is 'four'). These often alternate with lines of trimeter, the paired lines adding to form *ballad heptameter*, as in this example from Macaulay's *Lays of Ancient Rome*:

IAMBIC TETRAMETER / TRIMETER - di dúm (○●) × 4/3

Then óut| spake bráve| Horá|tiús,   ○● ○● ○● ○●
   The Cáp|tain óf| the Gáte: ○● ○● ○●
"To évery mán upón this éarth   ○● ○● ○● ○●
   Death cómeth sóon or láte."   ○● ○● ○●

We have already seen examples of trochaic, anapestic, dactylic, anapestic, and amphibrachic species of tetrameter (*pages 124–128*), but here is another interesting variety from *Lucy In the Sky With Diamonds*, by Lennon & McCartney, whose elongated 'trees' and 'skies' almost put it in the category of accentual verse (*see page 120*).

DACTYLIC TETRAMETER - dúm diddy (●○○) × 4

Pícture your|sélf in a| bóat on a| ríver   ●○○ ●○○ ●○○ ●○
   With tángerine| trée-ees and| mármalade| skí-ies ○ ●○○ ●○○ ●○○ ●○○
Sómebody cálls you, you ánswer quite slówly   ●○○ ●○○ ●○○ ●○
   A gírl with kaléidoscope| éyes   ○ ●○○ ●○○ ●

Longer feet (*see page 129*) can create great rhythms. Here is contemporary poet Julia Donaldson, with the first two lines from *Tyrannosaurus Drip*:

TERTIUS PAEONIC TETRAMETER - diddy dúm di (○○●○) × 4

In a swámp be|side a ríver| where the lánd was| thick with vég
Lived a hérd of| duck-billed díno|saurs who róamed the| waters édge.

PENTAMETER
five feet

Five feet make a line of *pentameter*, and five iambs form *iambic pentameter*, the beating heart of most traditional English metrical poetry since the 14th century. This is a *measured meter*, the 'heroic' line of English verse from Chaucer and Shakespeare to the present, used to translate the epic dactylic hexameter of Homer's *Iliad* and *Odyssey* and Virgil's *Aeniad* into English. Take these two lines from Shakespeare's *Sonnet 18*:

IAMBIC PENTAMETER - di dúm (○●) × 5

Rough winds| do sháke| the dárl|ing búds| of Máy,
And súmmer's leáse hath áll too shórt a dáte.

Examples of *trochaic pentameter* are very rare, so instead let's turn to another popular meter from classical Greek and Latin poetry, the *dactylic pentameter*. This line was made of two equal parts, each consisting of two dactyls and a stressed half-foot, the number of feet summing to five in total, and with the first half-foot always ending a word, to produce a *caesura* (*see page 136*). Classical quantitative meters do not translate well into English (*see page 121*), but here is an attempt at the form in English accentual-syllabic style:

DACTYLIC PENTAMETER - dúm diddy (●○○) × 5

"Whát is the| póint of you| Sír?" ¶ said the| Kíng, almost| víolently.
"Whý are there stárs in the ský?" ¶ then he láughed and stood sílently.

In the *elegiac couplet* (*see page 165*) a line of dactylic pentameter follows a line of dactylic hexameter. Ovid's *Amores*, a collection of erotic poems about love, begin with Cupid stealing a metrical foot from Ovid's epic hexameter, turning it into pentameter to create the compound form.

HEXAMETER
the six footer

Six iambic feet produce a hypnotic line, *iambic hexameter*, also known as an *alexandrine*, which tends to divide itself in half. Here is a sample from Michael Drayton's 15,000-line epic *Poly-Olbion*, published in 1612:

IAMBIC HEXAMETER - di dúm (○●) × 6

Consí|der, quóth| this Nýmph,| the tímes| be cúr|ious nów,
And nó|thing óf| that kínd| will án|y wáy| allów.
   The móre they hér persuáde, the móre she dóth persíst;
   Let thém say whát they wíll, she wíll do whát she líst.

The classical quantitative meter (*see page 121*) is the six-foot *dactylic hexameter*. In Homer's epic poems, any of the first four dactyls can be substituted (*see page 138*) with spondees (*see page 122*) while the sixth foot is a spondee or trochee. The Greek form was approximated in English by Henry W. Longfellow in his 1847 poem *Evangeline*. Notice his substitutions and final spondees.

DACTYLIC HEXAMETER - dúm diddy (●○○) × 6

Thís is the| fórest pri|méval. The| múrmuring| pínes and the| hémlócks,
Béarded with| móss, and in| gárments| gréen, indis|tínct in the| twílight,
Stánd like| Drúids of| óld, with| vóices| sád and pro|phétic,
Stánd like| hárpers| hóar, with| béards that| rést on their| bósoms.

Anapestic hexameter has a lovely galloping quality. W. B. Yeats used it for Book III of his epic *Wanderings of Oisin*, first published in 1889:

ANAPESTIC HEXAMETER - diddy dúm (○○●) × 6

And thére| at the fóot| of the móun|tain, two cár|ried a sáck| full of sánd ...
Leaning dówn| from the gém|-studded sád|dle, I flúng| it five yárds| with my hánd

HEPTAMETER & OCTAMETER
seven and eight feet

Seven feet form lines of exciting *heptameter*. These can often be divided into one part trimeter and one part tetrameter. Emily Dickinson [1830–86] often used iambic heptameter within ballad stanzas:

IAMBIC HEPTAMETER - di dúm (o●) ×7

Becáuse| I cóuld| not stóp| for Déath,| He kínd|ly stópped| for mé;
The cárr|iage héld| but júst| oursélves| and Ímm|ortá|litý.

Sevens and threes often go well together and here are two anapestic lines from Lewis Carroll's *The Hunting of the Snark*, published in 1876.

ANAPESTIC HEPTAMETER - diddy dúm (oo●) ×7

"He remárked| to me thén,"| said that míld|est of mén,|"If your Snárk| be a Snárk,| that is ríght:
Fetch it hóme| by all méans|—you may sérve| it with gréens,| and it's hán|dy for strí|king a líght.

Eight feet form an *octameter*. In Edgar Allan Poe's 1845 poem *The Raven*, the first line can be cut in half to form a double tetrameter whilst the second line is true octameter (with a few dactylic substitutions):

TROCHAIC OCTAMETER - dúm di (●o) ×8

Ónce, up|ón a| mídnight| dréary,| while I| póndered| wéak and| wéary
Óver| mány a| quáint and| cúrious| vólume| óf for|gótten| lore

Combining eight anapests produces a very long line, as in this example from Algernon Charles Swinburne's 1887 poem *March, an Ode*:

ANAPESTIC OCTAMETER - diddy dúm (oo●) ×8

Ere fróst-flower and snów-blossom fáded and féll and the spléndour of wínter had pássed out of síght,
The wáys of the wóodlands were fáirer and stránger than dréams that fulfíl us in sléep with delíght;

CAESURA
take a breath

A break or audible pause in the flow of a line is called a *'caesura'*, ¶, from the Latin *caedere*, 'to cut'. Caesurae can vary or support poetic rhythm, and create expressive contrasts, both metrical and rhetorical. Often marked with punctuation, they are like breath pauses between musical phrases. A caesura near the beginning of a line is termed *initial*, near the middle is *medial*, and near the end is *terminal*. In the extracts below from *Paradise Lost*, John Milton [1608–74] makes flexible use of initial and terminal caesurae:

INITIAL AND TERMINAL CAESURA - in iambic pentameter (o●) di dúm × 5

Séasons| retúrn,| but nót| to mé| retúrns
Dáy, ¶ or| the swéet| appróach| of Év'n| or Mórn.

Gó in| thy ná|tive ínn|océnce, ¶ relíe
On whát| thou hást| of vér|tue, ¶ súmm|on áll,

Medial caesurae are usually less idiosyncratic. They neatly aid stylistic/contextual counterpoint and, in the absence of strict meter, can help define rhythm (they are an ever-present feature in *Anglo-Saxon* verse, *see p. 167*). Here is Thomas Nashe's c. 1587 poem *Spring, the Sweet Spring*:

MEDIAL CAESURA (RHYTHMICAL) - in catalectic dactylic tetrameter (●oo) dúm diddy × 4

Spríng, the sweet| spríng, ¶ is the| yéar's pleasant| kíng,
Thén blooms each| thíng, ¶ then maids| dánce in a| ríng,

In Alexander Pope's 1731 *Moral essay*, caesura augments antithesis:

MEDIAL CAESURA (RHETORICAL) - in accentual

Cháste to her Húsband, ¶ fránk to all besíde,
A téeming místress, ¶ but a bárren Bríde.

STOP OR ENJAMB
at the end of the line

In a single line of verse, *end-stopping*, ⊙, marks the end of a complete phrase. This usually coincides with suitable punctuation, though sometimes the sense of the words alone dictates the pause. End stopping is a principle element of rhythm, sense, and form in most English poetry. Here are four end-stopped lines from Elizabeth Browning's *A Musical Instrument*, 1854:

> END STOPPING - in dactylic trimeter (●○○) dúm diddy × 4
>
> Whát was he| dóing, the| gréat god Pán, ⊙
>   Dówn in the| réeds by the| ríver? ⊙
> Spréading rúin and scáttering bán, ⊙
>   Splάshing and páddling with hóofs of a góat, ⊙

When a line runs onto the next and the reader feels little compulsion to pause, it is said to be *enjambed*, ✓, (from the French *enjamber* 'to stride'). Here are two enjambed lines from Maya Angelou's [1928–2014] poem *Rise*:

> ENJAMBMENT - in anapestic/quartus-paeonic dimeter (◡○○●) diddy dúm × 2
>
> Does it cóme| as a surpríse ✓
>   That I dánce like I've got díamonds ✓
> At the méeting of my thíghs?

Here are both devices, in a verse from Andrew Marvell's *The Mower to the Glo-Worms,* published in 1781:

> END STOPPING & ENJAMBMENT - in iambic tetrameter (○●) di dúm × 4
>
> Ye cóun|try cóm|ets, thát| porténd ✓
>   No wár| nor prín|ce's fún|erál, ⊙
> Shíning untó no hígher énd ✓
>   Than tó preságe the gráss's fáll; ⊙

SUBSTITUTION
changing feet

A poetic line which ends with an unstressed syllable is said to have a *feminine ending*, whereas one with a final stressed syllable is *masculine*. To aid *lineation* (the flow of lines) an iambic or anapestic line will occasionally end with an extra unstressed syllable. For example, this extract from Shakespeare's *Hamlet*, published in 1603, although written in iambic pentameter (5 iambic feet, 10 syllables per line), contains *hypermetrical* lines of 11 syllables:

ADDING FEMININE ENDINGS - to iambic pentameter (○●) di dúm × 5

Thus cón|science dóes| makeców|ards óf| us áll; ⊙	(10)	*m*
And thús| the ná|tive húe| of rés|olútion ✓	(11)	*+f*
Is síck| lied ó'er| with the| pále cást| of thóught, ⊙	(10)	*m*
And én|terprí|ses óf| gréat píth| and móment ⊙	(11)	*+f*

Note that the longer lines still consist of five feet, and that the addition of the unstressed syllable to the final foot changes it from an iamb into an amphibrach (*see page 128*). Deeper scansion of the above also reveals that this is not the only change in foot type. For example, a pyrrhic foot (*see page 123*) 'with the' appears in the third line, and a spondaic 'great pith' in the fourth.

This *substitution* of one foot for another is a commonly-used technique in metrical verse. A poet exchanges the expected foot for a different one, even of a different length. The swap is often found at the beginning of lines but can occur anywhere, any number of times. Here is Hamlet again:

SUBSTITUTION - in iambic pentameter (○●) di dúm × 5

To bé,| or nót| to bé;| thát is| the quéstion:— ⊙	(11)	*4th foot trochee, +f*
Whéther| 'tis nó|bler ín| the mínd| to súffer ✓	(11)	*1st foot trochee, +f*
The slíngs| and á|rrows óf| outrá|geous fórtune; ⊙	(11)	*no subs, +f*

Ór to| take árms| agáinst| a séa| of tróubles, ⊙   (11) *1st foot trochee, +f*
And bý| oppósing,| énd them?|—To díe|, to sléep ⌣   (11) *2nd amphibrach, 3rd trochee, m*
Nó móre;| and, bý| a sléep,| to sáy| we énd ⌣   (10) *1st foot spondee, m*
The héart|-áche, and| the thóu|sand nát|ural shócks ⌣   (10) *2nd foot trochee, m*
That flésh| is héir| to,—'Tís| a cón|summátion   (10) *no subs, +f*

Sometimes it can make sense metrically and dialectically to substitute the first foot of a line. For example, in the above extract, the opening trochaic 'Whether' (*facing page*) naturally follows a feminine ending. Substitution is also often used expressively, to signal a rhetorical shift, as in Hamlet's forceful opening spondee 'No more' (*above*).

Below, Emily Dickinson emphasizes the opening word of her 1891 poem *Hope is the thing with feathers* with a trochee:

INITIAL SUBSTITUTION - in iambic trimeter (○●) di dúm × 3

Hópe is| the thíng| with féathers ⌣   (7) *1st foot trochee, +f*
that pérch|es ín| the sóul ⊙   (6) *no subs, m*

And here, Robert Frost [1874–1963] uses some *trisyllabic substitution* (the substitution of a binary for a ternary foot, e.g. an anapest for an iamb) in his 1916 poem *The Road Not Taken*:

TRISYLLABIC SUBSTITUTION - in iambic tetrameter (○●) di dúm × 4

Two róads| divérged| in a yé|llow wóod, ⊙   (9) *3rd foot anapest, m*
  And sór|ry I cóuld| not tráv|el bóth ⌣   (9) *2nd foot anapest, m*
And bé| one trável|er, lóng| I stóod ⌣   (9) *2nd foot amphibrach, m*
And lóoked| down óne| as fár| as I cóuld ⊙   (9) *4th foot anapest, m*

Thus, with an ear for how language is spoken, metrical variation is part of poetic meter. It is used expressively, expanding and reinforcing meaning, and helping to naturalize a poem's rhythm. Ballads and nursery rhymes tend to vary less, as their meters are reinforced by musical rhythm (*overleaf*).

MORE COMPLEX RHYTHMS
and mixed meters

We have already seen how stresses and syllables create poetic rhythm. Yet something else underpins this art; something deeply connected to the musical origins of poetry. It is background beat, and we all meet it as children in the song and chant of nursery rhymes.

To take an example, *Hickory Dickory Dock* is a five-line accentual poem (*see page 120*), with varying syllable counts, and three stresses for lines 1, 2, and 5, and two for lines 3 and 4. However, when presented in semi-musical notation (*below*) we quickly discover the hidden 3:4 rhythm which is heard when the rhyme is actually spoken:

RHYTHMIC ACCENTUAL

I	2	3	I	2	3	I	2	3	I	2	3		
Híck--or---y		Díck--or---y		Dóck					The			(7)
móuse	ran	úp		the clóck					The			(6)
clóck	struck óne;		The móuse		ran dówn							(8)
Híck--or---y		Díck--or---y		Dóck								(7)

Notice how the stressed syllables fall on primary beats while the off-beats host unstressed syllables. In many places neither is marked. *Humpty Dumpty* has a similar rhythm, with lines 3 and 4 marking every beat:

I	2	3	I	2	3	I	2	3	I	2	3	
Húmp- - - -ty		Dúmp- - - -ty		sát	on	a	wáll					(8)
Húmp- - - -ty		Dúmp- - - -ty		hád	a	great	fáll					(8)
Áll	the king's hórs---es	and	áll	the king's mén								(10)
Cóuldn't	put Húmp-ty	to---gé---ther	a---gáin									(10)

Many accentual poems can be analyzed in this way. In *The Owl and the Pussycat*, by Edward Lear [1812–88], the waltzing rhythm is established from the start. It's almost impossible to read the first line without introducing pauses between 'went' and 'to sea', or between 'pea' and 'green boat':

I	2	3	I	2	3	I	2	3	I	2	3		
The	Ówl	and	the	Pús---sy---cat	wént		to	séa	in	a			(10)
	Béau--ti---ful	péa		green	bóat					They			(8)
	tóok	some	hó---ney	and	plén---ty		of	món---ey	wrapped				(11)
	úp	in	a	fíve	pound	nóte							(7)

Another way that poets vary the contours of metrical schemes is to mix their meters. William Wordsworth, in his 1804 ode on *Intimations of Immortality*, appears to change his meter on almost every line, whilst always retaining the lilting iambic foot as his base unit (*this poem also appears on page 165*):

MIXED METER	IAMBIC		
There wás| a tíme| when méa|dow, gróve,| and stréam,	pentameter	(10)	
The éarth,| and év|ery cóm|mon síght,	tetrameter	(8)	(10)
To mé| did séem	dimeter	(4)	(10)
Appá|relled ín| celés|tial líght,	tetrameter	(8)	
The gló|ry ánd| the frésh|ness óf| a dréam.	pentameter	(10)	
It ís| not nów| as ít| hath béen| of yóre;—	pentameter	(10)	
Turn whére|soe'er| I máy,	trimeter	(6)	(10)
By níght| or dáy,	dimeter	(4)	
The thíngs| which Í| have séen| I nów| can séel| no móre.	hexameter	(12)	

In the poem below, e e cummings [1894–1962] takes the opposite approach, varying his feet, whilst always ensuring there are four per line:

whát if a| múch of a| whích of a| wínd,	dactylic tetrameter	(10)
gíves the| trúth to| súmmer's| líe;	trochaic tetrameter	(7)
blóodies with| dízzying| léaves the| sún	dactylic tetrameter	(10)
and yánks| immór|tal stárs| awrý?	iambic tetrameter	(8)

Rhyme
and its schemes

The terms 'rhyme' and 'rhythm' both come from the Greek word *rhythmos* meaning 'flow', 'regular motion', or 'symmetry'. Rhymes bind poetic elements together, creating patterns across space and through time, implying and intensifying connections. Here's a rhythmic tail rhyme from the end of *The Cat in the Hat* by Dr. Seuss:

END OR TAIL RHYME - anapestic tetrameter (○○●) diddy dúm × 4

Then our mó|ther came ín| and she sáid| to us twó	○○● ○○● ○○● ○○● [a]
'Did you háve| any fún|? Tell me, whát| did you dó?'	○○● ○○● ○○● ○○● [A]
And Sá|lly and Í| did not knów| what to sáy.	○● ○○● ○○● ○○● [b]
Should we téll her the things that went ón there that dáy?	○○● ○○● ○○● ○○● [b]
Should we téll her abóut it? Now whát should we dó?	○○● ○○● ○○● ○○● [A]
Well, whát would you dó if your móther asked yóu?	○● ○○● ○○● ○○● [a]

To notate *rhyming schemes*, each new rhyme is given a letter when it first appears in a poem. In the example above, *a* rhymes with *a*, and *b* with *b*, while repeated end-words are notated with capitalized letters, *aAbbAa*.

Gerald Manly Hopkins' *The Windhover*, 1877, uses alliteration, consonance, end-rhymes, internal rhymes, imperfect rhymes and many other devices:

INTERNAL RHYMES - sprung rhythm, loose pentameter

I caúght\| this mórn\|ing mórn\|ing's min\|ion, king-
    dom of dáylight's dáuphin, dápple-dawn-drawn Fálcon, in his ríding
    Of the rólling lével underneáth him stéady aír, and stríding
High there, how he rúng upón the réin of a wímpling wíng
In his écstasy! then óff, óff fórth on swíng,
    As a skáte's héel swéeps smooth on a bów-bénd: the húrl and glíding
    Rebúffed the bíg wínd. My heárt in híding
Stírred for a bírd, — the achíeve of; the mástery of the thíng!

RHYME	DEFINITION	EXAMPLE
END OR TAIL RHYME, RIME COUÉE	A rhyme in the final syllable(s) of two or more lines.	The cow is of the bovine ilk One end is moo; the other milk. O. Nash
INTERNAL RHYME	Two or more rhyming words occur within the same line or across the center and/or end words of adjacent lines.	What would the world be; once beréft Of wét and of wildness? Lét them be léft G.M. Hopkins
CROSS RHYME	The end-word of one line matches a word in the middle of the following line or vice versa.	And he shall go where time lies still and frozen beneath eternal snow.
PERFECT, FULL OR TRUE RHYME	The sound of two words are identical except at the beginning.	light/night; fire/briar; names/flames; fish/dish; kind/mind; hole/mole
MASCULINE	Stress is on the final syllable of each word.	sublime/design; reveal/conceal;
FEMININE	Stress is on the second from last syllable of each word.	thúnder/asúnder; súltry/poúltry; tówers/flówers
DACTYLIC:	Stress is on the third from last syllable of each word.	cacóphony/heteróphony
PARTIAL OR HALF RHYME	Words which almost rhyme. Any species other than perfect rhyme: barn/large, craft/laugh, love/blush, etc	Courage was mine; and I had mystery; Wisdom was mine; and I had mastery: W. Owen
IMPERFECT RHYME	The otherwise perfect rhyming of stressed-unstressed syllables.	Lasting/sting; imagine/grin; summer/her; mountain/win; crystal/fall; narrative/live
ASSONANT RHYME OR ASSONANCE	Vowel sounds are identical but consonants differ.	love/move/prove; oar/oak; blows/notes; round/drown
CONSONANT RHYME	Outer consonants are the same but vowels differ.	night/nought; fell/fall/fool/foul/fail/feel; years/yours
ALLITERATION	Words in close succession have the same first letter or sound.	concordant/consonants/consistently/convolve and aurally/accord
EYE RHYME	A typographic rhyme between words with similar spellings but different sounds.	look/moon/o; thought/though; love/prove; brow/crow; hubris/debris; live/live
RICH RHYME	Rhyme between identical sounding words with different meanings.	their/there; bear/bare; foul/fowl; where/wear; eye/I; see/sea
DIMINISHING RHYME	A perfect chiming of two succesive words where the second is nested in the first.	report/port; emotion/motion; avail/veil; impale/pale; start/art; cracking/king

THE STANZA
unit of poetic form

Syllables combine to form words, words form lines, and lines form *stanzas* (*It.* for 'room'). Stanzas are the building blocks of poetic form, building space, shape, sense, and story in a poem, and aiding the reader's eye. Here are the first two stanzas of Emily Dickinson's *In the Garden* [1891]:

STANZA I

A bírd| came dówn| the wálk:
    He díd| not knów| I sáw;
He bít| an án|gle-wórm| in hálves
    And áte| the féll|ow, ráw.

STANZA II

And thén| he dránk| a déw
    From á| convé|nient gráss,
And thén| hopped síde|wise tó| the wáll
    To lét| a bée|tle páss.

The Greek word for stanza is *strophe*, which means 'turn' (literally, a complete turn in a dance). A poem formed from several stanzas is said to be *strophic*, which in music means several repeated verses (AAA) of the same melody, but with changing lyrics. Successive stanzas can function as introduction, development, and conclusion, much like a story's beginning, middle, and end (*see page 360*), or a logical argument (*see pages 190–198*).

When starting a poem, a poet faces a choice—whether to use a *fixed form*, a traditional pattern, or a *nonce form*, a unique pattern devised by the poet.

FIXED FORM - e.g. a VILLANELLE, see p.158, first two stanzas, by Dylan Thomas, 1952

Do nót| go gén|tle ín|to thát| good níght,   [A¹]
    Old áge| should búrn| and ráve| at clóse| of dáy;   [b]
Ráge, ráge| agáinst| the dý|ing óf| the líght.   [A²]

Though wise men at their end know dark is right,   [a]
    Because their words had forked no lightning they   [b]
Do not go gentle into that good night.   [A¹]

BLANK VERSE
fewer rules

Poetry which is not *stanzaic*, or broken into stanzas, is *stichic* (pr. *stik-ik*), and poems of unrhymed stichic lines written in regular meter are known as *blank verse*. It has been estimated that three quarters of all English poetry is in blank verse, mostly iambic pentameter. The lack of rhyme is well-suited to argument, emotion, and rhythmic speech. It was first adapted to English from the 11-syllable Italian form *verse sciolti da rima* ('verse free from rhyme') by Henry Howard, Earl of Surrey for his 1540s translations of *The Aeneid*. Christopher Marlowe [1564–93] then used it in *Tamburlaine the Great* before, coupled with rhyme and song, it became the great workhorse of Shakespeare's [1564–1616] plays and Milton's [1608–74] *Paradise Lost*.

Here is an example from Coleridge's *Frost at Midnight*, written in 1768:

BLANK VERSE - using iambic pentameter (○●) di dúm × 5

My bábe| so béau|tifúl!| it thrílls| my héart
With tén|der glád|ness, thús| to lóok| at thée,
And thínk| that thóu| shalt léarn| far ó|ther lóre,
And ín| far ó|ther scénes!| For Í| was réared
In the great city, pent 'mid cloisters dim,
And saw nought lovely but the sky and stars.
But thou, my babe! Shalt wander like a breeze
By lakes and sandy shores, beneath the crags
Of ancient mountain, and beneath the clouds,

Since the late 19th century, some poets have discarded meter as well as rhyme, resulting in *free verse*. This builds form and narrative using rhetoric, repetition, assonance, strophic and stichic line grouping, visual shape, trope, metaphor, and simile, but is not the subject of this book.

COUPLETS AND TRIPLETS
and the terza rima

The *couplet* is the simplest of all stanzas. Formed from any two lines rhyming *aa*, couplets take many forms. In an *equal couplet*, both lines have the same number of syllables and beats. Seventeenth-century poets, Shakespeare among them, often used sequences of couplets in iambic pentameter (known as *heroic couplets*) to give the feel of the classical heroic epics:

HEROIC COUPLET - iambic pentameter (○●) di dúm × 5

The Tíme| is óut| of jóint,| O cúr|sed spíte	[a]
That é|ver Í| was bórn| to sét| it ríght.	[a]

This is also an example of a *closed couplet*, one that forms a complete, balanced statement or sentence. The first line rises/calls; the second answers/falls. Closed couplets can become *epigrams*, like Coleridge's eponymous example:

CLOSED COUPLET - example in iambic pentameter (○●) di dúm × 5

What ís| an ép|igrám?| A dwárf|ish whóle,	[a]
Its bó|dy bré|vitý,| and wít| its sóul.	[a]

Unequal couplets have unequal line lengths, like the *poulter's measure*:

UNEQUAL COUPLET - e.g. the POULTER'S MEASURE, iamb. hex./hept. (○●) di dúm × 5/6

A twélv|ish twíst|ing líne,| a póul|ter's méa|sure kéeps,	[a]
With fóur|teen móre| right ún|dernéath| on whích| the óth|er sléeps.	[a]

Two couplets enjambed together are *open couplets*, as in this by Keats [1818]:

OPEN COUPLETS - example in iambic pentameter (○●) di dúm × 5

A thíng| of béau|ty ís| a jóy| for éver:	+f [a]
Its lóve|linéss| incréa|ses; ít| will néver ⸝	+f [a]

Pass ín|to nóth|ingnéss;| but stíll| will kéep   [b]
A bów|er quíet| for ús,| ¶ ánd| a sléep   [b]

A *triplet* is a three-line stanza of any length, rhyming *aaa*. It is often used for dramatic emphasis and variation in couplet-heavy verse. In *The Eagle*, Tennyson's powerful triplets draw out the bird:

TRIPLETS - example in iambic tetrameter (○●) di dúm × 4

He clásps| the crág| with cróok|ed hánds: [a]
Clóse to| the sún| in lóne|ly lánds,   [a]
Rínged with| the áz|ure wórld,| it stánds.   [a]

The wrínkled séa benéath him cráwls;   [b]
He wátches fróm his móuntain wálls,   [b]
And líke a thúnderbólt he fálls.   [b]

A *tercet* is any three-line unit of poetry, but when rhymed *aba* it is known as a *terza rima* (Italian for 'third rhyme'). Strung together in *chain rhymes*, *aba bab cdc ded efe* etc., stanzas of terza rima form the backbone of Dante's *Divine Comedy* and Chaucer's *Complaint to His Lady*. Four chained tercets with a concluding couplet, *aba bab cdc ded ee*, form a *terza rima sonnet*.

TERZA RIMA - in iamb. pent. from *Second Satire* by Thomas Wyatt [1503-42]

Ye dó| misséek| with móre| travául| and cáre.   [a]
    Make plaín| thy héart,| that ít| be nót| knottéd   [b]
With hópe| or dréad;| and sée| thy wíll| be báre   [a]

    From áll affécts whom více hath éver spótted.   +f [b]
Thysélf contént with thát is thée assígned,   [c]
    And úse it wéll that ís to thée allótted.   +f [b]

Then seek no more out of thyself to find   [c]
    The thing that thou hast sought so long before,   [d]
For thou shalt feel it sitting in thy mind;   [c]

THE BALLAD
the great quatrain

Any four-line stanza is called a *quatrain*. Hugely popular, many English poems are in quatrains: nursery rhymes, songs, and hymns. For example, Robert Burn's 18th century version of *John Barleycorn* begins like this:

THE BALLAD STANZA - iambic tetrameter/trimeter

QUATRAIN	There wás| three kíngs| intó| the eást,	○● ○● ○● ○●	[a]
	Three kíngs| both gréat| and hígh,	○● ○● ○●	[b]
	And théy have swórn a sólemn óath	○● ○● ○● ○●	[c]
	John Bárleycórn should díe.	○● ○● ○●	[b]

This quatrain is a *ballad stanza* (from the French *ballare*, 'to dance'), which alternates between lines of iambic tetrameter and trimeter. Its lines can rhyme *abcb defe* (*as above*), use a tighter cross-rhyme *abab cdcd*, or fall into couplets *aabb ccdd*. There are also versions which vary in line-length and meter (a 6-line version, rhyming *abcbdb*, is common). The earliest written English example of the form, *Judas*, dates to at least the 13th century:

Júdas,| thou móst| to Júr|selém,   Thrítti pláten of sélver thóu
    oure mét|e fór| to búgge;   bére up óthi rúgge.

Traditional ballads use everyday speech and song to tell stories of love, rural life, work, local events, the supernatural, and the like. The ancient Scottish Border ballad of *Tam Lin* shows the form:

O Í| forbíd| you, mái|dens á',   There's náne that gáes by Cárterháugh
    That wéar| gowd ón| your háir,   But théy leave hím a wád,
    To cóme| or gáe| by Cárt|erháugh,   Eithér their ríngs, or gréen mantlés,
    For yóung| Tam Lín| is thére.   Or élse their máidenhéad.

The ballad form was used for catchy hymns in the 15th and 16th centuries, when it became known as *common* or *short measure*. Then, between the 17th and 19th centuries, *Broadside ballads* flourished throughout Europe. Printed cheaply, posted on pub walls, and sold by peddlars, they often later became popular songs, passed on orally. Broadside ballads are journalistic, full of sensational news, disaster, love scandals, murder, and suicide. An example is the *Ballad of George Barnwell*, published in the 1650s. Here is an extract:

Most súdd|enlý| withín| a wóod	And fóurscore póund in réady cóyn,
he strúck| his Ún|cle dówn	out óf his Púrse he tóok,
And béat| his bráins| out óf| his héad,	And cómming únto Lóndon stráit,
so sóre| he cráckt| his crówn:	the Country quite forsóok.

Literary ballads developed throughout the 18th century. Oscar Wilde [1854–1900] adapted the form for *The Ballad of Reading Gaol* with two extra lines broadly rhyming *ababcb*, but perhaps the most famous example comes from Coleridge [1722–1834], in *The Rime of the Ancient Mariner*:

All ín| a hót| and cóp|per ský,	Dáy after dáy, dáy after dáy,
The blóod|y Sún,| at nóon,	We stúck, nor bréath nor mótion;
Right úp| abóve| the mást| did stánd,	As ídle ás a páinted shíp
No bígg|er thán| the Móon.	Upón a páinted ócean.

Much rap, performance poetry, and modern pop uses the ballad form. Here is a ballad variation from Benjamin Zephaniah's *Talking Turkeys*, 1994. Instead of 4-3-4-3 iambic feet, it uses 3-3-4-3 anapestic, much like a limerick:

BALLAD VARIATION - anapestic trimeter/tetrameter (○○●) diddy dúm × 3/4

So, be níce| to yu túr|key dis chrístmas	Be níce to yu túrkey dis chrístmas
Invíte| dem indóors| fe sum gréens	An spáre dem de cút of de knífe,
Lét| dem eat cáke| an lét| dem partáke	Join Túrkeys Uníted an déy'll be delíghted
In a pláte| of orgán|ic grown béans,	An yú will mek néw friends 'FOR LÍFE'.

FOUR QUATRAINS
four-line stanzas

Long measure is a common quatrain which contains four lines of four iambs with the same *abcb* rhyme scheme as the ballad. T. S. Eliot [1888–1965] used it for *Sweeney Among the Nightingales*, where the form's sincerity and natural openness help reinforce the poems irony:

LONG MEASURE - 4 lines of iambic tetrameter (○●) di dúm × 4

QUATRAIN

Ápe|neck Swée|ney spréads| his knées	[a]
Létting| his árms |hang dówn| to láugh,	[b]
Déath and| the Rá|ven dríft| abóve	[c]
Swélling| to mác|uláte| giráffe.	[b]

The circles óf the stórmy móon	[d]
Slide wéstward towárd the Ríver Pláte,	[e]
The zébra strípes alóng his jáw	[f]
And Swéeney gúards the hórnèd gáte.	[e]

When long measure has the rhyme scheme *abba*, it is called the *In Memoriam stanza,* after Tennyson's famous lengthy elegy *In Memoriam* [1850], forever associating it with the lyric of loss and lament, as in this extracted quatrain from Section LXXXV:

THE IN MEMORIAM STANZA - 4 lines of iambic tetrameter, rhyming *abba*

This trúth| came bórne| with bíer| and páll,	[a]
I félt| it, whén| I sórr|ow'd móst,	[b]
'Tis better to have loved and lost,	[b]
Than never to have loved at all	[a]

This is also an example of an *envelope stanza,* because the enclosed couplet *bb* is enveloped between another enclosing couplet, *aa.*

The *heroic* or *elegiac quatrain* uses iambic pentameter and has an alternating rhyme scheme *abab*. An example is *Elegy Written in Country Churchyard*, by Thomas Grey [1716–71] (an elegy in name but not in form, *see page 165*):

HEROIC QUATRAIN - 4 lines of iambic pentameter, rhyming *abab*

The cúr|few tólls| the knéll| of pár|ting dáy,	[a]
The lów|ing hérd| wind slów|ly óe'r| the léa,	[b]
The plóughman hómeward plóds his wéary wáy,	[a]
And léaves the wórld to dárkness ánd to mé;	[b]
Now fades the glimmering landscape on the sight,	[c]
And all the air a solemn stillness holds,	[d]
Save where the beetle wheels his droning flight,	[c]
And drowsy tinklings lull the distant folds;	[d]

Notice how the longer lines of the pentameter allow adjectives, fanfare and modifiers of all kinds to come rushing in to fill out the rhythm.

Ruba'i (plural *ruba'iat*) is a traditional Persian quatrain form, which was introduced to England in Edward FitzGerald's 1859 translation of the *Ruba'iat of Omar Khayyam*. Here are two quatrains (from over 1,000), which demonstrate the Ruba'i's rhyming scheme *aaba bbcb ccdc dded etc*:

RUBA'I - 4 lines of iambic pentameter, cross-rhyming with the next 4

Come fíll| the Cúp,| and ín| the Fíre| of Spríng	[a]
The Wín|ter Gár|ment óf| Repén|tance fling:	[a]
The Bírd| of Tíme| has bút| a lít|tle wáy	[b]
To flý|—and Ló!| the Bírd| is ón| the Wíng.	[a]
And lóok—a thóusand Blóssoms wíth the Dáy	[b]
Woke—ánd a thóusand scátter'd into Cláy:	[b]
And thís first Súmmer Mónth that brings the Róse	[c]
Shall táke Jamshýd and Káikobád awáy.	[b]

QUINTAINS
limericks and madness

Any poetic form built on five-line stanzas is called a *quintain*. The most widely recognized example in English verse is the *limerick*, which is constructed from three lines of anapestic/amphibrachic trimeter (lines 1, 2, & 5) and two of dimeter (lines 3-4). The rhyme scheme is strictly *aabba*, and the form seems to lends itself particularly well to wit or humour, with extra points awarded for uncanny or ridiculous rhymes, and nonsense or smut.

LIMERICK - Anon, catalectic amphibrachic trimeter/dimeter (○●○) di dúm di × 3/2

There wás a| young lády| named Whíte	[a]
Who trávelled| much fáster| than líght,	[a]
She sét out| one dáy	[b]
In a réla|tive wáy	[b]
And cáme back| the prévi|ous níght	[a]

Five-line stanzas also appear in other *nonsense verse* like 16th- and 17th-century *mad-songs* or *Bedlamite verse*. This form has five lines of variable meter (trochees and anapests) rhyming *abccb*, leaving an unrhymed *a*:

MAD-SONG STANZA - Anon. 16th C.

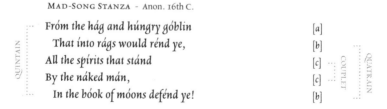

Fróm the hág and húngry góblin	[a]
That ínto rágs would rénd ye,	[b]
All the spírits that stánd	[c]
By the náked mán,	[c]
In the bóok of móons defénd ye!	[b]

A five-line stanza can be rhymed using the enclosing and enclosed couplets (*as above*), or it can rhyme *ababa*, or *aaaba*, or *abbba*, or it can be simply split into a triplet and a couplet, *aaabb*.

SESTETS
six lines

Stanzas of six lines, *sestets*, can be formed in many ways. Three couplets rhyming *aabbcc* are common, as is the Middle-English *romance stanza*, which rhymes *aabccb*. Scottish poet Robert Burns [1759–96] wrote over fifty poems in sestets; here is the first stanza of his *To a Mountain Daisy*:

THE BURNS STANZA ('STANDARD HABBIE') - iamb. tetr./dimeter (○●) di dúm × 4 / 2

Wee, mó|dest crím|son-típp|èd flów'r,	[a]
Thou's mét| me ín| an é|vil hóur;	[a]
For Í| maun crúsh| amáng| the stóure	[a]
Thy slén|der stém:	[b]
To spáre| thee nów| is pást| my ków'r,	[a]
Thou bón|ie gém.	[b]

Couplets added to a longer stanza can form an epigram or conclusion, and six lines of iambic pentameter rhyming *ababcc* form the sestet at the end of a *Petrarchan sonnet* (*page 156*), a six-line stanza also used by Shakespeare for his 1593 poem *Venus and Adonis*. Sir Walter Raleigh [1552–1618] opted for the same scheme in *The Lie*, but shortens the line to iambic trimeter, while William Wordsworth [1770–1850] used it in tetrameter to describe his famous daffodils in *I Wandered Lonely as a Cloud*:

QUATRAIN WITH END COUPLET - e.g. in iambic tetrameter (○●) di dúm × 4

Contín|uous ás| the stárs| that shíne,	[a]	QUATRAIN
And twín|kle ón| the míl|ky wáy,	[b]	
They strétched in néver-énding líne	[a]	
Alóng| the már|gin óf| a báy:	[b]	
Ten thóu|sand sáw| I át| a glánce,	[c]	COUPLET
Tóssing| their héads| in spríght|ly dánce.	[c]	

SESTET

SEPTETS, OCTAVES, & NINES
for royals and faeries

With seven lines of iambic pentameter rhyming *ababbcc*, the *Rhyme Royal* stanza was introduced into English poetry from late Medieval French court poetry by Geoffrey Chaucer [1343–1400]. He used it for high-minded and comic narratives like the *Parliament of Foules* and *The Canterbury Tales*, while Shakespeare used it for *The Rape of Lucrece*. Here is verse 132 from Book V of Chaucer's *Troilus and Criseyde*:

RHYME ROYAL - 7 lines of iambic pentameter (o●) di dúm × 5

And wíth| that wórd| he gán| to wáx|en réed,	[a]	QUATRAIN
And ín| his spéche| a lí|tel wíght| he quóok,	[b]	
And caste a-syde a litel wight his heed,	[a]	
And stinte a whyle; and afterward awook,	[b]	
And soberly on hir he threw his look,	[b]	COUPLETS
And seyde, 'I am, al be it yow no Ioye,	[c]	
As gentil man as any wight in Troye.'	[c]	

(SEPTET)

The scheme hinges on its center (like a musical scale's 4th and 5th), as the *bb* couplet expands the opening quatrain and suggests the *cc* couplet. The fifth line is the pivot—it can expand, amplify, or slow down the broader rhythm of the stanza. This openness makes it well-suited to shifting temporal experiences like dreams, visions, reverie, and trance. Milton added a foot at the end, to give a 12-syllable line (or *alexandrine, see page 134*).

With eight lines, *Ottava Rima* first appeared in Italy in the poetry of Giovani Boccaccio [1313–75], most notably in *The Decameron*. It uses feminine-ended (*see page 138*) lines of iambic pentameter (so *hendecasyllabic*, 11 syllables) and an *abababcc* rhyme scheme (rhyme royal with an extra fifth line). Simultaneously narrative and meandering, sincere and comic, Lord

Byron [1788–1824] called it 'half-serious rhyme' and used it for his long satirical poem *Don Juan*. Here is a stanza from Canto XVI, in which Don Juan, frightened by a ghost, reflects on his existence:

OCTAVA RIMA - 8 lines of iambic pentameter

Betwéen| two wórlds| life hó|vers líke| a stár	[a]
'Twixt níght| and mórn,| upón| the horí|zon's vérge	[b]
How little do we know that which we are!	[a]
How less what we might be! The eternal surge	[b]
Of time and tide rolls on, and bears afar,	[a]
Our bubbles; as the old burst, new emerge,	[b]
Lash'd from the foam of ages; while the graves	[c]
Of empires heave but like some passing waves.	[c]

OCTAVE · SESTET · COUPLET

The nine-line *Spenserian stanza* was invented by Edmund Spenser [1553–1599] for the *The Fairie Queen*, and was revived in the 19th century by Byron, Keats, Shelley and others. The rhyming scheme is *ababbcbcc*, essentially two chain-rhymed ballad stanzas *abab bcbc* with a concluding *c* to form a couplet. The stanza is formed of eight lines of iambic pentameter and a concluding line of iambic hexameter, a 12-syllable alexandrine. *The Faerie Queen* contains over 2,000 of such stanzas; here is one of them:

SPENSERIAN STANZA - 8 lines of iambic pentameter + 1 line of iambic hexameter

For wéll| I wóte| thou springst| from án|cient ráce	[a]
Of Sáx|on kíngs,| that háve| with mígh|tie hánd	[b]
And many bloody battailes fought in place	[a]
High reard their royall throne in Britane land,	[b]
And vanquisht them, unable to withstand:	[b]
From thence a Faerie thee unweeting reft,	[c]
There as thou slepst in tender swadling band,	[b]
And hér| base Él|fin bróod| there fór| thee léft.	[c]
Such mén| do Cháunge|lings cáll,| so cháng'd| by Fáe|ries théft.	[c]

SPENSERIAN · QUATRAIN · QUATRAIN · COUPLET · COUPLET

THE SONNET
fourteen lines of love

The *sonnet* is a 14-line closed poem in iambic pentameter, traditionally on a *lyrical*, or personal, theme, often love. Initially developed in Sicily (*sonetto*, 'a little sound/song'), it was popularized by Francesco Petrarca [1304–74], who divided the stanza 4:3 into an octave (split into two quatrains) followed by a sestet, rhyming *abba abba cdcdcd*, with the sestet occasionally varying as *cddcdc* or *cdecde*. Here is Thomas Wentworth Higginson's [1823–1911] translation of Petrarca's *Gli Occhi Di Ch' Io Parlai*:

PETRARCHAN SONNET · 14 lines of iambic pentameter (○●) di dúm × 5

Those éyes,│ 'neath whích│ my páss│ionate ráp│ture róse,	[a]
The árms,│ hánds, féet,│ the béau│ty thát│ erewhíle	[b]
Could my own soul from its own self beguile,	[b]
And in a separate world of dreams enclose,	[a]
The hair's bright tresses, full of golden glows,	[a]
And the soft lightning of the angelic smile	[b]
That changed this earth to some celestial isle,	[b]
Are now but dust, poor dust, that nothing knows.	[a]
And yet I live! Myself I grieve and scorn,	[c]
Left dark without the light I loved in vain,	[d]
Adrift in tempest on a bark forlorn;	[c]
Dead is the source of all my amorous strain,	[d]
Dry is the channel of my thoughts outworn,	[c]
And my sad harp can sound but notes of pain.	[d]

OCTAVE · QUATRAIN · QUATRAIN · ↄ · SESTET

Typically, the first and second quatrains outline and expand upon the subject of the poem (*exposition* and *development*). Then comes the *volta* or 'turn', ↄ, often signalled with a preposition '*and*', '*but*', '*while*', '*yet*', '*though*', or '*until*', after which the sestet opposes and resolves the subject (*conclusion*).

The *Spenserian sonnet* was developed by Edmund Spenser from the 9-line stanza he used for *The Faerie Queen* (*page 155*). The 14 lines are divided into three chained quatrains and a final couplet, rhyming *abab bcbc cdcd ee*, with the *volta* either after the first octave or before the final couplet.

The *Shakespearean sonnet* became popular around 1600. It is similar to the Spenserian, but easier to rhyme as it separates the three quatrains: *abab cdcd efef gg*. The *volta* is again at the start of the 9th or 13th line, with the final rhyming couplet often acting as an epigrammatic solution to the problem developed over the three quatrains. Here is Shakespeare's *Sonnet 18*:

SHAKESPEAREAN SONNET - 14 lines of iambic pentameter

Shall Í| compáre| thee tó| a súm|mer's dáy?	[*a*]
Thou árt| more lóve|ly ánd| more tém|peráte.	[*b*]
Rough winds do shake the darling buds of May,	[*a*]
And summer's lease hath all too short a date.	[*b*]
Sometime too hot the eye of heaven shines,	[*c*]
And often is his gold complexion dimmed;	[*d*]
And every fair from fair sometime declines,	[*c*]
By chance, or nature's changing course, untrimmed;	[*d*]
But thy eternal summer shall not fade,	[*e*]
Nor lose possession of that fair thou ow'st,	[*f*]
Nor shall death brag thou wand'rest in his shade,	[*e*]
When in eternal lines to Time thou grow'st.	[*f*]
So long as men can breathe, or eyes can see,	[*g*]
So long lives this, and this gives life to thee.	[*g*]

QUATRAIN · QUATRAIN · QUATRAIN · COUPLET

Some *sonnet variations* do not follow the rhyming schemes listed above. A famous example is *Ozymandias*, by Percy Shelley [1792–1822], which rhymes *abab acdc edefef*, an interesting fusion of the two classical forms. John Milton's *When I Consider How My Light Is Spent* is another example.

VILLANELLE

nineteen lines

The dreamy rustic *villanelle* (It. *villano* 'peasant' or 'villa') is a closed form of 19 lines of iambic pentameter, with five 3-line stanzas and a final quatrain:

VILLANELLE - 19 lines of iamb. pent: e.g. *The Waking*, by T. Roethke [1908-63]

1. I wáke| to sléep,| and táke| my wálking slów.   A¹   TERCET
    I féel| my fáte| in whát| I cán|not féar.   [b]
    I léarn| by gó|ing whére| I háve| to gó.   A²

2. We think by feeling. What is there to know?   [a]   TERCET
    I hear my being dance from ear to ear.   [b]
    I wake to sleep, and take my waking slow.   A¹

3. Of those so close beside me, which are you?   [a]   TERCET
    God bless the Ground! I shall walk softly there,   [b]
    And learn by going where I have to go.   A²

4. Light takes the Tree; but who can tell us how?   [a]   TERCET
    The lowly worm climbs up a winding stair;   [b]
    I wake to sleep, and take my waking slow.   A¹

5. Great Nature has another thing to do   [a]   TERCET
    To you and me; so take the lively air,   [b]
    And, lovely, learn by going where to go.   A²

6. This shaking keeps me steady. I should know.   [a]   QUATRAIN
    What falls away is always. And is near.   [b]
    I wake to sleep, and take my waking slow.   A¹
    I learn by going where I have to go.   A²

A little like a musical round, the 1st and 3rd lines of the first stanza, A¹ and A², are *refrains*, and repeat throughout the poem (*see too page 144*).

PANTOUM
strange refrains

The *pantoum* is another circular creature, this time from Malaysia via France. The English adaption has an *open form* composed with a variety of meters in interlocking cross-rhymed quatrains: *abab bcbc cdcd ... jaja.*

The second and fourth lines of each stanza repeat as the first and the third of the next, and the first and third lines of the first stanza become the fourth and second lines of the final stanza. The second half of each quatrain also has a more personal voice than the first half. Here's an extract from *The Blue Fly Sung in the Pane* by Austin Dobson [1840–1921]:

PANTOUM - example in dactylic trimeter (●○○) dúm diddy × 3

1.	Tóiling in| Tówn now is| "hórrid,"	A¹
	(Thére is that| wóman a|gáin!) –	B¹
	Júne in the| zénith is| tórrid,	A²
	Thóught gets| drý in the| bráin.	B²
2.	There is that woman again:	B¹
	"Strawberries! fourpence a pottle!"	C¹
	Thought gets dry in the brain;	B²
	Ink gets dry in the bottle.	C²
3.	"Strawberries! fourpence a pottle!"	C¹
	Oh for the green of a lane! —	D¹
	Ink gets dry in the bottle;	C²
	"Buzz" goes a fly in the pane! ...	D²
10.	To dash one with eau de Cologne,	I¹
	(June in the zenith is torrid; –)	A²
	And why should I stay here alone!	I²
	Toiling in Town now is "horrid."	A¹

BALLADE, TRIOLET, & RONDEAU
French song and dance

The solemn *ballade* is one of the three musical *formes fixes* of medieval French poetry (the other two were the *virelai* and the *rondeau*). The ballade uses 28 lines of consistent meter in three 8-line stanzas rhyming *ababbcbC*, with a closing four line *envoi* rhyming *bcbC*. The last line of the first stanza becomes a refrain, repeated as the last line of all other stanzas, including the *envoi*. Here is the end of Algernon Charles Swinburne's *A Ballad of Dreamland*:

BALLADE - 3 × 8 lines, with a 4-line *envoi*, example in iambic/anapestic tetrameter

3.	The gréen| land's náme| that a chárm| enclóses,	[a]
	It né|ver was wrít| in the tráv|eller's chárt,	[b]
	And swéet| on its trées| as the frúit| that gróws is,	[a]
	It né|ver was sóld| in the mér|chant's márt.	[b]
	The swá|llows of dréams| through its dím| fields dárt,	[b]
	And sléep's| are the túnes| in its trée|-tops héard;	[c]
	No hóund's| note wák|ens the wíld|wood hárt,	[b]
	Ónly| the sóng| of a séc|ret bírd.	C
ENVOI 4.	In the wórld| of dréams| I have chó|sen my párt,	[b]
	To sléep| for a séa|son and héar| no wórd	[c]
	Of trúe| love's trúth| or of líght| love's árt,	[b]
	Ónly| the sóng| of a séc|ret bírd.	C

The jaunty *virelai* is constructed from a 4-line refrain, rhyming AAAB, ABAB, or ABBA, followed by three tercets, rhyming *aab* or *abb*. The refrain repeats and another three tercets and refrain may or may not follow.

The *triolet* is an epigrammatic lyric form, originally sung as two melodies, matching its refrains. With no fixed meter or length, it is usually written in octaves with line 1 repeated as the 4th and 7th, and line 2 as the 8th:

TRIOLET - example in iambic tetrameter by Robert Bridges [1844-1930]

When first| we mét,| we díd| not gúess	A
That Lóve| would próve| so hárd| a máster;	+f B
Of more than common friendliness	[a]
When first we met we did not guess	A
Who could foretell the sore distress,	[a]
This irretrievable disaster,	+f [b]
When first we met? We did not guess	A
That Love would prove so hard a master.	+f B

The triolet is the basis for the *rondeau*, which originated from sung dance-rounds (rondels). The 12- and 15-line variations are the most common. Cut the second line of each stanza from Don Marquis' [1878–1937] 15-line example below to convert it to the 12-line form:

RONDEAU - example in iambic tetrameter (○●) di dúm × 4

Your rón|deau's tále| must still| be líght—	[a] R
[No bú|gle-cáll| to lífe's| stern fíght!]	[a]
Rather| a smí|ling int|erlude	[b]
Memór|ial tó| some trán|sient móod	[b]
Of íd|le lóve| and gá|la-níght.	[a]
Its manner is the merest sleight	[a]
[O' hand; yet therein dwells its might,]	[a]
For if the heavier touch intrude	[b]
Your rondeau's stale.	R
Fragrant and fragile, fleet and bright,	[a]
[And wing'd with whim, it gleams in flight]	[a]
Like April blossoms wind-pursued	[b]
Down aisles of tangled underwood;--	[b]
Nor be too serious when you write	[a]
Your rondeau's tail!	R

SESTINA
lyrical symmetry

The *sestina* is a closed form built on repetition. Mostly unrhymed, it uses any meter for its six 6-line stanzas and final 3-line closing *envoi*. Each stanza juggles the end-words in the next by a pattern: 1→2, 2→4, 3→6, 4→5, 5→3, 6→1. Here is an extract from *Sestina* by Elizabeth Bishop [1911–1979]:

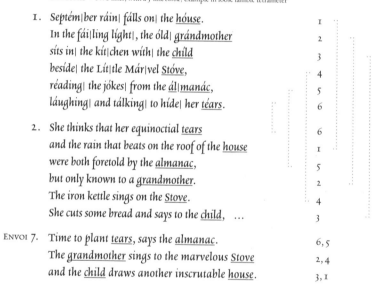

SESTINA - 6 × 6 lines, with a 3-line *envoi*, example in loose iambic tetrameter

1. Septém|ber ráin| fálls on| the hóuse.   1
   In the fái|ling líght|, the óld| grándmother   2
   síts in| the kít|chen wíth| the chíld   3
   besíde| the Lít|tle Már|vel Stóve,   4
   réading| the jókes| from the ál|manác,   5
   láughing| and tálking| to híde| her téars.   6

2. She thinks that her equinoctial tears   6
   and the rain that beats on the roof of the house 1
   were both foretold by the almanac,   5
   but only known to a grandmother.   2
   The iron kettle sings on the Stove.   4
   She cuts some bread and says to the child, ... 3

ENVOI 7. Time to plant tears, says the almanac.   6, 5
         The grandmother sings to the marvelous Stove   2, 4
         and the child draws another inscrutable house. 3, 1

After six stanzas all end-words have rotated through all positions, and then the final *envoi* reuses them in three lines, in the order: 6, 5; 2, 4; 3, 1. The sestina was developed by Arnaut Daniel [fl.1180–1200], one of the *Troubadours*, a southern European group of lyrical poets who sung their poetry over simple monophonic music, shaping the poetic experience.

CANZONE
heads and tails

Canzone, 'song', is the term for various Italian forms derived from medieval Provençal poetry. Stanzas contain between 8 and 20 lines of feminine-ended iambic pentameter or trimeter, with all stanzas in any one canzone identical. Each stanza is divided into a *fronte* (head), made of two matching *piedi* (feet) and a *sirma* (tail), sometimes divided into two *volte*. Canzone generally contain between three and seven stanzas. The opening stanza introduces a lyrical theme, the following stanzas elaborate on it, and the final stanza (sometimes just a *sirma*) concludes. The last line of a stanza often rhymes with the first line of the next.

In his translation of *Of The Gentle Heart* by Guido Guinicelli [1225–76], Dante Gabriel Rossetti [1828–82] shortens the 7- and 11-syllable Italian lines to 6 and 10 syllables to better suit English:

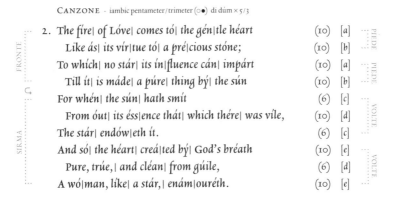

CANZONE - iambic pentameter/trimeter (o●) di dúm × 5/3

2. The fíre| of Lóve| comes tó| the gén|tle héart	(10)	[a]
Like ás| its vír|tue tó| a pré|cious stóne;	(10)	[b]
To whích| no stár| its ín|fluence cán| impárt	(10)	[a]
Till ít| is máde| a púre| thing bý| the sún	(10)	[b]
For whén| the sún| hath smít	(6)	[c]
From óut| its éss|ence thát| which thére| was víle,	(10)	[d]
The stár| endów|eth ít.	(6)	[c]
And só| the héart| creá|ted bý| God's bréath	(10)	[e]
Pure, trúe,| and cléan| from gúile,	(6)	[d]
A wó|man, líke| a stár,| enám|ouréth.	(10)	[e]

FRONTE — PIEDE / PIEDE
SIRMA — VOLTE / VOLTE

The full poem has six stanzas, each the same length and structure. Many other canzones open with a pair of quatrains, much like sonnets.

THE SAPPHIC ODE
love and devotion

The Greek poetess Sappho [c. 620–570 BC] wrote and sang oracular lyric poetry, often in three-line stanzas of mixed meter (trochee–trochee/spondee–dactyl–trochee–spondee, with an extra dactyl–spondee added to the third line). The Roman poet Horace [65–8 BC] adapted the form into Latin as three 11-syllable lines followed by a single 5-syllable line (an *adonic*). Here is a 1925 translation of Sappho's *Hymn to Aphrodite* by Edwin Marion Cox, which uses amphibrachs instead of dactyls:

> Shímmer|ing-thróned| immórtal| Áphro|díté,   ●○ ○● ○●○ ●○ ●●
> Dáughter| of Zéus,| Enchántress,| Í imp|lóre thée,   ●○ ○● ○●○ ●○ ●●
> Spáre me,| Ó quéen,| this ágo|ný and| ánguísh,   ●○ ●● ○●○ ●○ ●●
>   Crúsh not my| spírít.   ●○○ ●●

In English, Swinburne famously experimented with the stanza in his *Sapphics* (note the *anceps*, ⊙, a foot which can be either a trochee or a spondee):

THE SAPPHIC STANZA - mixed meter

13. Sáw the| Lésbians| kíssing a|cróss their| smítten
    Lútes with| líps móre| swéet than the| sóund of| lúte-strings,
    Móuth to| móuth and| hánd upon |hánd, her| chósen,
      Fáirer than| áll mén;

14. Ónly| sáw the| béautiful| líps and| fíngers,   ●○ ●⊙ ●○○ ●○ ●⊙
    Fúll of| sóngs and| kísses and| líttle| whíspers,   ●○ ●⊙ ●○○ ●○ ●⊙
    Fúll of| músic;| ónly be|héld a|móng thém   ●○ ●⊙ ●○○ ●○ ●⊙
      Sóar, as a| bírd sóars   ●○○ ●●

When reading a Sapphic, note how the emphasis falls more heavily in the later feet of each line.

ODES AND ELEGIES
passion, loss, lament

The modern *ode* developed from two ancient forms. The heroic *Pindaric ode*, from Pindar [522–443 BC], consists of an open-ended stanza (a *strophe*), its reverse-danced *antistrophe*, and finally a closed *epode*. Wordsworth's 1804 poem *Intimations of Immortality* encapsulates the idea within a stanza:

ENGLISH PINDARIC ODE - iambic pent./tetr./di./tri./hex.

There wás| a tíme| when méa|dow, gróve,| and stréam,	(10)	[a]
The eárth,| and év|ery cóm|mon síght	(8)	[b]
To mé| did séem	(4)	[a]
Apparelled in celestial light,	(8)	[b]
The glory and the freshness of a dream.	(10)	[a]
It is not now as it hath been of yore;--	(10)	[c]
Turn wheresoe'er I may,	(6)	[d]
By night or day,	(4)	[d]
The things which I have seen I now can see no more.	(12)	[c]

STROPHE ANTISTROPHE EPODE

The more intimate *Horatian ode* derives from Sappho via Horace and is a form of long/short line quatrain. Andrew Marvel [1621–78] shortened the first two lines to tetrameter for his *Ode upon Cromwell's Return from Ireland*:

ENGLISH HORATIAN ODE - iambic tetrameter/trimeter

He nó|thing cóm|mon díd| or méan	(8)	[a]
Upón| that mé|morá|ble scéne,	(8)	[a]
But wíth| his kée|ner éye	(6)	[b]
The áx|le's édge| did trý;	(6)	[b]

Classical *elegies* were written in *elegiac couplets*, alternate lines of dactylic hexameter (sometimes divided into halves or thirds) and pentameter.

CELTIC VERSE
the blacksmith's anvil

Irish verse is the oldest form of vernacular poetry in Europe, with the earliest written examples dating from the 6th and 7th centuries. Learned *Filidh*, seers, composed oral verse in Gaelic alongside ecclesiastical poets writing in Latin, sharing meters and forms. As with Anglo-Saxon verse (*opposite*), every line contains alliteration, with the alliterative syllables falling on stresses. Here is the 9th century poem *The Blackbird calling from the Willow*:

EARLY IRISH POEM - catalectic trochaic tetrameter (●○) dúm di × 4

ínt en| gáires| ásin| t-sáil	*The bird doth from the willow speak*
álainn| guílbnen| ás glan| gáir:	*lovely clear-toned little beak:*
rínn binn| búide fir| dúib| drúin:	*yellow bill of sleek black boy:*
cás cor| cúirther,| gúth ind| lúin.	*bright the song, the blackbird's voice.*

From the 6th to the 12th centuries, compositions often alternated sections of verse with prose (*prosimetrum*) as in *Buile Shuibne*, 'Sweeney's Frenzy', the story of a king who, cursed to madness by a saint, turns into a bird.

In the classical Bardic period [1200–1600] the traditional poetic forms were standardized, in particular the *Dan Direach*, which are composed in quatrains built from 'leading' and longer 'closing' trochaic couplets.

Later Irish poets captured some of these forms in English. Here are *hemistichs* from John Philpot Curran's [1750–1817] *The Deserter's Meditation*:

IRISH OCHTFOCLACH STANZA - catalectic dactylic dimeter (●○○) dúm diddy × 2

Bút as in| wáiling	*then for that reason,*
thére's nought a|váiling	*and for a season*
ánd death un|fáiling	*let us be merry*
wíll strike the| blów,	*before we go.*

ANGLO-SAXON VERSE
the push and pull of the oar

Anglo-Saxon verse was part of a rich, pre-Christian literary tradition of epic story, metaphysical fantasy, elegy, and magic. It is accentual with four primary stresses per line, often end-stopped, with each line divided in half with the weight of meaning in the first half. Evidence of the lolloping form survives in *Sir Gawain and the Green Knight* (late 14th C.) and *Beowulf* (8th–11th C.). Here is Beowulf's funeral (trans. Murphy & Sullivan):

ANGLO SAXON STYLE - accentual amphibrachal tetrameter

> The fírewind fáltered ¶ and flámes dwíndled,
> hót at their héart ¶ the bróken bónehouse.
> Her háir wáving, ¶ a Géatish wóman
> sáng for the Stálwart ¶ a sórrowful dírge

Both consonants and vowels are alliterated on at least two (though typically three) of the four stressed syllables (e.g. 'fire', 'faltered', 'flames').

A figurative device, or *trope* (*see page 252*), widely used in Anglo-Saxon, Old-German and Norse verse is *kenning* (from *kenna*, 'know, feel, show'). A kenning expresses one thing in terms of another: the sea becomes the *whale-road*; the ship a *sea-steed*; the body the *bonehouse*; in the Norse *Edda*, fire is the *sun of the houses*, and arms are *mountains of hawks*. Kennings can compound, so you can have a kenning of a kenning of a kenning:

COMPOUND KENNING - from *The Names of the Hare*, c. 1200, trans. S Heaney

> The stárer,| the wóod-cat,
> the púrblind,| the fúrze cat,
> the skúlker,| the bléary-eyed,
> the wáll-eyed,| the glánce aside ...

GHAZAL
song to the beloved

The *ghazal* is a poetic form originating in North Africa and the Middle-East around the 6th century. In the 12th century it spread into South Asia and India via Islam. Its theme is unrequited love, either because the love is forbidden or, especially within Sufism, the unobtainable beloved is God or a spiritual master. Ghazals frequently become intense, with the beloved referred to as a killer or assassin, and can include hyperbole and violence.

The form consists of five or more rhyming couplets and a refrain, with the last phrase of each line rhyming *aa ba ca da* etc. Notoriously hard to translate, the form is nevertheless evident in this version by Walter Leaf [1852–1927] of a ghazal by the Persian poet Hafiz of Shiraz [1316–90]:

GHAZAL - rhyming couplets in dactylic octameter, divided into hemistichs

Minstrel, awake the sound of glee; joyous and eager, fresh and free;
Fill me the bumper bounteously; joyous and eager, fresh and free.
  O for a bower and one beside; delicate dainty, there to hide;
Kisses at will to seize and be; joyous and eager, fresh and free.
  Sweet is my love, a thief of hearts; bravery, beauty, saucy arts,
Odours and unguents, all for me; joyous and eager, fresh and free.
  How shall the fruit of life be thine; if thou refuse the fruitful vine?
Drink of the wine and pledge with me; joyous and eager, fresh and free.
  Call me my Saki silver-limbed; bring me my goblet silver-rimmed;
Fain would I fill and drink to thee; joyous and eager, fresh and free.
  Wind of the West, if e'er thou roam; pass on the way my fairy's home;
Whisper of Hafiz amorously; joyous and eager, fresh and free.

The final verse of a ghazal often contains the poet's name (*as above*) or a hidden signature, a convention known as the *Maqta*.

TANKA & HAIKU
cutting through the moment

The classical *tanka* form, with its emphasis on nature, transience, and beauty, dominated Japanese poetry, or *waka*, in the 9th and 10th centuries. It has five lines with a total of 31 *on* (syllables) in the pattern: 5-7-5-7-7. From the 10th to 17th centuries the form became collaborative, as *renga*. A renga stanza splits the tanka into three opening lines, a *hokku*, plus two contrasting lines written by someone else, as shown in the verse below (*right*), taken from a longer *Haikai no renga* by master Sogi and his disciples.

TANKA - Ono no Komachi [825-900]

Though I go to you	[5]
ceaselessly along dream paths,	[7]
the sum of those trysts	[5]
is less than a single glimpse	[7]
granted in the waking world.	[7]

RENGA - Inō Sogi [1421-1502]

Some snow still remains
as haze moves low on the slopes
   toward evening.   - Sogi
Flowing water, far away
and a plum-scented village.   - Shohaku

By the 13th century, rules stated that a hokku must include a *kigo* (season word), appropriate to the season in which the renga was written, e.g. 'frog' for spring or 'rain' for summer, and also a *kireji* (cutting word) which, if placed at the end of a verse provides closure or return, but when used in the middle of a verse briefly cuts the stream of thought. By the time of Matsuo Bashō [1644–1694], the hokku had begun to appear as an independent poem, the 5-7-5-*on haiku*, which keeps a sense of 'opening without a closure'.

HAIKU - Matsuo Bashō

By the ancient pond	[5]
A frog jumping into it	[7]
The sound of water	[5]

HAIKU - Yosa Buson [1716-84]

An evening cloudburst—
sparrows cling desperately
to trembling bushes

POETIC DEVICES
rhetoric in verse

Rhetorical devices (or *figures*) are ways of patterning words, phrases, sentences and lines of verse to create deeper symmetry, meaning, and beauty. Studied by orators as persuasive aids *(see pages 237–291)*, they are also widely used by poets to enhance the vitality of their verses.

Repetition is the most common device, whether as *refrain*, *rhyme* *(see p.142-3)*, or *rhythm*, or as repeated consonants, in *alliteration* and *consonance* (e.g. *five/ feet* and *blank/think*), or as *assonance* in vowels (e.g. *black/hat*) *(see too pages 274–5)*.

> Betty Botter bought some butter, but she said, the butter's bitter
> If I put it in my batter it will make my batter bitter ...

Other common repetitions include *anaphora* (where several lines begin the same way), and *polyptoton* (when a word is used in more than one way, e.g. *'Please, please me'*). In *chiasmus*, from the Greek letter X (*chi*), sounds, words, phrases and grammar are repeated in reverse order:

CHIASMUS

| The wave of the particle | I mean what I say | Swift as an arrow flying |
| is the particle of the wave | and I say what I mean | fleeing like a hare afraid |

The first two examples reverse nouns and verbs, respectively, and exhibit *antimetabole*, total symmetry, while the third inverts adjective-simile-participle into participle-simile-adjective. Entire verses of the King James Bible, *Sir Gawain and the Green Knight* and Homer's *Odyssey* and *Iliad* are structured in this way, giving them a feeling of necessary balance.

Another family of figurative devices uses repetition to compare one thing to another, using *colour, imagery*, and *sensory clues* to invoke memories, and *simile* ('as' or 'like') and *metaphor* to draw parallels, e.g.:

METAPHOR - from *As You Like It* by William Shakespeare, [pub. 1623]

All the world's a stage,
And all the men and women merely players;

Words sometimes sound like the things they describe, a device known as *onomatopoeia*. Similarly, *portmanteau* mixes two words into one new one:

ONOMATOPOEIA & PORTMANTEAU - from *Jabberwocky* by Lewis Carroll [1872]

Twas brillig, and the slithy toves / did gyre and gimble in the wabe
All mimsy were the borogoves, / and the mome raths outgrabe.

Poets often extend comparisons via the human *personification* of animals, objects or ideas, e.g. 'the wind whispered'. Sometimes these personifications may even be addressed directly, as in *apostrophe* (e.g. 'O Moon!'):

APOSTROPHE - from *Holy Sonnet 10* by John Donne [1572–1631]

Death, be not proud, though some have called thee
Mighty and dreadful, for thou are not so;

Occasionally, the best way to draw a comparison is by *contrast*, which in its most binary form takes the form "not X". In *antithesis* (or juxtaposition) opposing situations are overlapped for effect, e.g.:

ANTITHESIS - *Eternity* by William Blake [1757–1827]

He who binds to himself a joy / Does the wingèd life destroy
He who kisses the joy as it flies / Lives in eternity's sun rise.

Poetic devices are the secret tools which poets use to enchant their audiences, but every poem still needs *atmosphere* (mood) and symbolic *narrative*, and at the core of every poem is the poet, with their unique creative and artistic *voice*. I hope these pages help you find yours!

BOOK IV

*Above: Logic, the truth-speaking huntress, with her questioning bow, syllogistic
sword, and arm of argument, crushing entire species of fallacies underfoot. From
the* Margarita Philosophica, *by Gregor Reisch, Freiburg, 1503. Opposite: Dialectic
catches a slippery fish and a forked-tongued dragon in her fine logical net. From*
Somma di Tutte le Scienze, *Aurelio Marinati, Rome, 1587*

LOGIC

THE ANCIENT ART OF REASON

Earl Fontainelle

Waterval by M.C. Escher [1961] is a beautiful visual representation of logical paradox (see p.218). All the individual elements of perspective make sense (the premises are true) and fit together on the page (the reasoning is valid), but the resulting image does not make sense (the conclusion is paradoxical).

INTRODUCTION

EVERYONE HAS HAD the experience of hearing a series of statements and thinking, 'That's logical'. Most of us seem innately to be able to reason from causes to effects. We exercise our rational faculty every time we cross the road and avoid an oncoming car. A small child, though, may be *unable* to make the connection between 'speeding car' and 'need-to-get-out-of-the-way'. So how do we get from the childhood state to one where we avoid the car as a matter of course? How do we create rules for *valid inference*?

While *reason* enables us to plan for the future, understand the past, and engage successfully with the present, *logic* is interested in the laws by which reason operates. Logicians want to know what makes one argument valid, and another plain wrong. This can be very useful, because people do not always think or speak the truth: they can be in error, they can lie, and they can 'rationalize' in crooked ways (*see page 384*).

It is for this reason that logic, rather than grammar, was considered by some to be the foundation of the trivium:

> Of all the arts the first and most general is logic, then grammar, and last of all rhetoric, since there can be much use of reason without speech, but no use of speech without reason. — John Milton, preface to The Art of Logic

This book explores the fundamental elements of practical logic and the process of reasoning in action. Along the way, the reader will be challenged to question everyday assumptions, to identify common logical fallacies, to wrestle with intractable paradoxes, and to take part in the ongoing search for truth.

DIALECTIC
and the Socratic method

We all have opinions. We all argue sometimes. In ancient Greece, when two or more philosophers used reasoned arguments to try to get to the truth of something over which they disagreed, they were said to be engaged in *dialectic* (from Gr. *dialegein*, to converse or dispute).

There are many ways to win an argument. The 5th-century BC Greek Sophists delighted in the arts of *oratory* (public speaking) and *debate* (oratorical competition), using *rhetoric* (clever linguistic devices) to persuade audiences and to demonstrate their own *arête* (excellence). However, Socrates [470-399 BC] argued that *truth* mattered the most, and that this could be best revealed through reason and logic in discussion.

To tease out the truth, Socrates employed a method which involved a number of steps:

> 1. Agatha asserts a THESIS: *"Justice should treat everyone equally".*
>
> 2. Socrates gets Agatha to agree to FURTHER PREMISES: *"Surely you would agree that someone who is mad is not responsible for their actions?"*
>
> 3. Socrates shows how these new premises imply the opposite of the original thesis: *"So Justice should not treat everyone equally."*
>
> 4. A NEW THESIS, more refined, is now advanced.

This technique was developed by Plato, Aristotle, and medieval and 19th century philosophers. Today it commonly takes the form:

> 1. THESIS: *I say! Don't you think ... Sheila is wonderful.*
>
> 2. ANTITHESIS: *On the contrary! I disagree ... She hurt Bill terribly.*
>
> 3. SYNTHESIS: *Let's try again! ... Yes, Sheila is complicated.*

While *dialectic* describes what people *do* every day as they dispute and reason back and forth, *logic* (from Gr. *logos*, 'reason' or 'speech') deals with the aspect of dialectic which is concerned with *validity*.

Over the centuries, the techniques by which the truth of statements and the validity of arguments have been determined and measured have changed immeasurably. Modern logical languages are so unforgiving that a single spelling mistake or wrong *Boolean operator* (*see page 224*) in a large computer program can bring a country to its knees.

These mathematical logical languages are not, however, the primary subject of this book. These pages instead mostly deal with the kind of logic we all use every day, the logic inherent in our spoken language, the logic that we use to convince children to brush their teeth, the logic we use to convince politicians to care for our future.

Some philosophers claim that true dialectic is a way of life resulting in a transcendent apprehension of truth. *The Seventh Platonic Epistle* sets the highest philosophic truth beyond the reach of words:

> *For it is not at all speakable like other subjects of study, but from much working together on the matter itself and living in company, suddenly a light, as it were leaping from fire, kindles in the soul, and (thenceforth) grows on its own.*

> Pl. Ep. VII (341c4-d1)

Left: Woodcut of teacher and student, Strassburg, 1499. The medieval tradition continued the Classical practice of philosophical dialectic, with teachers and students disputing together over logical problems. In modern times, mathematical logic has evolved into more of a solitary art, while conversational dialectic remains as alive as ever.

TRUTH AND FALLACY

two wrongs don't make a right

In logical reasoning the goal is less understanding *that* something is true and more understanding (or explaining) *why* something is true. For thousands of years, philosophers have held that in an *argument,*

TWO THINGS ARE NECESSARY FOR A SOUND CONCLUSION:

    A. *The premises must be true, and*

    B. *The reasoning must be valid.*

Validity depends on the types of inference made in the argument (the *form* of the argument), and has nothing to say about the truth of the premises or the conclusion. So, in fact,

AN ARGUMENT MAY BE VALID WITHOUT BEING SOUND:

    1. PREMISE: *If the grass is green, it's Monday.* ✗

    2. PREMISE: *The grass is green.* ✓

    ∴ THEREFORE: *It is Monday.* ✗ but valid

This unsound but valid *modus ponens* argument (*see p. 196*) is nonsensical because the initial premise is false. And similarly:

AN INVALID ARGUMENT CAN HAVE A TRUE CONCLUSION:

    1. *All flowers are plants.* ✓   2. *Roses are plants;* ✓

    ∴ *Roses are flowers.* ✓ but invalid

This argument is invalid because its middle term is undistributed (*see p. 191*).

Invalid reasoning causes flawed arguments, known as *fallacies*, and there are two main species of these sublogical creatures:

1. **FORMAL FALLACIES** are problems with the form of the argument. They involve invalid inferences, so are said to be formally invalid. One nasty formal fallacy is the CONCLUSION WHICH DENIES PREMISES.

   "No-one goes to that bar any more!" "Why?" "It's too crowded!" – Yogi Berra

2. **INFORMAL FALLACIES** arise from the matter rather than the form of the argument. Linguistic ambiguity, sneaky misdirection, and other problems can turn a validly formed argument into a fallacy. In the informal fallacy of CUM HOC ERGO PROPTER HOC ('With this, therefore because of this', *see too p. 209*) a false cause is imagined between events:

   "Every day I boil my kettle." "Hey! There are no elephants around here!"
   "How about that! Boiling my kettle keeps elephants away!"

The study of fallacies is important for the aspiring logician, and examples will appear throughout this book. Sometimes they are introduced into arguments by mistake; but they are also wielded by unscrupulous orators to win disputes by nefarious means.

Smart logicians can quickly identify the fallacies fed to them every day by parents, politicians, pundits, advertisers, and teenagers —all those who may have a vested interest in their deception.

REASONING

elementary, my dear

There are four main ways to form a logical conclusion:

1. **DEDUCTIVE REASONING** moves from the general to the particular, producing a necessary conclusion whose truth follows from that of the premises. It is the motor behind the *syllogism* (*see p. 190*), other instruments of traditional logic, and modern computers.

   1. *Mythical animals do not really exist.* ✓
   2. *Werewolves are mythical animals.* ✓
   ∴ *Werewolves do not really exist.* ✓

   Given the truth of the assumptions, a valid deduction will always lead to a true conclusion.

2. **INDUCTIVE REASONING** begins with the particular and proceeds to the general. Things are observed, then a rule or cause is proposed to account for them. This allows for innumerable general laws to be formulated which facilitate our daily lives, and permit science to advance by hypotheses, tests, and theories.

   1. *I see an apple falling from a tree.* ✓
   2. *I see it happen again and again.* ✓
   3. *I form a hypothesis to explain it.* ✓
   4. *Further experiments support my hypothesis and it is elevated to a theory, part of a law.* ✓

   The conclusion is probable, rather than certain, which is why, strictly speaking, no scientific theory is regarded as being true.

3. **ABDUCTIVE REASONING** infers the truth of the best explanation for a set of facts even if that explanation includes unobserved elements. It is the process of making educated guesses at why some given set or circumstances is the case. As such it benefits from the application of *Occam's Razor* (*see p. 215*). Diagnosticians and detectives commonly employ abductive reasoning.

> 1. *If it rains, the grass becomes wet.* ✓
> 2. *The grass is wet.* ✓
> ∴ *It is most likely that it rained.* ✓

The conclusion is probable but not exclusive; someone might have watered the lawn.

4. **ANALOGICAL REASONING** transfers information from a particular source to a particular target. It plays a central role in problem solving and cognitive perception by using comparison, similarities, and correspondences. It is always preceded by inductive reasoning:

> 1. *Many objects have been observed to share certain characteristics.* ✓
> 2. *We induce a class of these things by their common characteristics and name it 'apples'.* ✓
> 3. *We observe a target which shares characteristics we have found to be typical of apples.* ✓
> 4. *We reason analogically that this is also an apple!* ✓

The conclusion is only probable: it could be a plastic apple.

Analogical reasoning helps us observe patterns in the world and make on-the-spot decisions every day. However, if the wrong patterns are used, it falls into the **ANALOGICAL FALLACY** (*see p. 210*).

STATEMENTS AND ARGUMENTS
saying what's what

For the Greek philosopher Aristotle, the basic building blocks of argument were *statements*, made up of *subjects* and *predicates*, i.e. what we are talking about and what we are saying about it. Today, logicians recognize a number of basic types of statement:

1. **PREDICATIVE STATEMENT: S IS P.** *'Cats are mammals'.* The most simple statement, where S is the subject and P is the predicate.

2. **CONJUNCTIVE STATEMENT: P AND Q.** *'Animals and reptiles'*, as in **S IS P AND Q:** *'Crocodiles are animals and reptiles'.* Note that the predications can be separated out, e.g. *'S is P. S is (also) Q, etc'.*

3. **DISJUNCTIVE STATEMENT: P OR Q:** There are three kinds:
   i. **S OR Q (OR R OR …) IS P.** *'Either you or I (or Balthezar, or Mavis, or Myrtle, or …) will win'.* Can extend to cover all options.
   ii. **S IS P OR Q.** *'A person is dead or alive.'*
   iii. **S IS P, OR T IS Q.** *'Either I'll win or you'll do a headstand.'*

4. **CONDITIONAL/HYPOTHETICAL STATEMENT: IF S, THEN P.**

   'If the sun shines, the beach will be busy'. The first part is called the *antecedent*, the second the *consequent*. The logical/material link between them is called the *nexus*.

   THE NEXUS: The truth or falsity of *'If Robert has a vision all will be well'* depends on how we define the connection between Robert's visions and subsequent events. If this nexus does not hold, then the statement will be unsound and produce the informal fallacy of the **FLAWED NEXUS**. E.g. *'If music is playing, it is snowing'* is fallacious since, even if it happens to be true, there is no logical or substantive connection (nexus) between music and snow. (*Conditionals behave differently in formal logic, see p. 226.*)

5. COMPARATIVE STATEMENT: A IS LIKE B IN THIS RESPECT. '*Tangerines are like small oranges*'. This is *analogical reasoning* (*see p. 183*).

When making a comparative statement, beware the ANALOGICAL FALLACY, where someone mistakenly assumes that, because two or more things are similar in one way, they must be similar in others (*see p. 210*).

Once you have two or more statements, they can be combined to form *arguments*, which proceed from the known (the premises) to the previously-unknown (the conclusion). A common example is:

THE ARGUMENT FROM UNIVERSAL TO PARTICULAR.
ALL ⇒ SOME / ONE. '*All meerkats are cool, therefore this meerkat is cool*'.
If a universal statement is true, a particular version with the same subject and predicate is also true.

While it is valid to move from universal to particular, the reverse,
THE MOVE FROM PARTICULAR TO UNIVERSAL,
where a case or group of cases infer a more general rule, is an informal fallacy of
UNJUSTIFIED INDUCTION:

> *Many politicians break their campaign promises*
> ∴ *All politicians are liars.*

All politicians may indeed be liars; but we can't prove it like this.

"... and on that you have my word."

Propositions
value, quality, modality, quantity

In his logical writings—called collectively the *Organon* (lit., the 'instrument' or 'tool')—Aristotle set out the basic theory and practice of a far-reaching analysis of statements, their valid interactions, and their relationship to the realities they signify. Every classical Aristotelian proposition has four technical *characteristics*:

1. **VALUE**: *true* or *false*.

2. **QUALITY**: *affirmative* or *negative*. 'All stoats are mammals' is an affirmative proposition, while 'No stoats are reptiles' is a negative one.

3. **MODALITY**: *categorical* or *modal*. A statement of absolute fact, such as 'Ants are insects', is a categorical proposition, while an *obligation*, such as 'Politicians should serve the public good', or a *contingency*, such as 'Politicians may be corrupt', are modal propositions.

4. **QUANTITY**: *universal* or *particular*. A proposition such as 'All mammals are red' or 'No mammal is blue' is said to be 'universal', whereas a partial proposition such as 'Some skunks smell nice', or a particular proposition such as 'René is a skunk' is 'particular'.

So, for example, 'Every statement is either true or false' is true, affirmative, categorical, and universal; while '... except some paradoxes, which may be neither!' is true, negative, modal, and particular.

Intention and Imposition
sense and sensibility

Propositions in traditional logic are made up of *terms*, each of which has two possible *intentions* and three possible *impositions*:

INTENTION refers to the use of a term with regard to logical function:

> 1. FIRST INTENTION *refers to the real world (Slugs are slimy)*.
> 2. SECOND INTENTION *refers to the reflexive use of terms as regards their logical status or function ('Slugs' is a term referring to a class of beings)*.
>
> A lion is a feline. Feline is a genus. ∴ A lion is a genus.

Er, no! This is the fallacy of SHIFT OF INTENTION; a lion is a *member* of a genus.

IMPOSITION refers to the use of a term with regard to language itself.

> 0. NO IMPOSITION *refers to phonetics or spelling, ignoring the meaning of the term ('Slugs' has five letters)*.
> 1. FIRST IMPOSITION *refers to the real world (Slugs are slimy)*.
> 2. SECOND IMPOSITION *refers reflexively to the word as a word ('Slugs' is the subject of the statement 'Slugs are slimy')*.

The fallacy of SHIFT OF IMPOSITION occurs when we wrongly use the same term in two or more impositions:

> *Jupiter is a planet (first imposition). Planet is a word of two syllables (no imposition).*
> *∴ Jupiter is a word of two syllables (false, whichever imposition is understood).*

First intention and first imposition are the province of the everyday use of language. Logic is the art of analysing second intentions; grammar is the art of analysing second impositions.

Defining Terms
distribution, substance, and accident

Clearly defined terms are an essential part of the art of reasoning, while unclear or undefined terms are fatal to clear argumentation. Traditional logic crucially distinguishes between two types of term:

1. **Distributed** terms cover their entire class ('all hens', 'humankind').

2. **Undistributed** terms cover part of a class ('some ducks', 'a fox').

Pay close attention to the distribution of terms, as sneaky changes in distribution can invalidate an argument (*see p. 199*).

A second crucial distinction is between **Substance** and **Accident**.

1. **Substance** is that which exists in itself ('frog', 'mountain'). If any aspect of a substance is taken away, it ceases to be what it is.

2. **Accident** is that which exists in something other than itself ('sat', 'red'). Accidents are qualities or states of being in a particular way.

So, in defining a 'bird', we may mention wings and feathers as defining characteristics, 'substances', but must omit 'green and blue', as an 'accident' which only some birds have. Take another example:

> The tall Greek woman stood poised on the balcony in a long black ballgown.

Here the substance is 'woman', and remains so regardless of what accidents are predicated of it and however much the sentence is rephrased or simplified.

Confusing substance and accident can lead to absurdities, as Lewis Carroll [1832–1898] demonstrates in *Alice's Adventures in Wonderland*:

"Well! I've often seen a cat without a grin," thought Alice, "but a grin without a cat! It's the most curious thing I ever saw in my life!"

Here, the term '*grin*' is actually an accident disguised as a substance. An accident cannot remain when the substance has vanished.

Importantly, when we assert that it does, we commit the formal fallacy of CONFUSING SUBSTANCE AND ACCIDENT. Note that this is not be confused with the FALLACY OF ACCIDENT (*a sub-category—see p. 208*).

Above: In Alice's Adventure's in Wonderland *the Cheshire Cat can appear and disappear at will, sometimes leaving its grin behind.*

Substance, plus the nine different types of accident, make up Aristotle's *Ten Categories of Being*:

1. SUBSTANCE ('horse', 'tree')
2. QUANTITY ('fast', 'tall');
3. QUALITY ('white', 'lovely');
4. RELATION ('cousin', 'greater');
5. ACTION ('cuts', 'runs');
6. PASSION ('is cut', 'is run');
7. TIME ('yesterday', 'soon');
8. LOCATION ('in the car', 'here');
9. POSTURE ('lies', 'sits');
10. HABIT ('shod', 'armed').

These work as questions: *What is it? How much? What sort? Related to what? Doing what? Undergoing what? When? Where?* Some of the categories may seem dated today, but they still demonstrate an important principle: You can have a cat without a grin, but you can't have a grin without a cat!

Syllogisms

in or out

Aristotle believed that all categorical logical deductions (i.e. those dealing with general or universal terms like 'women', 'fishing', or 'freedom') were reducible to three-sentence structures called *syllogisms* (from Gr. *syllogismos*, deduction or reasoning about multiple terms). These consist of a major premise, a minor premise, and a conclusion:

EXAMPLE OF A SYLLOGISM

1. *All men are mortal*   *Major Premise*
2. *Socrates is a man*   *Minor Premise*
∴ *Socrates is mortal*   *Conclusion*

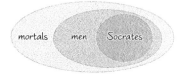

Where '∴' stands for 'therefore' and 'Socrates' stands for 'the class of all things that are Socrates'. The syllogism can produce necessary truths:

A. *If the premises are true,*   and B. *The form of syllogism is valid, then*
C. *The conclusion will be true.*

The three propositions of the syllogism have three *terms*: *major*, *minor*, and *middle*:

The **MAJOR TERM** is the predicate of the conclusion: 'mortal'
The **MINOR TERM** is the subject of the conclusion: 'Socrates'
The **MIDDLE TERM** is held in common by both premises: 'men'.

Each term appears twice in the whole syllogism, with the middle term linking the two premises but disappearing in the conclusion. The middle term *must* be distributed ('all men') in one or both of the premises, rather than being specific ('a man') or limited ('some men'), otherwise we fall into the formal fallacy of **THE UNDISTRIBUTED MIDDLE TERM**. So, in the example:

1. *All rich people are taxable.* ✓
2. *Some taxable people are poor;* ✓
∴. *All rich people are poor.* ✗

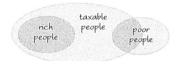

the middle term 'taxable' is undistributed since it does not in either instance encompass the total field of all taxable entities. Syllogisms with undistributed middles do not prove anything:

1. *Some violent anarchists are animal lovers.* ✓
2. *All cat lovers are animal lovers.* ✓
∴. *All cat lovers are violent anarchists* ✗

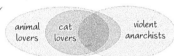

A good way to differentiate between syllogisms is to draw a logical diagram. In many cases a simple glance can quickly expose a fallacy.

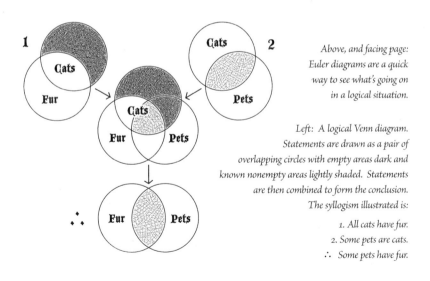

Above, and facing page: Euler diagrams are a quick way to see what's going on in a logical situation.

Left: A logical Venn diagram. Statements are drawn as a pair of overlapping circles with empty areas dark and known nonempty areas lightly shaded. Statements are then combined to form the conclusion. The syllogism illustrated is:

1. All cats have fur.
2. Some pets are cats.
∴ Some pets have fur.

A Square of Oppositions

all, some, or none

In his work *On Interpretation*, Aristotle describes a symmetry between statements of differing quality and quantity. Known as the *Table of Oppositions*, it has been shown as a fourfold diagram (*opposite*) since the work of Boethius. The two possible qualities (affirmative and negative) are multiplied with the two possible quantities (universal and particular) to get four simple types of categorical proposition.

In medieval times, mnemonic vowels were assigned to the four kinds of statements, derived from the Latin. Thus A and I are the first two vowels in *affirmo*, 'I affirm', while E and O come from *nego*, 'I deny'.

The Table shows the hidden relationships between various types of proposition. In summary, these relationships are:

CONTRARIES: *The upper statements are contrary; both cannot be true.*

CONTRADICTORIES: *The diagonal lines show statements which cannot both be true and cannot both be false.*

SUBCONTRARIES: *The lower two propositions do not necessarily contradict each other, but cannot both be false.*

SUBALTERNS and SUPERALTERNS: *The two universals at the top of the square automatically entail their lower counterparts.*

For Aristotle, and in traditional logic, all statements, universal (A and E) and particular (I and O), imply the existence of their subjects. So in the example on the opposite page the statement 'All *words are wise*' implies that words exist (*this is not the case in modern logic, see p. 195*).

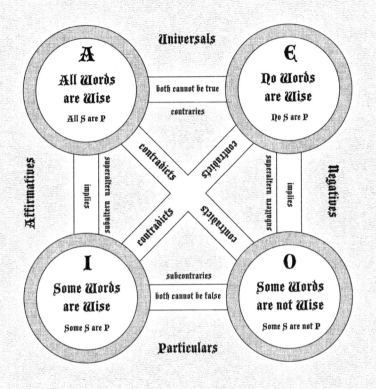

The Medieval Square of Oppositions

Two-way diagonals connect contradictories: so if A is true, O is false, and vice versa (same for E and I). One-way horizontals connect contraries: so if A or I is true, E or O is false, respectively. However, if E or O is false, we don't know the value of A or I, respectively. One-way verticals connect superalterns with subalterns, so A and E imply I and O, but not vice-versa (medieval logicians called this rule Dictum de Omni et Nullo—whatever is affirmed or denied of a logical whole must also be affirmed or denied of its parts).

Syllogistic Fallacies
misdeductions

A syllogism can go wrong in many ways. It may have four terms (Quaternio Terminorum), but even with three, out of 256 possible types, only 24 are valid in classical logic, and just 15 in modern logic. Using the vowels for the four types of proposition in the *Table of Opposites* (*see previous page*), medieval logicians devised mnemonics to learn these by heart:

Barbara AAA1	Cesare EAE2	Datisi AII3	Calemes AEE4
Celarent EAE1	Camestres AEE2	Disamis IAI3	Dimatis IAI4
Darii AII1	Festino WIO2	Ferison EIO3	Fresison EIO4
Ferio EIO1	Baroco AOO2	Bocardo OAO3	Calemos AEO4
Barbari AAI1	Cesaro EAO2	Felapton EAO3	Fesapo EAO4
Celaront EAO1	Camestros AEO2	Darapti AAI3	Bamalip AAI4

Syllogistic formal fallacies can be hard to spot. Here are three *Invalid Combinations of Positive and Negative Statements*:

Exclusive Premises: If both premises are negative, no connection is established between the major and minor terms.

> 1. No *aliens are human.* [E] ✓
> 2. No *humans have three eyes.* [E] ✓
> ∴ *All aliens have three eyes.* [A] ✗

Affirmative Conclusion from a Negative Premise: If either premise is negative, the conclusion must also be negative.

> 1. *All fights are trouble.* [A] ✓
> 2. No *trouble is worth dying for.* [E] ✓
> ∴ *All fights are worth dying for.* [A] ✗

The correct conclusion should be: No *fight is worth dying for.*

Negative Conclusion from Affirmative Premises: If both premises are affirmative, the conclusion must also be affirmative.

1. *All cows need grass.* [A] ✓
2. *All grass needs rain.* [A] ✓
∴ *No cow needs rain.* [E] ✗

Which is untrue; the conclusion is: *Therefore, All cows need rain.*

There are also three *Fallacies of Distribution*: We've already seen the fallacy of the **Undistributed Middle Term** (*see p. 181*). A second rule is that no term may be distributed in the conclusion if it is undistributed in its premise (although it can move from distributed to undistributed). Breaking this gives us the **Illicit Treatment of the Major Term**:

1. *All evil things are bad for you.* [A] ✓
2. *No chemicals are evil things.* [E] ✓
∴ *No chemicals are bad for you.* [E] ✗

Er, no! Some chemicals could still be bad for you, despite not being evil.

The third fallacy is the **Illicit Treatment of the Minor Term**:

1. *All cannibals are meat-eaters.* [A] ✓
2. *All cannibals are murderers.* [A] ✓
∴ *All meat-eaters are murderers.* [A] ✗

Neither premise has '*all meat-eaters*', so it can't be in the conclusion.

In modern Boolean logic, universal statements (*All fairies have wings*) do *not* imply the existence of their subjects, while particular statements (*some fairies have wings*) do. To assume the existence of the subjects of universal statements is to commit the **Existential Fallacy**. Disallowing it shaves the nine greyed syllogisms from the 24 opposite.

MODUS PONENS
everyday and direct

A simple and powerful form of deductive argument was identified by the Stoic logician Chrysippus of Soli [c.280–c.205 BC]. It is known as *modus ponens* ('the way of adding on'), and we use it every day:

> *If P, then Q; P; therefore Q.*

Here it is again, in a slightly expanded form:

> 1. *If P is true, then Q is also true.* 2. *P is true.* ∴ *Q is true.*

> 1. *If I touch the bubble, it will burst.* ✓ 2. *I touched the bubble.* ✓ ∴ *It burst.* ✓

Modus ponens is a powerful logical tool. Many examples of *modus ponens* don't immediately resemble the template above, but by using *expansion* (*see p. 200*) and examining the *nexus* (*see p.184*) we can quickly detect the validity-preserving *modus* hiding in everyday logic:

> *All fish can swim, so this fish can swim.*

can be rephrased as a classic modus ponens:

> 1. *If it is true that this is a fish (If P), then it is true that it can swim (then Q).* ✓
> 2. *This is a fish (P is true).* ✓
> ∴ *This fish can swim (Therefore Q is true).* ✓

Modus ponens is also iterative; arguments can be built on top of one another *ad infinitum*. The following argument, for example, is valid:

> *All logicians are clever. All clever people need pencils.*
> *Therefore, all logicians need pencils.*

We can use expansion (*see p. 200*) to show that this syllogism in BARBARA consists of two *modus ponens* arguments. Firstly:

> 1. If it is true that there are logicians (If P), then they are clever (then Q). ✓
> 2. Logicians exist (P). ✓ ∴ They are clever (Therefore, Q). ✓

(where the last two parts of the argument are implied rather than stated, as statements of mere existence often are); and secondly:

> 1. If clever people exist (If Q), then they need pencils (then R). ✓
> 2. Clever people exist (Q). ✓ ∴ They need pencils (∴ R). ✓

Iteration gives rise to *sorites*, a long chain of arguments attached one to another. It also gives rise to *sorites* paradoxes (*see p. 220*), one of the most intractable types of logical problem.

The *modus ponens* has an important formal fallacy of its own:

AFFIRMING THE CONSEQUENT (the 'then' part of the first line of an argument). Here, instead of arguing (validly):

> 1. If P, then Q. 2. P. ∴ Therefore Q,

it is argued (invalidly) that:

> 1. If P, then Q. 2. Q ∴ Therefore P.

> 1. If I touch the bubble, it will burst. ✓
> 2. The bubble burst. ✓ ∴ I touched it. ✗

This is incorrect; the bubble may have burst for any number of other reasons. This fallacy often shows up in political discourse:

> 1. If someone is a terrorist, they will be critical of our government. ✓
> 2. This man is critical of our government; ✓ ∴ This man is a terrorist. ✗

Modus Tollens
everyday and indirect

Modus tollens signifies 'the way of taking away'; it is the negative cousin of *modus ponens*, and takes the form:

    1. *If P then Q.* 2. *Not Q.* *Therefore, not P.*

    1. *If I touch the bubble, it will burst.* ✓
    2. *The bubble didn't burst.* ✓ ∴. *I didn't touch it.* ✓

The validity of *modus tollens* relies on the fact that, if a cause always leads to an effect, then if you don't have the effect then you don't have the cause either. (As with all conditionals, always check the *nexus, p. 184.*)

The *modus tollens* also has a nasty formal fallacy of its own:

DENYING THE ANTECEDENT (the antecedent is the 'If P' part). Here, instead of the valid version above, we get the sneaky:

    1. *If P, then Q.* 2. *Not P,* ∴. *Not Q,*

    1. *If I touch the bubble, it will burst.* ✓
    2. *I didn't touch it.* ✓ ∴. *It didn't burst.* ✗

which is again very useful
for political purposes:

    1. *If a man is a terrorist, he will*
    be critical of our government. ✓
    2. *This man is not a terrorist;* ✓
    ∴. *He won't be critical of*
    our government. ✗

"NOT SO FAST! HOW DO WE KNOW YOU'RE NOT TERRORISTS WITH WEAPONS OF MASS DESTRUCTION?!!"

EDUCTION
rearranging propositions

Sometimes things need rephrasing. In *Alice's Adventures in Wonderland*, the March Hare tells Alice that she should say what she means:

"I do", Alice hastily replied; "at least — at least I mean what I say — that's the same thing, you know." "Not the same thing a bit!" said the Hatter. "Why, you might just as well say that 'I see what I eat' is the same thing as 'I eat what I see'!"

CONVERSION reverses a proposition, turning the subject into the predicate and vice versa, e.g. "*I am Sam* = *Sam I am*". But watch out:

All men are monkeys = *All monkeys are men*

demonstrates the FALLACY OF FALSE CONVERSION, as the term '*monkeys*' has become illegally distributed. It has gone from a 'some' to an 'all'.

OBVERSION changes the quality of a statement from affirmative to negative (or vice-versa), and the predicate to its complement (non-):

Bucephalus is a horse = *Bucephalus is not a non-horse,*

taking care not to confuse "*a non-horse*" with "*not a horse*", or we will be committing the FALLACY OF ILLICIT OBVERSION (*see too litotes, page 260*).

CONTRAPOSITION reverses and negates: *All sharks are killers* = *All non-killers are non-sharks*". It is valid for A ('all') and O ('some ... not'), and invalid for E ('no') and I ('some') propositions (*see p. 192*).

LOGICAL EXPANSION
drawing out hidden logic

Annoyingly (for logicians at least), many premises vital to arguments are completely omitted in everyday speech, both on the assumption that they are already understood, and to keep sentences short. As a result, most arguments bear little resemblance to the traditional forms of deduction.

Logical expansion, however, restates an argument to reveal its hidden assumptions and make explicit its logical content. It is an essential tool for the aspiring logician to help discover and clarify the errors often lurking in an argument. Consider this one:

> *Flipper is a mammal because he is a dolphin.*

In traditional logic an abridged argument like this is known as an *enthymeme*. It is seen as valid if it can be expanded into a valid syllogism (*see p. 190*) even if it leaves out a large number of the elements of the syllogism itself. Of all the possible syllogisms which may be created from an enthymeme, only *one* need be valid for the enthymeme to be valid (*see too p. 240*). In this case, the enthymeme may clearly be expanded to a syllogism through the addition of the minor premise:

> *All dolphins are mammals.*

Expansions often reveal logical errors which can be developed into useful lines of attack.

Consider the latent assumptions here:

> MR. RABBIT: *Fellow council members, are you blind? Of course Mr. Fox's conservation policies will favour carnivores, since he himself is a carnivore.*

This may be expanded thus:

1. Mr. Fox *is a carnivore.*
2. *All carnivores support policies which favour carnivores.*
∴ *Mr. Fox's conservation policies will favour carnivores.*

The argument may now be attacked based on the latent premise (2); if it is false, then the argument is unsound:

MR. FOX: *This is illogical nonsense! Most carnivores are decent, fair, hardworking folk who support balanced policies that favour the entire forest, carnivores and non-carnivores alike. Your latent premise is false. Your argument does not hold.*

It can be helpful to remember that words like 'since' and 'because' often indicate the presence of a hidden premise. However, when digging them out, remember that premises may only be added if they really are implicit in the original argument; you cannot add extraneous material. Spotting latent premises is not always easy, but there are two conservation rules for logical expansion which can be very helpful:

TRUTH-VALUES MUST BE CONSERVED. *However we rearrange the statement* 'Flipper is a mammal because he is a dolphin', *we can never state that* 'Flipper is not a dolphin' *(changed truth value).*

DISTRIBUTION MUST BE CONSERVED. *We cannot go from a distributed to an undistributed term—from* 'All dolphins are mammals' *to* 'Some dolphins are mammals'—*or vice versa (changed distribution).*

Dilemmas
caught between two horns

Have you ever been impaled on the 'horns' of a *dilemma*, forced to choose between two or more mutually exclusive and undesirable options? A *logical dilemma* is a complex syllogism in three parts:

1. A Disjunctive minor premise, (either ... or); the 'horns'
2. A Compound hypothetical major premise, (if ... then; if ... then); the 'conjuncts'
∴ A Simple or disjunctive conclusion, (either 'therefore, P' or 'therefore, either P or Q')

For example, take this famous dilemma adapted from Aristotle:

1. Either we ought to practice logic, or we ought not.
2. If we ought, then we ought; if we ought not, then we still ought (because we need logic to justify why we ought not). ∴ We ought to practice logic.

The 'then' consequences in the second line are the 'conjuncts'—if any are false, the whole dilemma is false. The final choice between the conjuncts can be *simple*, as above, or *disjunctive/complex*. The Christian father Tertullian used the following complex dilemma to try to persuade the Stoic emperor Marcus Aurelius to stop persecuting Christians:

1. Either the Christians have committed crimes or they have not.
2. If they have, your refusal to permit a public enquiry is irrational; if they have not, your punishing them is unjust.
∴ You are either irrational or unjust.

The initial *disjunct* may present more than two options. If there are three, then we are dealing with a *trilemma*; if four or more, a *polylemma*. In all cases, however, the 'horns' must represent exclusive options: if there are any other possibilities, then the whole formulation is false and falls into the fallacy of IMPERFECT DISJUNCTION OF THE MINOR PREMISE, more commonly known as a FALSE DILEMMA or FALSE CHOICE.

For example, Archbishop John Morton was put in charge of levying taxes on the nobility for Henry VII. When reminded that some of the nobility might not be able to afford to pay, he replied that

> Either the nobles live lavishly, in which case they can be taxed; or they appear poor, in which case they are living frugally and must have savings which can be taxed.

Expanded to a full dilemma, the conclusion would be 'all may be taxed'. 'Morton's Fork' ignores the very real possibility that those who appear poor might actually be poor, and so offers a false choice.

Dilemmas can counter other dilemmas. The sophist Protagoras taught his student Euathlus rhetoric on condition that Euathlus would pay him upon winning his first court-case, but eventually Protagoras tired of waiting for his fee and decided to sue him for the money, reasoning:

1. Either Euathlus will win the case or lose.
2. If he wins, he will have to pay me because he owed me my fee subject to winning his first case; if he loses, he will have to pay me because I will have successfully sued him for the pay he owes me.
∴ Euathlus will have to pay me.

Euathlus, however, reasoned to opposite conclusions as follows:

1. Either I will win the case or lose.
2. If I win, I will not have to pay, because the court will have found in favour of me; if I lose, I will not have to pay because I will have lost my first court case.
∴ Either way I will not have to pay Protagoras.

Dealing with Dilemmas
go between, grasp, or counter

Politicians and parents regularly use abbreviated dilemmas to present complex circumstances as clean-cut either/or situations involving only two choices (especially when selling the lesser of two evils):

> *Either we record everyone's phone calls, or the terrorists grow stronger.*

There are various ways of dealing with such insidious devices:

ESCAPING BETWEEN THE HORNS. Are the two either-or options really exclusive? If you can find a third option then you can 'go between the horns of the dilemma'. In Plato's *Meno* (80e), Meno proposes that it is impossible to learn anything new. Socrates paraphrases the dilemma:

> *A man cannot search for what he knows (since he knows it, there is no need to search);*
> *nor for what he doesn't know (for he doesn't know what to look for).*

He then posits a third option: new knowledge is actually *recollection*, and escapes the dilemma by denying that the original options are exclusive.

GRASPING THE HORNS OF THE DILEMMA. If you can show that one or both of the major premises is false, i.e. the nexus of the hypothetical statement (the 'if ... then' part) is not valid (*see p. 184*), then there is no necessary connection between antecedent and consequent:

1. *People are either good, or they're bad.*
2. *If they're good, then we don't need laws to deter crime.*
   If they're bad, then laws to deter crime won't work.
∴ *Either way, laws to deter crime are useless.*

In this classic dilemma, a favourite of anarchists, some may agree with the first premise, but the second is flimsy. By grasping this horn firmly and showing its shortcomings we may counter it thus:

Laws do not deter crime, but fear of punishment does—in bad people, average people, and even in quite good people. So the second premise is wrong. Laws to deter crime are useful, as they threaten punishment to those who might otherwise commit crimes.

COUNTERDILEMMA. The most stylish and rhetorically-effective method of dealing with a dilemma is to counter, or rebut, it. Ideally, this should be done with a new dilemma constructed from the same premises as the old one, but with a new and opposite conclusion (*as shown on page 203*). A good example is the ancient Greek story of the mother who begs her son not to enter politics:

1. *If you enter politics, you will either act justly or unjustly.*
2. *If you act unjustly, the gods will hate you; but if you act justly, men will hate you.*
∴ *Entering politics guarantees that you will be hated.*

Her son counters her, effortlessly finding a valid reversed conclusion without changing the value of the premises:

1. *If I enter politics, I will either act justly or unjustly.*
2. *If I act unjustly, men will love me; but if justly, the gods will love me.*
∴ *Entering politics guarantees that I will be loved!*

LINGUISTIC FALLACIES
spoken with a forked tongue

Aristotle and his followers codified a group of informal fallacies known as fallacies *in dictione* (Lat. 'in language'), resulting from sloppy language:

AMPHIBOLY (Gr. 'thrown both ways'): Sometimes a proposition can be read in two or more ways, and it is impossible to tell which is meant:

> One morning I shot an elephant in my pyjamas.
> How he got into my pyjamas, I don't know. - Groucho Marx

This fallacy is rarely wielded deliberately; mostly it arises inadvertently.

COMPOSITION: This fallacy occurs when properties of constituent elements of a whole are illicitly attributed to the whole itself:

> 1. Hydrogen and oxygen are both gases at room temperature; ✓
> 2. Water is made up of hydrogen and oxygen; ✓
> ∴ Water is a gas at room temperature. ✗

DIVISION: In contrast to composition, this fallacy occurs when the properties of a whole are illicitly attributed to its parts:

> Nine plus nine is eighteen, which is an even number. ✓
> Since eighteen is even, nine must be even as well. ✗

The fallacy often occurs in statistical interpretation, where it can seem that a sample which stands out from a group is responsible for what is in fact due to the entire group. It's not the last roll of the dice which loses a gambler their money, but all the rolls weighed up cumulatively.

Ambiguity sometimes arises from distributive and collective predication to groups, so 'People drink more water than elephants' is true collectively but false distributively. A composition fallacy arises in going from the distributive to the collective sense; division goes the other way.

EQUIVOCATION: A favourite tool of comedians, this fallacy occurs when multiple meanings of a single word crop up in a single argument:

1. Fluff is light. ✓
2. Light travels faster than anything else in the universe. ✓
∴ Fluff travels faster than anything else in the universe. ✗

VERBAL FORM: Sometimes the form of words can suggest equivalence where there is none. Take the words 'inaudible', 'inadmissible', and 'inflammable': the prefix 'in' in the first two cases signifies 'not', but in the third case means 'extremely'. This fallacy often takes subtle forms arising from similarities in phrasing (especially sloppy use of verbal tenses) that hide different meanings:

1. Those who eat the least are the most hungry. ✓
2. Hungry people eat the most. ✓
∴ Those who eat the least eat the most. ✗

The problem here is the English tendency to use the present tense to signify both the future and habitual past action. Instead:

1. Those who HAVE EATEN the least are the most hungry. ✓
2. Hungry people WILL eat the most. ✓
∴ Those who have eaten the least will eat the most. ✓

Non-Linguistic Fallacies
built on false assumptions

The informal Aristotelian *extra dictionem* ('non-linguistic') fallacies all contain some false assumption. They tend to be trickier to spot than the fallacies *in dictione*, where the problems are purely linguistic.

ACCIDENT FALLACY: Much everyday human thinking relies on general statements (commonplaces or 'rules-of-thumb'). But these always have exceptions. This fallacy occurs when the exceptions are used to attack the validity of the rule (i.e. accident is confused with substance, hence the name, *see p. 189*). For example:

1. Humans are rational animals (*generally a useful rule of thumb*). ✓
2. Some humans are dead (*also true, but…*). ✓
∴ Dead people are rational. ×

This is a perverse reading of the first premise as a categorical statement rather than a rule of thumb; put another way, it confuses substance (human being) with accident (the state of being dead).

SECUNDUM QUID (literally, 'in this respect'): This fallacy occurs when it is assumed that a statement which is true in certain respects is true in all respects, or in other irrelevant respects. It is also known as 'converse accident' (as it reverses the accident fallacy) or 'hasty generalisation':

1. I have been to Paris three times, and ✓
2. Each time I was there someone was rude to me. ✓
∴ Parisians are rude. ×

Parisians may be rude, or maybe only three of them are.

FALSE CAUSE: This fallacy imputes causation to a relationship which may not involve any. It is especially popular with amateur moralists:

Firearms are EVIL; they KILL people!

This argument confuses an accident attendant on firearms (that they are used to kill) with their essential nature. A false cause is thus created for asserting that they are evil, rather than the correct conclusion, which is that some people do evil things with firearms.

Other forms of false cause are **CUM HOC ERGO PROPTER HOC** (*see p. 181*) and its sibling, **POST HOC ERGO PROPTER HOC** (Lat. 'after this, therefore because of this'), which assume that, because two events occur simultaneously (cum hoc) or sequentially (post hoc) they must be causally linked:

Last year, poverty rose in the same regions where welfare spending rose. Amazingly, it seems that welfare spending increases poverty! (CUM HOC)

We did the rain-dance and OMG it rained! This stuff WORKS! (POST HOC)

He was elected President, and car companies went bust. His fault! (POST HOC)

COMPLEX QUESTION: This fallacy occurs when one or more assumptions are smuggled into a question, before demanding a single answer. Often used in courtroom entrapment:

PROSECUTOR: *When did you meet the woman you would later murder?*

A plaintiff would be extremely foolish to answer this. The appropriate response is to demand a proper question.

More Informal Fallacies
devious devices

Some logical fallacies are really rhetorical tricks. Studying these fiendish figures can prepare and protect you against the slippery sleight-of-tongue served up by rhetoricians of all stamps every day.

THE ANALOGICAL FALLACY assumes that because two or more things are similar in one way, they must be similar in other ways:

> 1. *The universe is like a watch.* ✓ 2. *A watch is made by a watchmaker.* ✓
> ∴ *Therefore the universe was made by a universe-maker.* ✗

An analogical argument is only valid if there is an explicit premise stating that the things being compared are similar in the relevant respects. If that is true then it is also sound; if not it is valid but unsound. False analogies can be exposed by showing absurd differences between the analogous terms, using *reductio ad absurdum (p. 214)*.

> 1. *The universe is like a watch.* ✓ 2. *A watch can give you an itchy wrist.* ✓
> ∴ *Therefore the universe can give you an itchy wrist.* ✗

BEGGING THE QUESTION (*circular reasoning*) is a sneaky fallacy that occurs whenever the argument uses the conclusion as a premise. It assumes what it is trying to prove before it has proven it!

> AMY: *God exists because the Bible says so.*
> BILL: *But how do you know the Bible is true?*
> AMY: *The Bible IS the word of God; it's obvious.*

Such reasoning is not actually invalid but it begs the listener to ask the appropriate question concerning circularity:

BILL: *You can't use the Bible as a proof of God's existence when the only proof of its truth is that it comes from God, whose existence you have yet to prove.*

SHIFTING THE BURDEN OF PROOF is a favourite of every lawyer who can get away with it, as the burden of proof is an important component of courtroom logic:

PROSECUTOR: *Did you not visit the store beforehand to plan your robbery?*
DEFENDANT: *I visited the store, but only to do some shopping.*
PROSECUTOR: *But can you prove that you were not planning a robbery?*
DEFENDANT: *No, but ... um ....*

This fallacy demands that someone prove that they were *not* doing something, which is often impossible. This is why medieval logicians formulated the rule: *onus probandi incumbit ei qui dicit, non ei qui negat* ('the burden of proof is on the one who makes the accusation, not on the one who denies it'). Our defendant should have responded:

DEFENDANT: *You have no proof that I was planning a robbery. There is no need for me to prove my innocence, which is assumed.*

FALSE CHOICE is a pernicious fallacy where limited options are given as the sole possibilities (where in fact more exist):

Every nation in every region now has a decision to make: either you are with us, or you are with the terrorists. – George W. Bush, Sept. 20, 2001

Deal with this type of false dichotomy in the same way that you might a dilemma (*see p. 204*), either by going between its horns and demonstrating a valid third position (e.g. that it's possible not to be a supporter of either Bush or the terrorists), or by grasping the horns (e.g. showing that both sides are actually 'terrorists').

Fallacies of Misdirection
now watch closely

Some fallacies ignore the argument rather than refuting it honestly. These are forms of IGNORATIO ELENCHI ('ignorance of the argument').

THE IRRELEVANT THESIS is a tricky fallacy. It makes a valid point, but fails to address the issue in question.

> INTERVIEWER: *'Mr President, is it not true that under your term of office poverty has risen by 20%?'*
>
> PRESIDENT: *'In my term of office, we have in fact seen record corporate profits.'*

This fallacy is popular with politicians who wish to avoid answering a question; instead they deliberately miss the point.

THE RED HERRING fallacy tries to divert the course of argument by introducing irrelevant material. For maximum effect, the red herring should be something which is likely to get a strong emotional response.

> PROSECUTOR: *'Is it not true, Senator, that you expropriated enormous amounts of money from military contracts over the course of decades for your personal use?'*
>
> SENATOR: *'I served in the military, I love the military, and as far as I am concerned anyone who attacks the integrity of our military is a traitor.'*

Hearing this indignant speech, the audience may become roused by patriotic feelings, while the senator has ignored the question, and done so in a way which may cause the audience to forget it was asked at all.

THE STRAW MAN ARGUMENT is a common trick for dealing with an opponent who has strong support for their position. It takes the form of a deliberate misrepresentation of their position, which is then easily knocked down.

At the great 1860 Oxford evolution debate, Bishop Wilberforce is said to have asked his evolutionist opponent, Thomas Huxley,

WILBERFORCE: *You claim descent from a monkey; was this on your grandfather's or your grandmother's side?*

One response to a straw man is a concise statement of the real position:

HUXLEY (*poss.*): *Evolutionists do not claim that we are 'descended from monkeys'. We claim that apes, monkeys, and humans have common ancestors.*

A PERSONAL ATTACK (*argumentum ad hominem*) is also present, thinly veiled, in Wilberforce's statement. This nasty fallacy deliberately confuses someone's appearance, history, or character with their argument, whereas it is illogical to disagree with a person just because you don't like them. Huxley returned this curved ball in the manner befitting it:

HUXLEY: *I would sooner claim kinship with an ape than with a man who misuses his great gifts of oratory to stifle scientific debate.*

Appeals to the emotions have a long and successful history of undermining logical reasoning and are widely used by politicians. Classic EMOTIONAL APPEALS such as the APPEAL TO FEAR, the APPEAL TO PRIDE, the APPEAL TO HATRED, the APPEAL TO JEALOUSY, the APPEAL TO PITY, the APPEAL TO ANTIQUITY, the APPEAL TO COMMON CUSTOM, the APPEAL TO MODERATION, and THE APPEAL TO SUPERSTITION are all used daily on the floors of parliaments and in the media:

DEVELOPER: *If we, the leaders of the world, don't build this new airport then our great nation will decline! Our luck will leave us. Our place will be taken by France. We and others before us have always done the brave thing. I beg you, do not walk away now!*

TESTING AN ARGUMENT
some useful techniques

When confronted with a complex argument, or trying to develop one yourself, it can be a good idea to test it. Here are three ways to do this:

1. **REDUCTIO AD ABSURDUM:** To falsify a hypothesis, begin by assuming that it is true. If, based on that assumption, you can prove a contradiction (an 'absurdity'), then you may conclude that your original hypothesis is false. Conversely, to prove a hypothesis is true, assume that it is false and see if absurdities result. Here is a time-proven example from Euclid:

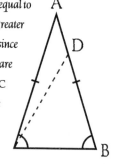

> Let ABC be a triangle having the angle ABC equal to the angle ACB. I say that the side AB is also equal to the side AC. For, if AB is unequal to AC, one of them is greater. Let AB be greater; and from AB the greater let DB be cut off equal to AC the less; Let DC be joined. Then, since DB is equal to AC, and BC is common, the two sides DB, BC are equal to the two sides AC, CB respectively; and the angle DBC is equal to the angle ACB; therefore the base DC is equal to the base AB, and the triangle DBC will be equal to the triangle ACB, the less to the greater: which is absurd. Therefore AB is not unequal to AC; it is therefore equal to it.

2. **THE CONSEQUENTIA MIRABILIS** ('admirable consequence'): The *Consequentia*, like the *Reductio*, tests a hypothesis by initially assuming it is false. If, on the basis of that assumption, you are then able to prove your hypothesis, you may conclude that it is true. Descartes' *Cogito*,

ergo sum ('I think, therefore I exist'), paraphrased here, rests on a form of this logical move:

> I am thinking. Granted that my thinking may be completely mistaken, I cannot deny that it is occurring. Applying the Consequentia, I assert: 'I am not thinking.' This cannot be true, as the statement 'I am not thinking' is itself the expression of a thought. Therefore I was right to assert that I was thinking.

3. OCCAM'S RAZOR: Abduction seeks a hypothetical cause which matches the known facts (*see p. 183*). When conducting such a risky undertaking, *Occam's Razor*, named after William of Ockham [c. 1287–1347], advises that a simple explanation is a better bet than a complex one. Newton gives the following 'philosophizing rule' at the beginning of the third part of the 1726 edition of *Principia*:

> Rule I: We should not admit extra causes of natural events beyond such as are both true and sufficient to explain the phenomena in question.

Beware of Occam's Overdose. The true reasons for things are often very complex indeed, and bizarre concatenations of events do occur all the time, so use Occam with due caution.

AXIOMS
logical foundations

All logical systems ultimately rest on a set of *axioms*, statements which are unproven and unprovable (within the system) and taken to be self-evident. The process of proving further statements is then built on these. Traditional logic rests on three axioms, *The Laws of Thought*.

THE THREE TRADITIONAL LOGICAL AXIOMS:

1. THE PRINCIPLE OF IDENTITY. *A thing is itself. 'I am myself'.*

2. THE PRINCIPLE OF THE EXCLUDED MIDDLE. *Every statement is either true or false. It cannot be 'sort of' true. Through changing circumstances true statements may cease to be true, and false statements may become true, but in the end 'My cat is either alive or it's not'.*

3. THE PRINCIPLE OF NON-CONTRADICTION. *No statement can simultaneously be both true and false. 'It cannot be true and false that my cat is alive'.*

Also these axioms seem self-evident and commonsensical, they do *not* hold true for every logical system. As we shall see in the following pages, Proposition 2 does not hold true for multi-valued logics (*see page 229*) and Proposition 3 does not hold true when we encounter a paradox (*see page 218*). Both 2 and 3 also run into trouble in quantum theory, particularly if the cat belongs to Erwin Schrödinger [1887-1961].

A fourth law of thought formally joined the other three in the 18th and 19th centuries after a long journey, via Plato, Aristotle, Cicero, Avicenna, and Spinoza, though it too is vulnerable to paradox:

4. THE PRINCIPLE OF SUFFICIENT REASON. *Nothing exists, happens, or is true without a cause which can make it so (a 'sufficient cause'). Something cannot be self-caused, since it would logically have to precede itself.*

These four axioms are by no means the only possible ones. For example, the four developed by Gottfried Leibniz [1646–1716] are similar to the traditional axioms, but also show intriguing differences.

LEIBNIZ'S FOUR FUNDAMENTAL AXIOMS:

1. THE PRINCIPLE OF IDENTITY (A = A). *'I am myself'.*

2. *If (all) A is B and (all) B is C, then (all) A is C. E.g. 'If all women are human beings', and 'All human beings are mortal', then 'All women are mortal'.*

3. *Something cannot be its own negation (A ≠ not A): So 'If I am mortal, I am not immortal (not non-mortal)'.*

4. *A positive statement of identity is equivalent to its reversed negation (A = B is equivalent to (not B = not A). This is contraposition (see p. 199). So if 'I am a human being' then 'That which is not a human being is not me'.*

"Well, if you insist on using logic I see little point in continuing this argument."

PARADOX
this is a lie

All systems of logic complex enough to be generally useful sooner or later encounter *paradoxes*, instances where logic comes to an impasse like a machine with a spanner in its works. A paradox is an argument which has a valid form and apparently true premises, but an apparently false or contradictory conclusion (*see too page 176*). Perhaps the most vexing example is THE LIAR PARADOX, which has bedevilled logicians for over two millennia. Here it is in its most simple form:

> This sentence is false.

If this sentence is true, then it's false (that it's false). On the other hand if it's false, then it must be true. In either case it's a false assertion that it's false, so maybe it's true that it's false after all! Perhaps the problem lies in the fact that the sentence refers to itself—maybe if we add a second line, the problem will go away:

> The following sentence is true.
> The preceding sentence is false.

But now the first sentence tells us to trust the second which tells us to distrust the first, so we should distrust the second, meaning we should trust the first after all. The logic is revolving endlessly around a contradiction, making it impossible to come to any conclusion. Maybe we should just ban words like 'sentence', but banning all metareferential statements would limit our ability to say things like 'This is a book is about logic'.

Metareferences are at the core of RUSSELL'S PARADOX, which was described by Bertrand Russell [1872–1970] in 1901:

Let R be the set of all sets that are not members of themselves. If R is not a member of itself, then its definition dictates that it must contain itself, and if it contains itself, then it contradicts its own definition as the set of all sets that are not members of themselves.

Russell was trying to join mathematical logic to the real world, via the development of a perfect logical system. But in 1931 a young mathematician named Kurt Gödel presented a paper titled *On Formally Undecidable Propositions* which changed logic forever. It outlined his *Incompleteness Theorems*, which showed that any logical system more powerful than the most basic must have limits, and that in any axiomatic system (of mathematics or logic), there will always be at least one proposition which cannot be proven within the confines of that system. In the terminology of traditional logic this translates as

In any system of logic, there will always be at least one statement which cannot be proved to be either true or false.

In other words, a paradox, with much in common with the self-referential Liar Paradox. In fact a 'Gödel question' may be formulated which will create a paradox in any logical system:

In system L (for Logic), this statement is false.

If L stands for traditional logic, with its four axioms (*see p. 216*) then if the statement is indeed false according to L, then it is true that it is false. So it is true. Which means it must be false, and so on. Today logicians accept that the paradox is unavoidable and work around it.

THE SORITES
and other famous paradoxes

Paradoxes of parts and wholes form an interesting group. One example, discussed by Plutarch [c. 46–120 AD], is **THE SHIP OF THESEUS**:

> *Over many years Theseus repaired his ship. At a certain point, every piece of the ship had been replaced. It was still Theseus' ship, yet no material from the original ship remained. How can this be? And if someone built a ship out of all the discarded parts, which then would be the real Ship of Theseus?*

Or consider another example, known as the **SORITES PARADOX**, attributed to Eubulides of Miletus [4th century BC]:

> *There is a big heap of sand. Take one grain away and it's still a heap, as we agree that removing one grain of sand does not change a heap to a non-heap. Continue to remove one grain at a time, until there is a 'heap' of two grains, and then, removing one, a single grain of sand. This is clearly not a heap, but we agreed that removing a single grain does not change a heap to a non-heap.*

Thus we have a heap which is not a heap, violating the axioms both of identity and non-contradiction (*see page 216*).

These paradoxes seem to depend on the vagueness of natural languages. Perhaps there is some (maybe unspecifiable) point at which a heap ceases to be a heap (or a ship ceases to be the same ship). The same is true for anything which is a collection of smaller things: e.g. a crowd, or a multitude, or a plethora, or a human body, whose cells are always being replaced.

We could try to solve this paradox with multi-valued logic: maybe there is a size of sand-pile for which it is neither true nor false that it is a heap, or maybe everything is either a heap or not a heap, but it's not clear which is which. Maybe reality, like language, is fuzzy (*see p.229*).

If you watch carefully, Eubulides uses fuzzy language to create some of his other famous paradoxes:

The Electra paradox (*Elektra*):

> Electra doesn't know that the man approaching her is Orestes, her brother.
> Electra knows her brother. So does Electra know the man who is approaching?

The Horns (*keratinês*) paradox:

> What you have not lost, you have. But you have not lost horns.
> Therefore you have horns.

Zeno of Elea [490–430 BC] designed paradoxes around problems of time, space, and infinity. His most famous is:

The **Achilles and the Tortoise** paradox:

> Achilles is racing a tortoise, which had a head start. He must first reach the spot where
> the tortoise was, but by the time he gets there the tortoise has moved on, and when
> he gets to its new location, it has moved on again, etc. How can he ever overtake?

Paradox is harnessed as a linguistic tool by many of the world's mystical traditions, to nudge students out of habitual ways of thinking and effect changes in their consciousness. The Zen *koan* is a classic example—a deeply paradoxical claim is made, and the student left to stew in the resulting lack of closure.

> Two hands clap and there is a sound.
> What is the sound of one hand?
>
> – Hakuin Ekaku

LOGICAL PROBLEMS
language and riddles

The human ability to reason with language has long been connected with the princely skills of problem-setting and problem-solving, and nowhere is this clearer than in so-called 'Logic problems'. Some of the earliest of these are riddles:

> *There is a house. One enters it blind and comes out seeing. What is it?*
>
> — Sumerian tablet, 1800 BC.

> *Four hang, four sprang, two point the way, two to ward off dogs, one dangles after, always rather dirty. What am I?* — Icelandic Hervarar Saga, c.1250.

The successful solution of a riddle can require a particularly agile mind, and often the answer 'comes in a flash', while quite the opposite approach works for puzzles such as this one:

> *There are seven houses; In each house there are seven cats; Each cat catches seven mice; Each mouse would have eaten seven ears of corn; If sown, each ear of corn would have produced seven hekat of grain. How many things are mentioned in all?* — Rhind Papyrus, 1650 BC

This is in fact a mathematical question (and mathematics is intimately related to logic). Little imagination is required to solve it, unlike this medieval problem, related to the Liar paradox (*see p. 218*):

> *Before you are two doors. One leads to heaven and the other leads to hell. Before each door stands a guardian, one who always tells the truth, the other who always lies. You can ask one of them one question. What should it be?*

This can only be solved using pure logic, as can its tougher cousin:

There are three gods on an island. One always tells the truth, one always lies, and one answers randomly. The gods answer "da" or "ja" in their own language but you don't know which means "yes" and which means "no." You have three questions to work out which god is which. What should they be? – George Boolos, 1996

Or try this one, based on an original by Albert Einstein [1879–1955]:

There are five different coloured houses, each with a man with a different nationality, favourite drink, food, and pet. The Englishman lives in the red house. The Swede keeps dogs. The Dane drinks tea. The green house is just to the left of the white one and its owner drinks coffee. The cabbage-eater keeps birds. The owner of the yellow house eats nuts while a man keeps horses next door. The man in the center house drinks milk. The Norwegian lives in the first house. The porridge-eater has a neighbour who keeps cats. The man who eats biscuits drinks beer. The German eats cheese. The Norwegian lives next to the blue house. The porridge-eater has a neighbour who drinks water. Who owns the fish? – after Albert Einstein

To solve problems like these logicians began to develop a special language of their own.

ANSWERS: A school; A cow; 19,607; Ask either guardian "What would the other guardian say if I asked them which was the door to heaven?", then choose the other door: 1. Ask any god "If I asked you 'Is that god Random?' would you say 'ja'?" 2. Ask a god who is not Random "If I asked you "Are you False?" would you say 'ja'?" 3. To the same god, "And if I asked if I spoke to Random? would you say 'ja'?"; The German.

BOOLEAN ALGEBRA
and true or false

At the heart of logic is the quest for knowledge about the truth or falsity of statements. Boolean algebra reduces truth and falsity to the numbers 1 and 0, and replaces words like 'and', 'or', and 'not' with *operators*, '∧', '∨', and '¬'. Logicians then convert statements into notation and study their behaviour using *truth tables*:

		AND	OR
P	Q	P∧Q	P∨Q
1	1	1	1
1	0	0	1
0	1	0	1
0	0	0	0

The truth table shows that 'if P is true AND Q is true' is only true when both P and Q are true. And that 'If P is true OR Q is true' is only false when P and Q are false.

In Boolean algebra '1 and 1' = '1' (as there is no digit higher than 1); and negation, '¬' or 'not', works by inverting a '1' into '0', or a '0' into '1'.

Boolean algebra mirrors many important logical transforms. Try substituting 0 and 1 into the equations below:

DOUBLE NEGATION $P \Leftrightarrow \neg\neg P$

"*I'm fine*" = "*I'm not not fine*"

TAUTOLOGY $P \wedge P \Leftrightarrow P$

"*I'm both well and I'm well*" = "*I'm well*"

$P \vee P \Leftrightarrow P$

"*Either I'm cool or I'm cool*" = "*I'm cool*"

Boolean algebra also allows you to flip logical statements just as you would mathematical equations:

COMMUTATION $P \land Q \Leftrightarrow Q \land P$
"I'm fit and happy" = "I'm happy and I'm fit"
$P \lor Q \Leftrightarrow Q \lor P$
"I'm good or I'm bad" = "I'm bad or I'm good"

ASSOCIATION: $(P \land Q) \land R \Leftrightarrow P \land (Q \land R)$
$(P \lor Q) \lor R \Leftrightarrow P \lor (Q \lor R)$

DISTRIBUTION: $P \land (Q \lor R) \Leftrightarrow (P \land Q) \lor (P \land R)$
$P \lor (Q \land R) \Leftrightarrow (P + Q) \land (P \lor R)$

And finally, it allows you to rephrase logical arguments in interesting ways, with some interesting results (*see too pages 226-7*).

MATERIAL IMPLICATION $P \rightarrow Q \Leftrightarrow \neg P \lor Q$
"If there's a shootout, then you'll die" = "There's no shootout, or you'll die".

TRANSPOSITION $P \rightarrow Q \Leftrightarrow \neg Q \rightarrow \neg P$
"If I shoot, then you'll die" = "If you haven't died, then I didn't shoot"

IMPORTATION $P \rightarrow (Q \rightarrow R) \Rightarrow (P \land Q) \rightarrow R$

DEMORGAN'S THEOREM $\neg(P \land Q) \Leftrightarrow \neg P \lor \neg Q$
"It's false that I'm hot and angry" = "Either I'm not hot, or I'm not angry"
$\neg(P \lor Q) \Leftrightarrow \neg P \land \neg Q$
"I'm neither slow nor stupid" = "I'm not slow and I'm not stupid"

The entire modern electronic world rests on simple logical processes made possible by the basic Boolean algebra shown on these two pages.

PROPOSITIONAL LOGIC
how to build a robot

Propositional logic dates back to Chrysippus of Soli [c.279–c.206 BC], and the Stoics. Reinvented by Pierre Abelard [1079–1142] in the 12th century, it was later taken further by Leibniz, George Boole [1815–64], and Gottlob Frege [1848–1925], among others.

Propositional logic essentially regards statements as its basic units and then examines the ways these are linked by operators ('and', 'therefore', 'not', etc). It cannot address the truth of a classical syllogism based on the traditional rules of subject-predicate relation, but instead excels at manipulating and transforming complex arguments to probe their validity.

In addition, propositional logic does not recognize the nexus in conditional ('if') statements (*see p.184*). So, while in everyday logic, "*If the Earth moves around the sun, then dogs are mammals*" is false, since the two statements (despite both being true) are not connected by a valid nexus, in formal logic, "*If two plus two equals five (F), then summer is the warmest month (T)*" is true, as is "*If two plus two equals five (F), then all circles are square (F)*". These strange results come from the truth-functionality of transposition and material implication (*see previous page, and table below*).

p	q	FALSE (contradiction) $\perp$	NOR (not or) $\downarrow$	Converse nonimplication $\leftarrow$	Negation (not p) $\neg p$	Material nonimplication $\nrightarrow$	Negation (not q) $\neg q$	XOR (exclusive or) $\oplus$	NAND (not and) $\uparrow$	AND $\wedge$	XNOR (exclusive nor) $\odot$	Q projection q	Material implication $\rightarrow$	P projection p	Converse implication $\leftarrow$	OR $\vee$	TRUE (tautology) $\top$
T	**T**	F	F	F	F	F	F	F	F	T	T	T	T	T	T	T	T
T	**F**	F	F	F	F	T	T	T	T	F	F	F	F	T	T	T	T
F	**T**	F	F	T	T	F	F	T	T	F	F	T	T	F	F	T	T
F	**F**	F	T	F	T	F	T	F	T	F	T	F	T	F	T	F	T

NAME	FORM	DESCRIPTION
Simplification	$p \wedge q \Rightarrow p$	p is true and q is true: therefore p is true
Conjunction	$p, q \Rightarrow (p \wedge q)$	p is true; q is true: therefore p and q are true
Addition	$p \Rightarrow (p \vee q)$	p is true: therefore p or q is true
Modus Ponens	$(p \rightarrow q) \wedge p \Rightarrow q$	If p then q; p: therefore q
Modus Tollens	$(p \rightarrow q) \wedge \neg q \Rightarrow \neg p$	If p then q; not q: therefore not p
Hypothetical Syllogism	$(p \rightarrow q) \wedge (q \rightarrow r) \Rightarrow p \rightarrow r$	If p then q, and if q then r; so if p then r
Disjunctive Syllogism	$(p \vee q) \wedge \neg p \Rightarrow q$	Either p or q, or both; not p: so q
Constructive Dilemma	$(p \rightarrow q) \wedge (r \rightarrow s) \wedge (p \vee r) \Rightarrow q \vee s$	If p then q, and if r then s; p or r: so q or s
Destructive Dilemma	$(p \rightarrow q) \wedge (r \rightarrow s) \wedge (\neg q \vee \neg s) \Rightarrow \neg p \vee \neg r$	If p then q, and if r then s; not q or not s: so not p or not r
Bidirectional Dilemma	$(p \rightarrow q) \wedge (r \rightarrow s) \wedge (p \vee \neg s) \Rightarrow q \vee \neg r$	If p then q, and if r then s; p or not s: so q or not r
Composition	$(p \rightarrow q) \wedge (p \rightarrow r) \Rightarrow p \rightarrow (q \wedge r)$	if p then q, and if p then r: so if p then q and r
Exportation	$(p \wedge q) \rightarrow r \Rightarrow p \rightarrow (q \rightarrow r)$	(if (p and q) then r) implies (if q is true then r is, if p is)
Importation	$p \rightarrow (q \rightarrow r) \Rightarrow (p \wedge q) \rightarrow r$	(if q is true then r is, if p is) implies (if (p and q) then r)
Commutation (and)	$p \wedge q \Leftrightarrow q \wedge p$	(p and q) is the same as (q and p)
Commutation (or)	$p \vee q \Leftrightarrow q \vee p$	(p or q) is the same as (q or p)
Commutation (equal)	$p = q \Leftrightarrow q = p$	($p = q$) is the same as ($q = p$)
Association (and)	$p \wedge (q \wedge r) \Leftrightarrow (p \wedge q) \wedge r$	p and (q and r) is the same as (p and q) and r
Association (or)	$p \vee (q \vee r) \Leftrightarrow (p \vee q) \vee r$	p or (q or r) is the same as (p or q) or r
Distribution (and)	$p \wedge (q \vee r) \Leftrightarrow (p \wedge q) \vee (p \wedge r)$	p and (q or r) is the same as (p and q) or (p and r)
Distribution (or)	$p \vee (q \wedge r) \Leftrightarrow (p \vee q) \wedge (p \vee r)$	p or(q and r) is the same as (p or q) and (p or r)
Double Negation	$p \Leftrightarrow \neg \neg p$	p is the same as (not (not p))
Tautology (and)	$p \Leftrightarrow p \wedge p$	(p is true) is the same as (p is true and p is true)
Tautology (or)	$p \Leftrightarrow p \vee p$	(p is true) is the same as (p is true or p is true)
De Morgan (and)	$\neg (p \wedge q) \Leftrightarrow (\neg p \vee \neg q)$	not (p and q) is the same as not p or not q
De Morgan (or)	$\neg (p \vee q) \Leftrightarrow (\neg p \wedge \neg q)$	not (p or q) is the same as not p and not q
Transposition	$p \rightarrow q \Leftrightarrow \neg q \rightarrow \neg p$	(if p then q) is the same as (if not q then not p)
Material Implication	$p \rightarrow q \Leftrightarrow \neg p \vee q$	(if p then q) is the same as (not p or q)
Material Equivalence I	$p = q \Leftrightarrow (p \rightarrow q) \wedge (q \rightarrow p)$	($p = q$) is the same as ((if p then q) and (if q then p))
Material Equivalence II	$p = q \Leftrightarrow (p \wedge q) \vee (\neg p \wedge \neg q)$	($p = q$) is the same as ((p and q) or (not p and not q))
Material Equivalence III	$p = q \Leftrightarrow (p \vee \neg q) \wedge (\neg p \vee q)$	($p = q$) is the same as ((p or not q) or (not p or q))

Above: The elements of propositional logic, where arguments are formed from symbols and logical operators.

EXTENDED LOGICS
more like the world

In the real world, things are rarely as binary as 'true or false', so in the 20th century, logicians like C.I. Lewis, Ruth Barcan, Lotfi Zadeh, and Saul Kripke extended predicate and propositional logic, making it more nuanced.

MODAL LOGIC applies qualifiers to logical statements. These qualifiers come in a number of different kinds:

> ALETHIC: *measure certainty; 'possibly', 'contingently', 'necessarily true'* ...
>
> DEONTIC: *consider ethical concepts; 'obligatory', 'ought', 'forbidden'* ...
>
> EPISTEMIC: *deal with states of knowledge; 'it is known that' or 'unknown'* ...
>
> DOXASTIC: *handle states of belief; x 'thinks that', 'will always think that'* ...
>
> TEMPORAL: *qualify in terms of time; 'was true', 'will be true'* ...
>
> PROBABILISTIC: *deal with degrees of likelihood; 'probable', 'unlikely'* ...

Modal logics are useful for analyzing everyday philosophies with their embedded webs of possible/impossible, permissible/impermissible, and necessary/contingent concepts. Take the tricky future conditional:

> *If it rains tomorrow I should stay at home!*

Its truth value is impossible to determine before tomorrow comes, unless we admit modals like 'probable'. Other arguments, like the *Ontological Argument for the Existence of God (see p. 231)*, rely on the modals 'possible' and 'necessary/must'. Modal logic can also treat ethical or aesthetic questions which lie outside the purview of traditional logic:

> *Mary believes that if you are beautiful you ought to be generous and kind.*

But there's not enough space to show the algebra for that here.

FUZZY LOGIC deals with grey areas of truth, using a (sometimes infinite) number of values between true and false; e.g. from a survey:

Very true [ ]   Mostly true [ ]   Partially true [ ]   Not at all true [ ]

Fuzzy logic is useful in the real and messy world, and allows logicians to work with statisticians, risk analysts, and other information crunchers.

QUANTUM LOGIC permits qubits to exist in a superposition of 1 and 0 (truth and falsity) until the system is observed. *Shor's algorithm* allows quantum computers to discover the answer to difficult questions without having to calculate—they simply freeze at the right answer. Mathematical physicist Roger Penrose has suggested our brains may likewise operate as quantum systems, explaining human intuition.

The mysterious relationship between reality and the language we use to describe it is at the core of the logical process (*see too page 219*):

'There's glory for you!'
'I don't know what you mean by "glory",' Alice said.
Humpty Dumpty smiled contemptuously. 'Of course you don't — till I tell you.'
'When I use a word,' Humpty Dumpty said, in rather a scornful tone, 'it means just what I choose it to mean — neither more nor less.'
— Lewis Carroll, Through the Looking Glass

Human infants acquire language fast and often ask 'why?' as soon as they can talk, thus both engaging in inductive reasoning (causes and effects) and associating words with things. Considering this mystery, the German philosopher Ludwig Wittgenstein [1889–1951] eventually concluded:

Whereof one cannot speak, thereof one must remain silent.

GOOD AND TRUE
logic and ethics

Logic is good at assessing statements of fact, but things get more tricky with modal statements involving words like 'ought' or 'should'. In particular, ETHICAL DILEMMAS ask you to consider how you should behave in a particular situation, and can reveal the way your rationality interacts with your character and your priorities:

> LIFEBOAT DILEMMA: *Your ferry has sunk in the middle of the ocean and you and five other adults are crammed into a tiny lifeboat which is leaking badly. With everyone bailing water the lifeboat can just stay afloat. A second lifeboat, in better condition, comes over and a friend who you met on the ferry invites you to join them, as there is room for one more. What should you do?*

Situations like this occur extremely infrequently in most people's lives, but they are the staple diet of scriptwriters and moviegoers.

> BOMBER DILEMMA: *An old psychiatric patient of yours has planted huge bombs all over a large town. If they go off thousands of people will die. He has been caught but is refusing to disclose the bomb locations unless you hand over your six-year-old daughter. You remember he has an intense terror of torture. The clock is ticking. What should you do?*

Dilemmas like these cleverly exploit the fact that, as Aristotle realized 2500 years ago, our natural human capacity for reason is not purely logical. In the same way that rhetoric can decorate a logical argument, everyday instincts, such as self-preservation, loyalty to friends and family, and social codes of behaviour, can play havoc with our logical faculty when we try and figure "what should I do?".

To help put goodness on a more logical foundation, 18th and 19th century ethical systems attempted to quantify the good:

Act only according to that maxim whereby you can, at the same time, will that it should become a universal law. – Immanuel Kant, 1785

Always act to maximise happiness for the most number. – John Stuart Mill, 1861

By and large, these maxims have become axiomatic to much modern ethical reasoning, seemingly even enabling 'the greatest good' in many difficult situations to be analysed and calculated (*see too pages 339–351*).

Logical systems are circumscribed; they can deal with matters under their purview, but they cannot 'see' outside their parameters. It has been argued by many thinkers, beginning with Plato, that certain important issues—the Good, the True, and the Beautiful—lie ultimately beyond the grasp of human thought and language. It may be that logic can prove to us truths about the highest realities (*as in the modal Ontological Argument, below*), but it cannot show us these realities in their entirety.

1. *It is possible that a supreme being exists.*
2. *In other words, a supreme being exists in some possible world.*
3. *But if it really is supreme, then it must also exist in every possible world.*
4. *And, if it exists in every possible world, then it must exist in the actual world.*
∴ *A supreme being exists.*

Indeed, the master logicians of the past indicate an understanding which ultimately transcends logic. From Aristotle to Boole, key thinkers have often erected their systems as ladders designed to be kicked away once successfully climbed. Hopefully, you too have now reached this stage, and can finally enjoy the full practice of dialectic, the search for Truth.

BOOK V

Above: Personification of Rhetoric from Gregor Reisch's Margarita Philosophica, *1503. Enthroned in the Roman Senate, Lady Rhetoric is surrounded by ancient authorities: Seneca (moral philosophy), Aristotle (natural philosophy), Emperor Justinian (law), and Cicero (Tullius). The lily and the sword coming out of her mouth represent her power to bring both peace and war, both mercy and judgment.*

RHETORIC

The Art of Persuasion

Adina Arvatu & Andrew Aberdein

illustrations by Merrily Harpur

Above: La Rhétorique, *French tapestry (ca. 1510–1520, Paris, Musée des Arts Décoratifs).
The personification of Lady Rhetoric is again majestic—seated on a throne, holding insignia
of royalty—and surrounded by practitioners of the art. No ancient or Church authorities
are present anymore, reflecting the growing self-confidence of Renaissance rhetoric.*

INTRODUCTION

RHETORIC is the *enfant terrible* of the trivium family. Like grammar and logic, it has an ancient pedigree; unlike them, it boasts a rather chequered reputation. At times the infamy even outstrips its ancestry. You cannot, for instance, dismiss someone's speech as 'grammatical' or 'logical,' but let it pack a wallop, and the cry of 'rhetoric!' deafens all. And that is because, from its inception millennia ago, the art of persuasion has been in tension with the truth. And philosophy. For what is to stop a good rhetorician from bending the truth to suit her case? Should rhetoric not make liars and bull-mongers of us all?

The most levelheaded answer ever given to that question remains Aristotle's. Between hard truth and bold-faced lie, he saw a whole domain—known in his day as the *polis*—where things were at best probable. We call it the public sphere, and it is where things need to get done and minds to be made up, where we argue about the right course of action, the most accurate account of events, or the good, the bad, and the uglies in charge of our political fates. If probabilities and values are the main currency in this sphere, then rhetoric and argumentation are its most efficacious tools.

That is why, for centuries, rhetoric was a staple of education in Europe and beyond. It had very useful skills to teach, which helped invent modern English (Shakespeare), steel a country against a terrible enemy (Churchill), move multitudes (Martin Luther King Jr.), or simply communicate effectively. So if you ever wondered about the subtle power that wins over hearts and minds, this little book is for you. And if you never did, it will get you started. For nothing may corrupt like power, but who wants to be powerless in the public sphere?

The Origins of Rhetoric
a charismatic art

Rhetoric began in ancient Greece as the be-all and end-all of public instruction and civic life. Early Greek philosophers known as the Sophists travelled around, offering to teach aspiring youth all they needed to know to succeed in the highly litigious life of the *polis*.

This ultimate art of leadership was rhetoric (Gk. *rhêtorikê technê*, the art of the *rhêtôr*, orator or politician, who regularly spoke in the Athenian Assembly and the courts). One Sophist's name became emblematic for it: Gorgias [ca. 485–380 BC]. Of Sicilian origins, he later plied his trade most profitably in Athens. Of his extant works, the most famous is the *Encomium of Helen*, where he sets out—half in jest—to vindicate the Greek beauty against the charge of starting the Trojan war.

Gorgias examines several scenarios as to what may have led Helen to run away with Paris—fate, force, *logos* (speech), or love—and concludes that she must have been coerced to do so, and hence was undeserving of the blame heaped on her by the poets. The *Encomium* did not clear Helen's name, as it bucked the dominant literary tradition. But it showcased the powers of rhetoric, and Gorgias' daunting skill at conceiving and delivering a seductive, if paradoxical speech. Indeed, of the fourfold argument about the probable causes of Helen's flight, Gorgias retains *logos* as the most powerful and likely one:

> *Speech is a powerful lord, who / with the finest and most invisible body / achieves the most divine works: / it can stop fear and banish grief / and create joy and nurture pity.*

The *Encomium* is a stunning display piece for such dominion. Hypnotically repetitive, rhythmic, euphonic, and metaphorical, it not only tells but also shows how speech, when carefully crafted, can act on the mind like a drug on the body.

Rhetoric's knack for mind-altering effects led Plato, Socrates' student and Aristotle's teacher, to start an all-out war against it. His dialog *Gorgias* marks the onslaught; in it, he denies the Sophists' claim that rhetoric was an art (*technê*), since it was not a form of knowledge, but rather an ease or cleverness with words acquired through experience (*empeiria*). Plato was thus taking aim at Gorgias' historical position that a good politician needed no expert knowledge apart from rhetoric. Then, in an *über*-rhetorical move, Plato compared rhetoric to cosmetics and cookery, all forms of flattery meant to please their ignorant audiences. Only philosophy (Socratic dialectic) could give honest advice or instruction about the good of the *polis*, and is hence the true political art.

And so began the age-old quarrel between philosophy and rhetoric, the latter now forced to wear a big scarlet letter (S for sophistry) on its sleeve.

ENTHYMEME
the rhetorical argument

Aristotle's sway over the development of Western rhetoric cannot be overstated. His *Rhetoric* mediates between the Sophists' overconfidence and Plato's wariness by conceding some Sophist points, redefining them, and using them to make rhetoric respectable. He thus grants that rhetoric is an art (*technê*) that can be taught and learnt; more importantly he sees it as a counterpart to *dialectic* (philosophical argumentation or logic), not its nemesis. Both are arts of communication that try to reason their way through difficult human problems with no final answers. Ergo, they are essential tools in situations where such difficulties arise, especially in ethical and civic life.

Rhetoric and dialectic differ in subject (persuasion *vs.* validity), application (matters of practical and public interest *vs.* universal questions), and audience (non-expert *vs.* expert). But their affinity is so strong that rhetoric too should be considered an argumentative art: "Persuasion," Aristotle argues, "is clearly a sort of demonstration, since we are most fully persuaded when we consider a thing to have been demonstrated." He calls rhetorical demonstration ENTHYMEME, after the Sophists, but takes it to work like the *syllogism* in logic, which is a *deductive argument* that draws a necessary conclusion from two propositions (premises) accepted as true:

> *All men are mortal. Socrates is a man. Therefore, Socrates is mortal.*

By contrast, an enthymeme leaves out a premise or even the conclusion if the speaker feels it is too evident (or just plain dubious) to state:

> *This man deserves punishment, for he is a traitor.* – Alexander of Aphrodisias

If the glove doesn't fit, the jury must acquit! — J. Cochran at the O.J. Simpson trial

If it's Borden, it's got to be good. — Borden Dairy slogan

The light that burns twice as bright burns half as long, and you have burned so very, very brightly, Roy. — Blade Runner

Because you're worth it! — L'Oréal strapline (drops one premise and the conclusion)

Enthymemes draw on commonly accepted notions (e.g. traitors should be punished), not logical truths. This does not make them less efficacious. Aristotle's analogy (*p. 256*) explains how and why they work: enthymemes are to rhetoric what syllogisms are to logic—technical means of reasoning from assumed premises to a conclusion. In brief, they are the very body of persuasive proof (*see too pp. 190-5, 200*).

A rhetorical situation has many limitations (social, cognitive, temporal, etc.); it is never ideal. Nor are enthymemes fallacy-proof. In fact, appealing to an audience's pity or fear (*ad misericordiam, ad baculum*), invoking an authority (*ad verecundiam*) or popular opinion (*ad populum*), attacking an opponent's character (*ad hominem*), while generally fallacies in logic (*see pages 212-3*), are admissible but highly regulated plays in rhetoric.

ETHOS, LOGOS, PATHOS
the three appeals

Aristotle defines rhetoric as "the faculty of observing in any given case the available means of persuasion." He divides these into *technical* (rhetorical) and *non-technical* (extraneous to the art: witnesses, forensic evidence, etc., persuasive means which precede the speaker's intervention). The three technical means of persuasion (or APPEALS) are based on the three key elements of the rhetorical situation: speaker, subject matter, and audience.

1. ETHOS is your *character* as communicated through your speech. It is an effect of what you say, not of what/who you are. To be persuasive, your *ethos* must inspire confidence, and rhetorical credibility comes from three projected qualities: *good sense, good morals*, and *good will*. Absent any one of them, says Aristotle, and you get less cred, which is why attacking an opponent's character, generally a fallacy in logic (*ad hominem*), is permissible and often successful in rhetoric.

2. LOGOS is your *argument*, covering both the 'what' (the substance) and the 'how' (the style) of your discourse, both the ideas and the words used to convey them. The mark of a persuasive speech is finding in any given case the best possible fit between the two.

3. PATHOS refers to the *emotions* of your audience (anger, pity, fear, patriotism, sympathy, etc.). Emotions colour judgements and affect outcomes, so to ensure a favorable reception of your *logos*, try to arouse in your audience those emotions that best fit your subject matter and further your cause.

A persuasive speech strikes a fine balance among appeals. Barack Obama's 'race speech,' which won him his presidential nomination in 2008, does so

with great poise. It is, for example, quite common for a speaker to use biography in their *ethos*. Obama does it too:

I am the son of a black man from Kenya and a white woman from Kansas...

But he uses it to tell an 'American story', meant to remind the audience:

that this nation is more than the sum of its parts; that out of many, we are truly one.

This is an appeal to his audience's patriotism (*pathos*). His *ethos* also embodies the idea of racial reconciliation and unity that he argues for in his *logos*:

the complexities of race in this country [are] a part of our union that we have yet to perfect.

But this perfection requires that Americans overcome racial polarization, so the final anecdote replays this overcoming in an emotional key (*pathos*):

By itself, that single moment of recognition between [a] young white girl and [an] old black man is not enough... But it is where we start... [T]hat is where the perfection begins.

THE FIVE CANONS
the persuasive process

Begun by the Greeks, the task of defining the main divisions of the art was completed by the Romans—chiefly Cicero [106–43 BC] and Quintilian [35–after 96 AD]. There are five such divisions (or *canons*), corresponding to the five steps of the persuasive process:

I. INVENTION (INVENTIO) is the brainstorming stage, when you find the ideas that will help you build a case. First, determine what is at issue (*stasis*, 'conflict'), by asking questions of *fact* (*did it happen?*), *definition* (*what happened?*), *quality* (*was it right/serious?*), or *policy/jurisdiction* (*how can it be solved? / is this the right venue to address it?*). This technique, known as *stasis theory* is a great tool for critical analysis and problem solving. And it's not just for lawyers: relationship offenders practice it with gusto, when they dispute the facts (*do you have proof?*), the definition (*flirting is not cheating*), the quality (*we were going through a rough patch*), or the solution (*you can't break up with me if I break up with you first!*).

Next, flesh out the issue by working out the relations that define it. This is done by using TOPICS (*topoi*, places), rules of thumb which ask you to *define* and *divide* it, *compare* and *contrast* it with others, predict outcomes based on *precedent*, *authorities*, and *language* (general *topoi*), or assess its *rightness*, *virtuousness*, or *goodness/advantageousness* (special *topoi*, associated with the three species of rhetoric: judicial, ceremonial, and deliberative; *see p. 248*). If same-sex marriage is the issue, a lot hangs on how you define marriage. Policy issues are generally complex, so you want to divide them and address one subissue at a time (is gun control constitutional vs. is it advantageous).

2. **ARRANGEMENT (DISPOSITIO)** is next, for a heap of ideas doth not a persuasive speech make. You need to put them in an order that will activate their suasive powers (*for the classical dispositio see overleaf, p. 246*). Jointly, invention and arrangement form the *argumentative* skeleton of a speech.

3. **STYLE (ELOCUTIO)** comes next, for "*it is not sufficient to know what one ought to say, but it is necessary to know also how one ought to say it*" (Aristotle). Style is invention at the level of words: it means finding the best language for your ideas. Rhetorical *figures*—the domain of style—make your speech take shape, and are thus the stylistic equivalent of invention *topoi*, which they follow closely. No one style fits all situations, and no stylistic virtue (e.g. the ancients' *ornateness*) is virtuous with all audiences.

4. **MEMORY (MEMORIA)** and, finally, 5. **DELIVERY (ACTIO)** (intonation, body language) deal with the *performance* side of persuasion. Memorizing and rehearsing will help you project confidence and authority, bond with your audience, and respond nimbly to any unforeseen change in the rhetorical landscape (*see too pp. 362–5*).

DISPOSITIO
arranging your ideas

Classical authorities had a clear recipe for how the content of a speech should be arranged: it should be divided into a set number of parts (five for Aristotle, six or seven for Cicero) in a set order. While this structure has often been criticized as unduly restrictive, it is still hard to beat.

1. EXORDIUM (or *prooimion*). The principal purpose of the first part of your speech is to establish who you are and why you are the right person to address this topic. As such, it is naturally the place for an *ethos* appeal, demonstrating your character and expertise.

2. NARRATIO (*diegesis* or *prothesis*). The second part of your speech is the basic story that all parties agree on. So set out the facts. Of course, since you're the one telling it, you can take the opportunity to present it in a light favourable to your cause, but you should postpone intrinsically controversial material until the next section.

3. DIVISIO (*partitio* or *propostio*). The proper place for contentious matters comes next, as you explain how your version of the facts differs from your opponent's. (Aristotle does not have a separate section for this purpose, which is why his speeches only have five parts.)

4. CONFIRMATIO (*pistis* or *probatio*). Once you have set out the terms of the debate, it's time to show why you're right. This starts with the confirmatio, in which you offer arguments in defense of your own side. *Logos* comes into its own here.

5. REPREHENSIO (or *confutatio*). Next, turn to your opponent's arguments, and show why they are no good. This rebuttal of competing views

is another *logos*-heavy section. (Cicero suggests that you may pause at this point for a DIGRESSIO, a sidebar addressing related issues. Later authorities mostly omit this optional extra component.)

6. PERORATIO (*epilogos* or *conclusio*). To conclude, end on a ringing appeal to your audience's emotions. This is the climax of the speech. Which emotions you appeal to depends, of course, on your subject matter: compassion when speaking for the defense, righteous anger when speaking for the prosecution, patriotism when rallying troops, and so forth. All of these are *pathos* appeals.

In practice, not every speech need contain every component, nor should all the components always receive equal weight or necessarily occur in this order. The echo of the courtroom and the assembly chamber is audible in the classical *dispositio*, but speeches (and written works) are composed for many other purposes. In particular, epideictic rhetoric (*p. 248*) often calls for a lighter structure—although you could construct a speech of praise with a lengthy *divisio*, in which you enumerate all the reasons people hate your subject, and an equally lengthy *reprehensio*, in which you rebut them, it may be better to pass over such regrettable matters in silence (an APOSIOPESIS, *p. 287*). The greater your experience with *divisio*, as with other supposedly rigid rules of rhetoric, the greater your confidence in knowing when to bend it.

Kairos

& the three species of rhetoric

KAIROS, in ancient Greek, meant the 'right time' or 'opportune moment,' and was always tied to circumstances. It was the crux of Sophistic rhetoric and Gorgias, the world's first pundit, made it a point of virtuoso pride to speak freely to the hour's most pressing concerns.

Aristotle kept *kairos* as a key rhetorical ingredient, but without the Sophists' zing. He put it under a general rule of appropriateness, *prepon*, to occasion, subject, and audience (*see decorum, opposite*). He thus defined rhetoric as the art and skill (*dynamis,* power) of finding '*in any given case* the available means of persuasion,' and identified its three species or branches as *judicial* (forensic), *epideictic* (ceremonial), and *political* (deliberative). Each branch has its own temporal markers: *past* for the facts of a case, *present* for praising or blaming, and *future* for pitching an idea or proposing a bill, respectively.

Tradition embraced Aristotle's solution, so *kairos* now means both the right season for speaking, and the right tense to speak in. Put proverbially:

To every thing there is a season, and a time to every purpose under the heaven. – Eccles. 3.1

A word fitly spoken is like apples of gold in pictures of silver. – Prov. 25:11

SILENCE

Decorum
for the rhetorically fit

DECORUM is a general rhetorical principle of appropriateness: if you want to be persuasive, you must fit your style to your subject matter, audience, occasion, and goal. This principle applies not only to the style of your speech but also to your style as a speaker: gestures, stance, facial expression, clothing and language, can exhibit decorum—or not. When Queen Victoria complained that Gladstone spoke to her as if she were a public meeting, she was accusing her prime minister of a failure of decorum. But it would have been just as much a failing if he had addressed a public meeting in a manner fit for private conversation.

Yet, taken too rigidly, decorum can breed conformity. And conformity can undermine your character (*ethos*) as a speaker, diminish the credibility of your argument (*logos*), and bore your audience. So optimal rhetorical decorum may call for an occasional dash of inappropriateness, to keep your audience from tuning out. Whence the *paradox (p. 268)* of decorum: to show respect for the limits of propriety in the very act of pushing them.

Hence decorum is not just about character. At its best, it is a precise calibration of the three rhetorical appeals (*p. 242*).

EPICHEIREME
& the Toulmin layout

Argument is essential to rhetoric, and often best expressed concisely. Nonetheless, in some contexts, such as forensic rhetoric, arguments need to be made explicit. If an *enthymeme* (*p. 240*) is an argument with something missing, an EPICHEIREME is an argument with extras. An epicheireme comprises five components, usually in the following order: a claim; a reason for that claim; a proof of that reason; an embellishment of the claim; and a restatement of the claim. For example, consider Robert Southey's justification for his attacks on Lord Byron (with added labels):

[Claim:] *I accused him;...* [Reason:] *because he had committed a high crime and misdemeanour against society,* [Proof of reason:] *by sending forth a work, in which mockery was mingled with horrors, filth with impiety, profligacy with sedition and slander.* [Embellishment:] *For these offences I came forward to arraign him. The accusation was not made darkly, it was not insinuated, nor was it advanced under the cover of a review.* [Restatement of claim:] *I attacked him openly in my own name.*

The most important feature of the epicheireme is that claims should not only have reasons, but those reasons themselves must have reasons (on some accounts, this is all that is required.)

A modern reinvention of the epicheireme is the Toulmin layout, devised by the philosopher Stephen Toulmin in the 1950s. This comprises six components: claim; data; warrant; backing; rebuttal; and qualifier. Here is one of Toulmin's most frequently cited examples:

Given that [D] *Harry was born in Bermuda, we can* [Q] *presumably claim that* [C] *he is British, since* [W] *anyone born in Bermuda will generally be British (on account of* [B] *various statutes...), unless* [R] *his parents were aliens, say.*

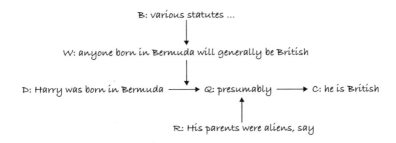

B: various statutes ...

↓

W: anyone born in Bermuda will generally be British

↓

D: Harry was born in Bermuda ——→ Q: presumably ——→ C: he is British

↑

R: His parents were aliens, say

The claim corresponds to that of the epicheireme but the data and warrant subdivide the reason, data being specific to the case in hand, warrant being a more general principle. The warrant is supported by the backing, which loosely corresponds to the proof of reason. The last two components are new: the rebuttal takes note of possible exceptions and the resultant force of the argument is given by the qualifier.

The beauty of the Toulmin layout is its versatility and explicitness: it can be used to make clear (often graphically) the structure and strength of an enormous diversity of arguments.

Bermudan you may be, but you'll always be our little boy...

METAPHOR
life is a box of chocolates

Rhetorical figures may be divided into *tropes* (figures of thought), involving a change in the meaning of words, and *schemes* (figures of speech), involving a change in word order. Tropes are often given pride of place. Indeed, classical rhetoric is a polite establishment wherein METAPHOR rules, IRONY (*p. 258*) secretly contends, and WORDPLAY (*p. 284*) yoricks away.

Metaphors are problem-solving tools which help us think through a complex or difficult experience in terms of another, simpler or more familiar. (The name comes from the Greek for 'transfer'; *metaphorai* are also means of public transport in Greece). Their function is above all heuristic, or practical, though aesthetic criteria do apply:

> *Love is a kind of warfare.* – Ovid

> *Love is a crocodile in the river of desire.* – Bhartrhari

A metaphor calls one thing by another's name based on a perceived likeness; it is a comparison between two things expressed definitionally:

> *Life is a box of chocolates, Forrest. You never know what you're gonna get.* – Forrest Gump

The comparison's point: life comes with choices, just like chocolates come in flavours. Forrest and most viewers remember this metaphor as a SIMILE (*p. 256*)—"Life is *like* …"—thus shoring up the view that the two tropes part on a technicality (metaphors lack comparison words: 'like,' 'as,' etc.).

But nothing is ever that easy in life and in rhetoric, as the similarity posited by metaphor may be between *relations* rather than things:

> *The hippo of recollection stirred in the muddy waters of the mind.* – Terry Pratchett

This metaphor is an ANALOGY (*p. 256*) or proportion: memory is to a clouded mind what a hippo is to a muddy river—a massive, luxuriating, barely stirring dweller. Metaphors have a *tenor* (or subject) and a *vehicle*: 'love' is the tenor and 'crocodile' the vehicle (*see facing page*). Often the tenor is left out, leading to an IMPLICIT metaphor:

> There is an ocean... And, somewhere in its depths, a Beast, stirring. – Salman Rushdie

We know, contextually, that shame is the ocean and violence, the Beast. They also form a COMPLEX metaphor, as they explore and illuminate each other. A good metaphor establishes connections where none were seen before. Its creative, generative powers are only matched by its expansiveness. Indeed, when pursued for many lines (an EXTENDED metaphor), it can lead to surprising findings:

> Love is a fire. / It burns everyone. / It disfigures everyone.
> It is the world's excuse / for being ugly. – Leonard Cohen

Generally, metaphor is not limited to nouns—or poets: weather is often 'beastly hot' (intensifier); one 'burns' with desire (verb), has a 'cold' heart (adjective), or believes 'blindly' (adverb); plans go 'south' (adverb), etc. It appears language is metaphors all the way down!

SYNECDOCHE AND METONYMY
specialized metaphors

If rhetoric is a toolkit, then metaphors are screwdrivers. But, as with screwdrivers, some metaphors have specialised applications. One of these is SYNECDOCHE: the metaphorical use of part for whole, or whole for part:

> *The slogan of progress is changing from the full dinner pail to the full garage.* – H.Hoover

> *I do not believe that Washington should do for the people what they can do for themselves through local and private effort.* – John F. Kennedy

Full dinner pails and full garages are part of prosperity, but not all of it. Conversely, the whole city of Washington has the government of the United States as a part. A close relative of synecdoche is METONYMY: the metaphorical use of an aspect or attribute for the thing itself:

> *The Red Flag was never flown throughout these islands yet, nor for a thousand years has the flag of any other alien creed.* – Michael Heseltine

> *One day you're a signature, next day you're an autograph.* – Billy Wilder

Red flags are associated with communists, but are not part of communism. Signatures and autographs look alike, but one is the attribute of a bureaucrat, the other of a celebrity.

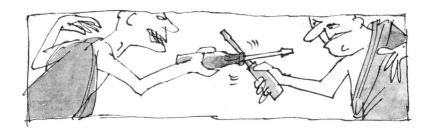

CATACHRESIS
runaway metaphors

Quintilian [c.35–100 AD] defines CATACHRESIS (*abusio*) as "the practice of adapting the nearest available term to describe something for which no actual term exists". The lack of a proper term for, say, the eye of a needle justifies the artifice of calling it an 'eye'. The need to fill such lexical gaps sets catachresis apart from metaphor (*translatio*), which is cavalier towards proper terms. Thus, common phrases like '*foot* of the mountain,' '*head* of the table,' '*lip* of a cliff,' etc., contain catachreses, whereas Hamlet's

I will speak daggers to her but use none. – William Shakespeare

should be a metaphor, since the transfer of 'daggers' from stabbing to speaking is prompted by the insufficiency of existing proper terms (e.g. 'words'), not their lack. Yet Hamlet's metaphor is also a catachresis, because it is perceived as extreme or 'abusive'. Once separated from metaphor as a form of coerced invention, catachresis is now mostly explained as a special kind of metaphor: either 'dead' (too clichéd and worn out to register as such, e.g. computer 'mouse'), or extreme—a far-fetched, eccentric, mixed, mangled, or even failed exemplar. Something like this sore thumb:

... We are riding hell for leather into a health-care box canyon full of spending quicksand, cactus tax hikes, policy briar patches, complete with CMS regulatory rattlesnakes, scorpions, and bad-news bears. – Pat Roberts

The involuntary humour of such runaway metaphors made comedian Stephen Colbert call them 'humaphors.' Here's an intentional example:

Hawaii made the mouth of her soul water. – Tom Robbins

For more stylistic fails, intentional or not, see *Pathologies of Style, p. 288.*

Simile and Analogy
comparison

SIMILE likens one thing to another, perhaps incongruously. It differs from metaphor in admitting that it is a comparison—where metaphor identifies two things, simile says they are alike:

> The stoical scheme of supplying our wants, by lopping off our desires, is like cutting off our feet when we want shoes. – Jonathan Swift

> To read without reflecting is like eating without digesting. – Edmund Burke

> Asking a working writer what he thinks about critics is like asking a lamp-post how it feels about dogs. – Christopher Hampton

Similes may be extended or explained by listing points of similarity:

> Operations of thought are like cavalry charges in a battle — they are strictly limited in number, they require fresh horses, and must only be made at decisive moments.
> – Alfred North Whitehead

> Trying to maintain good relations with the Communists is like wooing a crocodile. You do not know whether to tickle it under the chin or beat it over the head. When it opens its mouth you cannot tell whether it is trying to smile or preparing to eat you up. – Winston Churchill

This sort of simile is very close to ANALOGY, wherein a comparison is used to reason to some conclusion:

> Reading is to the mind what exercise is to the body. As by the one, health is preserved, strengthened, and invigorated; by the other, virtue — which is the health of the mind — is kept alive, cherished, and confirmed. – Joseph Addison

Confine the expression of popular feeling within rigid limits, surround it with iron bands, and a spark may cause a terrific explosion. Leave it free and like gunpowder scattered in the open air, even if set alight it will do no damage. – Jonathan Swift

Addison's first sentence echoes mathematical usage; it might be rewritten as *reading : mind :: exercise : body*. Indeed, rhetoric borrowed analogy from mathematics. For Greek mathematicians, a *logos* was a ratio and an *analogos* was a comparison of ratios, e.g. the proportion 5:7 :: 15:21. Unlike Addison's analogy, which yields at best a plausible conclusion, mathematical analogies are exact; for example, Archimedes proved that all circles satisfy *area : radius*^{2} :: *circumference : diameter*.

Exact analogies are not restricted to mathematics. They are central to the concept of case law: once a court determines that two cases are similar, it must apply the earlier judgement in the current case. That's how one manufacturer's liability for tainted ginger beer could establish another manufacturer's liability for defective underpants.

Analogy is also a conspicuous feature of much visual rhetoric. Political cartoons often make their point by drawing an analogy. As with verbal analogies, this can be taken too far, leading to visual *catachresis* (*p. 255*).

...our new range of intriguingly defective underpants...

IRONY
the great dissembler

In Greek comedy, the *eiron* was a dissembler who feigned ignorance and employed understatement in order to undercut the *alazon*, a vacuously noisy type, in a battle of wits. Our term IRONY preserves much of this meaning: it implies saying one thing and meaning something quite different, often the very opposite, with the intent not of deceiving anybody but rather of being rightly understood by the right audience. Irony is an intelligence test of sorts, and that is why 'getting it' is very important socially.

There are many kinds of irony: verbal, Socratic, dramatic, situational, etc. Verbal irony is the rhetorical trope *per se*, and the classic form that all the other are based on. At its simplest, verbal irony manifests as ANTIPHRASIS, which involves a concise and overt semantic reversal: Yeah, right!

Many define antiphrasis as one-word irony (e.g. calling a big guy 'tiny'), but the more important feature is its lack of subtlety. That is why it easily spills over into SARCASM, a bitter-biting-brutal takedown that relies heavily on delivery (intonation, facial expression) for its effect.

...I think I'll go for the sarcasm...

Mark Antony's oration over Caesar's slain body contains one of the most famous examples of antiphrasis jacked up to baleful sarcasm:

And Brutus is an honourable man. – William Shakespeare

The implication that Brutus is the very opposite of 'honourable' is clearer with every repetition of the phrase, which is used to incite mutiny.

Irony relies heavily on context and often consorts with other figures to make its point. An allusion (*p. 286*) to Pinocchio, say, can suggest that a person's emotional responses are wooden:

Sometimes your movements are so life-like, I forget you're not a real boy.

– The Big Bang Theory

Subtle or not, irony bears a straight face. It is why the opening of *A Tale of Two Cities* is often quoted for its masterly use of *anaphora* (*p. 275*) and *antithesis* (*p. 277*), but rarely for its irony:

It was the best of times, it was the worst of times, it was the age of wisdom, it was the age of foolishness, it was the epoch of belief, it was the epoch of incredulity, it was the season of Light, it was the season of Darkness, it was the spring of hope, it was the winter of despair, we had everything before us, we had nothing before us, we were all going direct to Heaven, we were all going direct the other way — in short, the period was so far like the present period, that some of its noisiest authorities insisted on its being received, for good or for evil, in the superlative degree of comparison only. – Charles Dickens

The main contrast is not between light and darkness, hope and despair, etc., but rather between overstatement (the hyperbolic claims being reported) and the narrator's understated, ironic conclusion: 'in short, the period was so far like the present period'—read, so very ordinary—that its noisiest authorities were right—read, wrong—to describe it superlatively. Dickens' narrator behaves like a true eiron.

MEIOSIS AND LITOTES
understatement

Sometimes less is more. Quiet understatement can speak louder than bold declaration. Together with *hyperbole* (*opposite*), it is one of the principal strategies of irony (*p. 258*). Most understatement takes the form of MEIOSIS:

> I am just going outside and may be some time. – Lawrence Oates

A *not uncommon* form of understatement is LITOTES, the denial of a negative term. In this *not unwitty* example, P. G. Wodehouse deploys it playfully:

> I could see that, if not actually disgruntled, he was far from being gruntled.

Like many rhetorical figures, litotes can be overdone:

> I am not, indeed, sure whether it is not true to say that the Milton who once seemed not unlike a seventeenth-century Shelley had not become... – Harold Laski

George Orwell was particularly critical of its overuse—it was he who drew attention to the egregious example above. He recommended that writers remember the following to cure themselves of the habit:

> A not unblack dog was chasing a not unsmall rabbit across a not ungreen field.

But both figures of understatement can be effective when used with discretion. Here the two are combined adroitly:

> In my late twenties, it was not unusual for me to wake up in a police cell wearing a paper suit. Waking to glazed tiles and a high barred window, and not knowing how one got there, is a bad way to start the day. – Jeremy Clarke

The first sentence exhibits litotes, the second meiosis; together they lend a certain wry irony to an otherwise melancholy image.

HYPERBOLE
overstatement

Sometimes nothing is so effective as unabashed exaggeration. This is HYPERBOLE. It is especially useful for invective, as in this splendid denunciation of one 19th century Canadian politician by another:

> *He is, without exception, the most notorious liar in all our country. He lies out of every pore in his skin. Whether he is sleeping or waking, on foot or on horseback, talking with his neighbors or writing for a newspaper, a multitudinous swarm of lies, visible, palpable, and tangible, are buzzing and settling about him like flies around a horse in August.* — Sir Francis Bond Head, describing William Lyon Mackenzie

The *tricolon* (*p. 281*) of *isocolons* (*p. 276*) and concluding simile (*p. 256*) demonstrate how helpful other figures can be in building up a good hyperbole.

As with meiosis (*opposite*), hyperbole is an intrinsically ironic figure. This can be comic in effect, unintentionally (*as above*) or on purpose:

> *There is only one cure for grey hair. It was invented by a Frenchman. It is called the guillotine.* — P.G. Wodehouse

> *If you live to be ninety in England and can still eat a boiled egg they think you deserve the Nobel Prize.* — Alan Bennett

SENTENTIA AND EXEMPLUM
shared wisdom

Often one's thoughts can best be expressed through the words of others:

> *It was prettily devised of Aesop, 'The fly sat upon the axletree of the chariot-wheel and said, what a dust do I raise.'* – Francis Bacon

Such pithy summaries are examples of SENTENTIA ('judgement')—a.k.a. *maxim, adage,* or *proverb* (*see pp. 366-7*). They express a general truth or commonly held view, and often embody a moral or practical rule of thumb:

> *An old saying and a true, 'much drinking, little thinking'.* – Jonathan Swift

> *There is a homely old adage which runs: 'Speak softly and carry a big stick; you will go far.'* – Theodore Roosevelt

...Got any homely old adages?....

Handed down through generations, maxims are often used as anonymous distillations of wisdom: 'they say…' Indeed, few will recall that *'seize the day'* is Horace's, even when they quote it in Latin—*'Carpe diem'*.

Thanks to their currency, maxims are great consensus builders and enthymematic material:

> O mortal man, nurse not immortal wrath. – Aristotle

By itself, 'it is not right to nurse immortal wrath' is a maxim; but by adding 'mortal man,' a reason is given ('for you are mortal'): the maxim is now an enthymeme (*p. 240*).

Rhetorical *exemplification* (Lat. EXEMPLUM, pl. *exempla*) aims to clarify or illustrate an idea. It is a short historical or fictional tale or anecdote, which serves to reinforce a moral point and get the audience to respond emotionally, not just assent intellectually to it:

> Old King Tarquin knew what he was about when he symbolised the surest way of enslaving a community by striking off the heads of the tallest poppies. – Lord Salisbury

Not every example is an exemplum. Bumblebee bats and blue whales are examples of mammals, but the story of the dodo—the flightless Mauritian bird that went extinct because it never learned to fear predators—illustrates rhetorically the dangers of being too trusting. Exempla aim for what is exemplary rather than classificatory, and illustrate a moral rather than logical category. Beloved by the ancients and medieval sermon writers, exempla remain a staple of motivational speeches:

> Americans, traditionally, love to fight. All real Americans love the sting of battle. When you were kids, you all admired the champion marble shooter, the fastest runner, the big league ball players, the toughest boxers. Americans love a winner and will not tolerate a loser. Americans play to win all the time. – George Patton

DISTINCTIO
definition and dissociation

The figure of DISTINCTIO specifies the meaning of key terms. Since so many words are potentially ambiguous, distinctio can be crucial in averting misunderstanding by spelling things out in more detail:

> When I mention religion, I mean the Christian religion; and not only the Christian religion, but the Protestant religion; and not only the Protestant religion, but the Church of England. – Henry Fielding

Distinctio is closely related to the strategy of DISSOCIATION, distinguishing two senses of a term that, one contends, have been mistakenly conflated:

> …there are two kinds of equality; there is the equality that levels and destroys and the equality that elevates and creates. – Benjamin Disraeli

Although dissociations can be made on many different grounds, they often distinguish between the apparent and the true senses of a term. Asserting that one's preferred sense is the true one is an example of DEFINITION:

> The true University of these days is a collection of books. – Thomas Carlyle

This strategy is particularly open to abuse:

> Ordinary temperance is just gross refusal to drink; but true temperance, true temperance is something much more refined. True temperance is a bottle of claret with each meal and three double whiskies after dinner. – Aldous Huxley

Definitions of this sort, where the positive (or negative) associations of a term are intended to survive a change in its substantive meaning, are called *persuasive definitions*. This approach is problematic: you may define your terms as you wish, but you do not get to keep all their past associations.

EUPHEMISM AND DYSPHEMISM
good and bad names

Giving a thing with a bad reputation a good (or at least neutral) name exemplifies the rhetorical figure of EUPHEMISM:

> Other nations use 'force'; we Britons alone use 'Might'. – Evelyn Waugh

> Sir Roderick Glossop ... is always called a nerve specialist, because it sounds better, but everyone knows that he's really a sort of janitor to the looney-bin. – P. G. Wodehouse

Euphemism can be all too easy to see through. If the renamed thing is still seen as bad, then the new term will also soon be seen negatively, so new euphemisms will be required for the old euphemisms, a process known as the 'euphemism treadmill'. Thus the terms 'idiot', 'moron', and 'cretin' originated as euphemisms for older words such as 'dullard', or 'fool', which, ironically, now seem less abusive than their replacements.

The converse of euphemism is DYSPHEMISM, giving something neutral or good a bad name:

> There is the milder kind of ridicule that consists in pretending that a reasoned opinion is indistinguishable from an absurd out-of-date prejudice. If you do not like Communism, you are a Red-baiter. – George Orwell

RHETORICAL QUESTIONS
erotesis, hypophora, and aporia

Is any figure better known than the rhetorical question? Is there only one sort of rhetorical question? Actually, no: both of these questions are rhetorical questions, but they are examples of significantly different figures. The standard rhetorical question is EROTESIS, a question which presumes its own answer:

> *If you're gonna ask if you can ask me a question, give me time to respond. Unless you're asking rhetorically, in which case the answer is obvious — yes.* – Ocean's Twelve

Erotesis is really disguised assertion—the speaker poses a question to which there is only one plausible answer: of course the rhetorical question is the

best known figure! But open questions can also be used rhetorically—just as long as the speaker is sure to supply the answer, as in the second question above. This sort of question is known as HYPOPHORA.

> *What is the best government? That which teaches us to govern ourselves.* – Goethe

And here's a neat double act—a hypophora answered with an erotesis:

> *What is conservatism? Is it not adherence to the old and tried, against the new and untried?* – Abraham Lincoln

In both erotesis and hypophora we already know the answer when we ask the question. But questions can be used rhetorically even when we don't know the answer. In particular, we can use a question to indicate that nobody knows the answer, an example of APORIA:

> *How many roads must a man walk down / Before you call him a man?* – Bob Dylan

How many indeed—who knows? Aporia covers such expressions of doubt, and can serve several purposes. It can be used to suggest that there is just no knowledge to be had:

> *Is there beyond the silent night / An endless day?*
> *Is death a door that leads to light? / We cannot say.* – Robert Ingersoll

Or set aside one question to focus on another (an implicit *præteritio, p. 267*):

> *I know not whether Laws be right, / Or whether Laws be wrong;*
> *All that we know who lie in gaol / Is that the wall is strong;*
> *And that each day is like a year, / A year whose days are long.* – Oscar Wilde

It can also be a polite way of casting doubt on an interlocutor's words:

> *I know that you believe that you understood what you think I said, but I am not sure you realise that what you heard is not what I meant.* – Robert McCloskey

PARADOX AND OXYMORON
and adynaton

Etymologically, PARADOX means 'contrary to popular opinion,' that is, against the grain of traditional wisdom. Technically, it denotes a statement (by extension, a situation) that seems to contradict itself, or runs counter to logic or expectations. Much like the physics of the Red Queen:

> *...here, you see, it takes all the running you can do, to keep in the same place. If you want to get somewhere else, you must run at least twice as fast as that!* – Lewis Carroll

The same 'law' was used in the 1960s to explain economic progress:

> *The United States has to move very fast to even stand still.* – John F. Kennedy

Paradox is not a *logical contradiction*, it does not ask us to believe A and not-A at the same time. Rather, it asks us to entertain the possibility that the truth, at least about the moral universe, lies in the tension between contraries. *Without contraries is no progression*, Blake once said, and history may bear that out:

> *Liberty was born in England from the quarrels of tyrants.* – Voltaire

> *To be prepared for war is one of the most effectual means of preserving peace.*
>
> – George Washington

A close relation of paradox is OXYMORON ('sharp-dull' in Greek). As its name suggests, it is a contradiction in terms, or a compressed paradox: e.g. *conspicuous absence, eloquent silence, old news, living dead*, etc. Romeo's jeremiad pushes this figure to the absurd:

> *O brawling love, O loving hate, [...] / O heavy lightness, serious vanity, / Misshapen chaos of well-seeming forms! / Feather of lead, bright smoke, cold fire, sick health...*
>
> – William Shakespeare

Sometimes, the contradiction is not apparent until some sharp-dull wit is applied to it:

> I do not know the American gentleman, god forgive me for putting two such words together. – Charles Dickens

If paradox and oxymoron are possible impossibilities, ADYNATON emphatically states the impossible, the absurd: *when pigs fly, not until hell freezes over, on St. Never's Day,* etc. Adynaton is emphasis in overdrive, and makes hyperbole (*p. 261*) look like Tom Thumb:

> Build a worm fence round a Winter supply of Summer weather; skim the clouds from the sky with a teaspoon; catch a thunderbolt in a bladder; break a hurricane to harness; [...] bake hell in an ice house; lasso an avalanche; [...] hang out the ocean on a grapevine to dry; put the sky to soak in a gourd; unbuckle the belly band of eternity and paste 'To Let' on the sun and moon, but never, sir, never for a moment delude yourself with the idea that you can beat [Ulysses S.] Grant.
>
> – Lt. Col. T. Elwood Zel

Præteritio and Apophasis
passing over in silence

It is often helpful to make clear what you are *not* going to say:

> I will not consider this important topic here and will also make no effort to survey the range of ideas … that fall within the particular tendency that I will discuss. – Noam Chomsky

This is PRÆTERITIO. There are many reasons for remaining silent, from limitation of space, as above, to the outright impossibility of saying more:

> Whereof one cannot speak, thereof one must remain silent. – Ludwig Wittgenstein

Præteritio also covers cases where the audience's imagination may well outdo the author's descriptive powers, as in this from Lord Salisbury:

> The agonies of a man who has to finish a difficult negotiation, and at the same time to entertain four royalties at a country house can be better imagined than described.

Or the audience may already know the score:

> Biggles tapped a cigarette reflectively on his case. 'You all remember the beginning of this affair, so I needn't go over it all again,' he began. – W. E. Johns

Yet Biggles does go over it all again, making his professed præteritio ironic (*p. 258*): such cases of saying exactly what it is that you won't say are sometimes distinguished as APOPHASIS. Examples abound in political discourse:

> I won't bring up the fact that your budget has been cut to smithereens, and the Department itself has in many respects been a shambles. – Sidney R. Yates

Most masterfully, one may successfully plant the idea one wished to convey without actually, technically, saying it:

> You might very well think that. I couldn't possibly comment. – BBC House of Cards

Zeugma

sharing a yoke

As a yoke joins together two oxen, so a verb may join together several *objects*, a *subject* several verbs, or a verb several subjects and objects. This figure is called ZEUGMA, from the Greek word for yoke. By making words do multiple duty, zeugma aids concision and points to relationships between the linked clauses.

Zeugma has several subspecies. In PROZEUGMA, the yoke comes first—one verb governs several objects, or several subject–object pairs:

> To be patriotic, hate all nations but your own; to be religious, all sects but your own; to be moral all pretenses but your own. — Lionel Strachey

> He would read with that intense application and delight, that he would forget himself, his wound, his confinement, his dinner. — Laurence Sterne

In DIAZEUGMA, a noun yokes together a string of verbs:

> They wouldn't even lift a finger to save their own grandmothers from the Ravenous Bugblatter Beast of Traal without orders signed in triplicate, sent in, sent back, queried, lost, found, subjected to public inquiry, lost again, and finally buried in soft peat for three months and recycled as fire lighters. — Douglas Adams

In HYPOZEUGMA, the yoke comes last. A verb may connect nouns, as in prozeugma, or a noun adjectives and adjectival phrases, as in this example:

> Desperate, lonely, cut off from the human community which in many cases has ceased to exist, under the sentence of violent death, wracked by desires for intimacy that they do not know how to fulfill, at the same time tormented by the presence of women, men turn to logic. — Andrea Nye

CONCESSIO

stooping to conquer

As its name suggests, CONCESSIO means conceding a point, but only to make an even stronger one. Here's Mark Twain in 1902:

> I am not finding fault with this use of our flag; for in order not to seem eccentric I have swung around, now, and joined the nation in the conviction that nothing can sully a flag. I was not properly reared, and had the illusion that a flag was a thing which must be sacredly guarded against shameful uses and unclean contacts, lest it suffer pollution; and so when it was sent out to the Philippines to float over a wanton war and a robbing expedition I supposed it was polluted, and in an ignorant moment I said so. But I stand corrected. I conceded and acknowledge that it was only the government that sent it on such an errand that was polluted.

Far from projecting weakness or defeat, concession makes you appear fair-minded and confident, by showing you can and will weigh both sides of an argument. Concessio boosts character and credibility (*see ethos, p. 242*). One author calls it 'rhetorical jujitsu,' since it uses the force of an opponent's argument against them. Sometimes, projecting goodwill and strength of character in the face of defeat is the sole purpose of concession:

> They asked [Abraham Lincoln] how he felt once after an unsuccessful election. He said he felt like a little boy who had stubbed his toe in the dark. He said that he was too old to cry, but it hurt too much to laugh. — Adlai E. Stevenson

As a 'nay' in the guise of a qualified 'yea,' concession is also an ally of irony:

> The Labour party is not dead, just brain dead. — Norman Tebbit

> Your president, President Clinton, is a great communicator. The trouble is, he has absolutely nothing to communicate. — Margaret Thatcher

PROCATALEPSIS
anticipating objections

Your audience will often start formulating their objections long before you've finished speaking. For this reason, it is helpful to anticipate and address such counterarguments, a figure known as PROCATALEPSIS:

> I can think of no one objection, that will possibly be raised against this proposal, unless it should be urged, that the number of people will be thereby much lessened in the Kingdom. This I freely own, and 'twas indeed one principal design in offering it to the world.
>
> — Jonathan Swift

> It may be objected, that many who are capable of the higher pleasures, occasionally, under the influence of temptation, postpone them to the lower. But this is quite compatible with a full appreciation of the intrinsic superiority of the higher.
>
> — John Stuart Mill

The great strategic value of procatalepsis is that it permits one to frame an objection in terms advantageous to one's argument, and answer accordingly:

> The argument is now put forward that we must never use the atomic bomb until, or unless, it has been used against us first. In other words, you must never fire until you have been shot dead. That seems to be a silly thing to say. — Winston Churchill.

REPETITION
epizeuxis, epanalepsis, anadiplosis, diacope

Repetition creates connections and patterns, which aid the speaker's memory and the audience's understanding. This is why it is key to many rhetorical schemes. Rhetoricians have distinguished many varieties. Simple repetition of a word is known as EPIZEUXIS:

> Yada, yada, yada! ... Blah, blah, blah!

EPANALEPSIS refers to ending one clause with the words that begin the next:

> Law enforcement is a protecting arm of civil liberties. Civil liberties cannot exist without law enforcement; law enforcement without civil liberties is a hollow mockery. – J. Edgar Hoover

In ANADIPLOSIS a sentence begins and ends with the same word (or phrase):

> War can only be abolished through war. – Mao Tse-tung

DIACOPE is repetition after an interruption. This example from a legendary master of the pause shows interruption by an epizeuxis:

> Never give in, never give in, never, never, never, never — in nothing, great or small, large or petty — never give in except to convictions of honour and good sense.
>
> – Winston Churchill

REPETITION
conduplicatio, anaphora, epistrophe, symploce

CONDUPLICATIO begins a new clause by repeating a key word or phrase from the last:

> *Those who have never dwelt in tents have no idea either of the charm or of the discomfort of a nomadic existence. The charm is purely romantic, and consequently very soon proves to be fallacious.* — Vita Sackville-West

There are also ways of repeating a word or phrase across any number of sentences or clauses: in ANAPHORA the repetition is at the beginning of each sentence; in EPISTROPHE it is at the end; and in SYMPLOCE it's both. Here is an example of anaphora in poetry:

> *Then none was for a party; / Then all were for the state;*
> *Then the great man helped the poor, / And the poor man loved the great;*
> *Then lands were fairly portioned; / Then spoils were fairly sold:*
> *The Romans were like brothers / In the brave days of old.* — Thomas Macaulay

The five *then*'s draw an implicit contrast between the early days of the Roman Republic with the fallen times in which Macaulay's narrator lives.

In the example of epistrophe below, the reader's attention is focused on the inevitability of the repeated notion, instinct:

> *Metaphysics is the finding of bad reasons for what we believe upon instinct; but to find these reasons is no less an instinct.* — F. H. Bradley

Lastly, here is a simple case of symploce:

> *Being young is not having any money; being young is not minding not having any money.* — Katharine Whitehorn

Parallelism
isocolon and parison

Besides repeating words or phrases, you can repeat the structure but change the words. There are several ways of doing this, but the easiest is Parallelism, the repetition of some formal feature, some number of times:

> *Some books are to be tasted, others to be swallowed, and some few to be chewed and digested.* – Francis Bacon

In Isocolon the repeated feature is the (approximate) number of syllables:

> *Kings will be tyrants from policy when subjects are rebels from principle.* – Edmund Burke

> *Gentlemen, you had my curiosity. But now you have my attention.* – Django Unchained

> *Reading maketh a full man; conference a ready man; and writing an exact man.*
> – Francis Bacon

Burke uses two 9-syllable clauses (on either side of 'when'), Tarantino two 8-syllable sentences (excluding 'Gentlemen'), and Bacon three 7-syllable clauses. These passages also exemplify Parison, a parallelism in which the grammatical structure is repeated. Although isocolon and parison are often combined, they can occur independently:

> *If you think twice before you speak once, you will speak twice the better for it.*

> *As many hands make light work, so several purses make cheap experiments.*

The first of these two quotations from William Penn comprises two grammatically distinct 9-syllable clauses—isocolon without parison; the second line two grammatically parallel clauses of significantly different length—parison without isocolon. Both are parallelisms.

Antithesis and Chiasmus
and antimetabole

Parallelism is a natural complement to ANTITHESIS, a figure that performs the analytically invaluable task of juxtaposing two contrasting ideas:

> The inherent vice of capitalism is the unequal share of blessings; the inherent virtue of socialism is the equal sharing of miseries. – Winston Churchill

> The disillusioned Marxist becomes a fascist; the disillusioned anarchist, a Christian.
> – Evelyn Waugh

These examples both exhibit isocolon and parison, as well as anaphora (*p. 275*)—other figures of repetition can reinforce a parallelism. Parallelism and antithesis may be combined in other ways, such as this *parallelism of antitheses:*

> Education makes a people easy to lead, but difficult to drive; easy to govern, but impossible to enslave. – Lord Brougham

An alternative to parallelism is CHIASMUS, in which the second clause reverses the grammatical order of the first:

> To resist was fatal, and it was impossible to fly. – Edward Gibbon

> Injustice is relatively easy to bear; what stings is justice. – H. L. Mencken

A close relative of chiasmus is ANTIMETABOLE, in which the reverse-order repetition is of words, not (just) grammatical structure:

> Think like a man of action, act like a man of thought. – Henri Bergson

> But if thought corrupts language, language can also corrupt thought. – George Orwell

> With my mind on my money and my money on my mind. – Snoop Dogg

Alliteration and Assonance
sound repetition

History repeats itself, they say, because we forget its lessons. Rhetoric repeats a lot, to make things—including history's lessons—memorable:

> *Now is the time to make real the promises of democracy. Now is the time to rise from the dark and desolate valley of segregation...* – Martin Luther King, Jr.

These lines use macro-repetition in the form of *anaphora* (*p. 275*) ('Now is the time'), but also *micro-repetition*. 'Dark and desolate' is an ALLITERATION— the repetition of a sound, especially a consonant, at the beginning of nearby words in a sequence. Poetry teems with examples:

> *In kitchen cups concupiscent curds.* – Wallace Stevens

Overdone, it can become a vice (PAROEMION) and thus a means of satire:

> *Puffs, Powders, Patches, Bibles, Billet-doux.* – Alexander Pope

Or it can help with memorizing the alphabet or recalling childhoods past:

> *David Donald Doo dreamed a dozen doughnuts and a duck-dog, too.* – Dr Seuss ABC

'Doo' ends with the same stressed vowel as 'too,' illustrating another form of micro-repetition, RHYME, more exactly INTERNAL RHYME (inline).

ASSONANCE consists in the repetition of the same or similar vowel sound in the stressed syllables of nearby words, as in 'fun in the sun,' or:

> *On a proud round cloud in white high night* – e e cummings

Micro-repetitions like these set the tone for the delivery of a speech, and the mood for its reception. And they are highly effective, for they are based on body rhythms—on walking, breathing, or a heart beating.

Onomatopoeia
a zizzer-zazzer-zuz

ONOMATOPOEIA is the kind of name that a thing would give itself, if a thing could name itself; it imitates the sound it names.

> It's sort of *whack, whir, wheeze, whine / Sputter, splat, squirt, scrape,*
>
> *Clink, clank, clunk, clatter / Crash, bang, beep, buzz...* – Todd Rundgren

Onomatopoeia is a powerful tool of linguistic invention, and rhetorically, it is used for both copiousness and brevity. COPIOUSNESS (Lat. *copia*), or a great abundance of ways and means of arguing, was the goal of traditional rhetorical instruction. Today, for better or worse, we tend towards brevity, and onomatopoeia zips right to the point:

> **Clunk Click Every Trip.** – UK seat-belt promotion
>
> *Plop, plop, fizz, fizz, what a relief it is.* – Alka Seltzer slogan

Add some micro- and macro-repetition (alliteration, rhyme, epizeuxis, etc.), and you get very special sound effects:

> *Once upon a time and a very good time it was there was a moocow coming down along the road and this moocow that was coming down along the road met a nicens little boy named baby tuckoo.* – James Joyce

Amplification

auxesis, climax, congeries, synonymia, bdelygmia

A critical goal of rhetoric is to focus attention on what you take to be most important. Strategies for achieving this are known as AMPLIFICATION. One example is AUXESIS, the substitution of stronger for weaker terms:

> I have brought before you, judges, not a thief, but a plunderer; not an adulterer, but a ravisher; not a mere committer of sacrilege, but the enemy of all religious observance and all holy things. – Cicero

This quote also exhibits CLIMAX, a sequence of increasing force, as in:

> Most people tire of a lecture in ten minutes; clever people can do it in five. Sensible people never go to lectures at all. – Stephen Leacock

These climaxes are loose tricolons (*p. 281*), but a climax may have more than three clauses. It is often most effective when combined with other figures:

> [Our aim] is victory, victory at all costs, victory in spite of all terror, victory, however long and hard the road may be; for without victory, there is no survival. – W. Churchill

> Peace is a daily, a weekly, a monthly process, gradually changing opinions, slowly eroding old barriers, quietly building new structures. – John F. Kennedy

Amplification is the main route to stylistic and argumentative abundance (*see copia, p. 279*). It often takes the form of a list, or CONGERIES. Where the items in the list are synonymous, or nearly so, the congeries is a SYNONYMIA:

> Stop you vandals! You home wreckers! You half-crazed visigoths! You pinstriped barbarians! – Douglas Adams

This, as a congeries of insults, has its own delightful name: BDELYGMIA.

TRICOLON
three part harmony

Good things come in threes: somehow, groups of three always seem more natural than pairs or larger groups. This is sometimes called the *Rule of Three*: if you have to have more than one thing, aim for three. In rhetoric, the corresponding figure is TRICOLON, a combination of three related items:

> A product of the untalented, sold by the unprincipled to the utterly bewildered. – Al Capp

> She was a woman of mean understanding, little information, and uncertain temper.
> – Jane Austen

Ideally, the three parts of a tricolon should be grammatically identical and equal in length, as in the most famous of Latin tricolons, Julius Caesar's *Veni, vidi, vici.* This is hard to do in English: "I came, I saw, I conquered" doesn't quite make it, since 'conquered' has one too many syllables. Here, a noted tricolon enthusiast comes close to a perfect classical example:

> Our generation's task is to make these words, these rights, these values—of life, liberty, and the pursuit of happiness—real. – Barack Obama (recalling Jefferson)

HYPERBATON
anastrophe, parenthesis, hysteron proteron

HYPERBATON is the generic term for a series of schemes that alter the standard or expected word order in a sentence. Its name is Greek for 'transposition.' In English, where word order is very important for conveying meaning, even small changes can have great effects. Given the standard *Subject–Verb –Object,* or *Subject–Copula–Complement* order, hyperbaton can be as simple as the inversion of subject-object, or subject-complement positions:

> *Clouded, this boy's future is.* – Yoda, Star Wars

A small-scale, single-word swap like this is often called ANASTROPHE (Lat. *inversio,* 'reversal'). It is used for emphasis, contrast, or both:

> *Some rise by sin, and some by virtue fall.* – William Shakespeare

> *Talent, Mr. Micawber has; capital, Mr. Micawber has not.* – Charles Dickens

Anastrophe can sometimes occur as a split-and-swap:

> *One swallow does not a summer make, nor one fine day.* – Aristotle

Splitting the verbal phrase 'does not make' and interposing an object has become clichéd as a shorthand argument against generalization, as it stresses the difference between a sign or property of a thing and the thing itself:

> *Stone walls do not a prison make, / Nor iron bars a cage;*
> *Minds innocent and quiet take / That for an hermitage.* – Richard Lovelace

Note also the inversion of the standard adjective-noun order ('minds innocent and quiet') for poetic and emphatic purposes, which is another typical form of anastrophe in English.

HYSTERON PROTERON, or the 'preposterous' scheme (as an Elizabethan rhetorician called it), is also a type of transposition that operates by inversion. It amounts to putting what comes later—logically or chronologically—first, such as the effect before the cause, the cart before the horse, etc.:

Let us die and rush into battle. – Virgil   **Find first, seek later.** – Jean Cocteau

Like *paradox* (*p. 268*), this scheme posits some truth beyond the absurdity (battle readiness is a readiness to die, invention cannot be premeditated). More often, however, hysteron proteron remains a logical fallacy:

We must explain the force of the horse by the motion of the cart-wheels, and hystero-proterise with a vengeance! – Samuel Taylor Coleridge

Other hyperbata disrupt syntactical flow by *insertion*, not by inversion. PARENTHESIS is the most frequent. It consists in interrupting the normal flow of the sentence by inserting some supplementary piece of information (a qualification, description, explanation, etc.), and placing it—as we just did and are now doing—within brackets, dashes, or commas:

Yours is the Earth and everything's that's in it,
And—which is more—you'll be a Man, my son! – Rudyard Kipling

HYSTERON PROTERON NEDDY!

WIT AND WORDPLAY
antanaclasis, syllepsis, polyptoton, paronomasia

G. K. Chesterton once quipped, "It is easy to be solemn; it is so hard to be frivolous." That's because WIT is a verbal and intellectual acuity that goes a long way by the shortest route (Aristotle called it "educated insolence"). It is not to be taken lightly, as any Shakespearean fool will tell you: "Better a witty fool, than a foolish wit."

WORDPLAY, the clever or playful use of words, can be witty (rhetorically apt) or foolish (rhetorically crude). Timing (*kairos, p. 248*), subject, audience, and goal are things to ponder before using your pun gun. Wordplay is not limited to puns or the four figures below. It also requires you to know your grammar, and be aware that language works thanks to—not despite—ambiguity, thanks to POLYSEMY (one word, multiple meanings), HOMONYMY (different words, same look and sound), and HOMOPHONY (different words, similar sound). If language were a mechanism, ambiguity would be its play or leeway. Witty wordplay uses it to make language do more work; foolish wordplay abuses it, and makes language break down.

Take ANTANACLASIS, the repetition of a word in two different senses:

> *...if we don't hang together, by Heavens we shall hang separately.* – Frederick Reynolds

The stated *antithesis* (*p. 277*) between 'together' and 'separately' draws attention to the play (polysemy) of 'hanging': solidarity *vs.* execution.

SYLLEPSIS too exploits polysemy, but elides instead of repeating, and makes one polysemic word (usually a verb) govern two or more objects. Structurally, it resembles *zeugma* (*p. 271*), but also stages a clash among the word's meanings, by yoking together cats and dogs, as it were:

> *Miss Bolo ... went straight home in a flood of tears, and a sedan chair.* – C. Dickens

Or stain her honour, or her new brocade, / ... Or lose her heart, or necklace, at a ball ... – Alexander Pope

POLYPTOTON repeats a word in various grammatical forms (*cognates*). Here's a complex polyptoton, playing off of the basic form '*x*-verb the *x*-noun', with a *double antanaclasis* at the end:

> *There are two types of people: those that talk the talk and those that walk the walk. People who walk the walk sometimes talk the talk but most times they don't talk at all, 'cause they walkin'. Now, people who talk the talk, when it comes time for them to walk the walk, you know what they do? They talk people like me into walkin' for them.* – Hustle & Flow

PARONOMASIA, or punning, consists in using words that sound alike but differ in meaning:

> *Immanuel doesn't pun; he Kant.* – Oscar Wilde

> *I am General Ising. And he's not an army man, either.* – Alfred Hitchcock

Puns use homophony—'can't'/'Kant' (the philosopher's last name), 'General Ising'/'generalising'—and are often *ironic* (*p. 258*), like punning on Kant's alleged incapacity to pun.

Epicrisis
anamnesis & allusion

There are very few dedicated figures of *ethos*, or *pathos*, because any trope or scheme, if well-built and aptly used, will make you cut a good figure, and raise your rhetorical credibility; many can also be used to create a favorable mood for the reception of your argument. EPICRISIS is one of the rare figures of *ethos*. It consists in invoking the authority of past authors, by citing, directly quoting from, and commenting on them:

> ... Archimedes, in explaining the principles of the lever, was said to have declared to his friends: "Give me a place where I can stand — and I shall move the world." My fellow inhabitants of this planet: Let us take our stand here in this Assembly of nations. And let us see if we, in our own time, can move the world to a just and lasting peace. – John F. Kennedy

ANAMNESIS does the same, except it quotes from memory:

> Archimedes promised to move the Earth if they would give him a point of support ... but in order to move the Earth it is still necessary to build the levers. – Leon Trotsky

Finally, ALLUSION is a passing reference to events, personalities, or sources that are common knowledge in a community. Archimedes' lever was so popular with revolutionaries of all times, especially American ones, that a mere allusion to it sufficed:

> The good opinion of mankind, like the lever of Archimedes, with the given fulcrum, moves the world. – Thomas Jefferson

Certain audiences will have recognized Kennedy's epicrisis as an allusion to Jefferson's allusion, with the U.N. as the 'given fulcrum' for world peace.

APOSIOPESIS
at a loss for words

Rhetoric offers many ways to arrange ideas and words, but sometimes silence is just as, if not more effective. This figure is called APOSIOPESIS, and has many uses. Sometimes the speaker simply has no idea how to continue:

It's bad enough when the bride decides she's got to join a cult in Devon, but as for this…

– Candia McWilliam

Sometimes it is impossible to continue:

The philosopher furiously hurling philosophical imprecations: 'What do you mean you're willing to be irrational? You shouldn't be irrational because…' – Robert Nozick

Nozick's philosopher is in a logical bind: he can't complete the sentence because he would need to give a reason for giving reasons. More mundanely, long lists can trail off into silence when no further details are required:

It makes sense to ask: 'Do I really love her, or am I only pretending to myself?' and the process of introspection is the calling up of memories; of imagined possible situations, and of the feelings that one would have if… – Ludwig Wittgenstein

(Is there a trace of *pathos* in the notoriously ascetic Wittgenstein's words?) An aposiopesis can also forestall a potential disclosure,

I sense something; a presence I have not felt since… – Darth Vader, *Star Wars*

or be used in anger, as in the famous threat from classical literature: Quos *ego…*, with which Virgil's angry Neptune chastises the winds. Literally, this translates as Whom, I…, but approximates to Moe Howard's Why, I *oughta…* (or Homer Simpson's Why, you little…). The threat is all the more effective (and broadcastable) for not being made explicit.

PATHOLOGIES OF STYLE
words, words, words

Style begins to suffer the minute it takes itself too seriously. When rhetoric omits the other canons (*p. 244*), trusting only in style, it gives up persuasion. The minute style is everything, style is nothing: it becomes mere ornament, often kitsch. In general, over-reliance on style misfires. All figures, if overdone or used inopportunely, can fail. Stylistic faults are usually called *vices*, in recognition of rhetoric's enduring bond with *ethics*. But we can also think of them as *pathologies*, grouped by specific symptoms.

In the *Too Many Words* category, we find style disorders like BATTOLOGY (tedious repetition), PLEONASM (word redundancy: 'free gift'), MACROLOGIA (longwindedness, or Polonius syndrome: see *Hamlet* 2.2.86–94), and TAUTOLOGIA (a failed *synonymia*, *p. 280*). For example:

> *I needed a new beginning, so I decided to pay a social visit to a personal friend with whom I share the same mutual objectives and who is one of the most unique individuals I have ever personally met. The end result was an unexpected surprise. When I reiterated again to her the fact that I needed a fresh start, she said I was exactly right… Etc.* George Carlin, "Count the Superfluous Redundant Pleonastic Tautologies"

Such disorders occur when *amplification* (*p. 280*) and *repetition* (*pp. 274–5*) go wrong, or too far. They often manifest as PURPLE PROSE—first diagnosed by Horace in *Ars Poetica*—and BATHOS (bombast, usually anticlimactic). Such is Signora Psyche Zenobia's predicament:

> *What a host of gloomy recollections will ever and anon be awakened in the mind of genius and imaginative contemplation, especially of a genius doomed to the everlasting, and eternal, and continual, and, as one might say, the— continued— yes, the continued and continuous, bitter, harassing, disturbing, and, if I may be*

allowed the expression, the very disturbing influence of the serene, and godlike,
and heavenly, and exalted, and elevated, and, purifying effect of what may be
rightly termed the most enviable, the most truly enviable — nay! the most benignly
beautiful, the most deliciously ethereal, and, as it were, the most pretty (if I may
use so bold an expression) thing (pardon me, gentle reader!) in the world — but
I am always led away by my feelings. In such a mind, I repeat, what a host of
recollections are stirred up by a trifle! Edgar Allan Poe

The *Wrong Words* category includes BARBARISM (use of foreign words to impress), SORAISMUS (mixing languages), SOLECISM (grammar mistakes typical of a particular sociolect: 'he ain't'), MALAPROPISM (e.g. Mrs Malaprop in Sheridan's *The Rivals*: 'He is the very pineapple of politeness'), BUSHISM (potent mix of other disorders in this category, not to be 'misunderestimated'), etc.

Perhaps the easiest to spot are the disorders of metaphor, which are induced by overreach (*catachresis, p. 255*), or mixing—wittingly or not:

Let your fingers do the walking!. Yellow Pages slogan

[Labour ministers] are going about the country stirring up complacency.

William Whitelaw

FROM COPIA TO COPY
rhetoric in the age of advertising

There is both awe and odium to rhetoric's history—and everything in between. An all-too-human institution, it began as a course of instruction for aspiring politicians in ancient Greece and soon became a lucrative trade, jealously opposed by Plato. Then came the Romans: Cicero and Quintilian. They made rhetoric ethically and pedagogically respectable—a must for a well-rounded education, not just a political career. *Rhetorica ad Herennium*, a pillar of medieval schooling, was based on their teachings. And later on their writings sparked the humanist revival of rhetoric in the Renaissance, which laid the cornerstone of modern liberal arts education.

Rhetoric's reach has always been a sore point, and Renaissance humanists disagreed too. Erasmus made *copia*, an abundance of persuasive means and skills, into its goal and crowning achievement, whereas Ramus restricted it to the study of style and delivery (*see the Five Canons, page 244*). But *copia* was more of an ideal than a calculable end, and the 17th and 18th centuries sided with Ramus: rhetoric was again cut off from logic and further reduced to a classification of figures of style ('tropes'). Tropology, mocked by the Romantics in the 19th century, led to rhetoric's institutional decline in the 20th.

So what of rhetoric today? It seems all but gone from curricula in the English-speaking world. Yet, rhetorical instruction continues, albeit in bits and under other names: communication, critical thinking, law, literature, marketing, public relations, etc. Even the sciences rely on it: models, some say, are scientific metaphors. In other words, rhetoric is dead, long live rhetoric! And that is just as well. For our pleonastically 'global' world is ruled by the 24-hour news cycle and total advertising. It is a world in which we are constantly being sold something, or simply sold ('*If you're not paying for it, you're it,*' is a principle of product marketing). A world, in short, in which *epideictic rhetoric* trumps the other two species—*forensic* and *deliberative* (*see page 248*)—on which journalism and political discourse traditionally rely.

Forensic rhetoric deals with the facts of the matter, with how this matter—whatever it may be—has come to pass; while deliberative rhetoric looks for the best course of action going forward. In contrast, epideictic rhetoric is all about advertising, (self-)display, praise and blame, about the values 'we' share and others do not. It is the species of rhetoric that 'tribal talk' is done in, as one author put it. It is also the most myopic kind of rhetoric, which never strays far from the present ('*I'm loving it*'), even when invoking the future ('*The future is bright. The future is Orange*'). It shuns reasons in favour of character and emotional appeals (*see p. 213 & p. 242*). Argument shrinks to slogan, as copy pushes out humanistic copia. Total advertising's allure, with its restricted and constricting rhetoric, is that it has one very simple answer—consumption—to all the complex issues of our world. That is also its fatal flaw.

BOOK VI

Above: Virtue Victorious over Vice. Sketch by Parmigianino (Girolamo Francesco Maria Mazzola), Florence, Italy, c. 1520. Opposite: Temperance, surrounded by the seven liberal arts; clockwise from lower left: Arithmetic, Music, Rhetoric, Astronomy, Geometry, Logic, and Grammar. Engraved by Philips Galle [1537–1612] from an original drawing by Pieter Bruegel the Elder [1525–1569], Netherlands.

ETHICS

THE ART OF CHARACTER

Gregory R. Beabout

with additional content by Mike Hannis

Above: Virtue, proceeded by Folly and followed by Glory. Engraving by Giulio Bonasone [1498–1580], Bologna, Italy. Courtesy of the Warburg Institute, London.

INTRODUCTION

Y OU CAN'T learn ethics from a book. To learn honesty, one must practice telling the truth. To learn justice, one must act in a just manner. The same is true of generosity, courage, kindness, patience, and all the virtues. This applies to any worthwhile complicated human endeavor. To learn to play the piano, you have to play the piano. To learn to play basketball, you need actual experience with a ball and a hoop. To learn to drive an automobile you'll need to get behind the wheel.

So, in cases where learning comes with practice, why *are* there instruction books? Besides, isn't ethics fundamentally different from skill acquisition? One can be masterfully accomplished at basketball or driving without being ethical. A trained physician has the skill to heal or to wound, and those who are artful in grammar, logic, and rhetoric can inspire or manipulate. Skill at using words, whether on the page, in one's mind, or in speech, seems entirely separate from ethics.

Or is it? Those who develop technical mastery in any domain eventually are faced with questions of deep purpose. How should one's skills be used? What goals are worth pursuing?

The ancient Greeks used the term *ethike* in debating how to live a good and worthwhile life. Tracing their arguments about the art of character and learning the history of moral philosophy won't make you ethical. Certainly reading this book on the good life won't make you richer or thinner or sexier. However, it just might help you on your journey to approach the authentic and ancient task of ethics: to craft a beautiful life.

WHAT IS ETHICS?
like this, not that

Ethics is an ancient term with a Greek pedigree. The philosopher Aristotle noted that, in Greek, *ethike* has meanings that are complex and ambiguous. Two Greek letters—*eta* and *epsilon*—are similar to the English letter *e* (*eta* has a faintly longer *ê*-sound than *epsilon*), and the Greek words *ethike* and *ethos* can be pronounced or spelled with either Greek *e*, slightly altering the meaning.

Spelled one way, *ethos* refers to the farm building where animals are kept. For example, in Homer's *Iliad*, the word *ethos* is used to designate the horse stable. Horses that run away tend to return (eventually) to this secure, stable location. Spelled the other way, *ethos* is a character trait, a personal quality that is reliable and persistent. In unusual circumstances, one may act out of character, but generally, *ethos* is stable, both in an individual life and in a community.

An excellent character trait (*ethike arête*) is an acquired personal quality that an excellent person "has". The Romans, seeking to translate into Latin the idea of a trait one has, called it a *habitus*. The excellent person "has it". In English, the meaning devolved; we tend to think that a habit is rote, routine, and perhaps sub-rational. That's not what the ancients meant at all. To be ethical is to have formed one's life in such a way that, through deliberate excellent actions, one has confirmed and consolidated those qualities of character and intellect that make for a worthwhile and beautiful human existence.

In conversation with Socrates, the military general Laches expressed the ambivalence we often feel about "ethics talk". As Laches put it:

When I hear someone discussing virtue and wisdom, especially a true man worthy of the topic, I am delighted beyond measure . . . but when a man's words and actions do not agree, it annoys me. – [88d-e]

Kant once quipped that two things provoke the most wonder and awe: the starry sky above and the moral law within. Humans have long huddled around the warm glow of a shared fire to trade tales of trial and truth that shed light on the eternal questions: Where are we going? Why? What makes for a good life? How does a human live well?

Many ancient stories contain sage advice about survival and human relations. They involve familiar stock characters: the mighty hero, the beautiful but boasting mother, the weak king, inseparable brothers, a jealous wife, the kind gentle shepherd, the rash fighter, and so forth. We meet a similar cast of characters in star-lore, fables, fairy tales, and folksongs. These provide a sort of field guide for social life. "Be aware of this one; be like that one; not like that one."

At its ancient core, ethics is not primarily about words or theories or knowledge or rules. It is the art of character. Reflection on the art of character and the requirements of conscience begins with and draws from the characters we've met during evening story time, and with the wonder that comes from gazing at the heavens.

CHARACTER AND CODES
virtues or rules?

Many ancient vows, such as the Hippocratic Oath (*see page 345*), involve a pledge to live according to a "*set of traits*". In contrast, contemporary "codes of ethics" tend to focus on specific *actions*, rather than considering a person's whole life and character. Modern codes are almost always framed as a "*set of rules*".

The terms "ethics" and "morality" have a complicated history. *Ethos* and *ethike* in Greek refer to character, not rules; Cicero translated these into Latin as *moralis*. Until the Renaissance, studies of ethics or morality focused on character formation and development, but during the European Enlightenment, philosophers began to narrow the moral debate to actions, aiming to discover the rational basis for determining right action, later focusing on either utility or duty (*see pp. 340–342*).

In the early 20th century, academic debates about *normative ethics* (discussion of which acts or action-types are right or wrong) gave way to discussions of *meta-ethics* (theoretical questions about the meaning of moral terms, the nature of moral judgements, and whether these are rationally defensible).

Of course, the ancient world had rules too. *The Code of Hammurabi* had 282 laws, including many that now seem problematic, such as "an eye for an eye, a tooth for a tooth." Certain passages resemble the

Bala

"Are you capable of distinguishing right from wrong?"

"Can you give me a hint?"

Mosaic Law and rules advanced by the Hittites, Assyrians, and others. Such lists prohibit and prescribe actions regarding trade, theft, killing, slander, the distribution of food, the duties of workers, and so on.

"WHEN'S HAPPY HOUR?"

Problems arise when ethics is conceived only in terms of rules. Life is complex, so no set of rules can be specific enough to cover every circumstance. A rule-based approach tends to encourage searching for loopholes and "gaming the system". Rules can conflict, and often require interpretation. If ethics is nothing but rules, then further rules will be needed to decide what to do when rules and interpretations conflict. Such problems show why it can be seen as better to understand ethics as having to do, first and foremost, with character. Actions shape character, including the action of following good rules.

> The law prescribes that the works of a courageous person be done (for example, that a soldier not break rank or flee), as well as those of a temperate person (for example, not committing adultery or wanton aggression) and those of a gentle person (for example, not striking people or verbally abusing them). Well-formed laws prescribe some things and forbid others. – Aristotle [1129b19-21]

Ethics consists in learning to live well. It is a quest to develop and excel in the traits needed to flourish, obeying good rules while acquiring the wisdom to distinguish between good and bad ones.

SOCRATES
stinging criticism

When he was young, Socrates [470–399 BC] studied the natural world, puzzling to understand the earth and the heavens. As he matured, his focus shifted. The logical methods of rational argumentation he learned from the "nature philosophers" were redirected to an inquiry about how to live an excellent human life.

Plato recounts that this change occurred after Socrates's impetuous friend Chaerephon asked the Pythian prophetess whether anyone was wiser than Socrates. Challenged by the answer that there is "none wiser", Socrates set off to seek someone wiser, meeting rhetoricians, politicians, and writers. Finding many of these fellow citizens full of fakery, he persisted in asking awkward questions (describing himself as a 'gadfly'), and unmasking those who claimed to know what they did not.

> *He among you is the wisest who knows that his wisdom is really worth nothing at all.* – Socrates, attrib. by Plato [Apology 23 b]

His stinging attacks were a nuisance, so charges were brought against him. At his trial, he defended himself by comparing the city of Athens to a great racehorse that had become sluggish until stung awake by his questioning. He exhorted his fellow citizens to share his quest for virtue, and by seeking to practice the virtues, to stir up a better life.

Socrates discovered only what is available to every reflective adult: the quest for authentic self-understanding involves acknowledging one's limitations. He engaged in dialogue as part of a life of honest self-examination, in order to better himself and his community. To fix your eyes on the stars takes focus, but it is harder to gaze intently into your soul.

Above: Socrates, whose role was, according to Plato, "to sting people and whip them into a fury, all in the service of truth," is eventually found guilty of impiety and corrupting the youth of Athens. He follows his rule of obedience to the law and carries out his own execution by drinking hemlock. 19th-century print.

Most of us blink and look away.

The poet, politician, and rhetorician who brought charges against Socrates perhaps worried that their questions and criticisms would destabilize the social institutions crucial to their power and prestige. The three accusers were part of the new class of "knowledge workers" in Greece's golden age, master wordsmiths who claimed expertise in a skill advertised as crucial for success. Socrates suspected them of caring more about wealth and power than character, conscience, and the common good.

The unexamined life is not worth living. – Socrates, attrib. by Plato [*Apology* 37e]

Understanding Socrates is not difficult. Living like Socrates is.

PLATO'S CAVE
shadow and light

Socrates left no written works, but his followers took on the task of *paideia*, the moral and cultural education of Greek citizens preparing for good leadership. One such follower, Isocrates [436–338 BC], is sometimes called the father of liberal education, because his school emphasized grammar, dialectical reasoning, and rhetoric as disciplines needed to excel in speech and to shape virtuous souls. Isocrates taught that good speaking (*eu legein*) is allied to good prudential action (*eu prattein*), and hoped that his fine written speeches might promote civic education.

The cross–town rival to the school of Isocrates was the Academy, founded by Plato. We have no textbooks from Plato's curriculum. Instead, we have dialogues, including Plato's masterful classic, the *Republic*, in which Socrates is depicted engaging in a wide-ranging conversation that includes a plan for educating a just soul. In one of the most famous sections, the "Allegory of the Cave," Socrates presents what he calls a "parable of the soul's education".

> *Imagine humans dwelling in a cave from childhood, fettered, only able to look in one direction at images on a wall.* – Plato [514a]

One prisoner is released. He turns to see a track of puppets, and behind it a fire. Realizing he has been staring at shadows, he ascends for the first time out of the cave, where he is overcome by the light of the upper world. Looking down, he notices shadows on the ground. As his eyes adjust, he is able to gaze upward, observing actual plants and animals, then the moon and stars, until finally he glimpses the overwhelming brilliant illumination of the sun. Recognizing that his life in the cave had been

Above: Plato's Cave. A lantern casts shadows of puppets on to a wall. Prisoners, living in the dark, see only the shadows on the wall, and mistake them for real things. Philosophers, meanwhile, stand beneath the lantern, considering the idea that they too may be but shadows, cast by a greater light.

a shadowy imprisonment in illusions, he feels compelled to return to enlighten his friends below of the dazzling upper world. This, of course, does not go well.

The art of guiding a soul toward the highest good, according to Plato, involves creating the conditions for a transformation of perspective, from the shadowy world of appearances (in which one is attracted to the shifting allure of wealth, pleasure, and power) to an increasingly deeper, more penetrating, enlightened vision of that "ever fixed mark," the highest good.

> *The journey upwards is the ascent of the soul. The last thing to be seen, and hardly seen, is the idea of the good.* – Plato [517b]

NICOMACHEAN ETHICS
crafting character

The most important ethics text ever published isn't really a book. Aristotle's *Nicomachean Ethics* [dated c.330BC] has been studied for millennia, but there is no reliable account of the development of its contents. Almost certainly, the text is based on lecture notes modified throughout Aristotle's career. If so, it is, as Alasdair MacIntyre observed, "the most brilliant set of lecture notes ever written".

Several ancient sources suggest that "Nicomachus" was the name of Aristotle's son, to whom the text may have been dedicated. Perhaps he played an editorial role, transforming the lectures into book form.

Aristotle says the lectures are "not suited for a young man". Instead, he addresses himself to a person experienced in life, a listener poised to take a leadership role in the life of a community. Such a person was likely well brought up, with a desire to pursue the common good, and in possession of a sense of what it is to live a beautiful, meaningful life. It is not a book intended for ethical theorists.

> *The present inquiry does not aim at theoretical knowledge, for we are inquiring not to know what goodness is, but to become good.* – Aristotle [1103b27]

For twenty years Aristotle was a student and then a young teacher at Plato's Academy, where he focused on rhetoric (*see pages 238-240*). After Plato died, Aristotle left Athens to spend several years doing biological field studies in the Greek islands, collecting and categorizing specimens of plants and animals. Against that background, the *Nicomachean Ethics* can be read as a "field guide" to human character, and this in two senses:

First and foremost, Aristotle aims to build up in his listener those qualities of character and intellect needed to flourish as a member of the human species. As Aristotle observed, the human being is a *zōon politikon*, a speaking animal whose powers of life are actualized not by mere instinct, but in a community through the development of language and the realization of rational powers of deliberation, judgement, and responsible action. Accordingly, the hero of Aristotle's story is the person of practical wisdom.

Secondly, the *Nicomachean Ethics* contains a familiar cast of characters: the boaster, the ironist, the boor, the buffoon, the coward, the rash man, the generous bountiful person, the glutton, the fool, the gentle one, the hothead, the unjust, the shameless, and many others (*see Theophrastus' Characters*, pages 356-7). Joining the conversation with Aristotle, we are invited to reflect upon which traits of character to purge from our habits, and which are integral to a beautiful life worth crafting.

Above: A procession of Shakespearean characters, representing a range of character traits. Which of these traits should we keep, and which should we purge? London, 1769.

Becoming Responsible

preconditions of virtue

In the *Nicomachean Ethics*, Aristotle presumes a listener who is a decent person of judgement with a well-rounded background, one who is able to discern which kind of knowledge is suitable for the context at hand.

> *It is the mark of an educated person to look for precision in each class of things just so far as the nature of the subject admits; it is evidently equally foolish to accept probable reasoning from a mathematician and to demand from a rhetorician scientific proofs.* – Aristotle [1094b25]

The subject of ethics presupposes an engaged participant who takes responsibility for their actions, the formation of their character, and their life. Our actions are up to us, at least some of the time, and to some extent; and although each of us is given specific tendencies as part of our biology and upbringing, our character-development depends in part on our voluntary actions and deliberate decisions.

We tend to praise and blame people for their voluntary actions, while feeling sympathy and pity for counter-voluntary ones which may result from *force* or *lack of knowledge*. Force can be either physical: "*I trod on your toe because the wind blew me*", or psychological: "*Threatened by violence, I acted strangely*". Lack of knowledge can involve either ignorance of relevant particularities: "*I didn't know it was your apple I ate*", or relevant principles: "*No one ever told me it's wrong to eat other people's apples*". Negligence, of particularities or principles, is excusable only when it is not voluntary, and culpable when it comes from lack of due care.

Decisions craft character. Each decision a person makes is a voluntary, all-things-considered judgement of how to act, something practical to which they are committed. In cases where the outcome is undetermined, unclear, or uncertain, deliberation will be required, involving attention to relevant particularities, multiple perspectives, and pertinent principles and purposes.

Living an unhealthy life will lead to physical deterioration, and in the same way a character can become 'sick' by doing actions that are greedy, self-centered, or thoughtless.

We are each responsible for our actions and (with some qualifications) our character states. Acting depends on us, and so does not acting. By each decision, each yes or no, we are ourselves responsible, to some extent, for who we become.

Above: Castle of Virtue, Italian, 16th C. Virtues need to be developed and protected.

HAPPINESS
and the good life

What makes for a good life? The poor may imagine it is money; the ill, health. In modern consumer cultures, happiness has become tied to getting whatever you want whenever you want it, so is viewed as a psychological state which "happens" when preferences are satisfied.

> People seem to get their suppositions about happiness and the good life from their own lives. – Aristotle [1095b15]

For the classical philosophers, the question "What is *eudaimonia?*"— or the Latin equivalent, "What is *beatitudo?*"—was a matter of prime importance. Rather than moment-to-moment experiences "happening" and bringing short-term pleasure, happiness is about the entire narrative of a life, unfolding through multiple chapters.

> The ultimate end of human acts is eudaimonia, happiness in the sense of living well. – Hannah Arendt

Considered this way, happiness has the quality of a goal, desirable in itself rather than for the sake of something else. Human purposes are often nested within deeper goals, and even when not quite aware of the motive, humans often act to aim at a target. Aristotle suggests that our ultimate target is not a quantifiable product like a trophy for the winner, but a quality of self-actualization in a complete life.

> He is happy who lives in accordance with complete virtue and is sufficiently equipped with external goods, not for some chance period, but throughout a complete life.
> – Aristotle [1101a10]

Accordingly, happiness is not preference-satisfaction; *eudaimonia* is a life of flourishing or well-being fitted to humanity, and especially to what is best in people. This raises a series of questions:

- *What qualities of character constitute a happy life?*
- *What dispositions count as virtues, not only in a social role, but in a human life?*
- *How is virtue distinguished from vice?*

Puzzling through these questions follows upon an understanding of happiness as well-being, and brings us closer to our ultimate goal:

Since happiness is an activity of soul in accordance with complete virtue, we must consider the nature of virtue, for perhaps this will help us see better the nature of happiness. – Aristotle [1102a1]

Above: Happiness—a Wedding Feast, Wenceslas Hollar [1607–77], after Pieter Bruegel the Elder.

Two Kinds of Goals
performance and results

Aristotle begins the *Nicomachean Ethics* by drawing an important distinction between two kinds of goals.

> *Some are activities. Others are products apart from the activities.* – [1094a3]

INSTRUMENTAL ACTIVITY aims at a specific end product: a carpenter builds in order to produce a house, and a painter's brushstrokes are directed toward a completed painting.

AUTOTELIC ACTIVITY, by contrast, is pursued for its own sake, often with a sense of internal purpose: the goal of the dancer is to dance. Autotelic activities include those pursued in the spirit of play, such as games which ignite energy and personal passion.

> *Play is a uniquely adaptive act, not subordinate to some other adaptive act, but with a special function of its own in human experience.* – Huizinga, Homo Ludens

> *The mystique of rock climbing is climbing; you get to the top of a rock glad it's over but really wish it would go on forever. The justification of climbing is climbing, like the justification of poetry is writing …* – Csikszentmihalyi, Flow

The two goals are well illustrated in Alasdair MacIntyre's story of a child, initially incited to learn the game of chess by bribes of candy, who finally becomes motivated instead by internal goals of analytical skill, strategic imagination, and competitive intensity. The mastery of any social practice involves a shift from mere results-oriented given-ends (where moral shortcuts can seem attractive), to a passion for performance-oriented guiding-ends. Research suggests that this shift strengthens integrity of character. Psychologist Martin Seligman identifies five elements crucial for human well-being:

P is positive emotion, E is engagement, R is relationships, M is meaning and A is accomplishment. Those are the five elements of what free people choose to do. Pretty much everything else is in service of one or more of these goals.

– Martin Seligman, Flourish

Building on this, Mihaly Csikszentmihalyi (*quoted opposite*) describes optimal human experience in a similar manner to Aristotle's description of *eudaimonia*: a musician who loses herself in her music, an athlete who is completely present in the experience of intense competition, or a scientist immersed in the investigation of a complex problem. In each case skills and challenges tend to be higher than average. The Taoist scholar Chuang Tzu described this as "walking without touching the ground" or "flowing", while the Stoics described the goal of human happiness as *eurhoia biou*: a smooth flow of life (*see too page 380*).

Left: Chinese philosopher Chuang Tzu, 4th century BC. Chuang Tzu and Hui Shi were walking beside a waterfall when Chuang Tzu said, "See how the minnows come out and dart around where they please! That's what fish really love!" Hui Shi said, "You're not a fish — how do you know what fish enjoy?" Chuang Tzu said "I know it by standing here beside the river."

Excellence of Character
cultivating virtue

Good character, like the acquisition of a skill, is developed through repeated deliberate decisions. Although some people are gifted with good looks, health, a good upbringing, and so forth, none of these fortunes guarantee good character—even the gifted can make a mess of their lives.

So what is excellence of character (Greek: *arête*; Latin: *virtus*)? Is it a feeling? Not quite. While some virtues refine feelings, there is a difference, since feelings can come and go, but excellence of character, once established through deliberate decisions, becomes relatively fixed as a stable trait. Is virtue a capacity? Not really. A child who is naturally outgoing has the capacity to grow up friendly, or perhaps annoying. In that way, the capacity of a child might be described as a sort of "first nature", while good character, once formed, becomes "second nature".

The virtues are acquired first by imitating those more excellent than oneself. By deliberately repeating and perfecting the good actions of an exemplary model, excellence of character is confirmed and consolidated in one's choices. We become what we repeatedly do.

> *Those things we have to learn before we can do them we learn by doing: humans become carpenters by building houses, and harpists by playing the harp. We become just by practicing just actions, self-controlled by exercising self-control, and courageous by performing acts of courage.* – Aristotle [1103a32]

A virtue is a disposition, an acquired personal quality that persists across time in various contexts. While Homer and the epic storytellers spoke frequently of physical virtues (the strength of Odysseus, the beauty of Helen), the excellences praised by ethicists are qualities of character.

These excellences involve a "balanced harmony" between too much and too little. As with physical exercise, where excess and deficiency can each harm, finding the "golden mean" is context-sensitive with variations relative to the person(s) involved:

> Virtue is the sort of disposition that is concerned with choice, lying in a mean of the
> sort relative to the context, determined by a rational principle, and by that principle
> by which a person of practical wisdom would determine it. – [1107a1]

So, for example, generosity is a virtue whereby a person is disposed to open-handedly offer money, time, or help to others without either acting like a miserly penny-pincher, or being wastefully extravagant.

Aristotle's lecture notes refer to a "chart" of virtuous traits, which scholars have been able to re-create from his discussion:

ACTION/FEELING	DEFICIENCY	MEAN	EXCESS
FEAR AND DARING	cowardice	courage	rashness
PLEASURES OF TOUCH/TASTE	insensibility	temperance	self-indulgence
GIVING AND RECEIVING	stinginess	generosity	extravagance
SELF-PRESENTATION	smallness	magnanimity	vanity
ANGER	lack of spirit	gentleness	crankiness
SELF-EXPRESSION	mock modesty	truthfulness	boastfulness
CONVERSATION	boorishness	wit	buffoonery
SOCIAL CONDUCT	cantankerousness	friendliness	obsequiousness

Above: Aristotle's list of virtuous traits, showing in each case the virtue as the mean
between a vice of deficiency on the left, and a vice of excess on the right.

THE CARDINAL VIRTUES
excellent hinges

The phrase "cardinal virtues" originates with Ambrose [340–397], bishop of Milan. Famous for his rhetorical eloquence, Ambrose delivered one of his greatest orations at the funeral of his brother. In the speech he identifies four excellent traits in his sibling, which he calls "*cardo*", Latin for "hinge". The name stuck, since these traits open the door to a good life, and excellence of character turns on them.

In art, common props and symbols traditionally identify these four excellences (*see opposite*). *Courage* is often shown wearing armor and escorting a lion as a sign of brave strength. *Moderation* pours the proper balance of water and wine between two jugs. *Justice* holds fair and balanced scales and a sword that protects and enforces righteousness. *Wisdom* or prudence gazes into a mirror of self-knowledge to approach the truth in its full complexity by recognizing multiple perspectives.

All other virtues can be said to hinge on these four excellent human traits. The theological virtues (*faith*, *hope*, and *charity*) flower from the four cardinal virtues, while other virtues are corollaries. For example, patience takes courage (to withstand difficulties in others); gratitude flows from justice (to recognize and respond to gifts granted).

HUMAN POWER	CARDINAL VIRTUE	GREEK	LATIN
fight/flight response	COURAGE	*andreia*	*fortitudo*
desire for touch and taste	MODERATION	*sôphrosunê*	*temperantia*
intelligence	WISDOM	*phronesis*	*prudentia*
social relations	JUSTICE	*dikaiosunê*	*iustitia*

Ambrose's fourfold structure also appears in more ancient texts:

Conduct oneself with courage in danger; moderation in foregoing pleasures; wisdom in choosing between good and evil; justice in giving each what is due.

— Cicero, De Officiis [I, ii, 5]

Wisdom is the leader: next follows moderation; and from the union of these two with courage springs justice. — Plato, Laws [631c]

In *The Republic* (IV), Socrates privileges these same four *arête*, assuming a wide acceptance of them as the core qualities in an excellent human. He says that these virtues perfect four fundamental powers of life in the human soul and the well-formed community. Moderation tempers and completes appetites. Courage brings order and excellence to the spirit. Justice is ordered balance within the soul and in relation to others. Wisdom or prudence is excellence in thought-guiding action.

Cicero giving his book to his son Marcus. Frontispiece to Cicero, De Officiis, *Venice, 1525.*

COURAGE
fight or flight

When animals sense a threat, they become alert and ready. Similarly, when faced by danger, humans will either run away, freeze, hold ground, or attack. However, human reflective power adds a layer of complexity. Rather than just reacting to circumstance, the virtuous person is self-possessed and in command of their primal responses. Some dangers are sudden and obvious, while others, such as illness, poverty, and abandonment, lurk and creep. Courage involves appropriating one's impulses and responding to each situation with the proper balance of apprehension and confidence.

Too much courage can lead to rash behaviour; too little, to cowardice. The courageous person has fortitude in the face of difficulties, including the practice of virtue itself (*see too page 374*).

> **Without courage, you can't practice any other virtue consistently.** – Maya Angelou

Women fighting Devils, Florence, 1460.

Moderation
temperance

We all get hungry—whether for food, possessions, excitement, attention, or power. However, developing a taste for the right things pursued in the right way, in the right amounts, at the right times, for the right reasons is not easy. Consumer culture may tell us that "greed is good" and "bigger is better", but this is a recipe for slavery, not liberation. Unbridled acquisitiveness becomes *pleonexia*, the insatiable and ruthless desire to acquire more and more, an infinite appetite for finite things. Unchecked ambition results in prideful *hubris*. As Epictetus [55–135 AD] noted:

> If one oversteps the bounds of moderation, the greatest pleasures cease to please.

To practice *sôphrosunê* (moderation) is to embody calm self-mastery:

> Self-knowledge is the very essence of moderation, and in this I agree with him who dedicated the inscription 'Know thyself' at Delphi. – Plato, Charmides [164d]

The first steps toward self-possession usually involve restraint, learning to recognize which inclinations need to be tempered, to achieve a balanced mean between self-indulgence (too little moderation) and self-denial (too much). As the saying goes, all things in moderation—even moderation itself (*see too the title illustration on page 295*).

> When a man is stimulated by his own thoughts, full of desire and dwelling on what is attractive, his craving increases even more. He is making the fetter even stronger. But he who takes pleasure in stilling his thoughts, practising the contemplation of what is repulsive, and remaining recollected, now he will make an end of craving, he will snap the bonds... – Buddha [563–483 BC]

JUSTICE
in the house

Humans are highly social animals, and our power to communicate (perfected in artful grammar, logic, and rhetoric) points to our need to cultivate a disposition that improves social relationships. Justice is the virtue that disposes one to give others their due.

> *Rational speech (logos) is for making clear what is beneficial or harmful, and hence also what is just or unjust. For it is special to human beings, in comparison to other animals, that they alone have perception of what is just or unjust.*
>
> – Aristotle [1253a15]

The character of 'Lady Justice' (*see opposite*) dates back millennia. In ancient Egypt, as *Ma'at*, she held a scale to measure the weight of each human soul against the 'feather of truth'. Later, Roman artists portrayed *Iustitia* by combining features of two Greek goddesses: *Themis* (who orders the seasons) and *Dike* (who balances custom and law). Although women in the ancient world could not vote or appear in court, Justice was nevertheless imagined as a fair and balanced woman.

By the early modern period she had gained a blindfold to portray (visual) impartiality, and a double-edged sword for truth, reason, and certain punishment. Lady Justice reminds the crowd that they can outnumber and eventually defeat any strong individual or group. The logic of *might makes right* gives way to the logic of custom, and eventually to a principle of defending and enforcing fairness and equality.

A deeper understanding of justice points beyond social conventions to more universal principles: equality, even-handedness, and shared liberty. Indeed, puzzles about how to treat equal cases equally have a long tradition, from Plato's *Republic* to *A Theory of Justice* by John Rawls [1921–2002].

From a public perspective, justice is the decisive criterion for moral action in social relations, whereas from a personal perspective, justice is complete virtue exercised in relation to others. Thus, the justice of one's character is revealed by the way one treats others when in a position of power or leadership, at home, at work, or abroad. Aristotle considered justice a key virtue, but also a special case since it encompasses all other virtues, rather than lying in a mean between specific vices of excess and deficiency.

Justice and its meaning are central to debates about ethics, including vast bodies of literature that take up questions about the equitable exchange of goods and the fulfillment of contractual obligations (*commutative* justice), the allocation of economic benefits and burdens (*distributive* justice), the appropriate punishment for criminals and victims (*restorative* justice), and the best type of institutions for cultivating balanced order in society (*political* justice).

Justice, blindfolded, holding scales and a sword; by Pieter Bruegel the Elder [1525–1569].

WISDOM
dear prudence

The most important of the cardinal virtues is *phronesis*, or practical wisdom. *Phronesis* is the habit of knowing the right action, at the right time, in the right way, for the right reason. This includes assessing what other virtues are applicable to a given situation - some commentators have called *phronesis* a 'meta-virtue'. A person who embodies this trait (the *phronimos*) has mastered the ability to see, judge, and act.

This virtue, of which some commentators have said that there is no real vice of excess, must at first be taught, but is then later developed by attention to experience and memory.

> *Wisdom is the daughter of experience.* – Leonardo da Vinci

> *Memory is the mother of all wisdom.* – Aeschylus

In addition, the wise person is open-minded, acknowledging their limitations with a cheerful willingness to learn more.

> *The cleverest of all, in my opinion, is the man who calls himself a fool at least once a month.* – Dostoevsky

Phronesis bestows both an understanding of first principles of general knowledge and good judgement, and a shrewd ability to apply what's appropriate to each situation. It involves being good at reasoning, evaluating evidence, and comparing alternatives. Cicero translated the term as *providentia*, meaning foresight. The medieval Latin schoolmen later contracted this into *prudentia*, referring to the ability to appreciate the uniqueness and complexity of any given situation, with appropriate awareness of the long-term risks and implications of each possible action.

Prudence. A woman puts out a fire before it spreads; a sick man is attended to; a merchant saves his gold; winter supplies are prepared and stored; the house is repaired. Engraved by Philips Galle [1537-1612] from an original drawing by Pieter Bruegel the Elder [1525–1569], Netherlands.

We have all met people lacking in prudence; they are shortsighted, thoughtless, distracted, negligent, and wasteful. Others twist their wisdom and become fraudulent, cunning, slick, sneaky, or deceitful. A few become pompous procrastinators, or profligate pedlars of proverbs (*see page 368*).

Just as a masterful athlete or musician knows almost by feeling what's appropriate in a given context, so the *phronimos* knows how to make emotion an ally of reason. They rely on their well-formed passions to shape good judgement, especially when timing matters and a quick decision is needed.

Wisdom is better than rubies; and all the things that may be desired are not to be compared to it. – Proverbs [8:11]

THE SEVEN DEADLY SINS
excess, inadequacy, and perversion

Dante Aligheri [1265–1321], in the *Divine Comedy*, has Virgil accompany him and his reader on a journey across seven terraces to diagnose and heal a broken soul. Dante argues that every virtue, as well as every vice, springs from love. Understood this way, sin is love that has wandered off the path; it is possible to love in a friendly and appropriate way, or in distorted ways. Dante's journey moves from the least serious disorders to the most serious. The easiest way to misdirect love is to place too much value on an earthly good, such as sexual pleasure (*lust*), food (*gluttony*), or possessions (*greed*). A less common, but more deadly, way to go astray is to lose interest in these, or in anything or anyone (*sloth*).

With regard to the destruction of one's character, it is even more deadly to practice a distorted defiant love that takes perverse delight in the downfall of others. This can be done in three (progressively disordered) ways: desiring revenge (*wrath*), taking jealous delight in the possessions of another (*envy*), or exalting oneself above all others (*pride*). Of the seven, the most deadly is pride or vainglory, which Dante defined as "love of self perverted to hatred and contempt for one's neighbour".

LATIN	VICE	MISDIRECTED LOVE	OPPOSING VIRTUE
luxuria	LUST	excessive love of sex	courtly love
gula	GLUTTONY	excessive love of food	temperance
avaritia	GREED	excessive love of material possessions	generosity
acedia	SLOTH	inadequate love of beginning anything	zeal
ira	WRATH	perverted love of revenge	patience
invidia	ENVY	perverted love of another's goods	kindness
superbia	PRIDE	perverted love of oneself	humility

Dante drew from several lists of vices and virtues. One such seven-part list joined the four cardinal virtues (*see p. 316*) with the three theological virtues (faith, hope, and charity). Gregory the Great [540–604] proposed another list of seven virtues that directly oppose the seven deadly sins, with humility at the root (*shown above*).

As to the Seven Deadly Sins, I deplore Pride, Wrath, Lust, Envy, and Greed. Gluttony and Sloth I pretty much plan my day around. – Robert Brault

Facing page: *The Seven Deadly Sins, Dietrich Meyer [1572-1658]. Superbia gazes at herself in a mirror beside a peacock, Avaritia clutches her treasure in front of a toad, Invidia bites her nails while snakes writhe in her hair and an angry dog yaps at her heels, Ira strides forth armed with a sword and an accompanying lion, Libido stands in for Luxuria, Ebrietas (intoxication) for Gluttony, and Otium (idleness) for Sloth.*

Left: *Triumph of Virtue over the Seven Deadly Sins, Venice, 1508. The sins are represented by animals, a goat for lust, a pig for gluttony, a toad for greed, an ass for sloth, a lion for wrath, a dog for envy, and a peacock for pride.*

HUMILITY AND GREATNESS
a sense of perspective

St. Gregory the Great insisted that humility is a key virtue, and this has never been more true than today. Many aspects of modern societies positively encourage an inflated sense of one's own importance, and an unreflective belief that it is perfectly legitimate to expect and pursue the satisfaction of one's every desire.

> Observe what has happened to the seven deadly sins of Christian theology. All but one of these sins, sloth, was transformed into a positive virtue. Greed, avarice, envy, gluttony, luxury and pride are the driving forces of the new economy.
>
> — Lewis Mumford

The resulting lack of humility distorts relationships not only between people, but also between human beings and the rest of the world (*see pp. 348–351*). Like other virtues, humility is a mean condition between vices of excess and deficiency. So, avoiding pride, conceit, and *hubris*, the vices of excess, does not mean retreating into exaggerated self-abasement, or hiding one's light under a bushel. It means developing a properly balanced sense of one's true importance in the world.

This is an area where classical priorities can be at odds with those of today. Every culture touched by Homer is taught, in one way or another, to admire a trait Aristotle called *megalopsychia*, "greatness of soul". Magnanimous individuals such as Odysseus conduct themselves with an almost preternatural awareness of their own excellence and carry themselves with a sense of grandeur. When Aristotle describes *megalopsychoi* he praises the grand elder who walks slowly, speaks in a deep voice, and carries himself with a sense of his own *gravitas*. But he also commends the ironist who, while aware of his status and accomplishments, knowingly presents himself with understated grace. Even in Athens, the proud swagger of the hero sometimes clashed with the gentle virtues of sophisticated society.

A virtuous person treats others respectfully, but without denying his or her own true worth. What does this mean in practice? Nowadays, we perhaps see humility as requiring us to treat others as equals, rather than in terms of respecting hierarchical power relations, as was often the case in former times. Questions about appropriate self-awareness and self-presentation still arise though, and are still important. Thinking them through can lead to the insight that being grounded and authentically humble is entirely compatible with greatness of soul. A great soul is, after all, also a humble one.

Humility, far from being opposed to magnanimity, serves to temper it, because humility makes us recognize great gifts. – Pope Francis

It's better to be looked over than overlooked. – Mae West

Pride leads her forces. From the celebrated Hortus Delicarum, Hohenburg *Abbey, Alsace, 1185, the first encyclopedia to be written by a woman.*

Social Virtues

gentleness, honesty, friendliness, and wit

Following Aristotle, Thomas Aquinas [1224/5-74], in the *Summa Theologica*, described the social virtues as those required in order to "behave well in the conduct of human affairs".

GENTLENESS: Gentleness defines the mean between excessive irascibility on the one hand and a lack of spirit on the other. A hot-headed person can quickly over-react to a perceived slight, while a bitter person can bottle it up until it explodes. The gentle person, with well ordered passions, finds the mean. Such a person gets angry about the right things, with the right people, in the right ways, at the right times.

Charity, cast out of the world by Self Interest (who has cut off her feet), is aided by a gentle and friendly poet. Peter Flötner, Nuremberg, early 1500s.

TRUTHFULNESS: We all prefer people who speak and act with integrity. Moreover, no society can function for long if people don't tell the truth, while expecting others to do so. Two stock characters from the ancient Greek stage typify excess and deficiency of this virtue: the *alazon* is a boaster who pretends to be greater than he is, and the *eiron* is a self-deprecator. Together, these two produce a humorous effect: the chubby bragger who overstates the truth is brought down a peg by the skinny, understated ironist. Their comic *hamartia* (missing-the-mark) brings into focus the target of truthfulness (*see too page 256*).

FRIENDLINESS: Friendliness is the disposition to treat strangers as future friends. Whether one's natural temperament is extraverted or introverted, one can develop an appropriate level of friendliness. A deficiency of friendliness results in a quarrelsome, cantankerous crank. An excess produces the annoyingly friendly, flattering, fawning, obsequious sycophant.

There's not a word yet for old friends who've just met. – Bob Marley

WIT: Our contemporaries might not think much about the ethics of having a good sense of humour, but the ancients offer timeless insight into this aspect of the art of character:

Those who carry humour to excess are vulgar buffoons, pursuing what's funny at all costs, and doing anything to get a laugh without concern for the pain caused to those who are the butt of their jibes; while those who can neither make a joke themselves nor appreciate good humour are boorish and stiff. The one who jokes tastefully is witty and quick. – Aristotle [1128a5]

You can pretend to be serious. You can't pretend to be witty. – Sacha Guitry

FRIENDSHIP
sharing the good life

Ancient philosophers reflected deeply on the nature of friendship and its place in a good life, for it is crucial to the rhetorical practice of citizen leadership, and indispensable to human flourishing.

> *Of all possessions a friend is the most precious.* – Herodotus

In classical antiquity, politicians and rhetoricians addressed fellow citizens as "friends". Thus, Mark Antony begins his funeral oration:

> *Friends, Romans, countrymen, lend me your ears.* – Shakespeare, *Julius Caesar*

Friendship is the central topic of Plato's *Lysis*, while Aristotle devotes more space to *philia* than to any of the virtues, defining it as reciprocated goodwill (*eunoia*, "good minded") with mutual awareness. He says that the proper objects of love are what is *useful* or *pleasant* or *good* in itself:

> *Friendship takes three forms, equal in number to the proper objects of love.* –[1156a6]

A **FRIENDSHIP OF UTILITY** is characterized by reciprocated goodwill where each party is useful to each other: examples include business partnerships, relationships among co-workers, and study partners.

A **FRIENDSHIP OF PLEASURE** centers on the delight that accompanies shared activity: a tennis partner or a theatre-going companion.

These are both *coincidental friendships*: the love is related to how useful or pleasant the other is, and last only as long as the utility or pleasure.

A **COMPLETE FRIENDSHIP** is between good people who are alike in virtue. Each is attracted to the other's excellence, desiring what's best for the sake of the friend's well being. Such friendships endure, since virtue persists, but are rare, since they develop over time, are tested through shared difficulty, and require sustained closeness.

Cicero translates *eunoia* as *benevolentia*, the idea that friends relate to one another with shared concern, wanting what's good for each other. In his dialogue *Laelius de Amicitia* he explores the nature of friendship by puzzling through questions such as "how far should a friend go to aid a friend?" and "should new friends ever be put before old friends?". He emphasizes the importance of trust, frankness, equality, graciousness, and kindness between friends.

> What sweetness is left in life, if you take away friendship? Robbing life of friendship is like robbing the world of the sun. – Cicero

Renaissance essayists such as Michel de Montaigne [1533–92] and Francis Bacon [1561–1626] also praised friendship in their writings (*and see p.373*).

Left: Illustration from The Paris Sketch Book of Mr M. A. Titmarsh, *by William Makepeace Thackeray [1811–63]. Does this look like a friendship of Utility? of Pleasure? or a Complete Friendship?*

Friendships build bridges between sexes, tribes, classes, and ages. Like Cicero, today we still question friendship: Do happy people need friends? What is a workplace friend? Can citizen friendships affect large, modern nation-states? Can an internet friend be a genuine companion? Can a favorite author be a friend?

GOOD SOCIETY

sphaera civitatis

A Spartan herald is recorded as once having said to the Persian king:

> *You understand a slave's life, but, having never tasted freedom, you do not know the sweetness of liberty.* – Herodotus [484–425 BC]

Athenian democracy was, ironically, built on slavery. But for those who were granted it, citizenship in the *polis* entailed sharing political power. A citizen was neither a slave nor a subject, but was *sui juris*, able to manage their own affairs. They enjoyed the abundance of civilized life and took part in the governance of the community's pursuit of shared goods. So the practice of citizenship, then as now, contained an internal motive to become informed and engaged, to cultivate eloquence, participate in public debate, and exercise the moral and intellectual virtues requisite for social life amongst a self-governing people.

> *All that is valuable in human society depends upon the opportunity for development accorded the individual.* – Albert Einstein [1879–1955]

What sort of education is required for civic virtue? Beyond the technical expertise needed to be a productive member of society, citizens require *artes liberales*: the skills worthy of a free person that perfect language, thought, and character.

> *Freedom is absolutely necessary for progress in science and the liberal arts.*
> – Baruch Spinoza [1632–1677]

The scope and degrees of citizenship have generated centuries-long debates. In ancient Rome, *civitas*, the political space constructed by a people to live a distinctively human life, extended beyond urban boundaries to include *res publica*, "public things", of all kinds (this many-layered phrase is the root of the English word "republic").

Diogenes of Sinope [412–323 BC] proclaimed "I am a citizen of the world". Augustine of Hippo [354–430 AD] later extended this to dual citizenship, encouraging peaceful contribution to the earthly political community while participating as pilgrims of the heavenly city.

Today, "global citizenship", emphasizing the solidarity across political boundaries required to address global problems, contends with "localism", which prizes connection to place and maximal local participation in shared decision-making. In addressing this modern dilemma, as much as for the timeless task of shoring up civic life against corruption, the classic virtues remain indispensable.

A constitutional democracy is in serious trouble if its citizenry does not have a certain degree of education and civic virtue. – Philip Johnson

SPHÆRA   CIVITATIS

Left: Title page of John Case's Sphaera Civitatis, *a popular Aristotelian treatise on politics, first published in 1588. "Elizabeth, Queen of the Angles, the French and the Spanish, defender of the faith," presides over the Ptolemaic universe. Inside the celestial sphere, with its stars, nobles, heroes, and counsellors, the planets rule the moral traits of good government: thus Majesty is ruled by Saturn, Prudence occupies the sphere of Jupiter, Fortitude is governed by Mars, Religion is the domain of the Sun, Mercy belongs to Venus, Eloquence to Mercury, and Abundance is the province of the Moon. At the center is "Immovable Justice."*

NATURAL LAW

a compass within

Is there is an innate moral law which guides human action? Plato and
Aristotle hint at the idea, and Sophocles [497–405 BC] captures it in a
speech delivered by Antigone to Creon:

> *These laws are not for now or for yesterday. They are alive forever, and no one*
> *knows when they were first shown to us.* – Sophocles, Antigone

Cicero later provided the classic Stoic expression of natural law
philosophy when he argued that Tarquin's rape of Lucretia was illicit,
regardless of human legislation:

> *Although there was no written law concerning adultery during the reign of Tarquin,*
> *it does not therefore follow that Sextus Tarquinius did not offend against the eternal*
> *law when he committed a rape on Lucretia. For, even then he had the light of*
> *reason from the nature of things, that incites to good actions and dissuades from*
> *evil ones; and which does not begin for the first time to be a law when it is drawn*
> *up in writing.* – Cicero, de Legibus

The apostle Paul wrote in his *Letter to the Romans* that every human has
a conscience, "a law written on the heart", and during the high middle
ages, Jewish, Christian, and Muslim scholars, from Baghdad to Cordova,
interacted in tolerant harmony while debating the obligations of this
natural law binding upon all.

One famous twentieth-century appeal to the idea of an objective norm
for human conduct appears in the letter written by Martin Luther King, Jr.
while imprisoned for protesting segregation laws:

How does one determine whether a law is just or unjust? A just law is a man made code that squares with the moral law or the law of God. An unjust law is a code that is out of harmony with the moral law. To put it in the terms of St. Thomas Aquinas: An unjust law is a human law that is not rooted in eternal law and natural law. Any law that uplifts human personality is just. Any law that degrades human personality is unjust. All segregation statutes are unjust because segregation distorts the soul and damages the personality. It gives the segregator a false sense of superiority and the segregated a false sense of inferiority.

– Martin Luther King, Jr.

Human laws can certainly be just or unjust, and King was surely right that this is connected with whether a law uplifts or degrades those governed by it. Yet such insights alone cannot establish that any law is really "natural". The segregationists also thought their beliefs reflected natural law, as indeed did Aristotle when he claimed that some people were born to be slaves. Every society has those who claim that its own laws and culture reflect "how things ought to be". Subcultures and resistance movements do the same.

Timeless questions of what it is for a human being to flourish, and to treat others well, must be contemplated afresh by every generation.

The greatest good for a human is daily to converse about virtue. – Socrates

In the modern era, this search for an ethic that transcends culture and context has given us the idea of universal human rights.

Human Rights
universal values

John Locke argued in 1688 that the sole justification of government was to protect individuals' "natural rights" to life, liberty, and property. He saw such rights as deriving from principles of natural law, which in turn could be discovered by discerning the will of God. This established the important principle that individual rights could transcend the authority of the state, but left it open for disputes over 'what God intended' to affect what rights people would have.

Immanuel Kant [1724–1804] later argued (*see p. 339*) that the claim that humans have certain fundamental rights could in fact be justified without appeal to any religious tradition. This cleared the way for modern universal human rights, but it would be another 200 years before they emerged into law.

In an effort to avoid any recurrence of the horrors of World War II, the Universal Declaration of Human Rights (UDHR) was adopted by the UN General Assembly in 1948 (*see the 30 articles, opposite*). For the first time, fundamental moral principles governing how we should treat one another were finally agreed to cover all human beings, as inalienable rights rather than as privileges of status or citizenship.

Since 1948 many other treaties and covenants on human rights have come into force, and the UDHR itself has gained the status of international law, meaning that every country's laws are supposed to be consistent with it. A moral right is not the same as a legal right, however, and the process of turning human rights from the former into the latter is far from complete.

Plato and Aristotle would have agreed that human affairs should be governed by universal moral principles, though their own cultural assumptions might have led them to disagree with many modern rights. Reaching agreement across cultures is hard, and debate continues, both about proposed new human rights and about some existing ones.

THE 30 ARTICLES OF THE UNIVERSAL DECLARATION OF HUMAN RIGHTS

1. Right to Equality
2. Freedom from Discrimination
3. Right to Life, Liberty, and Personal Security
4. Freedom from Slavery
5. Freedom from Torture and Degrading Treatment
6. Right to Recognition as a Person before the Law
7. Right to Equality before the Law
8. Right to Remedy by Competent Tribunal
9. Freedom from Arbitrary Arrest and Exile
10. Right to Fair Public Hearing
11. Right to be Considered Innocent until Proven Guilty
12. Freedom from Interference with Privacy, Family, Home & Correspondence
13. Right to Free Movement in and out of the Country
14. Right to Asylum in other Countries from Persecution
15. Right to a Nationality and the Freedom to Change It
16. Right to Marriage and Family
17. Right to Own Property
18. Freedom of Belief and Religion
19. Freedom of Opinion and Information
20. Right of Peaceful Assembly and Association
21. Right to Participate in Government and in Free Elections
22. Right to Social Security
23. Right to Desirable Work and to Join Trade Unions
24. Right to Rest and Leisure
25. Right to Adequate Living Standard
26. Right to Education
27. Right to Participate in the Cultural Life of Community
28. Right to a Social Order that Articulates this Document
29. Community Duties Essential to Free and Full Development
30. Freedom from State or Personal Interference in the above Rights.

THE GOLDEN RULE

do as you would be done by

The directive maxim Treat others as you would like them to treat you has been dubbed the "golden rule" at least since the 17th century, although versions can be found in the ancient codes of Egypt and Babylon, and in almost every world religion and wisdom tradition:

> *Regard your neighbour's gain as your own gain and your neighbour's loss as your own loss.* — Laozi, Dao de jing

> *Therefore all things whatsoever ye would that men should do to you, do ye even so to them.* — Bible, Matthew 7:12

> *No one of you is a believer until he desires for his brother that which he desires for himself.* — Sayings of Muhammad, Hadith 13

A prohibitive version, Do not treat others in ways you would not like to be treated, sometimes called the "silver rule," may be older:

> *Hurt not others in ways that you yourself would find hurtful.* — Udana-Varga 518

> *One should not behave towards others in a way which is disagreeable to oneself.*
> — Mahabharata, Anusasana Parva 113.8.

> *That which is hateful to you, do not do to your fellow. That is the whole Torah. The rest is elaboration. Go and learn.* — Torah, Shabbath 31a

DO UNTO OTHERS AS YOU WOULD HAVE THEM DO TO YOU.

But what if you're a masochist...?

DUTY
a little respect

Immanuel Kant argued that the Golden Rule need not be taken on scriptural authority, since it followed logically from a moral duty of *respect for persons*:

> Act in such a way as to treat humanity, whether in your own person or in that of anyone else, always as an end and never merely as a means. – Kant

> Do your duty as you see it, and damn the consequences. – George S. Patton

Deontology (from the Greek *deon*, duty) is the name for moral theories, like Kant's, which claim that certain actions are right or wrong in themselves, regardless of the consequences that may follow. Because he believed the "moral law" prescribed what one should do in all cases, Kant called it a *categorical imperative*. One expression of this, the *principle of universalizability*, asks whether the maxim guiding a proposed course of action is one that everyone should adopt:

> Act only according to that maxim by which you can at the same time will that it should become a universal law for all humankind. – Kant

A quick test, leading straight back to the Golden Rule, is the principle of reversibility: "Would I want my proposed action done to me?"

Telling lies, for instance, treats others as a means to one's own ends. It is also not something anyone could realistically wish everyone to do, so it violates both versions of the categorical imperative. However:

> DILEMMA: What if a raging man wielding an axe asks you which way his intended victim went? Would it really be wrong to lie?

UTILITY AND EQUALITY
consequences for all

Deontology holds that some actions, such as murder, are always wrong, no matter what. *Utilitarianism*, by contrast, is interested solely in outcomes. For a utilitarian, the end can justify the means: so perhaps killing one person to save ten might be right?

> DILEMMA: *A villain holds you and ten other people hostage, and then orders you to murder one of your fellow prisoners. You are told that if you do not do the murder then all ten of the others will be executed. What should you do?*

Jeremy Bentham [1748–1832], who coined the term utilitarianism, wanted ethics to be based solely on evidence, in the form of measurable consequences. Ethics was simply a matter of "summing up all the values of pleasure on one side, and those of all the pains on the other", thereby calculating the net impact on human happiness of any proposed action.

It is the greatest happiness of the greatest number that is the measure of right and wrong. – Jeremy Bentham [1776]

The hostage dilemma (*above*) illustrates some of the attractions of utilitarianism, but also some of its shortcomings. Not even Jeremy Bentham would really feel happy about killing his fellow prisoner. Just as with deontology's formal principles of duty, utilitarianism's

"It's a government funded study to find out how many wrongs make a right."

bald calculations often seem to miss something important.

Bentham saw utilitarianism as an emancipatory project, which could make society fairer and more equal. He wanted the pleasures and pains of *everyone* to be counted and measured on a single scale, not just those of men, of the rich and privileged, or of the well-educated. He felt it was the happiness that mattered, not how it was produced.

"Do you realize what Ethics has cost us this year?"

> Prejudice apart, the game of push-pin is of equal value with the arts and sciences of music and poetry. – Jeremy Bentham [c. 1775]

John Stuart Mill [1826–1873] later developed his own version of utilitarianism, which argued that "higher" pleasures such as poetry should be seen as better than "lower" pleasures such as push-pin (a popular bar game of the time).

> It is better to be a human being dissatisfied than a pig satisfied; better to be Socrates dissatisfied than a fool satisfied. – John Stuart Mill [1863]

Of course, while this version works well for poetry enthusiasts, it doesn't look so good if you prefer the joys of push-pin. Nobody wants to be seen as the pig. Is this just elitism, or an argument for good education and public subsidy of the arts? This debate continues today, in parliaments as well as universities.

ETHICS IN REAL LIFE
calculation or judgment?

A great deal of what passes for ethical deliberation these days is essentially utilitarianism. Whether a proposed action or policy would be right or wrong is widely seen to depend entirely on whether it will have a desirable outcome, all things considered. Since it's so hard to "sum up" all the different pleasures and pains felt by everyone affected by a given action or decision, such calculations often try and translate these into financial values, the better to add and subtract them.

> DILEMMA: *The time saved for thousands of commuting drivers by widening a congested urban highway is valued at more than the compensation owed to those whose houses will be demolished. Should the road be widened?*

But even if it were possible to put a price on everything, would it be right? Ethics is not just an exercise in cost-benefit analysis.

Ethical dilemmas can be approached several ways. A utilitarian perspective measures the *outcome*, a deontological perspective focuses on the *act*, and a virtue perspective considers the *character* of the agent:

> DILEMMA: *A runaway train is heading downhill towards five people working on the line. You can divert the train onto a disused siding where you know one homeless man is asleep on the tracks. What should you do?*

A pure Kantian would probably not divert the train, since this would deliberately kill an innocent person, an act which is always wrong. A pure utilitarian would probably be prepared to kill one innocent person in order to save five. A virtue ethicist would begin by applying practical wisdom in order to discern what other virtues (such as courage and justice)

"THAT'S IT, IN A NUTSHELL."

might be appropriate to this unfortunate situation, and then consider how to act in such a way as to embody them (requiring more detail than is specified here).

Virtue ethics is thus not well suited to giving quick answers to lurid hypothetical dilemmas such as these, which are designed to expose differences between "right" as valued by deontologists, and "good" as valued by utilitarians. They present a clear choice whether or not to do something that appears wrong, in order to avert an apparently greater evil. Real life ethical decisions tend to be less clear-cut, and more complicated. Many ethicists today seek to integrate useful aspects of modern moral theories with a renewed focus on virtue.

When determining moral responsibility, many ethicists also distinguish between a person's intention and foreseeable side effects. So, physicians sometimes prescribe palliative sedation to relieve suffering at the end of life, foreseeing unintended effects, including the death of a patient, and in military ethics, a tactical weapon, aimed at military target, may have the foreseen side effect of inciting fear and causing civilian deaths. Is foreseeing an outcome morally different than intending it?

DEPENDENCE
and caring for others

Many of the trickiest ethical decisions arise when not all the people involved are equal, healthy, rational adults.

> DILEMMA: *Your five-year-old daughter is too sick for school, but you have arranged to visit your aged father today. He lives alone, cannot hear the phone, and will become very anxious if you don't turn up. What should you do?*

Human flourishing involves self-governance and resilience, while justice requires us to respect the dignity and self-direction of others. But we do not come into this world as independent practical reasoners. If we achieve flourishing in this life, we do so only after long periods of dependence, relying on the generous care of others, whether in childhood, illness, disability, or old age. As Alasdair MacIntyre notes, English has no equivalent to the Lakota Sioux term *wancantognaka*, the virtue of open-hearted recognition of reliance on others.

Some feminist writers on *relational ethics* upend Plato's ordering of the Republic over the family, suggesting that ethics in fact has its origin in the home, especially in parental love. Building an understanding of ethics outwards from such relationships of care can throw a very different light on larger scale issues of social policy.

"I made this Valentine's card for you in school, mom. What the world needs is more love, and less homework."

Medical Ethics

first, do no harm

Utilitarian reasoning is not as dominant in medicine as elsewhere, partly because medical ethics has an ancient pedigree. This dates at least to the Oath written by Hippocrates (or one of his followers) between the 5th and 3rd century BC, in which physicians vow to comport themselves in a godly manner and never misuse their position.

Modern medical ethics proposes four action-guiding principles:

NON-MALEFICENCE: *Often expressed more pithily as "First, do no harm."*

BENEFICENCE: *The practitioner must act in the best interest of the patient.*

RESPECT FOR AUTONOMY: *The patient has the right to choose or refuse treatment. This includes the sub-principle of* INFORMED CONSENT: *the patient must be given all the information required for such decisions.*

JUSTICE: *Who gets what treatment should be decided fairly and equitably.*

It is not only possible but common for two or more of these principles to come into conflict, giving rise to complex ethical dilemmas:

DILEMMA: *A critically injured road accident victim refuses a blood transfusion, citing her beliefs as a Jehovah's Witness. Her relatives say she converted only recently, under pressure from a manipulative new boyfriend. Should doctors perform the transfusion?*

DILEMMA: *Two patients need a new kidney equally urgently, but only one is available. Which patient should get it?*

Difficult decisions like these are made by doctors every day.

ETHICS AT WORK
roles and responsibilities

In the case of doctors, ethics is clearly important. But ethical considerations apply whatever we do for a living. While we're used to hearing about "ethical consumerism", taking ethics to work with us is at least as important as taking them to the supermarket.

Sometimes the right course of action is obvious, and reflected in the rules of the job. Teachers shouldn't accept favours from students (or their parents) in exchange for better grades. Train drivers shouldn't drink on duty. Building inspectors shouldn't accept bribes to sign off unsafe structures. However, other cases are trickier:

SCENARIO: *A man is struggling to meet the costs of caring for his disabled child. He secretly takes home some out-of-date food from the grocery store where he works, against company rules. Is this wrong?*

DILEMMA: *A policewoman has a close cousin who is a single parent and occasional drug user. Should she tip her off about a forthcoming drug raid?*

People holding public office or managing public resources have clear responsibilities not to abuse their position. But private businesses run for profit also wield great power and can often do things which, while legal, may seem unethical.

SCENARIO: *A car company buys up local bus companies and shuts them down, increasing demand for its own products. Surely this is just business?*

SCENARIO: *A global water company buys the water supply infrastructure of a poor city and raises the price of water tenfold, making it unaffordable for many.*

Such matters are sometimes addressed by corporate social responsibility (CSR) policies, with varying degrees of effectiveness. But what happens if these kinds of unethical practices are intrinsic to the core business of the company and returns for its shareholders?

SCENARIO: *A pharmaceutical company specializes in buying up patents on old drugs still in widespread use, then raising the prices.*

Ethics are relevant to all employees, not just management, and the need to earn a living doesn't justify unethical behaviour. Conversely no-one should have to do things at work they wouldn't be prepared to do as a private individual, including turning a blind eye to wrongdoing:

DILEMMA: *Anna, an insurance saleswoman, discovers her colleague Barry is misleading elderly clients into buying expensive policies they don't need. She tells her boss, but he says she'll be sacked if she mentions it again, so she pretends not to know. Who's in the wrong?*

Many countries have "whistle-blower protection" laws to protect individuals who come forward in just these kinds of situation.

ETHICS AND ANIMALS
reaching out beyond the human

Most of ethics has always been about how to treat our fellow humans, and being human has often been defined by contrast with "beasts" or "dumb animals". Yet concern for animal suffering has a long history. The philosopher and mathematician Pythagoras [c.580–500 BC] was a vegetarian, apparently for ethical as well as health reasons:

> *As long as man continues to be the ruthless destroyer of lower living beings he will never know health or peace. For as long as men massacre animals, they will kill each other. Indeed, he who sows the seed of murder and pain cannot reap joy and love.* – Pythagoras [attributed by Ovid]

This kind of virtue-based argument, still common today, claims that someone who treats animals badly debases their character, and so will treat people badly too. Some utilitarians, such as Peter Singer [1946–], agree with Jeremy Bentham (*see p. 340*) that the pleasures and pains of animals should also be taken into account:

> *The question is not, can they reason? Nor can they talk? But, can they suffer?*
> – Jeremy Bentham [1780]

Mostly though, modern utilitarian reasoning has not been good for animals. Farming animals for food perhaps need not involve suffering, though most modern versions do:

> DILEMMA: *Over 50 billion chickens are killed and eaten worldwide by humans every year. Most have been kept in close confinement and actively prevented from having a normal chicken's life. Is this acceptable?*

Vivisection is another related matter:

DILEMMA: *Millions of animals suffer and die every year in the safety testing of chemicals, drugs, and consumer products. Is this justifiable?*

Both utilitarians like Singer and some Kantians (such as Tom Regan), have supported greater respect for animals on *extensionist* grounds. They argue that over the last 2500 years the circle of moral considerability has expanded from Athenian men to include women, the poor, and other ethnic groups: should this expansion not continue to include at least some animals? Exactly what this would mean, and which animals should be included, raises many questions, but most extensionists would start with those most similar to us:

DILEMMA: *Chimpanzees share 99% of their DNA with humans. Orangutans and gorillas face extinction. Should we extend basic legal rights (to life, liberty, and freedom from torture) to our closest cousins, the other great apes?*

ENVIRONMENTAL ETHICS
care for our common home

If applying traditional ethics to animals is difficult, then applying them to environmental problems is harder still. Yet there is clearly a strong ethical dimension to the current crisis in human relationships with the nonhuman world. Ethicists have puzzled over how to accommodate inspiring insights such as those expressed by Aldo Leopold:

> **A thing is right when it tends to preserve the integrity, stability, and beauty of the biotic community. It is wrong when it tends otherwise.** – A Sand County Almanac

One way of doing so is by way of ethical extensionism (*see p. 348*). Perhaps animals, plants, even landscapes and ecosystems, are due respect in their own right and (as Kant said about people) should never be treated merely as means to human ends.

> DILEMMA: *Across the world, trees are threatened by development. To facilitate their protection, should trees have legal standing in court, enabling lawyers to argue directly for their interests? If corporations and states can be treated as legal persons, why not the natural environment?*

"WE BELIEVE WE WILL BE ABLE TO TEAR DOWN THE ENTIRE ECOSYSTEM IN AN ENVIRONMENTALLY FRIENDLY MANNER."

This suggestion, made by Christopher Stone in 1972, might seem fanciful, but reflecting indigenous belief systems, the constitutions of Ecuador and Bolivia do now explicitly recognise rights for nature (or '*Pachamama*').

Another approach is to consider the interests of future humans:

DILEMMA: *What do our obligations to future generations require us to bequeath them?*

It's hard to know exactly what future people will value. But that's no reason not to leave them a natural world at least as wonderful as the one we enjoy today. If we take this obligation seriously, there's plenty of work to be done.

Environmental virtue ethics takes a different approach again, asking as usual what virtues are relevant to the problem, and what it would mean to embody them. Humility seems key (*see p. 326*), as does moderation (*p. 319*), and wisdom and courage will certainly be required. Some argue that it may be helpful to think in terms of a new virtue such as what Rosalind Hursthouse calls "right orientation to nature".

A virtue approach makes clear that working for ecological sustainability is not a matter of sacrificing the present for the sake of the future. Practicing ecological virtue and good stewardship contributes to human flourishing for everyone, right now.

LEARNING AND LIVING
ars recte vivendi

The liberal arts are traditionally divided into the *trivium* (three paths), involving the proper exercise of language (grammar, logic, and rhetoric) and the *quadrivium* (four paths), concerning number (arithmetic, music, geometry, and astronomy). Unlike the content-based *quadrivium*, the *trivium* are preliminary disciplines which are methods for dealing with subjects, roads that lead the lively mind to 'learn how to learn', and quest for wisdom hidden in the 'art of character' and the 'art of living'.

> *To compose our character is our duty, not to compose books, and to win, not battles and provinces, but order and tranquility in our conduct. Our great and glorious masterpiece is to live appropriately. All other things, ruling, hoarding, building, are only little appendages and props, at most.* – Michel de Montaigne [1533–1592]

Choosing the right word for any context requires good judgement; learning grammar requires temperance and an appreciation for deep structures of human awareness; learning dialectical argumentation requires patience and focus; persuasive communication, when practiced artfully, leads to larger questions of human action and purpose.

We can puzzle about human actions from a range of perspectives. Looking back at past actions raises questions as to whether obligations were met; looking ahead to future actions invites consideration of the most beneficial plan or policy. But ethics is more than debating which action is right; it involves reflection on a whole life, and the fundamental issue of what makes for a good one.

Consider your deepest longings. Desire prompts action, and action in turn refines and consolidates character, thus shaping future desires.

Accordingly, the human act of learning how to learn makes possible wise reflection and moral transformation.

Every human life is inevitably a self-portrait: the art of living is an art of character. Making a good and beautiful life thus requires crafting one's soul in excellence.

Above: The title page of the Margarita Philosophica *(The Pearl of Wisdom), by Gregor Reisch [1467–1525], showing the seven liberal arts as the leaves of the Tree of Knowledge.*

APPENDICES
& INDEX

Theophrastus's Characters

Theophrastus [d. 278 BC] studied under Plato and Aristotle, succeeding the latter as head of the Lyceum. *Characters*, a brief work attributed to him, outlines 30 characters derived from studies in ethics and rhetoric. With obvious value for writers and dramatists, it had a profound influence on European literature.

It makes no difference whether we consider the state of character or the man characterized by it – Aristotle

THE DISSEMBLER feigns ignorance, is two-faced, or describes the opposite of what is true. *He says Business is dreadfully dull; though at other times, when business is really dull, he reports a thriving trade.*

THE FLATTERER makes you cringe. To his hero, he says things like: *No man in Athens gets such attention.* Or, *You were the man of the hour yesterday in the Porch.*

THE GARRULOUS person talks at great length on matters irrelevant, trivial, or inappropriate. *And if you let him go on he will never stop*, regaling all with such gems as *I vomited yesterday* or *The price of wheat has gone down.*

THE BOORISH person knows nothing of propriety, he *wears his shoes too large for his feet; talks in a loud voice, and drinks his wine rather strong.* Worst of all, *Wearing a cloak which does not reach the knee, he will sit down.*

THE AFFABLE SELF-SEEKER or *smooth-boot* tries to please everyone but comes across as weak, unprincipled, or creepy.

THE SCALLYWAG is a *crier* and a *crook.* He *will turn his mother out of doors, be apprehended for larceny, and spend longer time in the lock-up than his own house.*

THE LOQUACIOUS character suffers from an *incontinence of speech*, enough to *outbabble the very swallows*, causing listeners to *forget what it is all about, or fall half-asleep.*

THE GOSSIP ends with saying, 'But mind you, this *must go no further'*, albeit he has been *running up to all the town to tell them of it.*

THE SHAMELESS individual is without conscience, and will *neglect reputation for the sake of base gain.* At the theatre, he *will see the performance without paying his own share.*

THE PENURIOUS person pays *too strict attention to profit and loss.* Tight fisted and mean, he *will pour a smaller libation to Artemis than any of the company* and forbid his wife to *lend a neighbour salt, or a lampwick, or aniseed, … or incense.*

THE BUFFOON revels in *obtrusive and objectionable pleasantry.* He *will lift his shirt to freeborn women; and at the theatre will applaud when others cease.* At prayer and libations *he will drop his cup, and laugh as if he had done something clever.*

THE TACTLESS person *should you bid him to a wedding, will inveigh against womankind,* and his timing is dreadful: *if you are sacrificing and put to great expense, that is the day he chooses to come and demand his usury.*

THE OFFICIOUS individual hinders and annoys. *He will undertake to show the path, and*

after all be unable to find his way. Fond of pointless questions and promises beyond his power.

THE STUPID man betrays a slowness of mind in word and deed, who after he has cast up an account, will ask one that sits by what it come to.

THE SURLY character exhibits a sullen rudeness of speech, who, When you ask him, 'where is so-and-so?' is like to reply 'Don't bother me'.

THE SUPERSTITIOUS man is fearful of unseen powers. If a cat cross his path he will not proceed on his way till someone else be gone by, or he have cast three stones across the street.

THE GRUMBLER is a thankless type, prone to undue complaining of one's lot. He is displeased with Zeus not because he sends no rain, but because he has been so long about sending it.

THE SUSPICIOUS man distrusts humankind. He will send one servant off to market and then another to learn what price he paid.

THE SLOB is shaggy as a beast, with hair well-nigh all over his body, and his teeth all black and rotten. Offensive habits include: spitting while talking, nose blowing at the table, nail biting during sacrifice, and hiccuping in your face.

THE ILL-BRED man annoys with bad manners. He Hinders you when you are at this moment about to set forth on a journey. Or says, before the servants, things like 'mammy, how went the day with you when you were brought to bed of me?'

THE PETTILY-PROUD person has a vulgar appetite for distinction. When he is invited out to dine must be next the host. It goes without saying he is apt to keep a pet monkey.

THE PARSIMONIOUS MAN has no honour when it involves expense. He will come home from market carrying his own buyings of meat and pot-herbs in the folds of his gown.

THE BOASTER is a pretentious fantasist. For example, though he live in a hired house he says to strangers that he is about to put it up for sale because it is too small for the entertaining of friends.

THE ARROGANT type will go speak to no man before the other speak to him. In his letters you do not find 'You would oblige me', but 'My desire is this', or 'I have sent to you for that.'

THE COWARD has fear in his soul. When battle commences he pretends that he forgot to take up his sword, and runs to the tent... hides it under his pillow and then spends a long time pretending to seek for it.

THE OLIGARCHICAL or anti-democratic spirit is a love of rule, covetous of power and gain. The one and only line of Homer's he knows is this: 'Tis ill that many rule; give one man sway.'

THE OPSIMATH or late-learner, undertakes activity too great for his age. At wrestling he'll take a throw with the youngsters. He borrows a mount for a ride, and by the way is thrown.

Some interesting characters. Proportions of Six Faces, by Albrecht Dürer [1471-1528]

CHARACTER AND STORY

All of us tell stories, whether in yarns, tales, jokes, anecdotes, gossip, journalism, or adverts. In *The Poetics*, the earliest extant writing manual [c. 335 BC], Aristotle writes that narrative stems from the author's imitation of humans 'in action', using 'spectacular equipment', i.e. an intriguing situation of sufficient magnitude to hold the audience's attention.

CHARACTERS

Aristotle says that action springs from 'personal agents' who 'possess distinctive qualities both of character and thought', and that these characters reveal their inner worlds through dialogue that expresses '*what they choose or avoid*'. The central character of a story is the protagonist (although in some stories, e.g. *Romeo and Juliet*, there are two protagonists).

PROTAGONIST

The actions of the protagonist cause change, either from '*good fortune to bad*' (in **TRAGEDY**) or '*from bad fortune to good*' (in **COMEDY**). In all cases, the protagonist absorbs a new idea and proves its capacity to bring change, embodying the familiar dialectic of *thesis-antithesis-synthesis*. For a story to maintain its momentum, a problem must act directly on the protagonist; it is only through their strength that it can be solved, only by overcoming their weakness or flaw that the story can achieve resolution.

FLAW

A character's flaw is the shadow of what they need. Initially, they hide from it, behind a behavioural facade. But as they gain knowledge the mask drops away and they have to face and overcome their deficiency.

In what Aristotle calls a comedy (not necessarily funny but ending with 'positive forces' ascendant), the character flaw is often some element of negativity (selfishness, cowardice, greed etc.), whereas character flaws in tragedy tend to be elements of goodness, crushed by egotism or a dark self (thus kindness becomes ruthlessness, sanity becomes madness).

The primary flaw of the protagonist is often the driving force of a story, as it embodies their need and the author's moral or ethical vision.

CHANGE

At its most simple, story is about action that brings about change, from the superficial change of blockbusters and detective stories (Batman and Sherlock Holmes don't change, but their *knowledge* of the story's problem does), to the inner transformation found in humanity's enduring healing stories (Odysseus changes from feckless warrior to loving husband, Pinnochio changes from lying puppet to honest child). Story can be seen as a strategy in how to address change, the constant of all life.

ANTAGONIST

In most stories, a flawed character is forced to take action, motivated by a desire or want, as they journey towards their goal, opposed by forces equal and opposite to their own. The antagonism can take the form of a character (Darth Vader or Moriarty), a force (a volcano or alien invasion), or an internal opposition (fear, madness, doubt), or combination. It is the capacity of the antagonist to oppose the protagonist that creates the tension of a great story. Hitchcock famously said 'The more successful the villain, the more successful the picture'.

SHOW, DON'T TELL

The central device of story is a puzzle, or problem, needing to be solved, but not too quickly. If a story explains itself, we can feel cheated, just as we tire of a character who *tells* us how they feel, or a plot which *tells* us what to think. Story engages via evidence (a character's behaviour, or thoughts demonstrated in action and dialogue), and lets *us* put the pieces together, bringing us into the story, by *showing* us how the villain's name makes the other characters shiver or how puppies cringe when he walks by, instead of *telling* us of his cruelty.

AUTHOR'S VOICE

Ancient Greek plays employed a chorus, a group of performers who commented on the dramatic action. Modern authors create a variety of effects by changing their language, e.g. between styles used in a fireside tale, an incredulous yarn, a somber elegy, a euphoric declamation, a curt report, or a salacious note.

FORESHADOWING

A writer can drop hints of what is to come, which may ripple backward through a story. Anton Checkov said that if a gun is shown on the mantlepiece in Act One, it should be fired by the end of the final act.

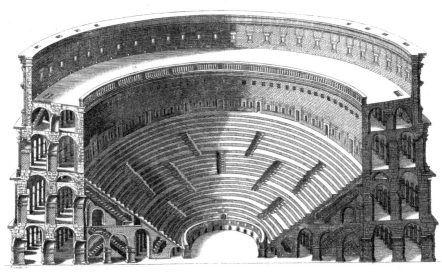

A Roman amphitheatre, engraving by Paul Weindl [1771-1811].

Three and Five Act Structure

Aristotle, in his *Poetics*, writes of plays in general that "A whole is what has a beginning and middle and end" (*protasis*, *epitasis*, and *catastrophe*).

THREE ACTS

In many plots, each of the three phases (beginning, middle, and end) closes with a surprise or **REVERSAL** (*peripatea*): a turning point of grave danger for the protagonist, which leads to a discovery or **RECOGNITION** (*anagnorisis*), a new path, and the next phase of the story. To model these reversals and mirror the dialectic model (*thesis-antithesis-synthesis*), plots are commonly divided into three acts. Acts are then themselves comprised of scenes, mini-stories that lead like a trail of breadcrumbs through the acts. Stories unfold in a setting or arena, populated by a supporting cast of characters, a community that changes with the protagonist.

BEGINNING

After introducing the characters and the setting, a problem pushes the protagonist into action (Frodo must destroy the ring, Alice/Gulliver must find their way home, Miss Marple must solve the crime). This reversal tends to occur towards the end of Act I, and is known as the *inciting incident*. It is the initial catalyst that forces the hero onwards, by revealing their problem.

MIDDLE

As the protagonist pursues their goal, they begin to recognize that what they *want* may

not be enough, that to reach resolution and defeat the antagonist's forces, their desire must become subsidiary to their *need*. This need is in direct relation to their flaw (if they are scared they need courage, if selfish they need compassion, if naive they need maturity etc). Towards the end of Act II the reversal takes the form of a *Crisis*, the lowest point of the story, where the hero appears to have failed (or in a tragedy where they appear to have triumphed).

END

In Act III the reversal is the *Climax*, the point of greatest stress for the hero which then leads to the climax and the resolution.

ACT I - EXPOSITION / THESIS
   Set up
   Flaw or need
   Inciting incident
   Second thoughts

ACT II - OBSTACLES / ANTITHESIS
   Obstacles & Complications
   Confrontation
   midpoint of journey
   Disaster
   Crisis

ACT III - RESOLUTION / SYNTHESIS
   Climax
   Final struggle
   Resolution

FIVE ACTS

In his *Ars Poetica*, written around 19 BC, the Roman critic Horace proposed that "A play should not be shorter or longer than five acts".

MIDPOINT

The five act model emphasizes the midpoint as the fulcrum or crux of the story (Hamlet proves his uncle's guilt, Cinderella meets her prince). The midpoint is the 'supreme ordeal' for the protagonist, the point where they gain an important, often dangerous, revelation. The remainder of the story describes the struggle to change, to be able to use this new knowledge.

SYMMETRY

Stories are symmetrical. In the first half, the protagonist journeys towards some transformative knowledge/event; in the second, they integrate this and return. Symmetry assert itself, with earlier acts being the opposite of later ones. A five act model shows this most clearly (*right*): Act I: no knowledge, Act V: full knowledge. Act II: doubting the need for change, Act IV: doubting the capacity to change. Act III itself divides into two, before and after the midpoint revelation.

SCENES

The structural principles of story repeat themselves fractally in the scene, a story's unit of action. Each scene is itself a mini story, containing its own set-up, conflict, crisis, climax, and resolution. In practice, however, the setup, climax, and resolution are often omitted, leaving the majority of scenes as pure conflict and crisis with other elements implied, as in the screenwriting adage '*arrive late, leave early*'.

A theatre of the middle-ages, from a 1493 edition of Terence's comedies, published in France by de Trechsel.

ACT I - EXPOSITION / ANTECEDENTS
  No knowledge of problem
  Early awakening, limited knowledge
  Awake to knowledge of problem

ACT II - COMPLICATION / RISING ACTION
  Doubts new knowledge, refuses problem
  Begins to overcome reluctance
  Accepts there is a problem

ACT III - ORDEAL / HIGH POINT
  Experiments with knowledge of problem
  MIDPOINT: *Key knowledge / breakthrough*
  Experiments with key knowledge

ACT IV - FALLING ACTION / REVERSALS
  Doubt, consequences of new knowledge
  Growing fear and reluctance
  Crisis, regression, worst point

ACT V - DENOUEMENT / RESOLUTION
  Final Choice; reawakening
  Final Battle; reacceptance
  Complete mastery; resolution

THE ART OF MEMORY · OBJECTS

In *Ad Herennium*, a book published c.85 BC, an unknown author covers the five parts of rhetoric (*inventio, dispositio, elocutio, memoria, pronuntiatio*). The section on memory begins: "Now let us turn to the treasure-house of inventions, the custodian of all the parts of rhetoric, memory".

In additional to our natural memory, we are told, there is also an artificial memory, which can be trained by using, in the words of Frances Yates [1899-1981], "*rules for places, rules for images, memory for things, memory for words*".

In the 15th and 16th centuries, books began to appear dealing with the "Art of Memory". A brief summary of the technique appears over the next four pages.

REMEMBERING A LIST OF ITEMS

The ancients long ago realized that the key to memory is visualization, and they knew that we remember images best when they are

An animal alphabet, useful for remembering words, from Ars Oratoria by Jac Publicius, published Augsburg, 1490.

"*... exceptionally base, dishonourable, unusual, great, unbelievable, or ridiculous*". Early authors on the subject tell us to "*... disfigure, stain with blood or mud, or assign comic effects to our images*".

With this in mind, let us attempt to commit to memory the following list of items: *a frog, a knife, a rubber band, a tomato, a cactus, a book, a pair of spectacles, a pen, some socks, and a rat.*

Following the ancient advice, imagine a bright green *frog*. It has been pierced through by a *knife*, its red blood dripping down the blade. Wrapped around the knife's handle is a fat yellow *rubber band*, which also attaches a large *tomato* to the handle, squeezing it hard. The tomato rests on a spiky *cactus* whose long spikes stick right through it, making its juice flow out and down on to a *book*, on which the cactus pot rests, partially fallen over, spilling sand and earth over the pages. On top of the book, magnifying it, is a *pair of spectacles*, one of whose lenses has been pierced by a huge and leaky *pen*. Around the pen are tied a pair of bright stripey *socks*, the toes of which are being chewed by a blue *rat*. Go through this three times ...

... or make up your own scenario. Medieval writers emphasized the importance of developing your own system, as personalization aids the process. Remember to make your images as vivid and shocking as possible—break them, splatter them, interpenetrate them, etc.

Build the picture, and you will find you can remember these items for days afterwards, as well as reciting them forwards and backwards, whether they represent a shopping list, a table plan, or the parts of a speech.

REMEMBERING WORDS

In preliterate societies, lengthy works of literature were regularly preserved via oral transmission. Today, such memory feats are rare outside the acting profession.

Imagine you needed to memorize the name of the Tonganese ambassador who is coming to dinner. She is called *Amanaki Tafolita Makelesi*. One way to do this, outlined in an anonymous 400 BC fragment, the *Dialexeis*, is to break down unfamiliar words into more familiar ones, so *Amanaki* might become a naked man holding a huge key, etc. But this will not always work if you need the correct spelling.

Numerous memnonic alphabets appear in the pages of medieval treatises on the art of memory. Some of these use animals to represent the letters of the alphabet, thus a lion for L, a snake for S, and so on (*see illustration, opposite, lower left*). Other such alphabets use objects which echo the shapes of letters, rather than their sounds, so a stepladder looks like A, as does an open compass (*see top right*).

By initially committing all of these objects to memory, and later building chains of objects from them (*as demonstrated opposite*), words may be exactly remembered, and, with practice, the entire operation can become surprisingly fast.

REMEMBERING NUMBERS

Long numbers may be remembered in the same way as words, by using a store of stock images for the digits 0-9, so stools and clover leaves for three, bricks and houses for four, stars, flowers or starfish for five, etc.

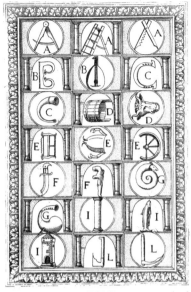

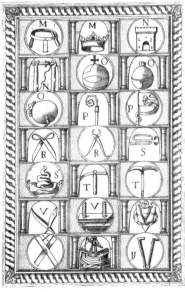

Right: Visual aids to the development of a memory alphabet from Rhetorica Christiana, *Rome 1579.*

THE ART OF MEMORY - PLACES

In his *Institutio Oratoria*, the Roman rhetorician Quintilian [c.35–c.100] describes the importance of *places* (*loci*) to the art of memory.

"*For when we return to a place after a considerable absence, we not merely recognise the place itself, but remember things we did there, and recall the persons whom we met ...*". This natural tendency, argues Quintilian, can be harnessed to the art of memory by creating a memory palace, with distinct places in it, ready for memory objects.

The practitioner is encouraged to imagine a large house, maybe one they already know well, and visit its rooms in a logical order.

In each room they should select five places for memory objects, (one in the center of the room, plus one in front of each wall).

For a simple memory task, maybe to fix the key points in a speech, one object may be placed in the center of each room. Perhaps a severed King's head in the center of one room (to stand for the dangers of revolution), a huge barnacle-encrusted anchor in the next room (to stand for the navy), and so on. By placing objects in this way and visualizing them a few times, the key stages of the speech may be remembered simply by moving through the house.

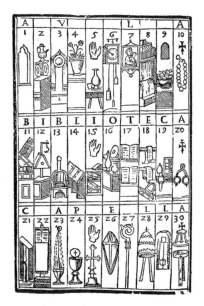 

Above: Pages from the Congestorium Artificiose Memorie *by Johann Horst von Romberch, Venice, 1533.*

To remember a speech in more detail, Quintilian recommends using more places: "*The first notion is placed, as it were, in the forecourt; the second, let us say in the atrium; the remainder are placed in order all round the impluvium, and committed to bedrooms and parlours, but even to statues and the like, ... so that as Cicero says, 'we use places as wax and images as letters'*".

And why use only one memory palace? The legendary memory system of Metrodorus of Scepsis [c.145–70 BC] employed 360 places, essentially the degrees of the zodiac, divided into the signs, decans and so on.

In the abbey memory system of Johann Horst von Romberch [c.1480–1532], all the buildings familiar to the monks were put to use as *loci* for memory objects, whether courtyard, library, or chapel (*opposite page, left*), or less familiar establishments like the barbers, armourers, or slaughterhouse, etc (*opposite page, right*). Romberch's technique uses ten places in each room, with the fifth place marked by a hand and the tenth place marked by a cross.

In the late Renaissance Robert Fludd [1574 –1637] stylized the art further in his memory theatre (*below*), with its five doors at the back of the stage and five pillars at the front (two circular, two diamonds, and one hexagonal).

Since the mid 16th century the ancient art of memory has largely fallen out of fashion, due to distaste for the nature of its weird imagery, and the easy availability of information.

Above: Memory theatre, from Robert Fludd's Ars Memoriae, London, 1621.

PROVERBS

All over the world you'll find that people pepper their speech with proverbs. These sayings reveal fascinating aspects of the common sense, morals, humor, wisdom, and history of their culture, and are vital when there is no written means of transmitting ideas and insights from one generation to the next. Proverbs are inevitably memorable, they are memes which have evolved and survived. They communicate concepts, and their use must be as old as language itself, indeed it has often been said that the best way to learn a language is to learn its proverbs.

Little verbal games are much used in many proverbs: alliteration (Forgive and forget), parallelism (Nothing ventured, nothing gained), rhyme (When the cat is away, the mice will play) and ellipsis (Once bitten, twice shy). Other tricks include repeated vowels (assonance), such as this Ethiopian example: Kan mana baala, a'laa gaala ('A leaf at home, but a camel elsewhere'). Proverbs also frequently employ metaphor (the squeaky wheels gets the grease) and hyperbole (All is fair in love and war), as well as paradox (For peace there must first be war) and personification (Hunger is the best cook) to make their points.

A proverb's frequent purpose is to make people pause for a moment and reflect. In Gaelic-speaking Ireland, for example, a fight caused by a bad comment might be stopped with It's often that a man's mouth broke his nose. The listener is thus made to reflect on the absurdity of the situation, for how can a soft mouth break a hard nose?

The word 'proverb' may be defined as a short sentence or phrase that conveys a nugget of common sense, a summary of practical experience or a rule of conduct. Several other words have similar meanings, for example, 'saying', 'aphorism', 'adage', 'maxim', or 'saw'. Paremiologists (academics who study proverbs) try to draw precise boundaries between these various terms, although in reality it can be difficult to tell them apart. They would define a maxim as a statement of general principle such as You're either part of the solution or you're part of the problem, while an aphorism has a moral or philosophical tone, such as Maladies are cured by nature, not remedies. Furthermore, an adage is described as an aphorism that has passed into general use, while another term, an apophthegm, is used for particularly cynically-worded sayings such as You could cut a better man out of a hedge.

As proverbs can employ all of these forms, they have a delightful fluidity. The best evidence we have for their antiquity is that surviving stone-age hunter-gatherer cultures such as those of the San in South Africa or the Australian aborigines use them in multitudes. Indeed, the earliest surviving book is a collection of sayings or proverbs written down in Egypt around the 25th century BC called *The Maxims of Ptahhotep*. This book covers a wide range of topics from table manners to beauty hints and ways of cultivating self-control, and the Egyptians produced many more including *The Instructions of Amememope*, circa 1300-1075 BC, which were an important source for the biblical *Book of Proverbs*. Ancient Sanskrit texts are also full of proverbs, and there are vast numbers of Chinese proverbs, including many attributed to the great fifth century BC philosopher Confucius. Indeed many of the best literary lines from Homer onwards have since become proverbs, and virtually all writers either used existing proverbs or gave the language new ones. Shakespeare gave more proverbs to the English than anyone else and often used John Heywood's *Dialogue Conteinyng The Nomber In Effect Of All The Prouerbes In The Englishe Tongue* of 1546 as a source, lifting from it such lines as *All's well that ends well*.

The use of rhetorical language, paradoxical statements, and purported logic in proverbs adds to their appeal, and helps them transmit their cultural insights; and the ambiguity inherent in so many is useful too, particularly for voicing sensitive opinions, such as political dissent. In Tsarist Russia people could thus express their contempt with such ironies as *When the Tsar spits into the soup dish, it bursts with pride*, but, inevitably, proverbs were also manipulated by people in power, including the Soviets, who tried to create politically correct ones such as *Good harvests come only from collective farms*. The impact of modernisation is always much celebrated, as in a recent offering from Haiti which declares that *A microwaved fish doesn't fear the lightning*.

Apart from the Egyptian examples, the earliest recorded proverbs are found in Sumerian and Akkadian collections, including one of 1800 BC which declares that *If a she-dog is too hasty it gives birth to blind puppies*. The popularity and longevity of proverbs is such that this

Above: Engraving by Pieter van der Heyden [ca. 1530–1572] of a 1558 drawing of by Pieter Bruegel the Elder, showing a senile or demented Everyman searching for who knows what in all manner of places.

one now turns up from Ethiopia to Holland to Afghanistan, and was also used by Erasmus in the 16th century. Indeed, all levels of belief are enshrined in proverbs, from Native American observations about how we should thank food before we eat it to the thousands found in the sacred texts of all major religions. Novelists and film-makers depend on them, and advertising gives them new outlets, from Volkswagen's *A pfennig saved is a pfennig earned* to Godiva Chocolatier's *Not only absence makes the heart grow fonder*.

These dollops of fun or good sense create such delightful verbal images that they colour every conversation, and roll so easily off the tongue that it would be impossible to live without them.

Pages 366–389 have been taken from Proverbs, Words of Wisdom, *by Alice O'Neill, Wooden Books/Bloomsbury Publishing 2015/16. Country codes are shown on page 410.*

WISDOM AND IDIOTS

WISDOM: Although Knowledge is not wisdom [EGY], Knowledge is harmony [EGY], and if you Know yourself you will know the Gods [EGY] for Knowing others is wisdom; knowing yourself is Enlightenment [CHI]. Actually, Knowledge is like water for the land [KYR], therefore Learn from the mistakes of others, so you don't have to make them yourself [ENG], for it's Better to know too much than too little [NOR]. Wisdom begins in wonder [GRE] but Wisdom only comes when you stop looking for it [HOPI], and since Knowledge takes up no space [SPA] and Learning is a treasure no thief can steal [IND], why not Open a school, close a prison [FRA], for when you Educate a woman, you educate a population [BURU]. To know all is to forgive all [FRA], so Leave half of what you know in your head [AFR AME], and be aware that Still waters run deep [ROM], for He who knows does not speak, while he who speaks does not know [GRE]. Of course, Not knowing is Buddha [JAP].

COMMON SENSE: They say To attain knowledge, add things every day; To attain wisdom, remove things every day [CHI]. And since All sense is not kept under the same roof [NOR], Even if you know a thousand things, always ask a man who knows something [TUR], indeed Seek education even if it means travelling to China [ARAB]; but go carefully, for In the desert of life the wise man travels in a caravan, the fool by himself [ARAB]. It's true that To get lost is to learn the way [AFR], but If you are on the road to nowhere, change the road [ASH], and don't give up, for Wisdom rides on the ruins of folly [DAN] and A disaster teaches more than a thousand warnings [TUR]. A wise man drinks little and believes less [BAS] because Wisdom is the lifelong attempt to acquire it [AME], indeed Only when a tree has grown can you tie your horse to it [AFR JABO]. Always remember, Everything is relative [RUS], so Everyone likes justice in another's house, none in their own [ITA], and never forget, Our first teacher is our heart [NAT AME].

IDIOTS: Beware wise-looking men, as Brains are not found in the beard [IND], and know that All seems the same to someone who knows nothing [EGY], just as In the unknown village the chickens have teeth [IVO]. Sadly, A fool grows without rain [HEB] and There is no royal road to learning [TUR], which is why so often The ignorant are the enemies of wisdom [ENG]. Remember, A person who knows little repeats it often [BER], so Fear a man who only knows one book [FRA], indeed Fear an ignorant man more than a lion [KUR]. Listen, A fool is known by his laugh [GER], and Every fool wants to give advice [ITA], but Try with all your might you'll not get milk from a bull [UKR], and A dog is no help in a smithy [TUR], so Only an idiot looks for a calf under an ox [TUR]. It's Better to leave those in error who love error [EGY], for By the time an idiot learns the game the players have dispersed [ARAB], indeed The dogs bark, the caravan passes on [TUR]. Remember, Even a broken clock is right twice a day [ENG], and Even the stupidest person seems wise if he keeps his mouth shut [FIN], which is why A wise man sits over the hole in his own carpet [PER].

ADVICE AND IGNORANCE

GIVING ADVICE: There's no price for good advice [SPA], which is why One word to the wise is enough [GRE], and He that speaks sows, whereas He that hears reaps [TUR]. Leading by example is better than giving advice [ARAB], so it's often best to Say little about what you know and nothing about what you don't [BAS], for No matter how much care is taken, someone will be misled [BURM]. For many the truth hurts [BAS], as Good medicine is bitter to the tongue; good advice is harsh to the ear [KOR], which is why If you advise a bear you deserve your fate [TUR], and Many people use a stick for a nobody and a hint for a nobleman [AFG]. A fool may say Do as I say, not as I do! [ENG] but Even a fool can give ideas to a wise man [AFR]. And remember, Never give advice in a crowd [ARAB].

HEEDING ADVICE: He asks advice in vain who does not heed it [FRA], so ask for what you want: Don't offer me advice; give me money [SPA]. Forewarned is forearmed [ENG] they say, so Learn from new books and old teachers [KUR], and if you can't read then Experience will show you, while a master points the way [EGY]. Remember, It's shameful never to ask [TUR] and It's better to ask twice than lose your way once [DAN], as He who seeks advice seldom errs [PHL]. Many a young prince is told that Listening to good advice is the way to wealth [PER], for A king with good counsellors has a peaceful reign [ASH]. Often, because Deep calls to deep [ITA], One piece of good advice is better than a bagful [DAN], and Crafty advice often comes from a fool [IRI]. Bear in mind that Another person's counsel is no command [ITA], and that you must Examine the advice, not who gives it [ARAB].

Remember, If you ask a lazy person to work he will only give you advice [TUR], but if you're lucky, you'll find The best advice is on your pillow [DAN] and The best word is left unsaid [SPA], for All that is known is not told [EGY].

IGNORING ADVICE: Only a bad child will not take advice [AFR], for There's none so deaf as those who won't hear [ITA], and There's none so blind as those who won't see [ENG], yet No enemy is worse than bad advice [GRE] because If the blind lead the blind, both will fall into the ditch [BIB], particularly as Advice most needed is least heeded [ENG]. Of course, The person on shore is always the champion swimmer [EGY] and Many will show you the way after the cartwheel breaks [TUR]. Remember, There is no right way to a wrong thing [TUR], and Advice after mischief is like medicine after death [DAN], so bear in mind that Wise men don't need advice and Fools won't take it [AME], so why not Go to the square and ask advice, then go home and do what you like [ITA].

SUBSTANCE AND APPEARANCE

SUBSTANCE: Things are what they are, It is what it is [JAP], for instance However long a log lies in the water it never becomes a crocodile [MALI], and You don't gather grapes from thorns, or figs from thistles [PER]. Nature abhors a vacuum [ROM], thus The pebble comes from the mountain [ARAB], and Each bay has its own wind [FIJI]. In nature there's no such thing as a lawn [ALB]; even if you try to Drive out nature with a pitchfork, she'll keep coming back [ENG]. Indeed, Nature follows its course and a cat the mouse [GRE], so Cats don't catch mice to please God [AFG]. Human nature is the same the world over [AME], just as The name given to a child becomes natural to it [AFR YORUBA]. Perhaps because of this Sometimes a person is nothing, and some aren't even that [FIN], so never forget, There's a prawn under every rock [THAI], and To him who watches, everything reveals itself [ITA].

APPEARANCE: It is widely held that As is the garden, so is the gardener [HEB], just as There is no smoke without fire [ITA], indeed What you see is what you get [ENG], so maybe Clothes make the man [GRE]. In most cases Joining tail to trunk reveals the elephant

[IND], in the same way that The background needs the foreground [MON], and Every hill has its valley [ITA]. So Appear always what you are and a little less [GRE], for In a flat country a hillock is a mountain [KUR]. And Don't judge a man until you have walked a mile in his shoes [KUR], as It takes all sorts to make the world [ENG], and All shoes are not made in the same batch [NOR], indeed Different ponds have different fish [INDO]. Remember, Appearances are deceitful [ENG], and Looks are nothing - behavior is all [IND], and since the Eyes are the window of the soul [ROM], What the eye doesn't see the heart doesn't grieve [ROM].

DISGUISES: Never judge a book by its cover [ENG], for A cowl does not make a monk [SPA] and Pretty clothes and fine faces don't make good people [CONG], indeed A fair skin often covers a crooked mind [DAN]. Perhaps Clothes do not make the man [ENG] after all, as Black souls wear white shirts [UKR], while A clever hawk hides its claws [JAP], and all too often Under the sheikh's turban there is a monkey [EGY]. Water can deceive the diver [EGY] as well, so don't be a fool: Don't think there are no crocodiles if the water is still [MALAY], and remember, A sweet potato doesn't advertise that he's tasty [MAORI], just as The tree with most leaves doesn't always have juicy fruit [BRA]. It goes without saying that Not all white liquids are milk [IND], just as Not all black objects are coal [BAS], and A sandal is not a shoe [AFG]. So look deeper, and see that The grey mare may be the better horse [ENG] despite the fact that A bad horse will eat as much as a good one [DAN], and watch out, There are often glowing embers under cold ashes [DAN]. Remember, Eat what you like but dress as others do [ARAB]: Goodness whispers, but evil shouts [BAL].

PAST, PRESENT, AND FUTURE

PAST: We all know how Time flies [ROM], how it is Here today and gone tomorrow [ENG], how No hand can catch time [IND]. Indeed, Time is precious [ENG], Time is money [AME], though all too often We want time badly, then use it badly [AME]. For example, Don't let yesterday take up too much of today [NAT AME], and Don't cry over spilt milk [ENG], for There are no birds in last year's nest [ENG]. In general, Hindsight is clearer than foresight [ENG], so remember, Four things do not return: spoken words, flighted arrows, past life, and lost opportunities [ARAB]; indeed, Even a god can't change the past [GRE], for A lost sheep can be recovered, but not lost time [BAS]. Despite this, No matter how hard the past, you can always begin again [ZEN]; and when you do, watch out, History repeats itself [ENG], which is why so often Things present are judged by things past [IND], and Today is the scholar of yesterday [ROM].

PRESENT: The early bird catches the worm [ENG], for so often in life it's First come first served [FRA] and If you get to the river early you drink the cleanest water [AFR]. Otherwise, you can tell yourself Better late than never [ENG], for Everything has its proper time, Even manuring cabbages [GRE]. Indeed, there's A time for adversity, a time for prosperity [TAM], and There's a first time for everything [ENG]—even The longest journey starts with a single step [CHI]. Aim to Experience each moment to its fullest [ZEN], for There's no time like now [ENG], and despite the fact that Time and tide wait for no man [ENG] and The tide must be taken when it comes [ENG], don't forget to Give time time [ITA], to Suit yourself to the times [GER], and remember that Time

brings roses [ENG]. Indeed, Those who are happy do not observe the passing of time [CHI], and One today is worth two tomorrows [ENG].

FUTURE: Worrying about the future ruins the present [ENG], so relax, Tomorrow is another day [ENG], and Tomorrow's winds will blow tomorrow [JAP], so Let us think of tomorrow when tomorrow comes [PER], though Tomorrow never comes [AME]. Of course, There are few paths without perils [ARM], so Be prepared for conflicts, as they have already begun [TIB] and however good your intention The food you give may come back as poo [AZTEC]. In the end Time heals all [ENG], for Everything has an end [UZB] and Things will work out [AME], All in good time [ENG]. Just remember The past is the future of the present [JAP]; indeed, We are only visitors to this time and place [AB AUS], With a sponge to wipe away the past, a rose to sweeten the present and a kiss to greet the future [ARAB], for Flowers bloom, flowers fall [CHI].

THOUGHT AND ACTION

THINKING: *Everyone who succeeds must first dream* [AFR], so remember that *Your head is not just there for a hat* [UKR], and that *If you fail to plan, you plan to fail* [AME]. At the very least, *Don't go out of your depth before you can swim* [ENG], because *If you know the road you can ride full trot* [ITA], and if you can't then *Ask those coming back for the best way forward* [CHI]. *A person in a hurry arrives late* [GEOR] whereas *Slow and steady wins the race* [ENG], so *First catch your hare* [ENG], because once you know how, *To know and to act are the same* [JAP]. That's why *Practice makes perfect* [ENG] and *Repetition is the mother of memory* [AME], and also why *A pleasant thought never comes too soon* [DAN]. So be aware that *A tree only moves if there's wind* [AFG], and *A watched pot never boils* [ENG], which is why you *Don't call a dog with a whip in your hand* [AFR] and *A big goat does not sneeze without a reason* [MALAW].

DECIDING: Some say that *The world is conquered with words, not swords* [GEOR], though this is *Easier said than done* [EUR], for *Fine words don't put porridge in the pot* [BOT]. Of course, *Thought is free* [ENG], and *Anything that releases you from a dilemma is useful* [AFR FULANI] but remember that *It's easier to think than to act* [GER], and *You don't get anywhere by running in your mind* [FIN]. Nevertheless, the mind is powerful, *Work doesn't kill, but worry does* [AFR], and *If you think something impossible, it will be* [TUR], just as *If the heart is unwilling it will make a thousand excuses* [INDO]. That's why *Where there's a will there's a way* [ENG], and *What isn't can yet be done* [GER] for *You already have all you need to become great* [NAT AME]. Above all, always try to *Do unto others as you would have them do unto you* [BIB], and *Never say never* [ENG]. Of course, *Smooth hands love the labour of others* [RUS], and the coward will always say "*When in doubt, don't*" [ITA], for *No choice is also a choice* [HEB], but even if *The spirit is willing but the flesh is weak* [ENG], generally, *Elbow grease is the best polish* [ENG].

ACTION: *A rocky field demands a pickaxe not a prayer* [NAT AME], so *Never put off for tomorrow what you can do today* [ENG], for *Even if the eyes fear, the hands will do the work* [RUS]. Of course, *Least said soonest mended* [ENG], and *Actions speak louder than words* [ENG], so it's mostly *Better to have less thunder in the mouth and more lightning in the hand* [NAT AME], for when you *Grasp a nettle like a lad of mettle, as soft as silk it will remain* [ENG]. In the same spirit, *Put your best foot forward* [ENG], aim to *Be the master of your will and the slave of your conscience* [HEB], and *If your destiny doesn't fit, then fit yourself to your destiny* [ARAB]. All *Actions have reactions* [KOR], so *Practice what you preach* [ENG] and remember that if *Brag is a good dog, Holdfast is better* [ENG]. Above all, *Act honestly and speak boldly* [DAN], *Tread gently on the ground and leave it as found* [ARAP], and *If you're in a hole, stop digging* [ENG].

FRIENDS AND ENEMIES

FRIENDS: *Be gracious to all men, but choose the best to be your friends* [GRE], for *A man is known by the company he keeps* [ENG]. Listen, for *When a stranger cares enough to speak, he becomes a friend* [ROM], and make time, for *Friendship is a plant which one must water often* [GER]. Never forget, *There's safety in numbers* [ENG], *If you play alone on the beach the sea monster will get you* [INU], so *Two heads are better than one* [ENG], and *A house can hold a hundred friends* [AFR]. *Old wine and friends improve with age* [ITA], so *Of friends the oldest, of everything else the newest* [KUR]. Indeed, *Nobody should forget old friends and old goats* [FAR], maybe because *Strangers forgive, friends forget* [BUL]. Treat your friends well, *If your friend is honey don't lick it all up* [EGY], for *Friends are lost by calling often or calling seldom* [SCO]. Take heed, *Many a friend is not known until they are lost* [ITA], and remember, a friend accepts another, *Warts and all* [ENG], because *The eyes of a friend do not see the warts* [AFG].

GOOD FRIENDS: *Life has no blessing like a prudent friend* [GRE], for *Iron sharpens iron, and one man sharpens another* [BIB], so *Hold a true friend with both hands* [AFR], and remember, *A cup of coffee brings forty years of friendship* [TUR]. A friend will tell you *The world is your oyster* [ENG] because *Like stars, a friend will guide you* [ARAB], just as *An old friend is like a saddled horse* [AFG], and *No camel journey is long in good company* [TUR]. *A real friend holds your hand in times of distress* [AFG], so *Share your path with a friend* [AFR], for *A friend who shares is a friend who cares* [ENG], and *A friend in need is a friend indeed* [ENG]. In fact, *Friendship is a single soul dwelling in two bodies* [GRE], thus *A true friend is like a mirror* [IND], so listen to friendly criticism, for *Without an opposing wind no kite can fly* [CHI].

BAD FRIENDS: Sometimes, *New friends can be as deceptive as spring ice* [RUS], for *Trusting some men is like having water in a sieve* [EGY], in other words, *If your friend is an ass expect nothing but kicks* [IND]. In fact, *Distance makes the heart grow fonder* [ENG], for *A hedge between keeps friendships green* [GER], but money doesn't: *Lend your money and lose your friend* [ENG]. Tellingly, *A friend to all is a friend to none* [GRE] as *Everybody's friend is everybody's fool* [GER], which is why *A man of many companions may come to ruin* [BIB], since *Bad company ruins good morals* [BIB]. So *Beware of a man's shadow and a bee's sting* [BURM], for *Cobras bite, whatever you call them* [IND], and *If you live in the river then make friends with the crocodile* [IND]. Remember, *A great talker can be a great liar* [FRA], so stay alert, for *A friend who leads one astray is an enemy* [GRE]; indeed, *An insider can bring down a kingdom* [IND]. Above all, bear in mind that *A wolf with no fangs doesn't lose its hunger* [CHI] and *Beware of the dog that doesn't bark* [NAT AME], *he'll be the first to bite* [GER],

ENEMIES: All too often *Close friends can become close enemies* [AFR], for *People with the same ideas can be enemies* [BURM], so *Keep your friends close and your enemies closer* [CHI], and never forget, *A friend looks you in the eye, an enemy at your feet* [KYR], while *A wise enemy is better than a foolish friend* [AFG]. Generally, you should *Eat an enemy for lunch before he has you for dinner* [EGY], *Use an enemy's hand to catch a snake* [PER], and if possible, *Give your enemy a hungry elephant* [NEP].

FIGHT OR FLIGHT

FIGHT: *Better death before dishonour* [JAP], for *You may as well die fighting as become a slave* [AFR]. *Pick your battles* [ENG], as *A hungry wolf is stronger than a well-fed dog* [UKR] and *Only an ignorant rat will fight a cat* [AFR], however much *Fortune favours the brave* [ENG]. *The bigger they are the harder they fall* [ENG], so *Meet roughness with toughness* [FRA], for *When the going gets tough the tough get going* [AME], and although *Attack is the best defense* [AME], never forget that *One man can guard a narrow pass* [CHI]. Often enough *Showing off is half the fight* [SWA], for you should *Deal gently with the bird you mean to catch* [ITA], as *The greatest victories spill no blood* [CHI] and *There's no need for poison if you can kill with sweets* [IND]. *Keep your eyes open* [ENG] and *Tread carefully* [ENG], for *A thousand good moves are ruined by one bad* [CHI] and *If you have no horse you have no feet* [KYR]. *Avoid chasing cowards lest they become brave* [TUR] and take care, *Loose lips sink ships* [ENG] just as *Ski tracks can be followed* [FIN]. Never forget, *The weakest man can cause hurt* [BURM], and *Blood does not wash out blood* [AFG], so you'll generally find that *If your fist is in*

his mouth, his fist is in your eye* [YEM]. Remember, *If a man bites a dog it will say he has poor teeth* [SUD], so *Better weight than wisdom you can't carry* [ICE], because *It ain't over till it's over* [AME].

PEACE: Often, *Discretion is the better part of valour* [ENG], so *If you won't bite, don't bare your teeth* [CHI]. Anyway, *The strong don't need clubs* [SEN], for *War is a bad chisel with which to carve out tomorrow* [SIERRA LEONE], and *No war has a cause that reason cannot settle* [ARM]. Wise up, *To live in peace, you must be on good terms with your neighbours* [ZIM], for *Only crows rejoice when grass-hoppers fight* [LESOTHO], so *Better a bad peace than a good war* [HEB]. And hope that *Peace does not need a guard* [SWA], for although *There's strength in unity and weakness in division* [TAN], *If the lion and the sheep lie down together the sheep won't get any sleep* [KEN]. Bear in mind that *The more you spend on peace, the less you spend on war* [KEN], so *If you can't beat them, join them* [ENG].

FLIGHT: *Evading the enemy takes true courage* [PHI]; *There are no atheists in foxholes* [AME]. However, although *Tottering is not necessarily falling* [SWA], and sometimes it's true that *Flight is the beginning of collapse* [HEB], at other times *It's better to live a coward than be a dead hero* [ENG], as *He that fights and runs away may live to fight another day* [ENG]. So *Who has no courage must have legs* [ITA], indeed *Fear lends wings* [GER], as *An old man will run through a thorn forest if he is being chased* [AFR], so *Find any port in a storm* [ENG] but remember, *The world's a small place for a fugitive* [KYR]. Why not *Watch and wait* [IND], for *A barking dog seldom bites* [ROM], and *Heroes only appear once the tiger is dead* [BURM].

Success and Failure

SUCCESS: *A good beginning makes a good ending* [ITA], just as *A small key can open big doors* [KUR]. Be patient, *Great oaks from little acorns grow* [ENG], as *Bean by bean, the sack gets full* [GRE]. Always *Take things one step at a time* [ENG], because *If you go as far as you can see, you'll see further when you get there* [PER], which is why *The true artist perseveres, whatever his critics say* [DUT]. So *Hang your clothes in the sunshine* [BAS], *Keep your eyes on the prize* [AME], and *Make hay while the sun shines* [ENG], because *Growing millet doesn't fear the sun* [UGA]. Be bold, for *Nothing ventured nothing gained* [FRA], and *Keep your options open* [ENG], for *The mouse that has but one hole is quickly taken* [TUR]. And *Don't use an axe to embroider* [MALAY] nor a *Sledgehammer to crack a nut* [ENG], because *Succeeds breeds success*, in fact *Nothing succeeds like success* [FRA], even though *The bigger a man's head, the greater his headache* [PER].

WARNING: *Don't count your chickens before they've hatched* [ENG], and *Don't say hurray until you've jumped the barrier* [RUS], for *The proof of the pudding is in the eating* [ENG], and all too often *A water pot only falls off your head when you reach your front door* [UGA]. Be prepared too, *A reed before the wind lives on while mighty oaks do fall* [ENG], and *If you want a rose, respect the thorn* [PER]. Don't daydream, *The road to hell is paved with good intentions* [ENG], just as *An imaginary mill grinds no flour* [BAS], indeed *As you make your bed so must you lie on it* [EUR], or as they say in America, *Garbage in, garbage out* [AME]. So bear in mind *Success comes from hard work* [BAS], as *Without working you won't get fish from the pond* [RUS], and *He who would eat the fruit must climb the tree* [SCO]. It's up to you, *Failure is the child of neglect* [ENG], and *If you snooze you lose* [ENG], so *If a job's worth doing, it's worth doing well* [ENG]. And don't play too clean, *Nice guys finish last* [AME], or too brash, *A barking dog catches no hares* [EST], or too fast, *Nothing so bold as a blind mare* [SCO]. And *Look before you leap* [ENG] as *Most shipwrecks happen in unknown waters* [EGY], and *Even good swimmers can sink* [MAD]. Remember too that *You can't unscramble eggs* [AME] and that *You're fine as long as there are no cows on the ice* [DAN].

FAILURE: Chin up! *Failure is the source of success* [CHI], for *Failure teaches you more than success* [RUS], and *He who never fails will never grow rich* [ENG]. Grin and bear it, for you *You can't be a good doctor if you've never been ill* [ARAB], and *Calm seas don't make good sailors* [AFR]. Moreover, *Even the best scribes make blots* [SPA], so learn to *Take the rough with the smooth* [ENG] as often *The obstacle is the path* [ZEN]. All in all, *Life is not a bed of roses* [SPA], for *Where wood is chopped, splinters fly* [POL], but when you do get hurt *Weeping washes the face* [IND]. Therefore *Suffer, suffer, suffer, and you will get the brightest crown* [FIN], and discover along the way that *Adversity makes a strange bedfellow* [ENG].

RICHER AND POORER

MONEY: If *The best things in life are free* [ENG], why do so many people think that *Money makes the world go round* [AME] and that *Money is power* [AME]? Maybe it's because *He who pays the piper calls the tune* [ENG] and *Money makes dogs dance* [FRA]. Or maybe it's as simple as *Money talks* [ENG], because *Money doesn't grow on trees* [ENG] and *There's no such thing as a free lunch* [AME]. Save it carefully, as *Many a mickle makes a muckle* [SCO], and *A penny saved is a penny earned* [ENG], for *Money has a way of taking wings* [BIB]. Sometimes, though, it's important to spend: *In for a penny, in for a pound* [ENG], they say, but please try to *Get the money honestly if you can* [AME].

RICHER: Watch out, for *When money's not a servant it's a master* [IND], and any gardener will tell you that *Good soil is worth more than gold* [EST]. You may be happier if you *Stay where there are songs* [GYP], and go where *Poor people entertain with the heart* [HAITI], because *It's always the idiots who have money* [EGY], despite the fact that *A fool and his money are soon parted* [ENG]. Remember, *Half of something is better than all of nothing* [ENG], but

Money isn't everything [ENG], so although *Every bird loves its nest* [ITA], it's funny how *Money can buy you a house, but not a home* [CHI]. And never forget, when you die *You can't take it with you* [ENG], for *You make a living from what you get, you make a life from what you give* [ENG], and *Even the poorest man has the sun and the stars* [FIN].

MODERATION: *Money won't solve all your problems* [SLO], but *Having enough is better than having too much* [BAS] for *The bigger your roof the more snow it collects* [PER], and *Many donkeys mean a lot of hay* [BAS]. Admittedly, there's *One law for the rich, another for the poor* [ENG], but *More slaves makes more thieves* [HEB], so *Better a small deal than a long quarrel* [NOR], and *Better your own copper than another man's gold* [GEOR]. That's because *Money is the root of all evil* [BIB], and *When money speaks, the truth stays silent* [RUS]. Remember, *All that glitters is not gold* [RUS], and *Pearls are worth nothing in the desert* [IND]. You know, *A bird wouldn't sing if it knew how poor it is* [DAN], so always *Count your blessings* [AME].

POORER: Life for the poor can be tough, for *The sated do not see the hungry* [BAS] and *Every rock strikes the feet of the poor* [AFG]. Indeed, *Beggars can't be choosers* [FRA], for a *Man with no money can do no nothing in a market* [FRA]. Lovers should bear in mind that *Love does much, but money does more* [FRA] and *When money goes out the door, love flies out the window* [ENG]. It's the same in Alaska, where *Unless you're the lead husky the view stays much the same* [INU], because *A man with no bread has no authority* [TUR], which is why *Small fish never sleep* [POLY].

HONOUR AND SHAME

HONOUR: *Honour once lost never returns* [DUT], for *Honour cannot be bought* [PHIL] which is why *A good name is the best treasure of all* [ITA]. It's *Better to be Poor with honour than rich with shame* [DUT] and it's also *Better to deserve honour and have none, than have honour and not deserve it* [POR]. *The measure of honour is in the person giving it* [HEB], so *There's no honour for an eagle in vanquishing a dove* [ITA], but *There is honour among thieves* [ENG] for *The thief thinks all men are like himself* [SPA]. *Do not lose honour through fear* [SPA], for *A hole is more honourable than a patch* [IRE], and *Where there is no honour there is no dishonour* [POR]. *Great honours can be great burdens* [ENG] for *Honour and reward are in different sacks* [POR] so all in all *Honour is better than honours* [FLEM]. Remember, *A prophet is not without honour save in his own country* [BIB], so *Keep your boasts until after the battle* [AFR], for *Honour often only blossoms in the grave* [FR].

RESPECT: In matters of integrity *Honesty is the best policy* [ENG], for *When a monkey can't reach a ripe banana he says it isn't sweet* [SUD]. Since *We are all guardians of our own honour* [IND], *If you've only a day to live spend half of it in the saddle* [KYR], for it is *Better to die on your feet than live on your knees* [MEX]. And pay attention, *He that respects not is not respected* [ENG], so *Respect others if you want to be respected* [PHIL], because *Respect is mutual* [ZULU]. Remember, *There is no shame in learning* [TUR] and *If you understand danger you'll not feel it* [TUR], which is lucky, as *The more the danger, the greater the honour* [ENG], for *No strength within, no respect without* [KASH]. Of course, *None but the brave deserve the fair* [ENG], so remember, *Every slip is not a fall* [USA] and it is *Better to retire in honour than advance in disgrace* [SERB].

SHAME: Shame is complex, *A clean conscience makes a good pillow* [ENG], but *Guilt is good for you* [JAP], for *If you fear shame, you fear sin* [HEB], thus someone *Who fears no shame comes to no honour* [DUT], and *A person with no shame has no conscience* [ENG], as *No sin is hidden to the soul* [IND]. So, *Light a candle rather than curse the darkness* [CHI], and be warned that *A long silence makes a big noise* [AFR]. Take note, *Dirty feet stain the carpet* [TUR] and *Shame lasts longer than poverty* [ENG], so *If you lie down with dogs you'll get up with fleas* [ITAL], just as *One scabby sheep infects a thousand* [ALTAY]; just remember, *Your mouth won't stink if you don't eat garlic* [TUR]. Take note, *A thief's a king until he's caught* [PER], because *Necessity knows no law* [AFR], and sometimes it's just *Either throne or coffin* [IND]. Indeed, *Shame can kill* [PHIL] so *Many lay their shame on the backs of others* [DAN], for *A man with an ill name is half-hanged* [ENG].

LOVE AND LAMENT

OVE: Take heed, *One cannot love and be wise* [ROM], for *Love is blind* [ENG], and *Love can make you blind and deaf* [ARAB], as *Love enters man through his eyes and woman through her ears* [POL]. Indeed, *The first love letters are written with the eyes* [FRA] after which *A letter from the heart can be read on the face* [SWA]. *No wind is too cold for lovers* [UKR], and *When one is in love, a cliff becomes a meadow* [ETH], for *Love makes the impossible possible* [IND], and *Love understands all languages* [ROM]. Remember, *The heart sees further than the head* [SWA], which is why *A life with love is happy; a life for love is foolish* [CHI], and it's best to have *One thread for the needle, one love for the heart* [SUD]. Interestingly, *Love can't grow garlic* [ARM], but *Garlic can grow love* [PAK], so put *Food before romance* [JAP], for *The way to a man's heart is through his stomach* [ENG], and *Love has to be shown by deeds not words* [SWA]. Like the sun, *Give more love than you receive* [SWA], for *Love begets love* [ROM] and *A loving heart has no equal* [SWA], indeed *Goodness of heart is more important than*

appearance [JAP]. *In love beggar and king are equal* [IND], for *All is fair in love and war* [ENG], and *The heart that loves is always young* [GRE]. Sometimes, *Stolen sugar is the sweetest* [IND], although for many *A mother's love is best of all* [IND]. There's someone for everyone, even *A mended lid for a cracked pot* [JAP], and since *Love makes the world go round* [ENG] of course *Love will find a way* [ENG].

LAMENT: *A broken hand can work but a broken heart can't* [AFG], as all too often, *Those who love us make us cry* [SPA], and *Although you can suffer without love, you can't love without suffering* [GER]. *Love is a despot who spares no one* [NAM], but it's *Better to have loved and lost than never to have loved at all* [ENG]. In most cases *Love hurts but doesn't kill* [MEX], so, because *The heart knows its own pain* [SWA], *Pain is obligatory, suffering optional* [AME]. Be careful, *Yield to your body's desires, and endure the disasters that follow* [RUS], for *He who marries for love, dies miserably of anger* [ITA], so watch out, *For a little love you pay all your life* [HEB]. Don't be jealous, *Diamonds are a girl's best friend* [AME], and *There is no love without jealousy* [ITA], although *Jealousy destroys love* [MEX], so all too often *A loving heart can change to hatred* [SWA], and *There's no medicine to cure hatred* [ASH]. *Hate burns its preserver* [SWA], so the sooner you *Learn to love your enemy* [SWA] and realize that *Anger is a luxury you can't afford* [CHI] the quicker you can *Move on* [ENG]. Often *A lovers' quarrel is love's renewal* [ENG] but *Many kiss the hand they would love to cut off* [SPA], so *If you have no big knife, kiss your enemy* [SWA]. At the very least *Love and let the world know, and hate in silence* [DUT].

MARRIED OR SINGLE

MARRY: *Marry first and love will follow* [ENG], but *Before you marry make sure of a house wherein to tarry* [ENG], for *You should only get married when you can build an igloo* [INU], together if possible, for *Teamwork holds you together, as four eyes see better than two* [GER]. Often, *Girls marry to please parents, widows to please themselves* [CHI], but even so *Marriages are not as they are made, but how they turn out* [ITA]. Thus *If your partner minds the children you'll catch more whales* [INU], and you should *Butcher the animals as your wife directs, as she knows your needs* [INU]. Remember, *Love is a flower which turns into fruit at marriage* [FIN], and much of *Love comes after marriage* [INU], for although *A happy man marries the girl he loves, a happier man loves the girl he marries* [AFR]. This is because *Once the home is set up, love is shown by deeds not words* [SWA], so even if *You only get married when you can sew well* [INU] you'll find that *If you love the vase, you'll love what's inside* [AFR], and that *Children are the reward of life* [AFR].

DALLY: *Love spares no one* [NAM], and *There is Magic in love* [ENG], thus *One wedding often brings another* [ENG]. You should *Follow your heart* [ENG], for *There is no love like the first love* [ITA] and *An early marriage brings long love* [GER], especially since *Marriages are made in heaven* [ENG]. But be aware, *The course of true love never did run smooth* [ENG], so don't *Marry in haste and be sorry at your leisure* [IRI], and *Never choose a spouse by candlelight* [FRA], for *It's much easier to fall in love than to stay in love* [AFR]. Remember, *Pretty paths can be crooked* [CAME], and if you *Marry beauty you marry trouble* [NIG], which is why *A marriage in May is rued for ever* [ROM]. And know

that *A kiss must last long enough to be enjoyed* [GRE] and that *Frequent kisses end in a baby* [HUN].

SINGLE: Actually, don't get married, *A good marriage lasts three days, bad ones until death* [ITA]; in fact *Marriage is the tomb of love* [RUS], and *Where there is marriage without love, there will be love without marriage* [AME]. Think it over, *Marriage is both heaven and hell* [GER], for *Marriages and ships always need mending* [GRE], as all too often *In marriage cheat who can* [FRA]. Remember, *If you marry a monkey for money, the money goes and the monkey stays* [EGY], so *Never marry for money, as ye'll borrow it cheaper* [SCO] and *Don't marry a woman with bigger feet than yours* [BOT]. *Marry late or never* [ENG], despite the fact that *A late marriage makes orphans* [BELGIAN], but watch out, if you *Always say no* [FRA], you'll see how *The choosy person ends up with the ordinary* [BAS]. *Marriage is a lottery* [ENG], and *A woman's heart is like the autumn sky* [JAP], so do you really want to *Marry and grow tame* [SPA], or be told that *A woman's work is never done* [ENG] or that *A woman's place is in the home* [ENG]? Take heed, *Who marries does well, who marries not does better* [ENG].

WORK AND PLAY

WORK: Hard work never killed anyone [HEB], although If you can't stand the heat, get out of the kitchen [ENG]. Be prepared to put the hours in [AME], for Work has bitter roots, but sweet fruits [ROMA], and It is working that makes the workman [ENG]. Mind you do it well, Measure seven times and cut once [RUS], for A worker is known by his work [FRA], and Fine work is its own flattery [SLO], so The work praises the workman [GER] if The labourer is worthy of his hire [BIB]. Pick your trade, Aim before you shoot [AFR], Acquire skill and make it deep [HAW], and bear in mind that He who likes his work, to him work comes easy [HEB]. Remember, If you look at the clouds your work will fail [MAYA], just as Weighty work is done with few words [DAN], so Go sure and steady [AME], Haste makes waste [ENG] and A stitch in time saves nine [ENG]; Rome wasn't built in a day [ROM]. Some trade tricks: If you're an anvil be patient, if you're a hammer be strong [KURD], Leap where the hedge is lowest [ITA], and Make a new bucket while you still have the old one [BER]. Never forget, The hardest work is to do nothing [AME], so Everybody must make his own arrows [INU], unless you're a teacher, as He who can does, he who can't teaches [ENG]. Timing is key, Don't put off today's work until tomorrow [AFR], but note, A windy day is

not a thatching day [IRI], and Launch the canoe when the breakers are calm [HAW]. Above all, be prepared, A bird caller must always be alert [HAW] just as A cat in gloves catches no mice [FRA]; and remember, Work loves fools [RUS] so A volunteer is worth two pressed men [ENG].

IDLENESS: Idleness is the root of all evil [GER] and Laziness is the mother of all vices [ALB], for The devil makes work for idle hands [ITA]. In addition The lazy pig does not eat ripe pears [ITA], just as Someone with no work in summer has no winter boots [POL], and He who looks for light work goes very tired to bed [HEB]. Excuses are the offspring of laziness [AFR], thus A bad dancer blames the floor [INDO], just as A poor writer blames his pen [SPA] and A bad workman blames his tools [ENG]. However, A bad excuse is better than none [SPA], and If ifs and ands were pots and pans, there'd be no work for tinkers' hands [ENG]. Just remember, You can't get something for nothing [ITA] and If you pay peanuts you get monkeys [AME], or you might even get a Jack of all trades and a master of none [ENG].

PLAY: When the cat is away the mice will play [ENG], since All work and no play makes Jack a dull boy [ENG], so don't Burn the candle at both ends [FRA] as It's the pace that kills [ENG], and hear this: An hour of play is worth more than a year of talking [POR]. So it's Better to play for nothing than to work for nothing [SCO] although If you work like an ant you'll eat sugar [YEM]. It's nearly always best if you Don't roll up your trousers before you reach the stream [KUR] and bear in mind that Barbers don't shave their own beards [AFR]. In any case, There's a time and place for everything [ENG], so Don't forget to breathe [AME].

HOPE AND DESPAIR

HOPE: Hope springs eternal [DAN], thus Every cloud has a silver lining [ENG], and Tomorrow is another day [ENG], for In the land of hope there is no winter [CHI]. Don't worry, If the sky falls we'll catch the larks [ENG], and If you die today you'll not sin tomorrow [YEM], so There's hope while your fishing-line is still in the water [NOR]. Live in hope [ENG], God will find a low branch for the bird that can't fly [KUR], so just Follow the river and you'll get to the sea [IND]. Hope keeps us alive [FRA], despite the fact that Hope is the mother of fools [POL], and He that lives on hope has a slender diet [SCO]. You know, even Crooked logs make straight fires [FRA] and Even foul water will quench a fire [MON], so Persevere and never fear [ENG], for the person Who digs lives [AUSTRIA] although Those who are declared dead live longer [GER]. Remember, A long hope is sweeter than a short surprise [HUNG], just as Hope keeps the poor alive, while fear kills the rich [FIN].

CONTENTMENT: Hope for the best and prepare for the worst [ENG], for it's Better to be one-eyed than blind [GER]. And Don't worry about tomorrow, because you don't know what may happen to you today [HEB]; Time will tell [GRE], for Time is a great healer [GRE], so Enjoy yourself, it's later than you think [CHI]. Also, Don't worry about unlaid eggs [GER], for Worrying never did anybody any good [SWE], instead Face your fears [ENG], for The death of fear is doing what you dread [SEQUICHIE]. In fact, Fear and hope are the parents of God [AZTEC] so if God doesn't need our prayers [AFG], at least Don't throw the baby out with the bathwater [ENG] but Be content with what God has given you [PHIL], for He has enough who is content [FRA]. Cross a bridge when it comes [ENG], and

remember, Who hides his grief finds no remedy [TUR]. As men fear snakes, snakes fear men [TIB], thus Every why has a wherefore [FRA], and Your feet take you where your heart lies [AFG].

DESPAIR: Just as Every rose has a thorn [ENG], Despair and hope are sisters [SLO], so He who hopes despairs [ROM]. No lamp burns until morning [PER], thus Shadows grow in moonlight [CHI], but never forget that The darkest hour is just before dawn [ENG]. Bad news travels fast [ENG], for Bad news is its own horse [BAS], just as Hunger drives the wolf out of the forest [FRA] and A bleating kid excites the wolf [ENG]. Be prepared, Misfortunes never come singly [FRA], After one loss come many [FRA], and Not all the buds on a bush will blossom [IND]. You're on your own, for Good fortune seldom knocks twice [ENG] and Most prayers go unanswered [NOR], so take care you don't Live by hope and die of hunger [ITA], as Grief is to the soul what a worm is to wood [TUR]. However much Despair gives courage to a coward [ENG], remember Despair never pays debts [AME], and You can't put out a fire with spit [ARM]. Pent up grief will burst the heart [ITA], so when New grief awakens the old [ENG], Drown your grief in pleasure [EGY].

STASIS AND CHANGE

STASIS: Only the wisest and the stupidest of men never change [CHI], for When you're finished changing, you're finished living [AME]. Old habits die hard [ENG], and Regret always comes too late [ITA], but It's no use crying over spilled milk [ENG], for you'll find It's just the same dog with a different collar [SPA], as Change alone is unchanging [GRE]. Therefore, although A leopard can't change its spots [ENG] and A dog's tail never straightens [EGY], The more things change the more they stay the same [GRE], for Nothing is carved in stone [ITA], and Never is a long time [ENG]. Take care [ENG] you Mind what you wish for [ENG], although If wishes were horses beggars would ride [ENG], and if you do Set a beggar on a horse he'll ride to the devil [ENG]; therefore be sensible, The dog only bites when you tread on its tail [CAME] so If it ain't broke don't fix it [AME], and Don't change horses in midstream [ENG]. Bear in mind that The past is the past [JAP], and When a man is out of sight the land remains [MAORI], for Beneath a lying stone no water flows [RUS], though Water flows but the stones remain [JAP].

CHANGE: It's never too late to change [GER], and A change is as good as a rest [ARAB]. That's why A squeaking wheel gets the grease [ENG], and A change of pasture makes fat calves [ENG], but remember that To change and to change for the better are two different things [GER]. Of course, Every action has its opposite [ENG], so When the wind is great, bow before it [CHI] and Let the wind choose the canoe's speed [SAM], for When the music changes so does the dance [AFR], or as the Scots say: Change of masters change of manners [SCO]. And remember, Those who don't dream are lost [AB AUS] so Throw caution to the wind [ENG], Everyone has their own way of eating yoghurt [TUR]. Live for today [CHI], say Easy come, easy go [ITA], C'est la vie! [FRA] or Today me, tomorrow thee [ENG], and aim to Be first at the feast, last at the fight [IND]. Therefore, Let the water you don't need flow [SPA], for All is flux, nothing stays still [GRE], and You can't step into the same river twice [GRE], as Nature admits of no permanence [ENG]. Some say Let it be worse as long as it is change [HEB], for If anything can go wrong it will [ENG], however The rain falls on more than one roof [CAME], and What was hard to bear can be sweet to remember [IND]. Therefore, Go with the flow [KOR], but be careful, Without the forest there will be no water, and without water there will be no rice [MAD], although If you wait long enough even eggs grow legs [ETH]. Remember that Many a sudden change takes place on a spring day [IRI], so Seize the day [ROM] and always bear in mind that all life on Earth has to Adapt or perish [ENG].

POWER AND HUMILITY

RULING: *People follow the ways of their kings* [ARAB], thus *A king and a crying child have their way* [JAP], unless *The mountains are high and the emperor is far away* [CHI]. Take heed, *The one who knows not how to dissemble, knows not how to rule* [ROM], and also know that *Every monarch is subject to a mightier one* [ROM], just as *Every power is subject to another power* [AFR SHONA], so *Rule the mountains to rule the river* [FRA]. Remember too that *Eagles don't catch flies* [DUT] and *Lions don't turn round when small dogs bark* [AFR], but *A little force can move large masses* [ICE]. Bear in mind that *Only billy goats are born to be masters* [NOR] and *Power often goes before talent* [DAN], so *A good king is better than an old law* [DAN].

HARD POWER: Alas, *The best apples are eaten by the bears* [TUR], for *Peace does not make a good ruler* [AFR], instead *Might makes right* [GRE], for *Pull someone by their ears and their head will follow* [IND], and *Flies don't land on a boiling pot* [ITA]. *Only a hand that can wield a sword may hold a scepter* [UZB], but *Much power makes many enemies* [ENG], and *No matter how big the whale a harpoon can kill him* [MALAY]. So, *He who continually uses an axe must keep it sharp* [AFR HAUSA], and *If a nail sticks up it is hammered down* [JAP], just as *A head on a spike no longer conspires* [NORSE]. Thus, while he *Who owns the stick will own the buffalo* [IND], in the end *He who lives by the sword dies by the sword* [BIB], and *When the tree falls, the monkeys scatter* [CHI].

SOFT POWER: *A good sword can keep others in their scabbards* [DAN], but it's also true that *The pen is mightier than the sword* [ENG], for *With sweet words you can lead an elephant* [PER], and in any case *The queen bee rarely stings* [POR]. Of course, *If you want obedience then only command the possible* [ARAB], and aim to delegate, for *Absolute power corrupts absolutely* [ENG]. Also, try to *Take out your anger on the saddle, not the donkey* [BAS], as *Zeal without prudence is frenzy* [ENG]. And observe too that *An honest magistrate has lean clerks* [CHI], as *A little with honesty is better than a great deal with knavery* [ENG].

HUMILITY: *He who has not served cannot command* [ENG], so *Don't forget what it is to be a sailor when you're a captain* [TAN]; *Cap in hand never did any harm* [ITA]. Inevitably, *Too humble is half proud* [HEB], and *Pride comes before a fall* [ENG], so *If you're on an elephant don't imagine there's no dew on the grass* [AFR], as *Even the tallest tree has an axe at its foot* [KURD] and *A small thistle still stings* [GRE]. Wherever you are, *There's always room at the top* [AME], for *No mountain is tall enough to block out the sun* [CHI], and *If the mountain won't come to Muhammad, Muhammad must go to the mountain* [ENG], for *A ruler is his people's servant* [YEM]. Aim to *Be a bee among flowers, not a fly on a trash-heap* [INDO], never forget that *We only borrow the earth from our children* [NAT AME], and that *Great trees afford wonderful shade* [CHI].

TRUE OR FALSE

TRUTH: Truth is heavy, so few men carry it [HEB], indeed A truth-teller finds all doors closed [DAN], for Whoever tells the truth will be chased out of nine villages [AFR], but still, it's Better to suffer for truth than prosper by falsehood [DAN]. A true word needs no oath [TUR], though Many a true word is spoken in jest [ENG] just as The worst insults are true [BAS]. Ask the truth from a child [AFG], as Whatever is in the heart will come to the tongue [PER], but be ready, Nothing hurts like the truth [ENG]; indeed it's best to Speak the truth with one foot in the stirrup [IND], for Truth is time's daughter [SPA]. Luckily, There is truth in wine [GRE] for The Truth lies at the bottom of a well [GRE]. All too often though, Truth is the first casualty of war [AME], as The truth is half a quarrel [IND]. Remember, Every fable is a bridge to truth [ARAB] but Truth is stranger than fiction [ENG], so Don't ask questions of fairy tales [HEB]; Not everything that is true is to be discussed [SPA].

FAULTS: A fault confessed is half-redressed [AFR], whereas A fault once denied is twice committed [FRA], for To justify a fault is a second fault [ROM]. Remember, Even a good man has his faults [ENG], so

Deal with the faults of others as gently as with your own [CHI]. Also be aware that Faults are thick when love is thin [DAN], and also that A man who falls into a well will seize even the edge of a sword [HAUSA] because Falling is easier than rising [IRI], so Don't look where you fell, but where you slipped [LIBERIAN].

LIES: Some liars tell the truth [ARAB], but even so, A half-truth is a whole lie [HEB] and A thousand probabilities do not make one truth [ITA]. Indeed, A little truth makes the whole lie pass [ITA], for Art conceals art [ROM]; but still, You can't ride two horses at once [ENG], just as You can't serve God and Mammon [ENG]. Remember, Until the lion can talk, men's tales will laud the hunter [AFR] and A pedlar always praises his wares [SPA], so even though Seeing is believing [ENG], A man with a big knife is not always a good cook [DAN], especially since What comes on the table must be eaten [GER]. Your mind can lie to you, for Even if your enemy is only an insect he will look like an elephant [TUR], and bear in mind that The eyes do not see what the mind does not want [IND]. So If you must lie then have a good memory [ARAB] for If you tell a lie in the next town it will be home before you [BAS]. Even if A lie has no author [IND], The smallest lies are deadly spears [AFR YORUBA], Falsehood travels and grows [DAN], and despite the fact that A lie has little legs [ENG], A lie will run halfway round the world before the truth has got its boots on [ENG]. Never forget, A guilty conscience is a powerful enemy, for the guilty person has the higher voice [NEP], so It's often best to keep your head down [ENG] and just accept that Everybody lies, apart from my mother and father [BER].

STRONG AND WEAK

STRONG MIND: *Strength is defeated by strategy* [PHIL] so *Being wise is better than being strong* [BIB], for *You don't have to cut a tree down to get its fruit* [CAMB]. Understand that *The strength of the bee is its patience* [WEL], so *Be master of mind, rather than mastered by mind* [JAP], and realize that *The forest needs the tiger just as the tiger needs the forest* [CAMB]. Know too that *Silence is a source of great strength* [CHI], and that *Our strength grows out of our weakness* [AME], in fact even *The weakness of the enemy makes our strength* [NAT AME], because *That which does not kill us makes us stronger* [GER]. Even so, *There's no point in an umbrella if your shoes leak* [IRI], for *You don't stumble over a mountain, but you do over a stone* [IND], so *Call the bear Uncle until you are over the bridge* [ROMA], and bear in mind *You can't clap with one hand* [AFG]. Remember, *He who acts honestly acts bravely* [ROM], and *A brave man gets his reward* [IRI], so *Plan your year in the spring, your day at dawn* [CHI], for *Fuel alone will not light a fire* [CHI].

STRONG BODY: *Be strong, for Only the strong will survive* [JAM], but *Attempt nothing beyond your strength* [ROM], for *It is the overload that kills* [SPA], as *Even the strongest eagles can't fly beyond the stars* [INU] and *Even horses die from hard work* [RUS]. Note that *You can only lean against something strong* [IND], which is why *A buffalo doesn't feel the weight of his horns* [IND], and just as *Big fish eat little fish* [ENG], *Little fish grow big* [FRA]. And *The strength of fish is in the water* [AFR SHONA] for *A river is made drop by drop* [AFG] and *A steady drop will carve the stone* [GER]. So persevere, *No pain no gain* [ENG], and *Where there's a will there's a way* [ENG], for *Big*

fleas have little fleas upon their backs to bite them [IRI], and *If you ride a camel you need not fear dogs* [BER]. Remember that *A cat is a lion in her own lair* and also that *An arch never sleeps* [IND].

WEAKNESS: *A chain is only as strong as its weakest link* [ROM], and *Who is brave enough to tell a lion that his breath smells* [BER]? Alas, *To the mediocre, mediocrity appears great* [IND], so *Weak souls always set out to work at the wrong time* [FRA] and *The weak go to the wall* [ENG]. Of course, *Every little helps* [FRA], because *A little help is better than a lot of pity* [IRI], but still, *Fleas jump on sickly dogs* [SPA] and *The cord breaks at last by the weakest pull* [SPA] so mind you *Hate not the man, but the weakness* [ICE], and *Endure the weaknesses of others by knowing your own* [JAP]. Remember, *A bully is always a coward* [ENG] and *A viper without fangs is a piece of rope* [IND], so *Make a weak man your enemy not your friend* [RUS] and *Keep your broken arm inside your sleeve* [CHI]. Bear in mind that *When the wine is in the wit is out* [ENG], so *It's better to limp than be footless* [NOR], and always *Better to stay on land than to cry for help from the water* [NOR].

KIND AND SELFISH

KIND: Generosity is wealth [AFR], they say, and Kindness is even better than piety [HEB], for Altruism is the mark of a superior being [EGY], and indeed Kindness is the soul's best quality [CHI], as Kindness nourishes both giver and receiver [AFR]. So Kindness is not just for the sake of others [JAP] because If you sow kindness you reap gratitude [ARAB], and Kindness begets kindness [GRE] as One good turn deserves another [ENG]. So Even if life is short, a smile only takes a second [CUBA] and certainly, A good word never broke a tooth [IRI], thus A word of kindness is better than a fat pie [ENG], and even if you're hungry Don't go where the food is plentiful but where the people are kind [BOT]. Forget injuries but never a kindness [CHI], indeed Write injuries in the sand, kindnesses in marble [FRA], except A forced kindness deserves no thanks [ENG]. Bear in mind too that Kindness is remembered, meanness is felt [HEB], so A kindness is easily forgot, an unkindness never [IND], and be aware that The sandal tree perfumes the axe that fells it [IND].

TOO KIND: Yours truly is not always true [ENG], and Too much kindness can lead to tiredness [SWISS], for often The kind hearted becomes a slave [BURM],

particularly if there is Too much kindness but not enough gratitude [TUR]. Just be aware that There is no honey without gall [SPA], so Speak softly but carry a big stick [AFR], and recall that the The hand of compassion is stung when it strokes a scorpion [PER]. Also be aware that To lend is to buy trouble [IND], for He that goes a-borrowing, goes a-sorrowing [ENG], as The greatest humiliation is helplessness [EGY] so Try to be envied rather than pitied [GRE]. Remember, He who depends on himself will attain the greatest happiness [CHI] because He travels fastest who travels alone [ENG], so generally It is better to buy than to receive [JAP], especially as The buyer's eyes are in the seller's hands [ITA].

SELFISH: No one calls on a miser [YORUBA], because Asking a miser for help is like trying to dig through seawater [ARM], just as A dog with a bone knows no friends [DUT]. Indeed, What you have, hold [ENG], for It is better to save than to beg [BAS], as Desire has no rest [ENG] and A person's desire grows day by day [HEB]. However, All suffering is caused by desire [CHI], so Grasp all and you lose all [ENG], as Gluttony kills more than the sword [ENG] and A glutton young becomes a beggar old [ENG]. Or you can Buy, buy, buy, and let the children pay the debts [FIN], for A selfish person will even take advantage of wind and clouds [JAP]. But He who has much is afraid of many [SPA], which is why Greed keeps men poor [MON], so Don't be a slave to your desires [ENG], but know that All that is not given is lost [IND] and No man is an island [ENG]. Remember, The miser's bag is never full [DAN], and Coffin carriers love the plague [JAP], but miser or not, After three days guests and fish smell [IND], and The guest who breaks the dishes is not forgotten [AFR].

YOUNG AND OLD

YOUNG: *You're only young once* [AME] so *Make the most of it* [ENG], *The world is your oyster* [ENG], although *Those whom the gods love die young* [GRE]. *Everything new is beautiful* [ITA], though *Nothing is so new it has not happened before* [DAN], so *Youth is the time to sow* [GER], for *The vigour of youth passes away like a spring flower* [ROM], yes, *Youth slips away as water from a sandy shore* [IRI]. *You have to learn to walk before you can run* [ENG], but *Green twigs bend easily* [TUR] so *Instructing the young is like engraving stone* [MOROCCAN], just as *The young cock crows as he hears the old one* [YORUBAN], for *What youth learns, age does not forget* [DAN]. *A new broom sweeps clean* [ENG], and *Diligent youth makes easy age* [ITA], but beware, *Young saint, old devil* [ENG]. In fact, *Youth is wasted on the young* [ENG], for many *Mysterious roads beckon to young people* [ANGOLA], indeed *Youth, ignorance, and impatience ruin people* [ARAB], and *Young folks think old folks fools, while old folks know the young are* [GER]. *You can't put an old head on young shoulders* [DAN], so *Never send a boy to do a man's job* [ENG], but remember, *When a palm branch reaches its height it must make way for a young one* [NIG], for *There is always something new out of Africa* [GRE].

OLD: *Walnuts and pears you plant for your heirs* [ENG], but *Old age comes for free* [NOR], so *The young rely on their parents, the old on their children* [VIET]. *Youth has a beautiful face, old age a beautiful soul* [SWE], for *Young twigs may be bent, but not old trees* [DUT]. *Elderliness is a richness* [BURU], so *An old man is put in a boat to give advice, not to row* [UGA], for *Taught by necessity, old people know a lot* [BAS]. *You don't teach the forest paths to an old gorilla* [AFR] any more than you'd *Teach your grandmother how to suck eggs* [ENG], indeed *Many a good tune is played on an old fiddle* [IRI] so *Cherish youth but trust old age* [PUEBLO], for it's *Better to be an old man's darling than a young man's slave* [ENG]. And even though *Old cows like young grass* [BURM], *It's better to have an old spouse than none* [TAN], for *A man grows old but his courage remains* [KYR]. *Young barber, old physician* [ENG], they say, for *We grow old fast, but wise only slowly* [CHI], for *Age doesn't make you wise, but it does make you slow* [FIN]. Of course, *Young men can die, but old men must* [ROM] for *When a lion grows old the flies attack him* [TAN] which is why *Old women get uneasy when dry bones are mentioned* [AFR], as *Old age leads to something worse* [NOR]. However, *Nobody is so old that he doesn't think he'll live for another year* [ROM], so even if *You can't teach an old dog new tricks* [ENG], *As we grow old our bad qualities keep us young* [FIN]. But it's also true that *Old sins cast long shadows* [ENG] so although *Everyone has seen a cradle, nobody knows their grave* [NOR].

HEALTH AND SICKNESS

HEALTH: A healthy mind lives in a healthy body [ROM], indeed A healthy mind makes a healthy body [JAP], which is why A person's health is in his feet [IRI]. Good health is the sister of beauty [MALT], so He who would be healthy, let him be cheerful [WEL], for Health is better than wealth [ENG]. Of course, When you're busy you are never ill [JAP], because Regularity is the best medicine [IND], but Life is uncertain, so eat the dessert first [FIN], for It's all one whether you die of illness or love [ITA]. Often, Health is only valued when sickness comes [ENG], as Illness gives you a taste for health [HUN], so remember, Prevention is better than cure [GER]. An apple a day keeps the doctor away [ENG], but Water is the oldest medicine [FIN], so Take good care of the well [SWA]. Never forget, Have a clean heart and you may walk near the altar [GRE], for If the heart be stout, a mouse can lift an elephant [TIB], but even The stoutest heart must fail at last [AME], so Your health comes first, you can hang yourself later [HEB].

HEALING: Laughter is the best medicine [AZE], just as A library is medicine for the mind [GRE] and Minor complaints are cured by eating [FIN]. Otherwise,

The sauna is the poor man's pharmacy [FIN], as It's better to sweat than to sneeze [SPA]. Feed a cold, starve a fever [AME], and bear in mind The medicine that hurts does you good [SWA]. Don't worry, For every ailing foot there is a slipper [BRA], so Don't hide the truth from your lawyer or your physician [ROM] as Hiding sickness prevents a cure [SWA]. Every patient is a doctor after his cure [IRI], but mind, Before healing others, heal yourself [AFR] and then Scratch people where they itch [ENG]. Console a sufferer, even an enemy [SWA], and remember There is no cure for old age [SWA], despite the fact that A creaking door hangs longest [ENG].

SICKNESS: Nothing tastes good to the sick [SPA], as Illness starts with the mouth [JAP], and Sickness comes in haste and leaves at leisure [DAN]. Sickness is everyman's master [DAN], indeed Sickness is our common lot [ENG], for Neither hat nor crown help against headache [SWE], and We are all in the laps of the gods [GRE]. If Sickness is awful, a relapse is worse [SICILIAN], which is why The worst ache is the present ache [LEB], and Mortals bear many ills [ROM]. Desperate ills require desperate remedies [FRA], and If sauna, liquor and tar don't help, the disease is fatal [FIN]. Note that An imaginary illness is even worse than a real one [HEB], because Those whom the gods would destroy they first make mad [GRE]. It's odd how Sickness is felt, but health not at all [ENG], so maybe An illness tells us what we are [ITA], which is why it's Better to have a sick body than an ignorant mind [GRE]. Remember, No one buys illness with money [LAT], for Sickness is the physician's feast [IRI], and If you eat caribou hair, you get an itchy bottom [INU].

LIFE AND DEATH

LIFE: *Life is a dream, but don't wake me* [HEB], *Life is but a bubble* [GRE], *Life is like licking honey from a thorn* [HUNG]. *Life is the flash of a firefly* [NAT AME], so *Nobody is quick enough to live life to the full* [SPA]. Even so, try to *Live life to the full* [SWE], for *As we live, so we learn* [HEB], and *Art is long and life is short* [GRE], thus *A good life keeps away wrinkles* [SPA]. *Life has its ups and downs* [AME], for *Life would be too smooth if it had no rubs in it* [ENG], but *It is one life, whether we spend it laughing or weeping* [JAP], so remember, *Life is for one generation; a good name is forever* [JAP]. *A person is lent, not given, life* [ROM] so *Live until you die, and don't panic* [BAS]. Indeed, *Live and let live* [ENG], and *Fear life, not death* [RUS], for *Living is harder than dying* [PHIL], and *He that fears death lives not* [ENG] so *Don't die before you die* [PER]. Or perhaps do *Die before you die* [AFG], for *Life is sweet* [ENG], and *What does the blind man know of the lotus flower's beauty* [IND]? With *A precipice in front of you, wolves behind you, such is life* [ROM], therefore *Live so the world will cry when you die and you'll rejoice* [CHEYENNE]. Remember, *The less you sleep, the more you get out of life* [HEB], also *Being thin is not death* [BEMBA], and *Bad breath is better than no breath at all* [AME].

DEATH: Despite the fact that *Birth is the remedy for death* [AFR], *There's no cure for old age* [SWA], and *One is certain only of death* [HEB], just as *The top of a tall tree will soon be firewood* [BURM]. *Approaching death is great, you just give up* [FIN], so don't worry, *Death kills worry* [LAT] anyway, and *When death is there, dying is over* [RUS]. Mercifully, *A nose doesn't smell its own head rotting* [IND] and *You only die once* [POR], for *Death is concise, like a good proverb* [RUS]; *Death is the great leveller* [ROM]. Indeed, *In death, everyone is equal* [PHIL], as *Death alone measures equally* [CZE], yes *Death combs us all with the same comb* [SWE]. *Death devours lambs as well as sheep* [ENG], *Death can carry a fat tsar as easily as a lean beggar* [RUS], *Death takes the poor man's cow and the rich man's child* [FRA]. *Death regards spring as winter* [RUS], for *Death keeps no calendar* [ENG], and since *Death rides a fast camel* [ARAB], it's *Best to send a lazy messenger to the angel of death* [HEB]. Often, *You only become important after death* [HEB], but if *There are skeletons in the closet* [PHIL], you'll find *Death is the revealer of secrets* [AFR HAUSA]. And *Death has the key to the miser's chest* [ASH], for *The shroud has no pockets* [EGY], so *Death pays all the debts* [ENG], indeed *Death rights everything* [MALT]. Conveniently, *Dead men don't bite* [ROM], and *Dead men tell no tales* [ENG] either, so *Look upon death as going home* [CHI], for *Even the dead in their vaults enjoy company* [MAD]. In the end, *Death defies the doctor* [SCO], for *When it's your time* [BRA], *Death is the last doctor* [SWE], and *You only sleep really well in your coffin* [IND]. Remember, *We don't even get death for free; as it costs us our life* [RUS].

Punctuation, Usage, and Abusage

COMMA: The comma divides opinion. However, to convey intended meaning, correct use is essential. Compare *Comfort ye my people* vs. *Comfort ye, my people.*

> **SERIAL COMMA** (aka *Oxford*, *Series*, or *Harvard comma*): Usually a matter of personal preference or institutional convention (and used throughout this book), it is also more common in the U.S. The serial comma is placed before the final conjunction (usually 'and' or 'or') in a series of three or more terms: *Red, white, and blue.* It *must* be used if its absence will create ambiguity: Compare *My dogs, Annie, and Peter.* vs. *My dogs, Annie and Peter.*

> **PARENTHETIC COMMAS:** These enclose parenthetic expressions: *Ashford, the most pleasant town in England, is 20 miles from Dover.*

> **COMMA BEFORE A CONJUNCTION INTRODUCING AN INDEPENDENT CLAUSE:** Not compulsory, but generally recommended. Compare *The abbey is in ruins, and the town around its walls derelict* vs. *The abbey is in ruins and the town around its walls derelict.*

SEMICOLON: One of the most underused punctuation marks; modernized by Venetian printer Aldus Pius Manutius [1449-1515], who also invented *italics* and pioneered the production of affordable bound books. A good rule is: if there is no conjunction joining independent (but closely linked) clauses then you may use a semicolon. *The sun was setting; an owl began to hoot in the wood.* – Beatrix Potter. *Language creates an imagined world; it also recalls, transforms, and exorcizes.* The semicolon can also be used with CONJUNCTIVE ADVERBS such as *however, moreover,* and *thus*: *The report proves nothing; however, it makes for interesting reading.*

COLON: A colon can join independent clauses if the second amplifies or explains the first: *She did not want to leave him: and yet she did not feel free with him.* – D. H. Lawrence. It can also introduce a quotation that supports the previous clause: *The wholefood store reminded Raven of a line from Dickens: 'It was the best of times, it was the worst of times'.* Or it can introduce a list: *Attendees will include: Bill, Jane, and Justin.* Use semicolons in the list when one or more items contain a comma: *Attendees will include: Bill, Head of Sales; Jane, Lead Scientist; and Justin, Director of Strategy.*

DASHES: The short HYPHEN glues two words into one, as in *Self-service, One-sided, Well-being.* The longer EN-DASH connects a range of numbers, as in *See pages 390–391* or *The 2015–2016 season.* The long EM-DASH can function like a colon: *And she—she belonged to nobody*, or as a pair of parentheses (brackets): *He had never seen—nor indeed heard of—soap.*

APOSTROPHE: Use 's to show POSSESSIVE SINGULAR OF NOUNS and most PERSONAL NAMES: *A witch's beauty. Tomorrow's weather. Bob's hat.* For PERSONAL NAMES THAT END IN 's' add 's only when you would naturally pronounce it: *Charles's friend, Dickens's novels.* When not naturally spoken, add the apostrophe only: *Jimmy Conners' best game. Griffiths' girlfriend.* Exceptions occur in place names and organisations: *St Thomas' Hospital* ('s' spoken but not written). For PLURAL NOUNS THAT ALREADY END IN 's' add the apostrophe only: *Girls' school. Two weeks' time. Horses' stable. Fans' rights.*

THAT OR WHICH: Of these RELATIVE PRONOUNS, WHICH refers to *things* only; THAT to *things and persons.* WHICH is *nondefining*: *The bicycle, which is broken, is in the yard* (the only bicycle in question); THAT is *defining*: *The bicycle that is broken is in the yard* (defines the bicycle in question). WHICH refers to the last thing mentioned: *The man wore a hat which covered his eyes.*

ITALICS: Use *italics* for EMPHASIS, such as asking your reader to pay *really close attention*, or CONTRAST: the word is *in*alienable not *un*alienable. Italics are also used to cite TITLES of books, films, journals, musical compositions, and other complete works, such as Tolstoy's *War and Peace* or Wagner's *Das Rheingold.* Finally, they are used in fiction for INTERNAL DIALOGUE, as in *She froze. He knows what I'm thinking.*

U.K./U.S./Canadian Spellings

-ISE or IZE: Most words ending -ise in the U.K. end -ize in the U.S. and CANADA.

> **U.K.:** *agonise, baptise, centralise, demobilise, etc.*
> **U.S. & CAN.:** *agonize, baptize, centralize, demobilize, etc.*
> **EXCEPTIONS:** *advertise, advise, apprise, chastise, comprise, despise, devise, disguise, excise, exercise, improvise, incise, prise, promise, revise, supervise, surmise, surprise, wise, televise.*

-RE: Words ending with a consonant then unstressed -re in the U.K. and CAN. often end with an -er in the U.S.

> **U.K. & CAN.:** *calibre, centre, fibre, goitre, litre, lustre, manoeuvre, meagre, metre, mitre, nitre, ochre.*
> **U.S.:** *caliber, center, fiber, goiter, liter, luster, manoeuver, meager, meter, miter, niter, ocher.*

-OUR: U.K. and CAN. -our endings are usually -or in the U.S.

> **U.K. & CAN.:** *colour, flavour, behaviour, harbour, honour, humour, labour, neighbour, rumour, splendour.*
> **U.S.:** *color, flavor, behavior, harbor, honor, humor, labor, neighbor, rumor, splendor.*
> **EXCEPTIONS:** When the 'our' sound is unreduced in pronunciation e.g. *contour, glamour* (but note *glamorous*), *velour, parmour, troubadour.*

-YSE: U.K. verbs ending -yse end -yze in U.S. and CAN.

> **U.K.:** *analyse, breathalyse, paralyse, catalyse.*
> **U.S. & CAN.:** *analyze, breathalyze, paralyze, catalyze.*

-AE & OE: Double vowels *ae* and *oe* become *e* in the U.S.

> **U.K. & CAN.:** *aeon, anaemia, anaesthesia, caecum, caesium, coeliac, diarrhoea, encyclopaedia.*
> **U.S.:** *eon, anemia, anesthesia, cecum, cesium, celiac, diarrhoea, encyclopaedia.*

-ENCE: Some -ence nouns end -ense in the U.S.

> **U.K. & CAN.:** *defence, licence, offence, pretence.*
> **U.S.:** *defense, license, offense, pretense.*

-OGUE: Some U.K. and CAN. nouns ending with -ogue can end with either -og or -ogue in the U.S.

> **U.K. & CAN.:** *analogue, catalogue, dialogue.*
> **U.S.:** *analog/analogue, catalog/logue, dialog/logue.*

-LL: A final U.S. l is often ll in the U.K. and CAN.

> **U.K. & CAN.:** *cancelled, counsellor, dialled, labelled, modelling, quarrelled, signalling, traveller, travelling.*
> **U.S.:** *canceled, counselor, dialed, labeled, modeling, quarreled, signaling, traveler, traveling.*

SILENT 'e': U.K. spelling often keeps a silent 'e' when adding suffixes; U.S. spelling typically does not.

> **U.K.:** *ageing, bingeing, likeable, liveable, rateable, saleable, sizeable, abridgement, judgement.*
> **U.S. & CAN.:** *aging, binging, likable, livable, ratable, salable, sizable, abridgment, judgment.*

SPECIAL CASES:

> **U.K.:** *annexe, aluminium, buses, cheque, cosy, disc, draught, grey, kerb, liquorice, mould, orientated, plough, pyjamas, smoulder, speciality, storey, sulphur, tyre, waggon, yoghurt.*
> **U.S.:** *annex, aluminum, busses, check, cozy, disk, draft, gray, curb, licorice, mold, oriented, plow, pajamas, smolder, specialty, story, sulfur, tire, wagon, yogurt.*
> **CAN.:** *annex, aluminum, busses, cheque, cozy, disc, draft, grey, curb, licorice, mould, oriented, plow, pyjamas, smoulder, specialty, storey, sulphur, tire, wagon, yogurt.*

PUNCTUATION WITHIN QUOTES: There are two views: The LOGICAL VIEW (*favoured in the U.K.*) asserts that only punctuation which is actually part of the quote should be placed within the quotation marks: *In Act V we learn that life is 'full of sound and fury'.* The CONVENTIONAL VIEW (*favored in the U.S. and CAN.*) places secondary punctuation (usually full stops and commas) *within* the marks: *In Act V we learn that life is "full of sound and fury."*

SINGLE OR DOUBLE QUOTES: The British use more single quotes than their American 'friends', reserving double quotes for "spoken" items: *Many of these 'experts' claim to know everything. One said "There's nothing I don't know!"* Single quotes come in to their own when a quotation has another 'inside' it: *"Theodore" said Winston. "Telling me to 'eat dirt' was really rather rude."*

VERB ASPECTS

Each of these verb aspects may be associated with specific verb endings in one or more world languages.

ACCIDENTAL: "I happened to knock over the chair"

ATTENUATIVE: A low-intensity action. "It glimmered."

COMPLETIVE: An action which takes place. "He spoke."

CONATIVE: Attempting. "I was trying to get to work."

CONCLUSIVE: Like the durative (below), but terminates with a static sequel in the perfective. "I had slept for a while."

CONTINUATIVE: Indicates an indefinite span of time or movement with a specified direction. "I am still eating."

CONTINUOUS: Ongoing. "I am eating" or "I know."

CURSIVE: Describes progression in a line through time/space. "He ran across the field."

DEFECTIVE: An action short of completion. "I almost fell."

DELIMITATIVE: Temporal boundaries. "I slept for an hour."

DISTRIBUTIVE: Expresses a distributed manipulation of objects or performance of actions. "He chopped off their heads one after another."

DURATIVE: Expresses an indefinite span of time, a non-locomotive uninterrupted continuum. "I slept for while."

EPISODIC: Something happened regularly, but not gnomically. "John rode his bike to work in the morning."

EXPERIENTIAL: Indicates a previous experience of performing the action. "I have gone to school many times."

FREQUENTATIVE: Implies repeated action. "It sparkled" rather than "It sparked." Or, "I run around" vs. "I run."

GNOMIC/GENERIC: Expresses a general truth. "Fish swim and birds fly."

HABITUAL: A subtype of imperfective, expressing a habitual tendency. "I used to walk home from work", "I walk home from work every day."

IMPERFECTIVE "I am walking to work" (progressive) or "I walk to work every day" (habitual). An ongoing action: combining progressive and habitual aspects.

INCEPTIVE or INGRESSIVE: The beginning of a new action (as opposed to the Inchoative). "I started to run."

INCHOATIVE: Focuses on the beginning of a new state (as opposed to the Inceptive). "She began to turn green."

INTENSIVE: Indicates a high-intensity action. "He glared."

INTENTIONAL: Tells us something about the reasons for the action. "I listened carefully."

ITERATIVE: Expresses the same action repeated several times. "I read the same books again and again."

MODERATIVE: Indicates a medium-intensity action. "It flowed," rather than "It trickled" (Attenuative) or "It gushed" (Intensive).

MOMENTANE: Describes a short-lived or sudden action. "The mouse squeaked once" (contrasted to "The mouse squeaked / was squeaking").

PAUSATIVE: Indicates a break in an ongoing action which frames the verb. "I stopped working for a while."

PERDURATIVE: An action extended beyond its wonted (or desired) length of time. "He talked and talked and talked. . ."

PERFECT (a common conflation of aspect and tense): Brings attention to the consequences of a situation in the past. "I have arrived."

PERFECTIVE: "I arrived at work." An event viewed in its entirety, without reference to internal temporal structure.

PROGRESSIVE: Describes an ongoing and evolving action. "I am eating."

PROSPECTIVE (a conflation of aspect and tense): Brings attention to the anticipation of a future situation. "I am about to eat," "I am going to eat."

PROTRACTIVE: Indicates an action which takes a very long time, perhaps much longer than normal. "The argument went on and on."

PUNCTUAL: An action which happened once. "I died."

RECENT PERFECT, or "after perfect." A recently completed action. "I just ate" or "I am after eating" (Hiberno-English).

REPETITIVE: indicates a continuum of repeated acts or a connected series of acts. "We were constantly shaking hands at the wedding."

RESUMPTIVE: "I went back to sleep."

REVERSATIVE: Directional change. "He turned them back."

REVERSIONARY: Indicates a return to a previous state or location. "They went back to the way they were."

SEMELFACTIVE: like Punctual, "I sneeze."

SERIATIVE: Indicates an interconnected series of successive separate and distinct acts. No real English equivalent.

STATIVE: Establishes an ongoing, but not evolving, state of affairs (a subtype of Continuous). "I know French."

TERMINAL: An inherently terminal action. "He stopped it."

TERMINATIVE, or cessative: "I finished eating."

TRANSITIONAL: Indicates a shift from one state to another. "He was becoming angry."

Index & Glossary

through (e.g. *I Am America (and So Can You!)*, Stephen Colbert) (cf. *enallage*).

Anadiplosis, *274*, (*an-uh-dip-LOW-sis*; Gk. doubling back): a sentence that begins and ends with the same word or phrase.

Analepsis: an interjected scene that takes the narrative back in time from the current point the story has reached.

Analogical fallacy, 183, 185, *210*: the use of an analogy which lacks relevance and evidence. "It's good to grow your own food!" "No, you sound like Chairman Mao".

Analogue: a story with similar characters, situations, settings, or verbal echoes to those found in a different story.

Analogy, *in logic*, 183, 185, 210, *in rhetoric*, 253, 256-7, (Gk. back reasoning): a comparison (among relations, not things) used to reason to some conclusion.

Anamnesis, *286*, (*an-am-NEE-sis*; Gk. reminiscence): quotation from memory. (q.v. *memory, the art of*)

Anapest, *127*, 130, 134-5, 142, 149, 152, (Gk. struck back): a metrical foot of two unstressed syllables followed by one stressed syllable (e.g. di di *dum*).

Anaphora, 170, 259, *275*, 277-8, (*an-AFF-oar-uh*; Gk. carrying back): repeated content at the beginning of several sentences.

Anastrophe, *282*, (*an-ass-tro-FEE*; Gk. turning back): small scale inversion of the usual word order in a sentence.

Anceps, *164*: a variable metrical unit, normally either a trochee or a spondee.

Anecdotal fallacy: informal fallacy. The use of an anecdote, sometimes a vivid one to distract from the argument. "Skiing keeps you so fit" "Yeah? My first husband *died* skiing!"

Anglo-saxon verse, 117, 120, 136, *167*: accentual verse with 4 stresses per line. Lines are hemistich - in two halves, separated by *caesura*. Alliteration on 2-3 primary stresses.

Antagonist, *358-360*: a character or some other entity that opposes the *protagonist* (cf.)

Antanaclasis, *284*, (*an-tan-uh-KLAH-sis*; Gk. breaking up against): repetition of a word in two different, often clashing senses; a figure of wordplay.

Antanagoge (*an-tan-uh-GO-ghee*; Gk. bringing up against): 1) the attenuation of a negative point by a positive one—a positive spin (e.g. sure, your glass is half-empty, but also half-full); 2) a countercharge to an opponent's charge (e.g. developing green technologies is expensive, but the cost of not developing them is far greater).

Antihero, a protagonist who is the antithesis of a conven-

tional literary hero (cf. *hero*).

Antimeria (*an-tee-MERE-ee-uh*; Gk. opposite part): using non-verb as a verb, a.k.a. 'verbing' (e.g. 'but me no buts'), or vice versa (e.g. 'having a good cry').

Antimetabole, 170, *277*, (*an-tee-muh-tab-OH-lee*; Gk. turning around): reverse-order repetition of words.

Antiphrasis, *258*, (*an-tee-FRA-sis*; Gk. opposite declaring): single word *irony*.

Antiquitatem, *argumentum ad*, 213: informal fallacy, 'appeal to antiquity'. "Buy this good old boot polish, ancient and trusted, tested by time!" Inverse of *ad novitatem*.

Antithesis, 136, *171*, *178*, *259*, *277*, 284, 358, 360 (*an-TITH-uh-sis*; Gk. placing against): juxtaposition of two contrasting ideas. Part of classical dialectic (q.v. *synthesis* and *thesis*).

Antonomasia (*an-ton-oh-MA-zee-uh*; Gk. naming instead): use of well-known nicknames (e.g. the Iron Lady) (cf. *eponym*).

Aphorism, 366, (Gk. delimitation), an astute saying, containing a cleverly observed element of truth.

Apodioxis (*app-oh-dye-OCK-sis*; Gk. chasing away): indignantly dismissing an argument as absurd (e.g. 'Piffle!').

Apophasis, *270*, (*app-oh-FAY-sis*; Gk. denial): saying what it is that you won't say.

Apophthegm, *366*: a cynically worded adage or saying.

Apoplanesis (*app-oh-plan-EE-sis*; Gk. leading astray): avoiding the issue by rapidly changing the subject (e.g. 'An excellent point, but—do you smell smoke?'). Related to *red herring*.

Aporia, *266*, (*app-OAR-ee-uh*; Gk. impasse): expression of doubt when posing a question.

Aposiopesis, *287*, (*app-oh-see-oh-PEE-sis*; Gk. becoming silent): breaking off into silence.

Apostrophe, 171, 390, (*app-os-tro-FEE*; Gk. turning away): directly addressing some non-present, or abstract entity— the reader, an idea, an inanimate object, etc. (e.g. 'O Canada! Our home and native land! True patriot love in all thy sons command.').

Apposition (L. put against): putting together two noun phrases with the same subject (e.g. 'Sir Robert Walpole, Britain's first prime minister').

Archetype: 13, an ideal pattern, in character, action, or a situation; often used in dramatic works to represent themes or motifs.

Argument: *in poetry*, a statement of a poem's major point/

theme, usually appearing in the introduction of the poem; *in logic*, 177, 178-181, 184-5, 188, 196-7, 200-1, 207, 209-10, 212-4, 218, 225-6, 228, 230-1: an argument is the basic type of expression in logic. Classically, it consists of one or more premises and a conclusion which is inferred from them (q.v. *dialectic*); *in rhetoric*, 237, 238, *240*, 242, 245, 246, 249, 250-1, 272-3, 280, 282, 286, 291; *in ethics*, 302, 348, 352

Aristotle, 66, *on grammar*, 57, 66, 78; *on logic*, 178, 184, 186, 189, 190, 192, 202, 206, 216, 230; *on rhetoric*, 237, 239-42, 245, 246, 248, 263, 282, 284; *on ethics*, 298, 301, 306-8, 310-15, 320, 326, 329, 330, 334, 335, 337; 356, 358, 360

Articles, 68-9, 76: words that tell us something about nouns (e.g. *the*, *a*, *some*, *this*).

Aspect, 81, *90-91*, *392*: the aspect of a verb expresses the status of an action, i.e. completed, or in progress.

Association fallacy: informal fallacy, just because two things share some property does not make them alike in other ways. "Blue is Conservative; the sky is blue; the sky is Conservative"

Assonance, 119, 143, 145, 170, *278*, 366, (*ASS-uh-nance*; L. responding to): repetition of the same or similar vowel sound in the stressed syllables of nearby words.

Asyndeton (*ay-sin-DIT-on*; Gk. unconnected): the omission of conjunctions, such as 'and', 'or', between words, phrases, clauses (cf. *polysyndeton*), (e.g. I came, I saw, I conquered).

Atmosphere, 171: emotion inspired by a work (= *mood*).

Aube/Aubade: a dawn-song sung by a person to hide the sound of his/her friends making love.

Author's voice, 359: the voice used by authors when they seemingly speak for themselves in a book.

Auxesis, *280*, (*AWK-see-sis*; Gk. increase): substitution of stronger for weaker terms; a scheme of *amplification*.

Axiom, *216-7*, 219, 220: a basic assumption which is taken as true, without proof, for a logical system. Without initial axioms, reasoning cannot begin.

Background beat, *in poetry*, 140-1

Baculum, *argumentum ad*: informal fallacy, 'appeal to the rod'. Replacing argument and reasoned refutation with the threat of physical harm, discomfort, blackmail, etc. A crude form of avoiding the issue, *Ignoratio Elenchi*.

Ballad, 120,125, 132, 135, *148-9*: a narrative poem in short, usually four line, stanzas; was often song. In pop music the term now refers to an emotive or dramatic love song.

Ballade, *160*: French verse form of three 8-line stanzas and a four-line envoi, rhyming *ababbcbC*, *bcbC*.

Barbarism, *289*, (Gk. speaking like a foreigner): awkward use of foreign words or pronunciation; hybrid language; a stylistic vice in classical rhetoric.

Bathos, *288*, (*BAY-thos*; Gk. depth): bombast, usually anticlimactic.

Battology, *288*, (*BAT-oll-odge-ee*; Gk. stammering talk): tedious repetition.

Bdelygma, *280*, (*dell-IG-me-uh*; Gk. nastiness): a list (=*congeries*) of insults.

Bedlamite verse: poems in the voice of 'Poor Tom' or his sweetheart 'Merry Mad Maud'.

Beginning, *of a play*, 360

Beowulf, *poetic meter in*, 120, 167; *Gnomic nature of*, 401

Blake, *William*, 13, 85, 94, 130, 171, 268

Blank verse, *145*: open form of non-stanzaic verse, unrhymed and usually in iambic pentameter. Appears frequently in plays of Shakespeare and poems of Milton.

Boethius, 3, 192

Boolean Algebra, 179, 195, *224-5*, 226

British, *accent*, 118; *punctuation and spelling*, 394-5

Cacophony: (Gk. bad sound): use of words that combine sharp, harsh, hissing, or unmelodious sounds (cf. *euphony*).

Caesura, 133, *136*: a significant pause (often for breath) in a line of verse, usually marked with a comma, colon or semi-colon.

Carroll, *Lewis*, 135, 171, 188, 229, 268

Cases, *grammatical*, 71, 74, 76, 86

Catachresis, 255, 257, 289, (*cat-uh-CREE-sis*; Gk. misuse): 1) dead metaphor. 2) forced, extravagant metaphor.

Catalectic, *124*, 126, 128, *136*, 152, 166: lacking one or more syllables in the first, or more often last, foot of a line (cf. *acephalous*, *acatalectic*, and *hypercatalectic*).

Catastrophe, 360

Celtic verse, 117, 120, *166*

Chain rhyme, 147, 155: interlinking stanza by carrying rhymes over from one stanza to the next (e.g. *aba bcb cdc ded...*).

Character, *of words*, 9-16 (q.v. *euphonics*); *as displayed through rhetoric*, 241-2, 246, 249, 272, 291; *ethical*,

230, 297-353 (see *ethics* and *virtue*); *characters of Theophrastus*, 356-7; *literary study of*, 356-361.

Chaucer, Geoffrey, 133, 147, 154

CHIASMUS, *277*, (*key-as-MUSS*; Gk. chi-shaped, i.e. X-shaped): two clauses in which the second clause reverses the grammatical order of the first.

Chinese, *language*, 58, 62, 64, 81, 98; *poetry* 117; *ethics* 313; *proverbs*, 367.

Chorus, 359: in Greek drama, a group of singers who stand alongside/off stage from the principal performers (cf. *hypocrites*).

Chrysippus of Soli, 196, 226, 230

Cicero, 3, 216, 234; *in rhetoric*, 244, 246, 247, 280, 290; *in ethics* 300, 317, 322, 331, 334; *on mnemonics*, 365

Circular structure: return to subject-matter, wording, or phrasing found at the beginning of the literary work.

CIRCULUS IN PROBANDO, 210: circular reasoning

CIRCUMLOCUTION (L. talking around): use of a descriptive phrase to talk in a roundabout way about a topic/person (e.g. 'you-know-who'; or 'ethically challenged' for 'corrupt'),(= *periphrasis*).

Clauses, 104-5; types of 106-7; in sentences, 109

CLIMAX, *of a speech*, 247, *280*, (*kly-max*; Gk. ladder): sequence of increasing force; *of a play*, 360

Closed form, 119, 156, 158: any poetic form where meter, stanza, rhyme, and other features are all fixed (= *fixed form*).

Colon, correct use of, 390 (q.v. *semicolon*).

Comedy, 114, 258, 358, (Gk. songs of merrymakers): *Ancient Greek origin of*, boisterous drama performed during major festivities such as at Dionysia; *Greek*, plays which contain satire, paradox, puns, crudity, and exaggeration in varying degrees. Notable surviving examples are by Aristophanes (c.446-386 BC); *In medieval/Renaissance*, any work in which the main characters avert disaster and have a happy ending; *Modern*, any work meant to be funny.

Comic relief: a humorous scene, incident, character, or dialogue occurring after some serious or tragic moment.

Comma, *correct use of*, 390

Complication, part of structure in a dramatic work, 361

COMPOSITIO, *266*: fallacy of 'placing together', a.k.a. *composition*. One is an odd number. two is made up of two ones. Therefore two is an odd number. Inverse of *divisio*.

COMPROBATIO (*com-pro-BAH-shee-oh*; L. approving): commend-

ing a virtue, especially in the audience (connected to *ethos*) (e.g. 'your kindness obliges me').

CONCESSIO, *272*, (*con-SESH-ee-oh*; L. giving way): conceding a point, in order to make a stronger one. *As a clause*, 106.

CONCLUSIO, *247*, (*con-CLUE-zee-oh*; L. shut together): the final stage of a classical speech (= *epilogos, peroratio*).

Conclusion, *in logic*, 180-3, 190-1, 194-5, 202-3, 205, 209-10, 218: in a traditional logical argument, the premises will give rise to a conclusion, which is inferred from them. The conclusion is the result of the reasoning process; *in rhetoric*, 240-1, 256-7 (q.v. *enthymeme*).

CONCLUSION WHICH DENIES PREMISES, *181*: formal fallacy. In traditional logic no conclusion can deny its own premises.

CONDUPLICATIO, *275*, (*con-dew-plick-AH-shee-oh*; L. doubling up): beginning a new clause by repeating a key word or phrase from the last.

CONFIRMATIO, *246*, (*con-firm-AH-shee-oh*; L. firm together): the stage of a classical speech in which arguments are offered (= *pistis, probatio*).

CONFUSING SUBSTANCE AND ACCIDENT, 189: formal fallacy. When qualities of things are treated as things in their own right, substance and accident have been confused.

CONFUTATIO, *246*, (con-few-TAR-shee-oh; L. overthrow altogether): the stage of a classical speech in which opposing arguments are rebutted (= *reprehensio*).

Conjugations, 64-5, 81

CONJUNCTION FALLACY: formal fallacy. The mistaken assumption that the probability of multiple conditions ocurring will be higher than for any of the single conditions alone.

Conjunctions, 68, 95, 98-9, 106; *in logic*, 227

CONSEQUENTUM: informal fallacy, the fallacious use of the desirability or undesirability of an argument's outcomes. "If P then Q will happen, and we don't like Q, so P must be false".

Consonance: *170*, the repetition of consonant sounds in successive words (e.g. tomorrow matters for Timmy, the end well found), (cf. alliteration).

Content words, 68

CONTINUUM: informal fallacy. The fallacy of the beard, Sorites, etc. Wrongly rejecting a claim because it is not precise. Human language often blurs boundaries, but such vagueness does not automatically create invalidity.

Contraction: reducing the number of syllables in a word (= elision), (q.v. *syncope* and *synaeresis*).

CONTRADICTORY PREMISES: formal fallacy. Premises which

contradict each other imply anything (the 'principle of explosion').

Copia, 279-80, *290*, (*COE-pee-ub*; L. plenty): stylistic and argumentative abundance; the goal of rhetorical instruction in the Renaissance and after.

Counterplot: a plot intended to thwart another plot (cf, *plot* and *subplot*).

Couplet, 146-7, 119, 150, 152, 153, 157, 165: a 2-line, rhyming stanza in any meter.

Courage, 297; *Aristotle on*, 314, 315; *in character theory*, 360; *one of the four cardinal virtues*, 316-18; *in other branches of ethics*, 342, 351; *proverbs about*, 374, 385. (q.v. *justice, moderation*, and *wisdom*).

Crumenam, *argumentum ad*: informal fallacy, 'the appeal to wealth'. Assuming someone's wealth is an indicator of possession of the truth. Inverse of *ad Lazarum*.

Cum hoc ergo propter hoc, 181, *209*: informal fallacy, 'with this, therefore because of this'. Assumes that two or more events which occur together are causally linked, simply because they occur together. Should not be pushed too far, as often, co-occurrence *is* evidence of a causal link.

Dactyl, 121, *126*, 133-4, 136-7, 143, 159, 164-6, (*DACK-till*, Gk. finger): a metrical foot of one stressed syllable plus two unstressed syllables - *dum* di di.

Dative, 65, 71: grammatical case for a noun to which something is given, e.g. "She gave Elsa a glance".

Debate, 11, 213, 246, 300, 320, 332, 337, 341; *Sophist*, 178

Declension, *grammatical*, 64-5, 70-1, 76-7

Decorum, 249, (*deck-OAR-um*; L. appropriateness): general principle of propriety, which requires that a speech fit its occasion, audience, and goal.

Defective induction, 208: the inductive fallacy, or 'jumping to conclusions' or 'hasty generalization'. "1, 3, 5 and 7 are prime; 9 is square; 11 and 13 are prime. So all odd numbers are either square or prime."

Definition, 264: advantageously choosing the sense of an ambiguous term in rhetoric.

Democracy, 332

Denouement, of a play, 361, = end.

Denying the antecedent, *178*: informal fallacy. Assuming in a conditional (if P then Q) sentence, that because the antecedent (P) is false, the consequent (Q) must be too.

Deontology, *in logic*, 228; *in ethics*, 339-40; *in real life*, 342-343

Determiners, 67, 68-9, 102

Deus ex machina: (Gk. God from the machine): narrative device involving unrealistic or unexpected intervention to rescue protagonists or resolve conflict.

Deuteragonist, a sidekick who accompanies the lead protagonist; often the subject of *subplots*.

Diacope, *274*, (*dye-ACK-ob-pee*; Gk. cutting through): repetition after an interruption.

Dialectic, *178-9*, 231, 239, 240, 304, 352, 358, 360, (*die-UH-leck-tick*; Gk. debate craft): the art of debate by question and answer; the characteristic mode of reasoning in philosophy; the art of considering arguments and seeking the truth via *thesis, antithesis*, and *synthesis*.

Dialysis (*dye-AL-ub-sis*; Gk. splitting apart): a disjunctive argument, in which two or more alternatives are considered (e.g. 'If it moves, salute it. If it doesn't move, pick it up. If you can't pick it up, paint it.').

Diazeugma, *271*, (*dye-ub-ZYOOG-muh*; Gk. yoking through): a zeugma in which one subject governs a string of verbs.

Dicto simpliciter: informal fallacy. A fallacy of accident in which exceptions are taken to invalidate rules. "I saw a cat with three legs, therefore cats cannot be defined as four-legged animals". Reverse of *Compositio*.

Diegesis, *246*, (*die-UH-gee-sis*; Gk. narrative): = *narratio*.

Digressio, *247*, (*die-GRESS-see-ob*; L. stepping aside): a digression in a speech.

Dilemma, *logical*, 202-5, 211, 227; *ethical*, 230, 333, *339-51*; *proverbs about*, 372

Dionysius Thrax, 2, 57, *60*

Dipodic verse: Strongly metrical verse with only two feet per line. Rap lyrics are often dipodic.

Dipody: combining two metrical feet to form a new one (q.v. *syzygy*).

Dirimens copulatio (*di-ree-MENS cop-yew-LA-shee-ob*; L. separating combination): conceding a point, to preserve an appearance of balance (e.g. 'I have the body of a weak, feeble woman; but I have the heart and stomach of a king, and of a king of England too...') (cf. *antanagoge, concessio*).

Dispositio, 245, *246*, 247, 362, (*dis-POE-zish-ee-ob*; L. placing apart): one of the five rhetorical canons: the arrangement of the ideas in a speech.

Dissociation, 264: distinguishing two senses of a term that, one contends, have been mistakenly conflated.

Distance: how close a reader or audience feels to the

characters and events in any given work.

Distich (*dis-Tick*): a unit of two verse lines, usually a couplet (cf. *hemistich*).

DISTINCTIO, 264, (*diss-tink-SHEE-oh*; L. distinguishing): specification of the meaning of key terms.

DISTRIBUTION, *188-191*, 195, 199, 201, 206, 225, 227: terms which cover the whole of their class are called distributed terms, (e.g. 'all penguins' or 'no penguin').

DIVISIO, 246-7, (*dee-VIZ-ee-oh*; L. forcing apart): the stage of a classical speech in which the issues dividing the parties are set out (= *partitio, propostio*).

DIVISION FALLACY, *206*: informal fallacy. The English love cricket. Tom is an Englishman. Therefore Tom loves cricket. Inverse of *compositio*. ·

DONKEY FALLACY: informal fallacy. Those bad guys are attacking that argument, so it must be good and true.

Dramatic irony: when the audience is aware of the plot, or sections of it, but the characters are not.

Dramatic tension: level of involvement, uncertainty, and interest experienced by an audience.

DYSPHEMISM, *265*, (*diss-FUH-mism*; Gk. bad speech): giving something neutral or good a bad name (converse of *euphemism*).

ECPHONESIS (*eck-foe-KNEE-sis*; Gk. speaking out): exclamation of extreme emotion (e.g. "Sufferin' succotash!").

Eiron, 258, 328: dissembling/self deprecating character from Greek comedy who undercuts the *alazon*.

Elision: the omission of one or more sounds (vowel, consonant, or syllable) from words or phrases, often used to aid adherence to a metrical scheme or rhythm (e.g. oft, o'er, gonna), (q.v. *syncope, synaeresis*, and *epenthesis*).

Ellipsis, 366: dropping words without impeding the reader's ability to understand meaning (e.g. 'I will away').

ELOCUTIO, *245*, 362, (*ell-oh-KEW-shee-oh*; L. speaking out): one of the five rhetorical canons: style; finding the best language for your ideas.

EMPEIRIA, 239, (*em-PEER-ee-uh*; Gk. experience): hands-on know-how.

ENALLAGE (*en-ull-a-GEE*; Gk. changing): using one grammatical form where another would be expected (e.g. 'mistakes were made') (cf. *anacoluthon*).

ENARGEIA (*en-ar-GHEE-uh*; Gk. clear): set of figures aimed at achieving a vivid description, to reach an audience emotionally (e.g. 'Picture it! Sicily 1922...'); a virtue of style in classical rhetoric.

Encomium of Helen: work on Rhetoric by Gorgias, 238

ENCOMIUM, *238*, (*en-COE-me-um*; Gk. eulogy): a speech of praise; *Encomium of Helen* by Gorgias, 238

Endstopping, *137*, 167: when a line of verse ends without running on (grammatically) to the next.

English, old, 62, 65; *middle*, 64, 65; *modern*, 62, 65; *as a Germanic language* 60-1

Enjambment, *137*, 146: when a line runs or 'strides' into the next (e.g. I sing it in / My heart this / Joyful song).

ENTHYMEME, *200*, *240*, *250*, 263, (*enth-ee-MEEM*; Gk. in mind): shortened argument, similar to syllogism, but missing a premise or/and the conclusion (cf. *syllogism*).

ENUMERATIO (*ee-new-mare-AH-shee-oh*; L. counting out): listing a series of related points.

EPANALEPSIS, 274, (*ep-an-uh-LEP-sis*; Gk. taking up again): Starting a clause or sentence the same way that the previous clause or sentence ends.

Epenthesis: insertion or development of sounds within words (e.g. pronouncing film 'FIL-um') (cf. *elision* and *infixation*).

Epic hero: main character in an epic poem; typically one who embodies the values or virtues of his or her culture (e.g. Odysseus in *The Odyssey*). Cf. *protagonist*.

Epic verse/poetry, 114, 133, 134, 167, 314: long and often dramatic narrative poetry with grand, noble, mythological, or nationally important themes (e.g. ancient Indian *Ramayana*, Greek *Iliad*, and Milton's *Paradise Lost*) (cf. *lyric poetry, q.v. heroic couplets/lines/odes*).

EPICHEIREME, 250-1, (*ep-ee-kai-REAM*; Gk. undertaking): an extended argument, with five components, usually in the following order: 1. a claim; 2. a reason for that claim; 3. a proof of that reason; 4. an embellishment of the claim; and 5. a restatement of the claim.

EPICRISIS, 286, (*ep-ee-CRY-sis*; Gk. deciding upon): invoking the authority of past authors.

EPIDEICTIC, 247, *248*, 291, (*ep-ee-day-ICK-tick*; Gk. showing upon): the branch of rhetoric focused on speeches of praise or censure.

Epigram, *146*, 153, 157, 160: a short, witty poem or component of a poem. Also a proverbial saying. As an adjective, *epigrammatic* is used of poems and remarks when they are characteristically witty and memorable.

EPILOGOS, 247 (*ep-ee-LOW-goss*; Gr. reason upon): = *peroratio*.

Epilogue: a conclusion added to a literary work.

Epimone (*ep-IM-oh-nee*; Gk. staying upon): refrain, leitmotif, slogan; persistent repetition of a phrase/word to sway a crowd.

Epiplexis (*ep-ee-PLECK-sis*; Gk. striking upon): indignant upbraiding, often by means of erotesis (e.g. 'Why died I not from the womb?').

Episodic: occurring in a long string of short, individual scenes, stories, or sections, rather than a sustained plot.

Epistrophe, *275*, (*ep-is-tro-FEE*; Gk. turning upon): repeated content at the end of several sentences.

Epitasis, 360: middle of a play (q.v. *protasis, catastrophe*).

Epithet (*ep-ee-THET*; Gk. placing upon): an adjective or adjectival phrase that qualifies a noun, literally or figuratively (e.g. 'a much-maligned band').

Epizeuxis, *274*, 279, (*ep-ee-ZYOOK-sis*; Gk. fastening upon): repetition of a single word, with no intervening breaks.

Eponym (*ep-OH-nim*; Gk. given as a name): a name used for the properties for which the name's owner is famous (e.g. 'Machiavellian').

Equivocatio, *207*: equivocation. The fallacy of using the same word or words in two or more distinct significations in a single argument.

Erasmus, 106; *on rhetoric*, 290

Erotesis, *266*, (*erro-TEE-sis*; Gk. questioning): a question which presumes its own answer.

Ethics (gk. *ethike*): *in the liberal arts*, 1, 352; *in logic*, 230-1; *in rhetoric*, 288; *classical* 302–5; *Nicomachean* 306-15; *cardinal virtues*, 316-323; *seven deadly sins*, 324-5; *other virtues*, 326-31; *natural law*, 334-5; *human rights* 336-7; *golden rule*, 338-9; *deontology & utilitarianism*, 339-343; *relational*, 344; *medical*, 345; *vocational*, 346-7; *animals*, 348-9; *environmental*, 350-1.

Ethos, *242-3*, 246, 249, 272, 286, 298-300, (*EE-thos*; Gk. character): appeal to character; one of the three technical means of persuasion (cf. also *logos, pathos*).

Eudaimonia, *310*-313: happiness in the sense of living well.

Eunoia, 330-1, (*yew-NOY-uh*; Gk. thinking well): goodwill that a speaker aims to demonstrate and instill in the audience.

Euphemism, 265, (*yew-FUH-mism*; Gk. good speech): giving something with a bad reputation a good (or neutral) name (converse of *dysphemism*).

Euphonics, *definition of*, 1, 9-14; *practical application of*, 15-51

Euphony (Gk. good sound): attempting to group words together harmoniously, to create an easy and pleasing flow.

Exclusive premises, *194*: formal fallacy. Two negative premises generate no necessary conclusion.

Exemplum, *263*, (*eck-ZEM-plum*; L. sample): a short, historical or fictional narrative used to make a moral point.

Existential fallacy, *195*: formal fallacy. Arguing from a universal (All X / No X) to an existential (therefore X exists) (Aristotle did not thinks this was fallacious).

Exordium, *246*, (*eck-ZOR-dee-um*; L. beginning from): the introductory stage of a classical speech (= *prooimion*).

Exposition, 156, 360-1: background information put into a dramatic work, about setting, characters, history, etc.

Fallacy, *180-1*, 184-5, 187, 189, 191, 199, 203, 241-2, 283; *syllogistic* 194-5; *modus* 196-8; *linguistic* 206-7; *non-linguistic* 208-9; *informal* 210-213; *183-5*: a fallacy in logic refers to a lack of validity in the reasoning process. It is not the same as a falsehood, which refers to one or more untrue premises.

Fallacy fallacy: formal fallacy. The mistaken assumption that just because a logical argument contains a fallacy, its conclusion must be wrong.

False choice (*Imperfect Disjunction* or *Bifurcatio*), 203, 211: formal fallacy. A disjunctive (either/or) premise must state the only possibilities; if another exists, the disjunction is false.

Farce (L. stuffed): a form of low or bawdy comedy.

Feminine ending, 138, 139: a line of verse which ends on an unstressed syllable.

Feminine rhyme, 143: rhymes the second from last syllables of successive words.

Figurative language: a deviation from ordinary or standard use of words to achieve some special meaning or effect.

Figure, rhetorical, of thought and speech, 170, 245, *252*, *examples of*, 252-87 (q.v. *trope, scheme*).

Flaw, in character, 358, 360

Fludd, Robert, *memory palace of*, 365

Foot, *spondee*, 122; *pyrrhic*, 123; *trochee*, 124; *iamb*, 125; *dactyl*, 126; *anapest*, 127; *amphibrach*, 128; *amphimacer*, 128; *paeonic*, 129: a metrical unit, comprised of stressed and unstressed syllables, in varying combinations, used to measure and represent poetic meter. The system is inherited from ancient Greek literature and the different metrical feet retain their Greek names (q.v. meter).

Foreshadowing, *in structure of liierary work*, 359

Framing fallacy: informal fallacy, a.k.a. 'loaded question'. Posing a question in a misleading way to give a bad conclusion.

Free verse, 145: poetry with no conventional meter or form.

Gender, *in language*, 70-1, 74, 76: of an object, can be masculine, feminine, or neutral.

Genitive, 65, 69, 71, 87: grammatical possessive case of noun, e.g. in Peter's house, Peter takes the genitive.

Ghazal, *168*: Poetic form of couplets and a refrain, originating in North Africa and the Middle East.

Gnomic poetry: verse containing short statements (gnomes) pertaining to general truth or morality (e.g. 'Thus did Ecgtheow's son, so famous for battles and valiant deeds, act as a brave man ought' - Beowulf).

Gorgias, 238-9, 248

Grammar (gk. a letter), *in the liberal arts*, 1-3, 55; *introduction to*, 57-9; *inflection*, 60-2, 64, 70, 81, 98; *development of English*, 62-3; *rules of*, 64-5; *categories and terms*, 66-9; *declension*, 70; *nouns and pronouns*, 70-5; *adjectives*, 76-9; *verbs*, 80-95; *adverbs* 96-7; *conjunctions and prepositions*, 98-100; *subject and predicate*, 101; *phrases*, 102-3; *clauses*, 104-7; *sentences*, 108-9; *slang and dialect*, 110-11.

Greek, language, 60; words in English, 62

Haiku, 169: Japanese poetic form. Three lines of 5-7-5 'on' (approximate to syllables). Syllabic meter. No rhyme. Used for meditative/lyrical/transcendental themes.

Head word, *in grammar*, 102-3

Headless = *acephalous*, 127.

Hemistich, 166, 168: a half-line of verse followed and preceded by a *caesura*.

Hendiadys (*hen-dye-UH-diss*; Gk. one through two): using two words joined by 'and' to express one idea (e.g. 'nice and easy' for 'nicely easy').

Heptameter, *132, 135*: a metrical line of seven feet.

Hero, 360, the main focus of narrative attention in a literary work; typically a character who combats adversity through bravery, ingenuity, moral force, or strength (cf. *antihero*).

Heroic couplet, 146: two successive lines of rhyming iambic pentameter; *heroic line*, 133; *heroic ode, 165; heroic quatrain*, 151

Heterometric stanza: a stanza with lines containing different numbers of syllables (cf. *isometric stanza*).

Hexameter, 126, 133, *134*, 141, 155, 165: a metrical line of six feet.

Holorhyme: a line/stanza that rhymes in its entirety: "Ms Stephen, without a first-rate stakeholder sum or deal / Must, even, with outer fur straight, stay colder, some ordeal".

Homer, 97, 126, 133, 134, 170, 298, 314, 326

Hominem, *argumentum ad*, 213: informal fallacy, 'argument against the man'. The personal attack. The use of an opponent's appearance, character or background to discredit them. A form of *ignoratio elenchi*.

Homoeoteleuton (*hoe-me-OH-tell-YEW-ton*; Gk. like ending): a sequence of words with similar endings (e.g. 'Got myself a cryin', talkin', sleepin', walkin', livin' doll').

Homonymy, *284*, (*hoe-MON-uh-me*; Gk. same law): the capacity of a word or phrase to carry multiple unrelated meanings; cf. *amphiboly*.

Horace, 164, 165, 263, 288, 361

Horismus (*hoh-RIZ-mus*; Gk. boundary): a concise and memorable definition (e.g. 'A horse is dangerous at both ends and uncomfortable in the middle') (or a dissociative definition).

Humility, 325, 351; *virtue of, 326-7; in proverbs*, 383.

Hypallage (*hype-ull-a-GEE*; Gk. under changing): an epithet incongruously applied to a noun other than the one it would be expected to modify (e.g. 'he smoked a pensive cigarette') (cf. *personification*).

Hyperbaton, *282*, (*high-PAIR-bat-on*; Gk. overstepping): group of figures that alter the standard or expected word order.

Hyperbole, 168, *261*, 269, 366 (*high-PAIR-bo-lee*; Gk. excess, literally over-thowing): unabashed exaggeration.

Hypercatalectic, *124*, 126, 130: a metrical line of verse which contains one or more additional syllables at the start or end of the line (cf. *acephalous* and *acatalectic*).

Hypocrites (Gk. one who plays a part): the classical Athenian word for an actor.

Hypophora, 266, (*hype-OFF-uh-rub*; Gk. under carrying): answering one's own question.

Hypothesis, 182, 214 (q.v. *reasoning* and *thesis*).

Hypotaxis (*hype-o-TACK-sis*; Gk. under arrangement): the arrangement of phrases or clauses in a relation of subordination with the help of conjunctions such as 'because' or 'therefore' (cf. *parataxis*).

Hypozeugma, 271, (*hype-o-ZYOOG-muh*; Gk. yoking under): a zeugma in which the yoke word comes last.

Lazarum, *argumentum ad*: informal fallacy, 'the appeal to the poor' (the biblical Lazarus having been a poor man). The fallacy that poor, simple people are less subject to corruption or vice than the rich. Inverse of *ad Crumenam*.

Letters, *innate qualities of*, 9-12, 50; *in memnonics*, 363, 365 (cf. *alphabet*).

Limerick, 128, 149, 152: a five-line rhyming poem, usually with an anapestic or amphibrachic meter.

Lineation, 138: the manner in which line breaks are inserted in a poem for expressive/rhythmical purposes.

Linked verse: poems written collectively by more than one person (often in large groups, e.g. *renga*).

Litotes, 260, (*lie-TOE-tease*; Gk. small): understatement by the denial of a negative term (e.g. 'he was not unfriendly').

Locative, 71: grammatical case indicating location (e.g. I drive *down a track*).

Logic, the formalization of the ways in which reasoning functions: *arguments*, 184-5; *propositions*, 186; *terms*, 188-9; *syllogisms*, 190-5; *modus ponens/tollens*, 196-8; *expansion*, 200-1; *dilemmas*, 202-5; *fallacies*, 206-213; *axioms*, 216-7; *paradox*, 218-221; *problems*, 222-3; *Boolean*, 224-5; *propositional*, 226-7; *extended*, 228-9; *in ethics*, 230-1. 'Logic (in its broadest sense) is the science of verbal expression and [argumentative] reasoning. Sometimes the term 'logic' is used with more restricted extension, and limited to rules of [argumentative] reasoning' (John of Salisbury, *Metalogicon I*.10).

Logos (*LOW-goss*; Gk. reason, word): *in logic*, 179; *in rhetoric*, 238, *242-3*, 246-7, 249, 257, appeal to reason; one of the three technical means of persuasion (cf. also *ethos*, *pathos*); *in ethics*, 320.

Long measure, 150

Lyric poetry: poetry expressing personal thoughts or feelings, typically spoken in first person (cf. *epic verse*). In ancient Greece lyric/melic poetry was sung to music played on the lyre (*lyrikos* = adj. form of *lyra*). Reemerged in early 19th century Europe as the dominant poetic form. The term derives from one of the three broad categories of poetry formalized by Aristotle: *lyric*, *dramatic* and *epic*.

Macrologia, 288, (*mack-ro-LODGE-ee-uh*; Gk. long-worded): longwindedness, prolixity.

Mad song, 152, a verse form of five-line stanzas. Variable accentual meter. Rhymes *abccb* etc. Used for nonsense, oddities and madness.

Malapropism, 289, (*mal-uh-PROP-ism*; F. awkward): comical misuse of words, after Mrs Malaprop, a character in Sheridan's *The Rivals*, 1775.

Masculine ending, 138: a line of verse which ends on a stressed syllable, cf. *feminine ending*.

Masculine rhyme, 143: rhymes the last syllable of each word.

Masked man: formal fallacy. Denying identity based on relative or subjective properties: "I know my father; I do not know that masked man; therefore, that masked man is not my father".

Maxims, 336; *in logic*, 231; *in rhetoric*, 262-3; *in ethics*, 333, 338-9

Meiosis, 260, (*my-OH-sis*; Gk. lessening): unaffected understatement.

Meme, 366, an idea or pattern of thought that replicates like a virus by being passed along from one thinker to another.

Memoria, 245, 362, (*mem-OAR-ee-uh*; L. memory): one of the five rhetorical canons: memorizing what one has to say; more generally the skills of enhancing one's memory.

Memory, *art of*: 362-5

Mnemonics, the art of memory, 245, 362-365

Merism (*merry-zum*; Gk. diving into parts): listing all the parts rather than the whole; a strategy of *copia* (e.g. 'lock, stock, and barrel').

Metabasis (*met-uh-BAY-sis*; Gk. going after): a linking device recapping what was said and previewing what will follow (e.g. '...and with that settled, let us now turn to...').

Metafiction: fiction which uses reflexive techniques to break or blur the barriers between author, character and reader.

Metanoia (*met-uh-NOY-uh*; Gk. change of mind): correcting your own statement to either strengthen, or weaken it (e.g. 'one of the best—no, the best').

Metaphor, 145, 171, 239, *252-5*, 256, 289, 290, 366 (*met-uh-FOR*; Gk. transfer): calling one thing by another's name in virtue of some similarity or relation discovered through their comparison.

Meter, 118-121, 122-9, 130-5: the measurement of regular rhythm in verse.

Metonymy, 254, (*met-ON-ee-me*; Gk. change of name): the metaphorical use of an aspect or attribute for the thing itself.

Metum, *argumentum ad*, 213: informal fallacy, 'the appeal to fear'. An *Emotional Appeal*. "If you X you will die".

Midpoint, of a play, 360-1 (= *epitasis*, high point).

Milton, John, 13, 136, 145, 154, 157, 177

Mimesis: 'to imitate'. In ancient Greek poetics, the process by which the arts come to truth through imitation and stylization of humanity and nature.

MISERICORDIAM, *argumentum ad*, 241: informal fallacy, 'the appeal to pity'. "Give me a better grade; my mother is sick".

MODERATION, one of the four cardinal virtues, *316-17*, 319; *in environmental ethics*, 351; *proverbs about*, 376. (q.v. *modum*).

Modern English: the English language as spoken between c. 1450 and the modern day.

MODUS PONENS, deductive argument, 180, *196*, 198, 227.

MODUS TOLLENS, deductive argument, *198*, 227.

MODUM, *argumentum ad*, 213: informal fallacy, 'the appeal to moderation' or false compromise. "You say it's spelled with an A; I say it's Z; so the correct answer is probably around M."

Monologue: a character speaking aloud, or narrating an account, to an audience with no other characters on stage.

Mood, *of verbs*, 81, 89; *of literary and oratory works*, 130, 171, 278, (q.v. *atmosphere*).

Morpheme, 67, 98: phonetic building blocks of words.

Motif: a conspicuous recurring element with symbolic significance which appears frequently in the narrative of a literary work (q.v. *epimone*).

MYCTERISM (*mick-TARE-ism*; Gk. sneering): an insult accompanied by an appropriate gesture (e.g. 'Not this again!' <Rolls eyes>).

NARRATIO, 246, (*nuh-RAY-shee-oh*; L. relating): the stage of a classical speech in which uncontroversial facts are set out (= *diegesis, prothesis*).

Naturalism: a literary movement seeking to depict life as accurately as possible, without artificial distortions.

NATURALISTIC FALLACY, 'is-ought': informal fallacy, occurs when someone argues for what ought to be the case on the basis of statements about what is the case.

NECESSITY: formal fallacy. Imputing unwarranted necessity. "All bachelors are unmarried; John is a bachelor; so John cannot marry". In fact John's marital status can change!

NEGATIVE CONCLUSION FROM AFFIRMATIVE PREMISES, 195: formal fallacy. Can occur when all premises are affirmative.

NO TRUE SCOTSMAN: informal fallacy, reinforcement of a blunt assertion. DAD: "No Scotsman puts sugar on his porridge". KID: "But uncle Angus puts sugar on his". DAD: "Ah yes, but no true Scotsman puts sugar on his porridge!"

Nominative, 65, 71: grammatical case applied to the noun doing the action if the verb is active, or receiving the action if the verb is passive.

NON CAUSA PRO CAUSA, 209: 'non-cause in place of a cause'. The informal fallacy of *False Cause*.

NON SEQUITUR: 'it does not follow'. A general term for any invalid inference, where the conclusion is not entailed by the premises.

Norman French, influence on English language, 62

Noun phrase, *70-1*, 76

Nouns, 64-5, 66, 68, 69, *70-3*, 74-5, 78

NOVITATEM, *argumentum ad*: informal fallacy, 'appeal to the new'. "It's newer, so it's better!" Inverse of *ad antiquitatem*.

Nursery rhymes, rhythm and meter of, 120-1, 124, 139; background rhythms of, 140-1

Obstacles, *for characters in a play*, 360

Octameter, 135: a metrical line of eight feet.

Octave, 154, 156, 160: any eight-line stanza, although most often two quatrains, the first eight lines of a sonnet.

Ode, 135, *164-5*: an elaborately structured poem praising or glorifying an event or individual.

ODIUM, argumentum ad: informal fallacy, the appeal to hatred'. "Prisoners should dig roads because prisons are full of scumbags!"

On, 169: Japanese phonetic units similar to English syllables but different in that they can contain two distinct sounds.

ONOMATOPOEIA, 10, 14, 171, 279, (*on-oh-mat-oh-PEE-uh*; Gk. making of words): naming a thing with an imitation of its sound, e.g. splash, plop, crash, swish, etc.

ONUS PROBANDI, 211: informal fallacy, shifting the burden of proof. "Prove me wrong, otherwise I'm right".

Open form, 119, 159: metrical poetry with a variable rhyme or stanza scheme (cf. *closed form*, *blank verse*, *free verse*).

OPERATOR: 179, *224,7*: a term with a defined function in relating logical propositional elements to one another in a syntactically valid way. They are the 'connecting terms' which link logical thoughts together. Examples are 'and', 'or', 'not', 'if ... then', and 'therefore'.

Oratory, 178, 213: the art of public speaking.

Ordeal, in dramatic/literary work, 361

Ottava rima, 154-5: a rhyming stanza form, originally from Italy, of 8 lines, usually in iambic pentameter.

Overwhelming exception: asserting something as an exception to a rule, when it falsifies the rule. "We are a loving peaceful people, except when we are at war."

Oxymoron, 268, (*ock-see-MORE-on*; Gk. sharp-dull): a contradiction in terms or compressed paradox.

Paean (*PAY-ahn*): a song/chant of praise, triumph, or imploration.

Paeon 129, 132, 137, (*PEE-uhn*): a type of quaternary foot.

Palindrome: a device used since antiquity where a word, phrase, number or sequence reads the same backwards as forwards. Earliest from 79 AD Herculaneum (e.g. 'noon', 'race car', 'able was I ere I saw Elba', 'madam, I'm Adam').

Pantoum, 159, Malayan closed verse form adapted to English.

Paradox (*pa-ra-DOCKS*; Gk. contrary to received opinion): *in euphonics*, 48; *in logic*, 176, 216, *218-222*. A paradox is a syntactically-valid proposition or argument with apparently true premises which generates self-contradictory or apparently false results. *In rhetoric*, 249, *268*, apparent self-contradiction, or running counter to expectations.

Parallelism, 276, 366, (*pa-ra-lell-ism*; Gk. beside one another): the repetition of some formal feature, some number of times.

Parataxis (*pa-ra-TACK-sis*; Gk. alongside arrangement): the opposite of *hypotaxis*; juxtaposition of clauses or phrases without subordinating conjunctions.

Parenthesis, *283*, (*pa-renth-UH-sis*; Gk. placing beside): a species of *hyperbaton* that interrupts one sentence with another (or with a word or phrase).

Parison, 276, (*pa-rees-ON*; Gk. exactly balanced): a *parallelism* in which the grammatical structure is repeated.

Paroemion, 278, (*pa-REE-me-on*; Gk. near like): overdone *alliteration*.

Paronomasia, 284, (*pa-ro-no-MA-zee-uh*; Gk. naming beside): punning.

Particular *logical statement* ("this", "a", "some"), 182-3, 185, *186*, 192-3, 195.

Partitio, *246*, (*par-TISH-ee-oh*; L. dividing into parts): the stage of a classical speech in which the issues dividing the parties are set out (= *divisio, propostio*).

Pathetic fallacy: human feelings or activities ascribed to inanimate objects or non-human phenomena in the natural world.

Pathos, *242*, 247, 286-7, (*PAY-thos*; Gk. feeling): appeal to emotions; one of the three technical means of persuasion

(cf. also *ethos, logos*).

Pentameter, 125, *133*, 136,138, 140, 142, 145-6, 151, 153, 154-6, 158, 163, 165: a metrical line of five feet.

Periphrasis (*perry-FRA-sis*; Gr. round about declaring): = *circumlocution*.

Peroratio, 247, (*perro-RAY-shee-oh*; L. speaking through): the final stage of a classical speech (= *conclusio, epilogos*).

Personification, 171, 366: the ascription of human attributes, such as emotions, to inanimate objects or abstract entities (e.g. 'gloomy clouds threatened miserable rain'), (= *prosopopoeia*).

Petitio principii, 210: also known as *"Begging the Question"* Giving an argument's conclusion as a premise.

Petrarchan sonnet: a sonnet form named for Francesco Petrarca [1304-74]. Two quatrains (an octave) followed by a sestet.

Philippic (*fill-LIP-ick*; Gk. concerning Philip): a speech of bitter invective, after Demosthenes's attacks on Philip II of Macedon.

Phonetics, 58, 187

Phonographic alphabets, 58

Phrase, *noun*, 70-1, 76; *verb* 80, 91; *five phrases* 102-3, 104-5; *in a sentence*, 108

Phronesis, 316, 322, (*fro-KNEE-sis*; Gk. thinking): practical wisdom or prudence; for Aristotle the faculty of knowing what one ought to do and how to achieve it; good sense as projected by the speaker in an ethos appeal.

Pistis, 246, (*PISS-tiss*; Gk. belief): = *confirmatio*.

Plato, *on euphonics*, 11,13; *quotes by*, 75, 90, 105; *on grammar*, 76; *on logic*, 178, 204, 216, 231, 302; *on ethics*, 304-6, 317, 319, 321, 330, 334, 337, 344.

Pleonasm, 288, (*PLEA-on-asm*; Gk. superfluity): use of redundant words.

Pleonexia, vice of, 319

Plot, *three- and five-act*, 359-60: the structure, and relationship, of actions and events in a work of fiction.

Plurium interrogationum, 209: informal fallacy, 'of too many questions'. A fallacy which smuggles several questions into a single one, and then demands a simple answer. A specialised form of *petitio principi*.

Poetic license: the freedom to depart from the norms of common discourse, literal reality, or historical truth.

Poetics, Aristotle's, 360, 362

Point of view: the way a story gets told and who tells

it; the character whose eyes we currently see through, whose voice we hear.

Polis, 237, 238, 332, (*POE-liss*; Gk. city): names the form of political organization (city-state) in ancient Greece; by extension, the community of discourse, or public sphere, in which rational debate occurs.

Polyptoton, 170, *284*, (*pol-ip-TOE-ton*; Gk. many falling): repetition of a word in different grammatical forms.

Polysemy, 284, (*pol-ee-SEE-me*; Gk. many signs): the capacity of a word or phrase to carry multiple related meanings. (cf. *homonymy*).

Polysyndeton (*pol-ee-sind-IT-on*; Gk. many binding): the use of unnecessary conjunctions between words or phrases or clauses (e.g. 'East and west and south and north/The messengers ride fast').

Populum, *argumentum ad*, *213, 241*: informal fallacy, 'the appeal to the populace'. An emotional appeal such that if lots of people do/say/believe it, then it must be true.

Portmanteau, 171

Post hoc ergo propter hoc, 209: informal fallacy, 'after this, therefore because of this'. The false assumption that because an event followed another event, there must be a causal link between them. Closely related to *Cum Hoc Ergo Propter Hoc*.

Praeteritio, 267, *270*, (*pritt-air-ISH-ee-oh*; L. passing over): giving reasons for remaining silent.

Predicate, *grammar* 101; *logic* 184-5, 188, 190, 199, 226, 228: a statement made about a subject. In the sentence 'You and your family are en route to Mars', 'You and your family' is the *subject* and 'are en route to Mars' is the predicate. The predicate always contains at least one verb (often the copulative verb 'to be').

Premise, *logic*, 178, 180-1, 183, 185, 190, 194-5, 200-1, 210, 218: a statement adduced in a logical operation; several premises are usually adduced to infer a conclusion. False premises may well lead to false conclusions, but this will not necessarily effect the validity of the argument; *in rhetoric*, 240-1 (q.v. *enthymeme*).

Prepositions, grammatical, 68, 98, 100

Probatio, *246*, (*pro-BAH-shee-oh*; L. proving): = confirmatio.

Procatalepsis, 273, (*pro-cat-UH-lep-sis*; Gk. taking up beforehand): anticipating and addressing counterarguments.

Prolepsis (*PRO-lep-sis*; Gk. preconception): use of an epithet before it is strictly applicable (e.g. 'I bet on the losing horse'), (or = *procatalepsis*).

Pronouns, *in grammar*, 65, 67-68, 70, *74-5*, 78: stand in for nouns, e.g. he, she, it, etc.

Pronuntiatio, 362, (*pro-nun-shee-AH-shee-oh*; L. announcing forth) = *actio*.

Prooimion, 246, (*pro-OI-me-on*; Gk. prelude; Latinized as *procemium* or *proem*): = *exordium*.

Propositio, 246, (*prop-oh-ZISH-ee-oh*; L. setting forth): = *divisio*.

Proposition, *in logic*, 186, 190, 192, 194, 199, 206, 216, 219: a statement in logic, normally declarative (not a question or a command), and non-subjective/non-evaluative; *in rhetoric*, 240.

Propositional Logic, 226-227

Prosody, 118, the study of poetic meter and the art of versification.

Prosopopoeia (*pro-soh-poh-PEE-uh*, Gk. making face): = *personification*.

Protasis, 360

Prothesis, 246, (*prowth-EE-sis*; Gk. placing before): = *narratio*.

Proverb, *definition of*, 262, *366-7*; *speaking proverbially*, 248; *examples of*, 366-93

Prozeugma, 271, (*pro-ZYOOG-muh*; Gk. yoking before): a zeugma in which the yoke word comes first—one verb governs several objects, or several subject–object pairs.

Pun, 284, a play on two words similar in sound but different in meaning.

Punctuation, *usage and abusage of*, 394

Pyrrhic, *123*, 138, (*Pee-rik*): a metrical foot of two unstressed syllables.

Quadrivium, 2-3, 352

Qualifiers, *in grammar*, 67, 76; *in logic*, 228

Qualitative verse: poetry which counts stressed syllables at regular intervals as either the only (accentual) or combined (accentual-syllabic) component of its meter.

Quantitative verse, 121: the type of metrical poetry written in Ancient Greek (and other syllable-timed languages) which counts syllable length, not stress.

Quantity: see *Distribution*.

Quaternio terminorum, 194, 'four terms': formal fallacy. A syllogism must have precisely three terms in order to be valid.

Quatrain, 119, 148, *150-1*,158, 163, 165, 166: a stanza of four

pentameter).

Syncope (*SIN-kuh-pee*): a form of elision; the omission from a word of either a consonant (e.g. 'ne'er') or unstressed vowel (e.g. 'hastening' to 'hast'ning').

Synecdoche, 254, (*sin-eck-DOE-kee*; Gk. taking with something else): the metaphorical use of part for whole, or whole for part.

Synonymia, 280, 288, (*sin-oh-NIM-ee-uh*; Gk. naming alike): a sequence of synonyms (cf. *congeries*).

Syntax, *in grammar*, 57

Syntax: *in logic*, refers to the rules governing the validity of the formal language, regardless of meaning.

Synthesis, *178*, 358, 360 (Gk. putting together): resolution. The creation of something new from two or more entities. Part of classical (or Socratic) dialectic (q.v. thesis, antithesis).

Systrophe (*sis-tro-FEE*; Gk. turning together): indirect definition by enumeration of properties (e.g. 'Quadruped. Graminivorous. Forty teeth, namely twenty-four grinders, four eye-teeth, and twelve incisive…') (cf. *horismus*).

Syzygy (*SIZ-ee-jee*): in prosody, can refer to counting two metrical feet as one for the sake of scansion (cf. *dipody* and *elision*).

Tanka, 169: traditional Japanese five-line poem.

Tautologia, 288, (*tau-toe-LODGE-ia*; Gk. saying the same): tedious repetition of the same idea in different words; failed *synonymia*.

Tautology, *in logic*: a statement or formula which is true in every possible interpretation is tautologous. According to some modern thinkers, all valid deductive reasoning is tautologous.

Techne, 238, 239, 240, (*TECK-nay*; Gk. craft): a practical skill.

Temperantiam, *argumentum ad*: see *modum*.

Tenor, 253, (*TEN-uh*; L. that which holds): the subject of a metaphor, whether expressed or not; that which a metaphor refers to (cf. *vehicle*).

Tenses, of verbs, 81, *82-3*, 91, 207

Terms, *in grammar*, 66-7, 70-71, 76-7; *in Logic*, 180, 187, 198, 190-91, 194-5

Terza rima, 146: open form of 3-line stanzas in pentameter, rhyming *aba bab cdc ded efe ... ee*. Used in Dante's 'Divine Comedy'. Narrative and lyrical.

Tetrameter, 121, 124, 126-7, 128, *132*, 135, 136-7, 139, 141, 142, 147, 148-9, 150, 153, 160-1, 162, 165, 166: a metrical

line of four feet.

Texas Sharpshooter Fallacy: informal fallacy, ignoring differences in data while stressing similarities. Its name comes from a story about a 'gunman' who repeatedly fires at a barn door, then paints a target on the largest cluster.

Theme, 156, 163, 168: a central idea or statement that unifies and controls a literary work. A piece may contain multiple themes.

Thesis, 178, 212, 358, 360: a proposition. Part of classical (or Socratic) dialectic (q.v. *thesis, antithesis*).

Theophrastus, the characters of, 356-7

Thomas Aquinas, 328, 335

Thorn line: a line without rhyme in a generally rhymed passage. There are ten 'thorn lines' among the 193 lines in Milton's irregularly rhymed 'Lycidas'.

Three act structure, 360

Tone, 278: the means of creating a relationship or conveying an attitude or mood in a literary work.

Topos, 244, (*TOE-poss*; Gk. place): one of a number of generic argument patterns, adaptable for specific circumstances (= *locus*).

Toulmin layout, 251

Tragedy, 114, 358, 360: A serious play in which the chief character passes through a series of misfortunes leading to a catastrophe.

Tragic hero: originally the main character in a Greek or Roman tragedy; typically an admirable character undone by a tragic mistake.

Tragicomedy: A experimental literary work containing elements common to both comedies and tragedies.

Translatio, 255, (*trans-LA-shee-oh*; L. carrying across): = metaphor.

Tricolon, 261, 280, *281*, (*try-COE-lon*; Gk. three limbs): a series of three phrases/clauses, of roughly the same length and grammatical structure.

Trimeter, 121, 125, 128, *132*, 135, 137, 139, 141, 148-9, 152-3, 159, 163, 165: a metrical line of three feet.

Triolet, 160-1: closed form of 8 lines of accentual-syllabic verse with any meter. Rhymes *ABaAbbAB* (*A+B* = refrains). Used for lyrical/light verse/imagistic themes.

Triplet/tercet, 119, *146-7*, 152, 158, 160: Three-line stanzas of any meter, rhyming *aaa* or *aba*. Semantically linked , often a complete statement

Trivium, The, history and nature of, 1-2, 57, 177, 237, 352

Trochee, 124, *(TRO-key)*: A metrical unit (or "foot") containing one stressed syllable followed by one unstressed syllable (e.g. STATEment, RIVer, WONder).

TROPE: *In poetry*, 145, 167; *in rhetoric*, *252*, 258, 274-283, 286, 290. One of two kinds of rhetorical *figure*. A figure of thought, involving the changing of the meaning of a word, or the use of a word in a non-literal sense (cf. *scheme*). Tropes commonly used in poetry include *metaphor*, *metonymy* and *simile*.

TRUTH, 180-1: *in logic*, truth refers to a statement's correspondence with a particular reality. In modern logic, 'soundness" is preferred to 'truth' when referring to arguments and their conclusions.

TU QUOQUE: an *ad hominem* fallacy invoking hypocritical behaviour in an opponent relating to the conclusion. "How can you argue X when you're doing Y?"

TWO WRONGS: DON'T MAKE A RIGHT: informal fallacy. "You stole a banana from Sue!" "I know, but Sue stole it from Eric!"

UNDISTRIBUTED MIDDLE TERM, 91: formal fallacy. Where the middle term is not universal ('all') in at least one premise.

UNIVERSAL, *logical statement ("all" or "no")*, 185, *186*, 192-3, 195: logical use of a term; *truth*, 231; *values in ethics*, 336.

UTILITY, 2, 300; *in friendship*, 330-1; *in ethics*, 300, 330-1, 340

UTILITARIANISM, *340-3; medical*, 345; *animal*, 348-9.

VACUOUS TRUTH FALLACY: the use of empty sets in an argument. E.g. saying "I ate up all the turnip on my plate" to Mum when Nanny didn't feed you any turnip.

VALIDITY, 176, *179*, *180-1*, 182, 185, 186, 188, 190, 194, *196-200*, 204-5, 208, 210-11, 212, 218, 226: logical validity refers to the correctness of the process of reasoning, rather than to the content of the propositions involved. Thus an argument may be valid but untrue; *in rhetoric*, 240.

VALUE, *in binary, true or false, logic*, 186, 193, 201, 205; *in multi-value logic*, 228-9.

VEHICLE, 253, (L. carrier): the image that carries the weight of the comparison in a metaphor; that which the tenor is compared to (cf. *tenor*).

Verb, 80-95; *tense*, 82-3; *form* 84-87; *voice*, 88; *mood*, 89; *aspect*, 90; *phrases*, 91; *auxiliary and modal*, 92; *Transitivity*, 93; *finite and copular*, 94; *or not*, 95

VERBOSITUM, *argumentum*: 'wordy argument'. The use of excessive and obfuscatory verbiage to hide the weakness of an argument.

VERECUNDIAM, *argumentum ad*, 241: 'The appeal to shame'. A proposition is claimed to be true simply because a respected figure says it is true. The shame enters when the opponent accepts this false authority.

Vernacular: (Lt. native, indigenous): the everyday or common language of the people.

Verse sciolti da rima, 145

Verse: poetry as distinct from prose. The word 'verse' is used interchangeably with 'poetry'. Also a traditional word for *stanza*.

Versification: the art or technique of writing verse.

VICE, 46, 377, 382; *in ethics* 294, 311, 315, 324-6 (q.v. *virtue*); *rhetorical*, 278, 288

Villanelle: a 19 line poem (6 stanzas of 3 lines each) with rhyming refrains and a concluding quatrain, all in iambic pentameter. Also a French dance with sung lyrics.

Virelai: a French verse form often used in song and dance.

VIRTUE(S), *Addison on*, 256; *Aristotle on*, 310, 330; *definitions of*, 314-15; *graphic depictions of*, 294, 296, 309; *virtue ethics vs utility*, 342-3; *cardinal*, 316-323; *courage*, 318; *moderation*, 319; *justice*, 320-321; *wisdom*, 322-323; *humility*, 326-7; *friendship*, 330-1; *civic*, 332-3; *and the seven deadly sins*, 324-5; *social*, 328-9; *proverbs*, 377.

Visual poetry, 116

Vocative case, 71: in grammar, who/what is addressed.

Volta, 156-7, 163: the 'turn' in a poem, particularly a sonnet.

Vulgate: the use of informal, common speech, particularly of uneducated people. Similar to the use of *vernacular*.

WISDOM, *one of the four cardinal virtues, 316-17, 322-3, 338, 342, 351-3; in rhetoric* 262-3; *proverbs about, 368*;

Wit, the art of, 329

Words, *ancient origins of*, 9-14; *order of in grammar*, 64.

Wrenched accent: the forcing of an accent onto a non-accented syllable (e.g. 'in my imagination' becomes 'in my imagina-shee-aan').

ZEUGMA, 271, 284, *(ZYOOG-muh*; Gk. yoking): using one word to govern two or more objects (cf. *syllepsis*).

References

Further Reading: Liberal Arts: *The Seven Liberal Arts in the Middle Ages*, edited by David Wagner, 1986; *The Classical Trivium*, by Marshall McLuhan, 1943; *The Trivium*, by Sister Miriam Joseph, 1948. **Grammar:** *The Complete Guide to Grammar*, by Fergusson and Manser, 2010; *The Bloomsbury Grammar Guide* by Gordon Jarvie, 1993; *Usage and Abusage* by Eric Partridge, 1946; *The Oxford Companion to the English Language*, 2005. **Poetics:** *The Ode Less Travelled*, by Stephen Fry, 2007; *The Poet's Manual and Rhyming Dictionary*, by Frances Stillman, 1972; *Poetic Meter and Poetic Form*, by Paul Fussell, 1979; *Poetry, The Basics*, by Jeffrey Wainwright, 2004; *Rules for the Dance*, by Mary Oliver, 1998. **Logic:** *The Logic Book* by Bergmann, Moor & Nelson, 1990; *How to Win Every Argument*, by Madsen Pirie, 2006; *The Annotated Alice*, Martin Gardner, 1999. **Rhetoric:** *Rhetorical Style*, by Jeanne Fahnestock, 2011; *Farnsworth's Classical English Rhetoric* by Ward Farnsworth, 2011; *The Elements of Eloquence*, by Mark Forsyth, 2013; *Winning Arguments*, by Jay Henrichs, 2010; *Words Like Loaded Pistols*, by Sam Leith, 2012; *Rhetoric: A Very Short Introduction*, by Richard Toye, 2013; *Silva Rhetorica* at rhetoric.byu.edu. **Ethics:** *After Virtue*, by Alasdair MacIntyre; *Intelligent Virtue*, by Julia Annas; *Ethics: The Essential Writings*, by Gordon Marino; *The Quest for a Moral Compass*, by Kenan Malik, 2015; *Happiness and Virtue Ethics in Business*, by Alejo Sison; *The Virtues in Medical Practice*, by Edmund Pellegrino; *Ecological Ethics*, by Patrick Curry.

Proverbs Codes

AB AUS - Aboriginal Australian	CHI - Chinese
AFG - Afghan	CONG - Congolese
AFR - African	DAN - Danish
AFR AME - African American	DUT - Dutch
ALB - Albanian	EGY - Egyptian
AME - American	ENG - English
ANG - Angolan	ERI - Eritrean
ARAB - Arabian	EST - Estonian
ARAP - Arapaho	ETH - Ethiopian
ARM - Armenian	FAR - Faroese
ASH - Ashanti (Ghana)	FIN - Finnish
AZE - Azeri	FLEM - Flemish
BAL - Balinese	FRE - French
BAS - Basque	GEOR - Georgian
BER - Berber	GER - German
BIB - Bible	GRE - Greek
BOS - Bosnian	GYP - Gypsy
BOT - Botswanian	HAW - Hawaiian
BRA - Brazilian	HEB - Hebrew
BUL - Bulgarian	HUN - Hungarian
BURM - Burmese	ICE - Icelandic
BURU - Burundian	IND - Indian
CAME - Cameroonian	INDO - Indonesian
CAMB - Cambodian	INU - Inuit
	IRI - Irish

ITA - Italian	POLY - Polynesian
IVO - Ivory Coast	POR - Portuguese
JAM - Jamaican	ROM - Roman
JAP - Japanese	ROMA - Romanian
KASH - Kashmiri	RUS - Russian
KEN - Kenyan	SAM - Samoan
KOR - Korean	SCO - Scottish
KUR - Kurdish	SLO - Slovenian
KYR - Kyrgyz	SPA - Spanish
LEB - Lebanese	SUD - Sudanese
MAD - Madagascan	SWA - Swahili
MALAW - Malawian	SWE - Swedish
MALAY - Malaysian	TAM - Tamil
MALT - Maltese	TAN - Tanzanian
MALI - Malian	TIB - Tibetan
MEX - Mexican	THAI - Thai
MON - Mongolian	TUR - Turkish
NAM - Namibian	UGA - Ugandan
NAT AME - Native American	UKR - Ukrainian
NEP - Nepali	UZB - Uzbek
NIG - Nigerian	VIET - Vietnamese
NOR - Norwegian	WEL - Welsh
PER - Persian	YEM - Yemeni
PHIL - Filipino	ZEN - Zen Buddhist
POL - Polish	ZIM - Zimbabwean

Illustrations are credited where they appear, except for:

Pages 7-51: Cartoons © Merrily Harpur, 2001.

Pages 64, 71, 81, 107, 111, 207, 299, Arthur Rackham [1867-1939].

Pages 69, 73, 84, 88, 93, 94, 99, 100, 105: Johannes Lencker [1523-85].

Page 98: *Parts of Speech*, Rome, [1516].

Page 115: *Dancing Muses*, Zoan Andrea, [1497].

Page 175: *Waterfall* © M.C. Escher Company, [1961].

Pages 180-1, 185-6, 197-8, 201, 205, 217, 224: © Cartoonstock.

Pages 189, 199, 218, 229: from *Alice*, John Tenniel [1820-1914].

Pages 215, 235-291: Cartoons © Merrily Harpur, 2015.

Pages 300-1, 336, 338, 340-1, 343, 344, 346-347, 350: © Cartoonstock, 2016.

Page 303: *Socrates drinking the hemlock*, © Alamy, 2016.

Page 335: American Indian, © 123rf, 2016.

Page 349: Gorilla, © Shutterstock, 2016.

Page 351: Joel Pett cartoon, © New York Times, 2016.

Page 368: *Foolish behaviour*, Dutch, [c.1600].

Page 369: *Arrival of the King*, woodcut, Guido Delle Colonne [15th C.].

Page 370: *Reynard the Fox*, woodcut, Sebastian Münster [1488-1552].

Page 371: *The Decision of the Flowers*, Henry Moses [1782-1870].

Page 373: *Tossing the Pancake*, George Cruikshank [1792-1878].

Page 374: *Battle*, woodcut, Guido Delle Colonne [15th C.].

Page 375: *Haymaking*, medieval woodcut.

Page 376: *Michaelmas Day*, George Cruikshank [1792-1878].

Page 377: *Golden Head Golden Head*, Dante Gabriel Rossetti [1828-82].

Page 378: *Allegory of Venus*, Granger, [1496].

Page 379: *Poliphilo & the Nymphs*, *Hypnerotomachia*, Venice, [1499].

Page 380: *Sloth*, Pieter Bruegel the Elder [1525-1569].

Page 381: *Hope*, Pieter Bruegel the Elder [1525-1569].

Page 382: *War in Heaven*, wood engraving [14th C.].

Page 383: *The Basilisk & the Weasel* Wenceslaus Hollar [1607-1677].

Page 384: *Ladies in Parliament*, 1885, George Cruikshank [1792-1878].

Page 385: *Big Fish Eat Little Fish*, Pieter van der Heyden [1530-1572].

Page 386: *Avarice*, Pieter van der Heyden [1530-1572].

Page 387: *Fear and Hope are Vision*, William Blake [1757-1827].

Page 388: *Adam and Eve*, Pierre Lombart, [1660].

Page 389: *The Dancing Deaths*, from Schedel's *Liber Chronicarum*, [1493].